XENOCRACY

Xenocracy

State, Class and Colonialism in the Ionian Islands, 1815–1864

Sakis Gekas

berghahn
NEW YORK • OXFORD
www.berghahnbooks.com

First published by
Berghahn Books
www.berghahnbooks.com

© 2017, 2024 Sakis Gekas
First paperback edition published in 2024

All rights reserved. Except for the quotation of short passages
for the purposes of criticism and review, no part of this book
may be reproduced in any form or by any means, electronic or
mechanical, including photocopying, recording, or any information
storage and retrieval system now known or to be invented,
without written permission of the publisher.

Library of Congress Cataloging-in-Publication Data

Names: Gekas, Sakis, author.
Title: Xenocracy : state, class, and colonialism in the Ionian Islands, 1815-1864 / Sakis Gekas.
Description: First edition. | New York : Berghahn Books, 2017. | Includes bibliographical references and index.
Identifiers: LCCN 2016026098 | ISBN 9781785332616 (hardback : acid-free paper) | ISBN 9781785332623 (ebook)
Subjects: LCSH: Ionian Islands (Greece)--Politics and government--19th century. | Ionian Islands (Greece)--Social conditions--19th century. | Social classes--Greece--Ionian Islands--History--19th century. | Social change--Greece--Ionian Islands--History--19th century. | Ionian Islands (Greece)--Economic conditions--19th century. | Ionian Islands (Greece)--Colonial influence--History--19th century. | Great Britain--Colonies--Administration--History--19th century. | Great Britain--Territorial expansion--History--19th century. | Imperialism--History--19th century. | Congress of Vienna (1814-1815)--Influence.
Classification: LCC DF261.I6 G44 2016 | DDC 949.5/5072--dc23 LC record available at https://lccn.loc.gov/2016026098

British Library Cataloguing in Publication Data
A catalogue record for this book is available from the British Library

ISBN 978-1-78533-261-6 hardback
ISBN 978-1-80539-127-2 paperback
ISBN 978-1-80539-391-7 epub
ISBN 978-1-78533-262-3 web pdf

https://doi.org/10.3167/9781785332616

*To Eirini
and our son Yanis
Because H is for History*

Map Greece and the Ionian Republic, 1856.
Courtesy of www.davidrumsey.com.

Table of Contents

List of Illustrations		viii
Acknowledgments		x
Introduction		1
Chapter 1	The First Greek State and the Origins of Colonial Governmentality	23
Chapter 2	Building the Colonial State	51
Chapter 3	Law, Colonialism and State Formation	79
Chapter 4	Colonial Knowledge and the Making of Ionian Governmentality	101
Chapter 5	'A True and Hateful Monopoly': Merchants and the State	130
Chapter 6	State Finances and the Cost of Protection	174
Chapter 7	Building a Modern State: Public Works and Public Spaces	199
Chapter 8	'Progress': State Policies for Ionian Development	227
Chapter 9	Poverty, the State and the Middle Class	250
Chapter 10	The *Literati* and the *Liberali*: The Making of the Ionian Bourgeoisie	287
Conclusion.	1864: The End of Colonial Rule?	325
Bibliography		337
Index		365

Illustrations

Tables

4.1	Ionian Islands population, exempting foreigners	110
4.2	Ionian Islands natural movement, 5-year averages	110
4.3	Ionian Islands working population, according to sector	114
4.4	Corfu population (1830–32)	124
6.1	The finances of the Ionian State, 1821–34	178
6.2	Public expenditure, 1847–48	192
9.1	Number of recorded 'paupers' in the Ionian Islands	266
10.1	Schools and pupils in the Ionian Islands, 1828	292
10.2	Schools and pupils, 1834	296

Figures

Map	Greece and the Ionian Republic, 1856	vi
0.1	Corfu, in front of the Maitland rotunda, Kerkyra 1856–60	xii
4.1	First page of the 'Blue Books of Statistics', 1828	106
5.1	Ionian State Imports–Exports, 1827–57	132
5.2	Total value of imports, exports and transit trade	132
5.3	Value of olive oil exports	134
5.4	Exports of currants in quantity and value	136
5.5	Currants exports, 1827–63, amount and percentage of total exports	137
5.6	Value of cotton imports and percentage of total imports	143

5.7	Value of grain and total imports and percentage of grain imports	146
7.1	'View from the New Fortress'	209
7.2	Views of main street in Corfu	211
7.3	Napier's plans for a multipurpose civic building and a market in Lixuri	214
8.1	Man in Corfu	238
9.1	The peak of the cholera outbreak, Corfu 1855	272

Acknowledgments

I knew I was going to write about the history of Corfu only after I left the island to go to England. *Xenocracy* therefore has travelled with me for a while; and with some of the people who shaped the research and writing of the book we go back a long way. Geoffrey Crossick especially and Kevin Schürer, supervisors and mentors at the University of Essex, played a most crucial part at the early stages of the project and believed in its completion. Patrick O'Brien at the LSE shaped the economic history side of the book and helped me frame anything I was doing within a Mediterranean and global context; Giorgio Riello and Colin Lewis read and commented generously on earlier drafts of chapters. With Tony Molho, Mathieu Grenet and especially with Manuel Borutta at the European University Institute we exchanged ideas about the colonial Mediterranean and Manuel offered a fascinating comparative vantage point on colonialism. All colleagues at York University History Department continue to offer a wonderful environment that enabled the completion of the book and I am grateful to them.

Tom Gallant has been following the progress of the research project on British colonialism in the Ionian Islands since its very beginning. The ongoing conversation with Tom is a source of inspiration that has affected the research and writing behind the book. The book, however, as all books, is the product of conversations, presentations, conference papers and invited lectures; in them many historians have shaped the writing of this book through their work and/or their comments. Among them, Tassos Anastassiadis, Roderick Beaton, Filippos Carabott, Eleni Calligas, Maria Christina Chatziioannou, Katherine Fleming, Simon Gunn, Gelina Harlaftis, Robert Holland, Maurizio Isabella, Kostas Kostis, Antonis Liakos, Paris Papamichos Chronakis, Prasannan Parthasarathi, Socrates Petmezas, Evangelos Prontzas, Michalis Sotiropoulos and Konstantina Zanou.

Librarians and archivists rarely receive the credit they deserve for making our work possible; I need to thank archivists especially in the Corfu and Kefalonia libraries and archives, and the ones at National Archives in London and the Gennadios Library in Athens. I also have to thank the reviewers for improving earlier drafts of the book and Chris Chappell and Caroline Kuhtz at Berghahn Books for the efficient and smooth transformation of chapters, images and figures from files into a book. I would also like to thank Alexia Travlou and the Ephorate of Antiquities in Corfu, who kindly gave permission to use the images of Corfu that officer Major Shakespeare captured for the first time in camera in 1856 and are now held at the collection of Mon Repos Museum in Corfu.

My sister Olga and my parents Agapi and Elias are probably the most important reason for going to Greece especially, now that their grandson has already started telling his own stories; to Yanis and to his mother the book is dedicated for giving meaning to the present and making it worthwhile to reflect on the past.

Sakis Gekas
Toronto, August 2016

Figure 01 Corfu, in front of the Maitland rotunda, Kerkyra 1856–60. Fotografikes Martyries. Mouseio Paleopolis-Mon Repo, Kerkyra. Eforia Archeotiton Kerkyras, Elliniko Ypoyrgeio Politismou kai Athlitismou

 Introduction

In the last few years the words colony and protectorate dominate discussions and writings on the current state of Greece, as the famous country remains locked into an unprecedented (in peacetime) crisis. Since 2010 the collapse of the Greek economy has meant record unemployment and financial dependency, perhaps for years to come; this catastrophe has triggered a rhetoric that talks about loss of sovereignty since the country has become a 'debt colony' and a 'protectorate'. In the nineteenth century, Ionians invented a word for the period of British rule and called it *xenokratia* – xenocracy.[1] Chiotis, Ionian historian and author of a book titled *History of the Ionian State* wrote in 1877:

'Ionian liberals compared the acts of the Ionian government to the works of a malicious xenocracy' and 'the attitude of English in [our] country seemed to them as a xenocracy established through violation of a treaty for the destruction of the Greek State'.[2] The word xenocracy appeared probably for the first time in an article of the radical newspaper *Anagenissis* [Regeneration], where Ionians and the Ionian 'people' were called to set aside their differences and fight united as brothers to paralyse the destructive force of xenocracy and its instruments'.[3] In fact the term 'western xenocracy' was so ingrained in the politics of the time that the Ionian Parliament in 1850, the first following the liberal reforms of high commissioner Seaton that extended the franchise, castigated western xenocracy when they declared 25 March – Greek Independence day – a national holiday for Ionians.[4]

This was the first period in Greek history when colonialism, protection, dependency and foreign rule were notions that went beyond the metaphorical and polemic ways in which the words are used today, and this is where the beginnings of Greek dependency and its colonial (or 'colonial') condition can be traced. The semi-colonial state that formed under British protection in the Ionian Islands – the Seven Islands or *Eptanisa* as Greeks call them – and the involvement of the Great Powers in the 1821 revolution against the Ottoman Empire that created an independent Greek Kingdom hardly makes sense without understanding French, Russian and especially British involvement in the Ionian Islands.[5]

The book *Xenocracy* shows how a protectorate state that was created by Britain under conditions of colonial rule gradually became ungovernable due to the political and economic contradictions of British colonialism. The modernizing attempts of British and Ionian officials created state institutions but failed because of deficits in public finances, conflicting interests among Ionians, and the oscillations of British colonial officials between autocratic and liberal forms of rule. From the 1840s onwards a liberal middle class became hegemonic in politics, commerce and the public sphere of Ionian societies. Some of those liberal Ionians, the more radical, demanded the unification of the islands with Greece, which was achieved in 1864; this was a case of decolonization that set a precedent in British and imperial politics in the Mediterranean, especially in the case of Cyprus in the twentieth century. As the book shows, the Ionian State depended on colonial administrative categories, an expensive bureaucracy and increased military spending, a fiscal administration and on enforcing, or being seen as able to enforce, public order to exercise power effectively. The liberal discourse of progress and 'enlightened' rule explains the infrastructure and public works project that in theory would render British rule benevolent and even acceptable to Ionians. The contradictions and asymmetries of the Ionian State protectorate reached an impasse in the 1850s; a crisis of legitimacy forced decolonization and the cession of the islands to Greece, on the occasion of the change of dynasty after the expulsion of King Otto in 1862. Decolonization of the islands in 1864 owed much to the ten-year constitutional struggle of the radicals and other liberals and to a lesser extent the rather timid mobilization of the Ionian people against British rule; nevertheless, the decision to cede the Ionian Islands to Greece was a decision made by the British in their own time and on their own terms, notwithstanding the political developments in Greece and the overthrow of King Otto in 1862.

The book delves into the history of the Ionian State and society to raise central issues and inform current debates on the history of British colonialism: economic development under colonial rule, and the transformation of local economies to accommodate British interests; the perception of modernity and its impact on colonized societies; law, colonialism and the function of a colonial state; and the formation of a bourgeoisie in colonial societies through commerce, education, bourgeois virtues and a civil society. The book argues that the making of the Ionian bourgeoisie coincided with the formation of the Ionian State and civil society; in fact antagonisms but also negotiation between Ionians and foreigners often took place within the state in those clearly stratified Mediterranean island societies. During the fifty years of British rule the Ionian State failed to change the basic institutions of the rural economy and tackle the constant indebtedness of peasants; such was, after all, the typical colonial approach of non-intervention, avoiding jeopardizing the much-needed support of local elites. The progressively deteriorating fiscal condition of the Ionian State stalled any public works projects; only a few were completed in the early years of the protectorate but even these were abandoned later. The arrival of a new generation of liberal Ionians in commerce, politics and state administration created a public sphere and substituted the old political class when they rose to prominence through the new media of newspapers, and in spaces such as commercial and voluntary associations.

There were a few British at the top levels, but it was mostly Ionians who administered and ran the colonial Ionian State; these officials introduced liberal reforms that shaped this hybrid semi-colonial polity.[6] The history of the Ionian State offers another perspective to the history of liberal modernity, characterized by bureaucratic practices, statecraft, commerce, consumption patterns and the rise of civil society,[7] which has not been studied in the colonial context of the British Mediterranean. The only exception is the study of British–Ionian colonial encounter drawing on concepts from historical anthropology and social history.[8] Civil society was the work of Ionian merchants, intellectuals, lawyers, civil servants and some British colonial officers who followed liberal values and principles. Ionians created a public sphere of political parties and groups, philanthropic and literary societies, clubs and social events. A study of the ways in which the Ionian State was organized under colonial rule, and the power relations exercised on the islands by the British and Ionians alike, can tell us about the ability of British colonial rule to adapt but also to coerce indigenous populations to achieve the most effective and costless rule possible.

The Making of the British Mediterranean

The book avoids a rigid distinction between colony and independent state when studying the impact of British rule on the islands, but raises the broader implications this 'case' has for the history of colonialism. Schematically, there were two types of colonies in the British Empire, those with 'responsible government', such as Canada and Australia, whose white European settlers enjoyed representative institutions and a large degree of autonomy over legislation; in the other type of colonies, such as Ceylon, the West Indies and West Africa, British governments in London exercised full authority over legislation and administration, even where a legislative council of appointed locals existed, albeit in a largely decorative role.[9] The Ionian Islands belonged to wartime conquests or acquisitions, what has been called the 'dependent Empire'.[10] While the Ionian State was born in conditions that resembled a crown colony, it ended being closer to the type 'responsible government'. Whichever category of colony we chose, however, the concept of 'informal empire', which explains how British influence presided over a number of territories that at some point became colonies and whose subordinate position was defined by the 'imperialism of free trade',[11] is suitable only to an extent, since the Ionian Islands did not transform into a colony. The definition of the protectorate as 'polities in which indigenous authorities and occupying forces share sovereignty and authority' reflects the political and social organization of the Ionian Islands during the period of British rule;[12] the case study of the Ionian State offers also a comparative vantage point to the history of French colonial Mediterranean, in Tunisia for example.[13]

Throughout the history of the British Empire, forms of rule adapted to local conditions with improvisation and ingenuity, but were met with varied success.[14] In 1815, the Treaty of Paris presented British imperial administration in the Ionian Islands with a new set of problems, equivalent to the capture of Ceylon in 1796 and the challenge of setting up a colonial government entirely separate from the East India Company in India.[15] The fifty years that followed the Napoleonic wars buttressed the foundation of an 'Anglo-Mediterranean order' and coincided with the heyday of liberal imperialism under the Pax Britannica,[16] a regime that extended to parts of the world previously under absolutist and despotic rulers; the Ionian Islands, Gibraltar, Malta and Sicily (for a few years) were some of the Mediterranean outposts of British rule that, together with Cyprus and Alexandria later in the century, formed a field of experimentation in colonial practices. The transition from despotism to more liberal forms of rule in the colonies – and in areas such as the Ionian Islands – was far from even or rapid. Ionian societies became a colonial 'laboratory', where colonial schemes in administration and social and economic organization were applied in more daring and controversial ways than those reserved for straightforward colonies.

The period 1780–1830, the 'dawn of the Second British Empire', also saw the 'massive expansion of British dominion, of techniques of governance and exploitation', and historiography has generally followed this periodization.[17] High commissioners and the imperial administration experimented with forms of rule to facilitate imperial policies but also to minimize and/or accommodate local pressures and above all avoid conflicts.[18] Colonial governors and other officials often had no other guide than their experience and they trusted it more than reports from their predecessors or even their superiors; as a result, places such as the Ionian Islands became ground for experimenting with forms of government and colonial institutions. Colonial officers drew on their personal experience from appointments on the colonial circuit, such as administering Upper Canada, Ceylon or India, and on their networks and personal connections from before their term in the Ionian Islands. This partly explains the despotism and the hierarchies that colonial governors imposed in those 'European societies, in Malta, Canada and the Ionian Isles',[19] although these three areas are rarely used within the same historiographical context; the observation however reflects the colonial circuit that many governors followed. Colonial officials wrote about how they reached crucial decisions on thorny issues and how experience shaped their policies. The changes introduced by British and Ionian colonial officers followed the same liberal modernizing project behind regulatory practices in West European and colonial cities.[20] Ionian liberals pursued the same agenda and aimed primarily at improving British protection and not uniting with the Kingdom of Greece, a political aim that only achieved some coherence and prominence in the 1850s; besides the issue of union, Ionians innovated in public policy with the tacit approval or endorsement of British colonial officials.

The project to organize the state under autocratic rule behind a facade of a representative assembly laid the foundations for the failure of the British protectorate, but also exposed the contradictions of the Treaty of Paris in 1815. The pledge of high commissioners to improve living conditions and moral standards that would legitimize British colonial rule remained an empty promise, especially after 1840; the Ionian economy adjusted to British requirements but the Ionian State fell into deficit under the heavy costs of protection, extravagant spending on salaries, and financial mismanagement. Despite the various versions of rule tried by different commissioners and their Ionian counterparts, ranging from autocratic to liberal, depending on the ideas and disposition of each commissioner, increasingly local pressures became insurmountable. This was a progressively failing protection, which in the end was not desired by the majority of Ionians of different classes and occupations, even in Corfu, which got the most out of the protectorate. The British had failed to win the tolerance – if not the support – of Ionians, and the prospect of a new king and dynasty in Greece in 1863 impelled the British to cede the islands and secure their influence over Greece, as a united territory. Despite these failures of the Ionian State, other forms of indirect rule such as the protectorate, or colonial rule in all but name, were applied later in the nineteenth century in Cyprus (1878) and Egypt (1882). The Ionian Islands case therefore allows for an alternative reading of nineteenth-century British colonialism in the Mediterranean.

The Ionian State and Colonial Governmentality

The Protectorate of the 'United States of the Ionian Islands' was only nominally independent; according to the Ionian Islands constitutional charter of 1817 the islands were placed under the 'exclusive and immediate protection of HM King of Great Britain'. This phrase symbolically and constitutionally relegated Ionians to semi-colonialism, the condition that best describes the experience of a protectorate and the British–Ionian colonial encounter. Herzfeld came up with the term 'crypto-colonialism' and identified the 'paradox' that Greece is both spiritual ancestor of Europe and political pariah in the European present.[21] The historical if not the intellectual origins of this paradox can be found in the British colonial rule over the Ionian Islands. The tension between the esteemed ancestor status and the corrupt and politically immature pariah (or 'history's spoiled children' as one famous historian from the Ionian Islands called Greeks),[22] emerged for the first time in the Ionian Islands. In the nineteenth century, French and later British colonial officials struggled with Greek political identities and national aspirations. The outbreak of the Greek Revolution complicated Ionian allegiances and shaped their Greek national identity, but it was in the British protectorate that Ionian Greeks came to represent the 'other' that had to be governed, modernized, and occasionally punished for being, well, Greek – which in many a colonizer's mind meant undisciplined, politically immature and potentially troublesome.

The logic of colonial rule, what Partha Chatterjee calls 'the rule of colonial difference', distinguished the colonizers from the colonized, was based on the power of the metropole over its subject peoples, and underpinned colonial governmentality in the British Empire.[23] Colonial governmentality is the notion that encapsulates the sophisticated system of surveillance and bureaucracy that the Ionian State developed. Ionians became involved in this system of government as state employees, beneficiaries or adversaries to state policies and practices. In its early days the Ionian State employed practices and strategies of government that resembled distant British colonial outposts of the long eighteenth century, where the colonial was formed largely independently from the metropolitan imperial centre and was rather performative, especially in colonial frontiers, rather than rigidly institutional.[24] The Ionian Islands colonial 'frontier', seen under the notion of governmentality explains how in the nineteenth century rationality became the main organizing principle that shaped relations between government and the people, transforming the 'art of government'.[25] No other 'method' was more instrumental in the expansion of state knowledge about its territory and population than the engineering of social statistics by government bureaucracies, that often resembled a mechanism for profiling and labelling people; 'nowhere was this more apparent than in the colonial world, where ... European observers and administrators succumbed to the false allure of objectivity'.[26]

The case of Ionian governmentality forces us to think comparatively about the heuristic value of the notion. India has become the focus of a number of recent works on colonial governmentality.[27] Historians have looked at the application of ideas on social and economic organization to understand the impact of British rule on nineteenth- and twentieth-century India. The liberal project that drove regulatory practices in West European (particularly British) and colonial cities was also in the minds of those who introduced changes in the Ionian Islands between the 1830s and 1860s – state officials and British commissioners who created commercial, legal and urban governance institutions, literary societies and philanthropic associations. The concept of colonial governmentality explains how the Ionian State promoted attempts to control and regulate people's daily lives to conform to aspects of European modernity.

The Ionian Islands and the History of the Greek State

All states, mighty empires as well as little-remembered kingdoms, come and go,[28] and their histories remind us of their ephemeral life regardless of their ostensible invincibility. The republican waves that the French Revolution unleashed reached the shores of the islands in 1797; foreign intervention created the Septinsular Republic, an autonomous state under Russian–Ottoman Protection, essentially the first Greek State. The Ionian State created expectations among Greeks everywhere and contributed to the emergence of national consciousness; it even helped move towards the Greek war of independence. Commissioners Maitland and, after him, Adam implemented the shift in British foreign policy from the state of neutrality in 1821 towards the Greek war of independence to the official recognition of the actions of Greek insurgents as constituting a state at war; the proximity of the Ionian Islands to the war zone increased the importance the islands held for the Greek Revolution. Years before the outbreak of the 1821 revolution, the Ionian Islands State proved that an independent state in the Mediterranean was a real possibility, not just an imagined project.

This book offers a decentralized reading of the history of the Greek State. Conventional historical accounts begin with the revolution and the war of independence from the Ottoman Empire (1821–28) that led to dependence on Russia, France and Britain;[29] as the narrative goes, Greeks became more independent than they had even been under Ottoman rule, but the state that emerged still fell short of what utopian revolutionaries such as Rigas Fereos (Velestinlis) had envisioned.[30] As this book argues, this process of informal dependency started before the Greek Revolution in the Ionian Islands, little known for their history but well visited for their beauty. Greece emerged – in chronological order – first with the Septinsular or Ionian Republic (1800–1807), a state created under Ottoman and Russian protection, the periods of French Republic (1797–99) and Imperial rule (1807–14, mostly for Corfu), and as the British Protectorate of the United States of the Ionian Islands (between 1814 and 1864). *Xenocracy* explains how this Greek State formed in the nineteenth century under semi-colonial conditions between 1797 and 1864, and especially during the period of British protection, 1815–64 and therefore seeks to contribute to our knowledge on the socio-historical process of modern state formation in South-eastern Europe.[31]

The formation of Greek states in the nineteenth century – the Septinsular Republic, the Ionian State, the Greek Kingdom, the Principality of Samos and the Cretan Republic – belongs to a tradition or rather practice of empires granting autonomy to borderlands regions out of necessity and diplomatic pragmatism. Within the Ottoman Empire this flexibility is exemplified in the Republic of Ragusa, for centuries under Ottoman suzerainty and subject to a tribute tax but practically independent, and the principalities of Wallachia and Moldavia, which in the eighteenth century were granted to members of the Phanariot Greek Orthodox elite to administer.[32] These states emerged on the periphery of Europe and at the intersection of European states with the Ottoman Empire. The creation of a state in a region that managed to secede from the Ottoman Empire as post-revolution Greece did, with the heavy influence of Russia, Britain and France, was a bright exception, not the norm at the time.

This book's narrative de-centres the dominant Atheno-centric view of the history of the Greek State that considers 1821 as the beginning of Greek state formation. Historians of art and literature are comfortable enough to date the beginnings of modern Greek art and literature to the period of Venetian rule in Crete and the Ionian Islands (in the works of Cornaro, Theotokopoulos, Solomos and others); other historians however are reluctant to think beyond the conventional view of the state born out of the revolution, and trace the origins of the nineteenth-century Greek State not just in the post-revolution and post-Ottoman Greece but in the legacy of Venetian rule and the British protectorate in Ionian societies. The Ionian State was part of the post-Napoleonic wars European order; this order was disrupted by the Greek war of independence. The book compares the two states in order to highlight the different trajectories and the alternative state-formation projects that were under way in the fist half of the nineteenth century. Comparing the Ionian State and the Greek Kingdom economies and societies shows how the two converged towards the formation of a national economy and the development of legal systems; it also shows the class antagonisms and the legacy of Venetian and Ottoman institutions and forms of rule. In many ways this is an argument for writing the history of the Greek State by looking at the regions that gradually constituted it.

The Ionian State functioned for fifty years under British-protected colonial rule, but it succumbed to the contradictions of colonial liberalism and local radicalism. Successive forms of foreign domination truncated the liberalism on which Ionian aspirations were founded – a romantic if not utopian political project. The British Protectorate of the Ionian Islands has been regarded as a 'transitional' system of peripheral significance.[33] Historians, even accomplished ones, fail to avoid the cardinal sin of the profession and consider transitional what at the time seemed indefinite; such was the case with the Ionian State until the early 1860s, when the change of dynasty in Greece offered an opportunity for the handing over of the Ionian Islands to the Greek Kingdom. The Ionian State dissolved in 1864 after the ousting of the first king of Greece, Otto – an event that triggered the chain reaction for a change of monarchy. Greece passed under British financial and political clout for nearly a century, as the Ionian islands' societies started the long but smooth road towards integration with the 'motherland', and the peculiar life of this Mediterranean state ended in the name of national unification.

The Ionian colonial bourgeoisie

The Ionian bourgeoisie emerged during the nineteenth century through commercial prosperity (defined broadly in gains from trade), university education abroad (mostly in law, medicine, philosophy and, less so, the sciences) and an awareness of national consciousness. It was the petite bourgeoisie who assumed the role of avant-garde in the fight for the unionist-nationalist cause. In all accounts, particularly those by Greek scholars who have been most keen to study the unionist movement, one can find numerous references to the class identity of unionists and their enemies. The object of these studies, however, is usually more the struggle for union rather than the class in which unionists belonged. The book looks at the language and the discourses available at the time, especially in the way people defined themselves and other social strata, by drawing on these available discourses. A discursive approach to class 'assumes that there is no pre-given relationship between class as structural fact and class as social identity'.[34] Class identities did not spring up once industrial capitalism had been established or, in our case, once commercial capitalism was advancing; in the Ionian Islands class identities evolved out of conflicts of interest, negotiation, and the formation of hegemonic relations of power as they played out in the field of state authority.

As the book shows, it was the Ionian bourgeoisie's relationship with the state (complementary or antagonistic) and their educational and social background that produced the distinct characteristics of what is often termed a liberal middle class. The meaning of middle class-ness differs according to national and linguistic contexts, however, recent approaches to study the middle class draw cases from various regions around the world contributing and pointing towards a global history of middle classes.[35] Despite local and regional particularities there is little doubt that the nineteenth century saw the 'rise of the bourgeoisie' and increased the importance of the middle ranks in society; in Corfu and other Ionian cities bourgeois were particularly aware of that and often compared themselves to other 'civilized' parts of the world that shared a similar worldview, habitus and hierarchies.

This book shows how the Ionian bourgeoisie formed in the 1830s–40s as a result of the education they received, their liberal aspirations to form a state under the rule of law, and the advances in the commercial economy that heightened class antagonisms; and, above all, it was the result of contradictions in the constitution of the semi-colonial state. The process of class formation can be seen in the adoption of a liberal philosophy, encapsulated in the issue of free trading of grain and the deregulation of the grain market. Liberalism has always been, after all, the philosophy of the commercial bourgeoisie par excellence, and even if liberalism and the bourgeois worldview were not always identical, they were certainly compatible in the rest of nineteenth-century Europe as well.[36]

The formation of the Ionian bourgeoisie was a process, not an end result or a fixed condition; Ionians, a few British, and other foreigners on the islands who worked for the state or became merchants, lawyers or agents of foreign companies, formed a liberal, semi-colonial bourgeoisie that was split on a number of issues, one of which was the issue of union with the Greek Kingdom. This dynamic definition of the bourgeoisie as a project as well as a class identity explains the contradictions in Ionian class politics during the period of British rule. Modernity in the Ionian State was an aspiration, as well as a condition, expressed by Ionians and British, who were involved in state-building for almost fifty years (more if we include the years of the Septinsular Republic, important as they were for the fermentation of Ionian governmentality). Many Ionians participated in international commercial and intellectual networks during their period of studies abroad, and they were experienced administrators. Besides these unifying elements, the rise of the Ionian bourgeoisie in politics and society reflected their economic standing; but it was not an even process because of the previous history of each island and the gradual realization that they shared collective fortunes. Class was an identity linked with the religious, national and local identities that Ionians fashioned in their newly created public sphere. For these reasons the book does not propose a blueprint of (British) colonial modernity against which the Ionian middle classes will be judged, but exposes the contradictions inherent in any colonial project and traces the actions of protagonists who had the economic, educational and symbolic capital to participate in and create a public sphere.

Middle-class Ionians used the available discourses of nation, society and class to assert their identity against other classes as well as the British and Ionian State authorities. The transportation system of steamships, which connected the islands' ports with Trieste, Livorno, and other cities, ensured the steady flow of people, products, ideas and fashions. Beliefs, values, modes of political discourse and agency but also lifestyle distinguished the Ionian State middle classes from other classes and from Ionian elite groups of previous decades; it also distinguished them from the Greek bourgeoisie in the Greek Kingdom and the Ottoman Greeks in major Ottoman cities.[37] This book is part of a project to integrate the history of the Ionian Islands with the post-revolution

Kingdom of Greece during the period 1833–1862 and examine how two Greek states and their bourgeoisies formed in parallel before they merged. Once the Ionian Islands became part of Greece in 1864, many Ionians settled in Athens and germinated Athenian society with their ideas; and they excelled in politics, the university and public administration.[38] It was thus educational and broadly social capital, as well as economic, that enabled Ionians to produce but also consume a colonial modernity much earlier than other parts of the empire, such as India for example.[39]

The response of middle-class Ionians to the British colonial project was diverse; educated, informed about European – mostly Italian, but also French and British – ideas of economic and social organization, middle-class Ionians adapted the colonial project to their realities and agendas. Against the backdrop of British-inspired discourses of a corrupt Venetian-Ionian past, middle-class Ionians willingly adopted this image to fuel their own ambitious rise in politics and the Ionian public sphere. Through this contrast a distinctive Ionian 'middle class-ness' emerged. Many Ionians joined the Greek Kingdom integration project with ambivalence in the 1840s but with enthusiasm in the 1850s. After fifty years in the Ionian State (1815–64) a fragmented middle class emerged, navigating its way through various forms of state control, its Venetian past, its British colonial present and its Greek future. The Ionian bourgeoisie, especially the most liberal and radical amongst them, managed to empower themselves against both the (initially) superior Ionians of the previous generation, many of whom collaborated with the British until the end, but also against the lower classes. The age of reform, which began after Venetian rule ended with the integration of the islands with the Greek Kingdom, began a new trajectory for these island – but far from insular – societies.

Chapters and Sources

The challenges that historians face when paying attention to the 'circuit of ideas and people, colonizers and colonized',[40] are addressed here by showing the impact of colonial rule on both Ionians and British during the formation of the Ionian State. The pages that follow interrogate critically the sources produced by British and Ionian officials, intellectuals, the Ionian bourgeoisie as well as the 'common people', all filtered through the Ionian State bureaucracy, to discuss the most important aspects of economic and social transformation in the semi-colonial state until it dissolved in 1864 into the Greek Kingdom, taking it deeper under the British hegemonic influence, which lasted until the 1940s.

Chapter 1 demonstrates the crucial years following the end of Venetian rule in 1797 and the various forms of rule and occupation that shaped the Ionian Islands' politics and society and laid the foundations for Ionian governmentality that developed during the period of the Ionian State. The importance of the constitutions of 1800 and 1803, and the economic and diplomatic developments of the time, are discussed because they form the basis for the idiosyncratic federal state that followed during the period of the protectorate.

The first few years of the transition from an occupied territory to an area of the Protectorate and the United States of the Ionian Islands were crucial. Chapter 2 discusses the first two challenges the British administration and Maitland personally faced; the plague outbreak in Corfu and Kefalonia of 1816 and the uprising in Lefkada in 1819, which in turn stalled the establishment of an Ionian militia. When the Greek Revolution broke out in 1821, martial law was also imposed to prevent Ionians from breaking Ionian neutrality – part of the British policy on the issue – and thwart any rebellions on the islands. The chapter shows how efficient the Ionian State mechanism was in battling disease, disarming the population and suppressing even the slightest threat to tranquillity on the islands; in these tasks Ionians in positions of authority were quick to offer their services.

Chapter 3 shows the ways in which the tenacious class structure of the Ionian Islands under British rule 'produced' the institutional and in particular legal framework that is so important in any process of state formation. Law reform was among the priorities of many colonial powers in search of legitimacy, efficient bureaucratic administration and ordering practices for the control of the population. In the Ionian protectorate the project of legitimization failed when nationalism and the radical unionists prevailed, but the construction of an efficient, even if expensive, bureaucracy was quite successful. High commissioner Maitland based his ideas about legal reform and governance on his previous experience as a colonial administrator, and saw similarities between the 'tribes' of Ceylon (Sri Lanka), Maltese society and the Ionian Islands, where Maitland ended his career in British colonial office. British officials drew comparisons between Ionians and other subjects of the empire, and portrayed Ionians as the 'Mediterranean Irish'.

Chapter 4 shows how Ionian State officials conducted population registers for colonial administrative purposes but also held a meticulous record of petitions to the local and central authorities that reveal the language, concerns, requests, pleas, demands and motivations of Ionians of all classes. After 1827, population registers were constructed annually for the Blue Books of Statistics. This collection of knowledge formed the backbone of colonial policy in the Ionian Islands, and in the empire as a whole. The 'Blue Books' were compiled in all colonies of the British Empire with the aim to provide imperial officials with the knowledge that they considered important for optimal government. These books recorded population, revenue, trade, shipping, currency, public works, legislation, civil servants, enumeration of schools, prisons, hospitals and lunatic asylums, in an impressive attempt to impose colonial uniformity on vastly different societies. These series were published and evaluated by Parliament, and were intended to provide an imperial compass; British commissioners took into account the wealth of information to be found in the registers. The detailed accounts submitted to the Colonial Office accompanied the colonial statistics, and from the early 1840s onwards indicate a more systematic approach to Ionian administration and closer cooperation between the Colonial Office and the commissioner in Corfu.[41] Information was collected by Ionian staff on the islands, and by the bureaucrats of the British Empire in the Colonial Office. Sometimes with accuracy and sometimes in approximation, officers collected information about the population and the economy of the colonies as well as 'grey areas' such as the protectorate of the Ionian Islands, which until about the 1860s enjoyed a special – even if peculiar and occasionally embarrassing – status in this transitional period of the British Empire. This is the reason why the Ionian Islands have escaped strict categorization, since they formed neither a colony nor an independent state.

The 'Blue Books' were part of the imperial knowledge accumulated through measuring, recording and classifying population in 'statistics'; the ability to use this information for colonial projects of control and development is what distinguished the modern state from previous forms of record keeping and measurement. Venetians compiled 'cadastral' sources for centuries, but the Venetian *Proveditore* or Governor never used these sources to achieve the sophisticated level of colonial governance of nineteenth-century colonial rule. Ionians quickly adopted measurement and the detailed record keeping of population, land, production, climate, customs and geography in a fine example of local governmentality.[42] Later in the nineteenth century, colonial statistics informed Parliament and shaped colonial policy. Historians have demonstrated the importance of census and statistics for colonial governmentality in settler colonies, the tropics and South Asia, but not for European lands.[43] Statistics were part of a technology of domination, and as such developed in most colonial regimes, especially in India, one of the 'investigative modalities' that were crucial to the operation of colonial power, together with the historiographical, the observational/travel, the survey, the enumerative, museological and surveillance.[44] In the Ionian Islands one could add to these modalities the juridical, given the importance that all commissioners paid to the introduction of codes and the modernization of legislation in Ionian societies. British colonial officials regarded the islands as a colony, and applied a homogenizing model borrowed from the colonies that aimed at improving the quality of administration. This attitude made perfect sense from an administrative point of view, especially for the period until 1849 and the Seaton reforms, which allowed free press, extended the franchise by a few thousand people, and paved the way for radical unionist politics. British officials calculated people, production and trade, the 'population' and the 'economy', for the Ionian Islands, using the same methodology used for Caribbean islands and other colonies, although the historical trajectory of Ionian economic and social structures was worlds apart from those in the Caribbean or the dominion of Canada.

Chapter 5 argues that the ambiguous state of Ionian independence manifested itself most vividly in the political economy of the Ionian State and especially in the relationship between merchants and the state. Responding to the call by Cooper and Stoler for more complex engagement with colonial institutions and the work that colonial states do beyond the political aspects of decision making on the economy, including the creation of racial and economic categories, this chapter looks at the categories of inclusion and exclusion in the labour economies. 'Labour' and 'trade', however, were not entities with fixed meanings across time and space in the British Empire, but can serve as key concepts in understanding the political economy of colonialism at the time and for the Ionian Islands. It is more productive and historically accurate to focus on the forms of power that specific institutions projected and reproduced in the 'field' of economy as much as anywhere else.

Chapter 6 shows the ways in which the finances of the Ionian State were crucial for Ionian attitudes to the protectorate, which did not have control over its own finances but was constrained by the semi-colonial relation with the British Empire. The revenues of the Ionian State from import and export duties determined the capability of Ionian governments to pay for public works and promote the modernization project that British commissioners and Ionian liberals shared. The Ionian budget was a high priority in both Corfu and London since, according to British principles, colonies and dependencies had to pay for their expenses, including those incurred by the British army. The case of the Ionian

Islands shows the fiscal impact and the limits of development in regions under colonial rule or, in the case of the Ionian State, semi-colonies.

Chapter 7 conducts an investigation of Ionian public works and estimates the amounts spent, since this project was at the heart of colonial modernity. Public works of infrastructure and communication integrated the islands' rural population into urban markets, transferring even more power to the commercial – administrative – military hubs of Corfu, Zante and Argostoli. British and Ionian officials designed and ordered the construction of a dense and efficient road network in Corfu and Kefalonia. They also redesigned and attempted to modernize and impose order on Ionian cities, with impressive results for both their architecture and their functionality. Ionian State governments oversaw the integration of new and old groups in Ionian cities, the arrival of the Parga refugees, the Maltese colonial migrants and the coexistence of Christians and Jews in Corfu. The Ionian Islands were far from united, coherent or politically and socially stable. Ionians developed distinct and often competing regional, insular, identities as well as a common identity as Greek Orthodox subjects since Venetian times; the cities of Zante and Corfu were more diverse because of Catholic and Jewish populations, foreign merchants, officers and soldiers who settled during the period of Venetian rule, and Maltese workers and Parga refugees who enriched Corfu urban society in the 1810s. The most important aspect of Ionian identity however was not regional or 'national' but was based on class and defined by the strong division between town and country. Class differences were a direct result of the islands' mode of production, the cash crops that since the sixteenth century integrated the Ionian economy with the European mercantilist system. A Venetian colonial administration with the indispensable help of Ionians produced a system that allowed for abuse of power, unaccountable allocation of resources to *rentiers* (such as tax farmers) and surplus extraction from the semi-impoverished and chronically indebted farmers of the cash crops olive oil and currants. By the time the British took over in the 1810s the 'state' was fragmented, inefficient, poor, and badly in need of reform and modernization.

Chapter 8 demonstrates how the Ionian State promoted the islands' development through the necessary institutional framework and what is in today's jargon called 'structural reforms' in the Ionian economy. In the 1820s, the government also strived to promote agriculture, recognizing that increased exports would mean increased revenues. Parliament passed the first act promoting economic policy in April 1823.[45] This was the first of a series of measures adopted to promote agriculture but also 'arts' and 'commerce'. The resolution created a parliamentary committee, which pledged to enquire about obstacles that were hindering agricultural progress, consider what measures could be taken to alleviate these obstacles, and investigate where land could be cultivated or improved. Other duties included suggestions for the consolidation of landed property. The resolution also called for the publication, in both Italian and Greek, of the committee's conclusions introducing a new mode of governance that was accountable, transparent and, in theory at least, open to deliberation. Projects such as the savings bank and the societies for the improvement of agriculture were part of the same concept seeking to improve Ionian economies but also societies; this process also included regularization and control of the key professions and occupations of the cities, such as doctors and porters, but also of fishermen. These groups and individuals promoted their interests in a negotiation with the state through petitions, an invaluable source for historians to understand how Ionians perceived their condition and their relationship with the state authorities. By the end of the period, Ionian officials were skilled enough to devise projects of colonial governmentality in education, agriculture and prison reform, to mention only some of their contributions to public policy examined in the book. None of these reforms, however, was enough to quench the thirst of the more 'radical' Ionians for unification and an end to 'xenocracy' in the Ionian Islands. Chapter 9 looks at how the British-Ionian state and the Ionian and British elite introduced practices that strove to regulate economic and social life. This ideology coincided with practices followed in Britain during the same period. The model of social organization adopted as well as the practices to implement it were the same, namely the ones followed by the British bourgeoisie. The increasing use of police force in the towns to remove the pariahs of Ionian society pushed them further towards its fringes, and shows the unwillingness and inability to improve the conditions of poverty through philanthropy, and the necessity to introduce more stringent measures. The question of poverty in the Ionian Islands during the period would have to consider the deterioration of living conditions for the majority of the population. The increase in the number of the urban poor reflected the recognition of beggars and vagabonds as a social problem, and was primarily the result of the worsening economic condition on the islands and the difficulties of securing a living by relying on agricultural production; it was also the result of the more systematic recording of poverty. The Ionian State and the urban elite responded in different but complementary ways to the problem of poverty as it became more visible in Ionian towns. Ionian liberals, with the assistance of the state, consolidated their exercise of power in the public sphere with regulations, discourses and practices of social control. The coercive means of criminalizing begging, confinement and hard labour for anyone over twelve years old was the joint project of the state and the Ionian liberal bourgeoisie to achieve social control through philanthropy but also through force. Philanthropy emerged as a voluntary institution of bourgeois activism. In Corfu and the other Ionian islands, the agenda of philanthropy was far wider than simply distributing aid to the poor, and was founded on the principle and practice of voluntary organization by merchants, lawyers, state officials and military officers. These groups played a pivotal role at a moment of crisis and social upheaval caused by the outbreak of cholera in the suburbs of Corfu in 1855.

The meaning of 'middle class-ness' differs according to national and linguistic contexts, however recent approaches to the study of the middle class draw cases from various regions around the world contributing and pointing towards a global history of middle classes.[46] During the period of transition from the Ottoman and Venetian context to the Greek State, merchants (and less so intellectuals) were often regarded as the diaspora bourgeoisie who contributed in various ways to the formation of modern Greece, and who gradually during the nineteenth century transferred their economic and political power to the Greek State. Greek historians and political scientists have underestimated the agency and the role of the Greek bourgeoisie in its own making;[47] instead they opted for other factors, following mostly an old-fashioned dependency theory approach and tools drawn from political science and anthropology: comprador capitalism, foreign influence, clientelism and political patronage.[48] The Greek (and Ionian) urban world was so fragmented, especially in the nineteenth century, that a Greek national bourgeoisie sounds implausible and unconvincing, just like elsewhere in Europe, where bourgeoisies were distinguished by their local identities and civic pride.[49] What distinguished some Ionians as a bourgeoisie was not only their commercial-economic, financial and shipping activities (as a conventional definition of a colonial bourgeoisie would suggest), although these were undoubtedly present; but, as Chapter 10 specifically and the book show, it was the educational and social background that produced the distinct characteristics of a liberal middle class and defined the relationship between the Ionian bourgeoisie and the state (complementary or antagonistic). In the Ionian Islands case, the term 'bourgeoisie' in the broader sense than the strict Marxist definition of class reflecting the capitalist relations of production is more appropriate, because it avoids the tripartite definition of upper, middle and lower class; many Ionian bourgeoisie were upper class and many upper class Ionians did not share the worldview that could be found among the bourgeoisie in other European and Mediterranean cities. On the other hand, given the peculiarities of each island, it is also fair to speak about the Ionian middle classes to describe the formation of a class of lawyers, merchants, politicians and after 1848 journalists as well as civil servants with conflicting aspirations about their state and society's fortunes; at the same time these same people shared lifestyle, dress, language, social norms, a common education and above all their attitude towards British rule over their country – what liberal and radical Ionians called *xenokratia* or 'xenocracy'. It was this attitude that ultimately drove some of them apart, dividing them into reformists and radical unionists.

This structure of chapters reflects, and aspires to capture, some of the key moments and developments in the process of state and class formation in the Ionian State. Rather than follow a strict chronological sequence it follows a thematic order that does highlight the changes during the terms of different high commissioners, as they undoubtedly mattered. The politics of the bourgeoisie were inextricably linked with the building and development of the colonial state to the extent that the bourgeoisie formed the state and at the same time they were shaped by it. The various sources that are used in each chapter – government documents, newspapers, publications, contemporary accounts of travellers and officials, but also the petitions of Ionians of different classes – show the negotiation and conflicts that emerged in the process of class and state formation. The overwhelming presence of British colonial power should not mask the agency of different groups of Ionians, most active among them, the middle class, who embraced ideas of liberalism, state and social reform, national integration and unification with Greece, and thus broke away from their traditional Venetian-era structures and their British colonial present, looking into a Greek future, for better or for worse for them.

Notes

1. The first book to use the term was published at the end of the nineteenth century by G. Filaretos, *Xenokratia kai Vasileia stin Ellada* (Xenocracy and Monarchy in Greece), in 1897. The term was also used in one reference for the history of education in the Ionian Islands; E. Yotopoulou-Sicilianou, 'I Eptanisiaki paideia sta chronia tis ksenokratias', *Kerkyraika Chronika* XV, 1970, 101–121.
2. P. Chiotis, *Istoria tou Ioniou Kratous*, vol. B, p. 26 and 35–36.
3. *Anagennisis*, No 12, 25/6/1849.
4. *Fileleftheros*, No. 30, 19/3/1851.

5 For the role of Russia in the making of modern Greece see Lucien J. Frary, *Russia and the making of modern Greek identity, 1821–1844*. Oxford: Oxford University Press, 2015.
6 The concept of semi-colonialism is rarely used in cases other than China but it is probably more appropriate in cases of state projects such as protectorates. Hobson went into more speculative detail than Lenin and anticipated a joint invasion of China by the financiers of the great powers; Jurgen Osterhammel, 'Semi-Colonialism and Informal Empire in Twentieth-Century China: Towards a Framework of Analysis', in Wolfgang Mommsen (ed.), *Imperialism and After: Continuities and Discontinuities*. London: Allen & Unwin, 1986, 290–314.
7 Simon Gunn and James Vernon (eds), *The Peculiarities of Liberal Modernity in Imperial Britain*. Berkeley: University of California, 2011, 12.
8 Thomas W. Gallant, *Experiencing Dominion: Culture, Identity and Power in the British Mediterranean*. Notre Dame: University of Notre Dame Press, 2002.
9 David Sutherland, *Managing the British Empire: The Crown Agents, 1833–1914*. Royal Historical Society: Boydell Press, 2004, 1.
10 Andrew Porter, 'Introduction', in A. Porter (ed.), *The Oxford History of the British Empire, Vol. 3*. Oxford: Oxford University Press, 1999, 4.
11 John Gallagher and Ronald Robinson, 'The Imperialism of Free Trade', *Economic History Review*, 2nd series, 6 (1953): 1–15.
12 Heather Streets-Salter and Trevor Getz, *Empires and Colonies in the Modern World. A Global Perspective*. Oxford: Oxford University Press, 2016, 5.
13 Julia A. Clancy Smith, *Mediterraneans. North Africa and Europe in an age of migration, c. 1800–1900*. Berkeley, CA: University of California Press, 2011.
14 Porter, 'Introduction', 18. Darwin writes that 'coercion and collaboration were two sides of the same coin', and one needs to pay close attention to the conditions on which British expansion aiming at trade or dominion depended. In any case, 'this was almost never possible without some form of alliance or understanding with the rulers and peoples who claimed or controlled the area concerned'; J. Darwin, *Unfinished Empire: The Global Expansion of Britain*. London: Bloomsbury Press, 2012, 8, 228.
15 Helen Taft Manning, *British Colonial Government after the American Revolution, 1782–1820*. New Haven, CT: Yale University Press, 1933.
16 Robert Holland, *Blue-Water Empire: The British in the Mediterranean since 1800*. London: Allen Lane, 2012.
17 C.A. Bayly, *Imperial Meridian: The British Empire and the World, 1780–1830*. London and New York: Longman, 1989, 2.
18 R. Hyam, 'The Primacy of Geopolitics: The Dynamics of British Imperial Policy, 1793–1863', *Journal of Imperial and Commonwealth History* 27(2) (1999): 27–52.
19 Bayly, *Imperial Meridian*, 8.
20 Patrick Joyce, *The Rule of Freedom: Liberalism and the Modern City*. London: Verso, 2003.
21 Michael Herzfeld, 'The Absent Presence: Discourses of Crypto-Colonialism', *South Atlantic Quarterly* 101(4) (2002): 899–926. For another critique, see Gourgouris, *Dream Nation*.
22 K. Kostis, *Ta kakomathimena paidia tis istorias*.

23 Catherine Hall (ed.), *Cultures of Empire: Colonizers in Britain and the Empire in the Nineteenth and Twentieth Centuries*. Manchester: Manchester University Press, 2000, 7.
24 Kathleen Wilson, 'Rethinking the Colonial State: Family, Gender, and Governmentality in Eighteenth-Century British Frontiers', *American Historical Review* 116(5) (2011): 1294–1322.
25 Historians influenced by Foucault, 'use the term liberalism to capture a new mentality and method of government that emerged in the late eighteenth and early nineteenth century. Far from being wedded to a particular set of ideas or the ideology of a political party, this mentality was the product of new forms of knowledge and expertise. In turn, they produced and justified new techniques of rule over those subjects deemed capable of self-government (the informed, industrious, healthy, and self-improving individual) as well as those others found incapable of it. Some have claimed that it is possible to identify eras of liberal government that stretch from the late eighteenth century through to the late twentieth. As a political technology that extends far beyond the realm of politics and the work of the state, liberalism here is a diffuse rationality, generated by many actors from multiple sources and evident in a panoply of everyday practices and material environments. It is seemingly everywhere and nowhere'. Gunn and Vernon, *The Peculiarities of Liberal Modernity*, 9.
26 Jürgen Osterhammel, *The Transformation of the World*, Princeton: Princeton University Press, 2014, 29.
27 See David Scott, 'Colonial Governmentality', *Social Text* 43 (1995): 191–220; Peter Pels, 'The Anthropology of Colonialism: Culture, History, and the Emergence of Western Governmentality', *Annual Review of Anthropology* 26 (1997): 163–83; U. Kalpagam, 'Colonial Governmentality and the Public Sphere in India', *Journal of Historical Sociology* 15(1) (2002): 35–58; Joyce, *The Rule of Freedom*.
28 Norman Davis, *Vanished Kingdoms: The Rise and Fall of States and Nations*. London: Penguin, 2011.
29 Thomas W. Gallant, *Modern Greece*. London and New York: Arnold, 2001; Richard Clogg, *A Concise History of Modern Greece*. Cambridge: Cambridge University Press, 2nd edn, 2002; John S. Koliopoulos and Thanos M. Veremis, *Modern Greece: A History since 1821*. London: Wiley-Blackwell, 2010; Κωστής, *Τα κακομαθημένα παιδιά της ιστορίας*.
30 P.M. Kitromilides, 'An Enlightenment Perspective on Balkan Cultural Pluralism: The Republican Vision of Rhigas Velestinlis', *History of Political Thought* 24 (2003): 465–79.
31 Tassos Anastassiadis, Nathalie Clayer (eds), *Society, Politics and State Formation in Southeastern Europe during the 19th Century*. Athens: Alpha Bank Historical Archives, 2011.
32 M. Şükrü Hanioğlu, *A Brief History of the Late Ottoman Empire*. Princeton, NJ: Princeton University Press, 2008, 8–9. Christine Phylliou, *Biography of an Empire: Governing Ottomans in an Age of Revolution*. Berkeley and Los Angeles: University of California Press, 2011.

33. John Petropoulos, 'Introduction', in N. Diamantouros et al. (eds), *Hellenism and the Greek War of Liberation (1821–1830)*. Thessaloniki: Insitute for Balkan Studies, 1976.
34. S.A. Smith, *Like Cattle and Horses: Nationalism and Labour in Shangai, 1895–1927*, Durham, NC and London: Duke University Press, 2002, 9.
35. A.R. López and B. Weinstein (eds), *The Making of the Middle Class: Toward a Transnational History*. Durham, NC: Duke University Press, 2012.
36. A. Mitchell, 'Bourgeois Liberalism and Public Health: A Franco-German Comparison', in J. Kocka and A. Mitchell (eds), *Bourgeois Society in Nineteenth-Century Europe*. Oxford: Berg, 1993, 350.
37. Haris Exertzoglou, 'The Cultural Uses of Consumption: Negotiating Class, Gender and Nation in Ottoman Urban Centers during the 19th Century', *International Journal of Middle East Studies* 35(1) (2003): 77–101.
38. Helen Gardikas-Katsiadakis, 'Ioannis A. Valaoritis: The Life of a Typical Greek Nineteenth-Century Bourgeois?', in P. Carabott (ed.), *Greek Society in the Making, 1863–1913: Realities, Symbols and Visions*. Aldershot: Ashgate, 1997, 55–69.
39. Sanjay Joshi, *The Middle Class in Colonial India*. New Delhi and New York: Oxford University Press, 2010.
40. F. Cooper and A.L. Stoler, 'Between Metropole and Colony: Rethinking a Research Agenda', in Frederick Cooper and Ann Laura Stoler (eds), *Tensions of Empire: Colonial Cultures in a Bourgeois World*. Berkeley: University of California Press, 1997, 34.
41. M. Paximadopoulou-Stavrianou, *Politeiografika Ionion Nison epi Agglikis Kyriarchias 1815–1864. Oi etisies ektheseis tis Armosteias pros to Ypourgeio ton Apoikion*, Vol. I. Athens: Etaireia Kefalliniakon Istorikon Erevnon, 1997.
42. One such example is the book by E. Theotoky, *Details Sur Corfou*, Corfu, 1826.
43. Pels, 'The Anthropology of Colonialism'.
44. B.S. Cohn, *Colonialism and its Forms of Knowledge: The British in India*. Princeton, NJ: Princeton University Press, 1996.
45. Risoluzione del II parlamento (12 April 1823).
46. López and Weinstein, *The Making of the Middle Class*.
47. Koliopoulos and Veremis, *Greece, the Modern Sequel*. Γ.Β. Δεϱτιλής, Ιστορία του Ελληνικού Κράτους [History of the Greek State], Athens, 2006.
48. Diamantouros, *I aparches sygkrotisis sychronou kratous stin Ellada*. The 'failure' of the Greek bourgeoisie to live up to its expected role and reputation is an argument that has returned forcefully as the Greek crisis has deepened. This argument, despite its ambivalent empirical foundation, raises the question of whether there was ever a Greek national bourgeoisie – or middle class, as it is sometimes called – and whether this is another fictitious concept introduced by analysts and (some) historians.
49. There is only one work that has stressed this aspect of the Greek bourgeoisie and has opened an avenue in Greek social history that has not been taken up: Yannitsiotis [Yannis Yannitsiotis, 'Social History in Greece: New Perspectives', *East Central Europe* 34–35 (2007–8): 1–2, 101–30].

 Chapter 1

THE FIRST GREEK STATE AND THE ORIGINS OF COLONIAL GOVERNMENTALITY

The Republic of the Seven Islands

On 16 June 1797 two frigates and two brigs carrying fifteen hundred French soldiers under the command of General Gentili landed on Corfu. Their mission was to establish a republican government in the name and the interests of the French Republic.[1] On 17 October 1797 the Republic of Venice expired with the Treaty of Campo Formio that Napoleon Bonaparte imposed on Austria, and the Ionian Islands passed under French rule. Napoleon's troops abolished the aristocratic government in Corfu, and appointed for the first time municipal councils with representatives from different classes, both from legally constituted groups and those aspiring to acquire political status under the new regime; soon after on the other islands the old regime crumbled as soon as the French landed. The French Republican army ruled for a year and a half (1797–99) and introduced revolutionary changes that brought a liberal and democratic wind to the islands.[2] Ionians, however, soon became disillusioned when the French imposed heavy taxation and extracted loans to serve the army's needs. When the French arrested thirty grain importers from Corfu and kept them in prison for several days, their families yielded to French demands for more cash as new taxes added to existing ones.[3]

Napoleon's campaign in Egypt signalled the beginnings of modernity for the Eastern Mediterranean and the Middle East;[4] the case can be made for Greek history as well. The scramble between France, Britain, Russia and the Ottoman Empire for the Eastern Mediterranean intensified during the Napoleonic Wars. In January 1799 Britain, Russia and the Ottoman Empire formed an alliance to block French expansion in the Eastern Mediterranean and undermine French presence in the region by claiming the Ionian Islands; encouraged by displaced Ionian landowners, disgruntled merchants and the Church, who despised the 'atheist' French, an 'unholy alliance' of a Russian-Ottoman fleet landed on Kythera in September 1798 and then on the other islands one by one, finally claiming Corfu in February 1799. After a year of negotiations and efforts to impose order on the islands, the Treaty of Constantinople was signed on 21 March 1800, creating the Septinsular Republic under Ottoman sovereignty and Russian protection. The new state was modelled after the Republic of Ragusa, the 'jewel of the Adriatic'.[5] The state of Ragusa and its centuries-long success resonated with diplomats of the time and served as the model for the Septinsular Republic, as Ragusan merchants and ship owners were already losing to Ionian commerce and shipping, which had enjoyed Russian and Ottoman protection since 1774 and the Treaty of Kucuk-Kainarci, that game changer for Greek shipping and Greek history in the Black Sea. This is why the Septinsular Republic generated expectations in Russia of state-building in the Adriatic and the western Balkans that could lead to an autonomous Slav State embracing Bosnia, Herzegovina, Serbia and Montenegro, predating (to an extent) the Kingdom of Yugoslavia.[6]

The Septinsular Republic was modelled according to the Republic of Ragusa because of the commercial success, military impartiality and diplomatic neutrality that translated into state formation; international and regional developments, however, quickly derailed such plans but left the aspiration of national self-determination. The Septinsular Republic (1800–1807) unified the islands as a state entity for the first time, and formed a Russian-Ottoman protectorate with a constitutional and federal dimension, laying the foundations for the Ionian State under British protection. The constitutions of this period (1800, 1803, 1806) did not express the wills of the nation for self-determination and independence, however they did introduce a federal organization, Greek as the language of the state, civil liberties, and – especially – provided the scaffolding of a state bureaucracy distinct from the Venetian period. It was the 1817 constitutional charter, pledged by the British when they assumed control and provided 'protection' for the Ionian Islands, that created a political – as in 'national' – consciousness, and later in the nineteenth century opened a space for negotiation between British colonial officials and Ionian liberals, which the more 'radical' ones gradually occupied.

The first constitutional texts in the Ionian Islands were published in a form of Greek that integrated Italian and French terms and concepts of political terminology that were simple enough for most people to understand. This reform represented a break from the domination of Italian in law and administration; however, this was not completed until 1852 when the Greek language was implemented as the language of the state.[7] The political institutions that were established during this period make the Septinsular Republic the first Greek State, a state whose language was Greek. The first constitution of 1800 was printed in Greek by the patriarchal press in Constantinople in a dialect that borrowed heavily from Italian for technical terms in administration. The constitution of 1803 was published in Italian, and a Greek translation followed in 1804. In the preamble the committee declared in Italian – an obvious contradiction – that the language of the state should be Greek, an 'exiled' language: 'the noble, rich and harmonious Greek dialect, having been exiled by the long dominion of the Venetians, should be recalled to the State and become the language of government and the interpreter of the active citizens'.[8] Political rights were granted to individuals according to property that was calculated in capital, land, education, or professional expertise and specialization, the cornerstone of a liberal state that remained in the constitutional charter of 1817 and the reforms of 1849.

The creation of a republic under conditions of protection laid the foundations for a constitutionally sanctioned political hegemony of a privileged group of Ionians who later in the nineteenth century challenged British protection. The Ionian Republic, the first Greek state with some sort of independence filled educated and revolutionary Greeks in the Ottoman Empire with hopes, and generated expectations in European cities among 'diaspora' Greeks. After French republicanism, Russian-Ottoman protection followed and brought a conservative backlash. Government offices returned to the hands of the old nobility, who saw their privileges restored. The new regime aspired to unify the islands as a single administrative entity (the basic presupposition of a modern nation-state) – a process that the Ionian State continued during the nineteenth century.

The constitutions of 1800 and 1803 laid the foundations for the offices of government, the 'ministries'.[9] The first constitution included general statements on commerce, shipping and religion, but made provision that 'every General or Grand Council will elect the respective Municipal Authorities of the Island and will be responsible for the Economy, Commerce, Shipping and Public Health'.[10] This government structure remained practically the same, apart from a few other important portfolios such as education added later on in the Ionian State. The constitution of 1803 included important provisions on religion, introducing tolerance and therefore (limited) religious freedom to minority religions such as the Roman Catholic rite and the Jewish religion; it also declared the Eastern Greek Orthodox religion as the state religion.[11] An important provision that lasted until 1810 declared that those who had already served or were serving as lawmakers, senators, judges or top officials could get elected.[12] Maintaining the same people in power served a practical political purpose; the state needed immediately people versed in the art of government, and there were few individuals with those qualifications who could oversee the transition in those troubled times. One of them was Francisco Zoulati, who drafted and presented the constitution of 1803 to the Senate for approval, influenced by the principles of the Enlightenment and political philosophy, the intellectual origins of the constitution.[13] Zoulati (1718–1805) was a fervent supporter of liberal ideas during the period of the French Republic, and he was most likely aware of the translation of Beccaria's work by Koraes, if not aware of the original.[14] Zoulati was also involved in the literary and educational associations in Corfu that saw the transition from the last Venetian period to the French and British periods of rule. The language in the draft for the constitution is also one of the first – if not the first – condemnation of 'xenocracy', which Zoulati blames for having deprived Ionians from 'science' (επιστήμη); here lie the roots of the anti-foreign, anti-xenocratic movement that led to the demand for union with Greece in the 1850s.

Building a Federal State

French republicanism was followed by a period of anarchy and social turmoil until 1803 when the old political order was restored. Elites in Corfu, Zante and Kefalonia offered their support for the next occupation in line – French initially, Russian, then French again, and British afterwards. When the British took over the southern Ionian Islands in 1809–10 and Corfu in 1814, they were aware of the radical political events of the previous years. These elites preferred a strong British administration to a weak and volatile local government that would prove unable to impose order.

The formation of a federal state needed a strong central government to impose its authority, but that required a leap of faith from the Zante elite, since there was no reason why they should have capitulated to Corfu, when the authority of Venice had vanished. The Corfu government tried to restore order and force all factions on the islands to accept the new status quo. This, however, was a complicated challenge. *The Times* reported in October 1800 that the islands of Zante and Kefalonia had practically seceded from the provisional government of Corfu:

> Letters from Corfu mention that the Islands of Cephalonia, Zante & c. have entirely separated from the Provisional Government established at Corfu and declared themselves independent. As there is but feeble Russian garrison at Corfu, it cannot interfere in the concerns of the other Islands. It is added that the new plan of Government proposed for those

Islands does not meet with the approbation either of Russia or the Porte. These Islands have given themselves to the most dreadful anarchy, and assassinations are very frequent in them.[15]

Kefalonia presents the best example of how the conflict was resolved. The Russian plenipotentiary was blunt when he met Kefalonia's elite families and tried to reason with them to form a local council and restore order: 'The memory of the terrible chaos that had plunged the island must convince them how destructive the constant disturbance of private and public affairs is and the conflict of violent passions'.[16] Faced with continuing violence and anarchy, the powerful families did exactly that; they met in council and elected delegates for the Legislative Assembly and the Senate of the state. Restoring order on the island was extremely difficult without the powerful families – the Anninos and Metaxas families especially – since villagers could not be simply dragged into the conflict but had enough reasons of their own to rebel; a young, weak and 'under foreign control' state could impose its authority and realize its federal plan only with the consent of its most powerful citizens.

Political changes and increased taxation pushed Kefalonia villagers to revolt; the islands were already a hotbed for factional conflict throughout the eighteenth century. Kefalonia was in a state of 'anarchy' for three years. In Venetian times, in Kefalonia just like on the other islands, tithe collection was leased to tax farmers who, together with landowners and often with the use of violence, subjected villagers to ever-increasing taxes. Until the Septinsular Republic and modern state formation, annual visits or rather raids of tax collectors with the protection of the army were the norm. When a government committee from Corfu headed by S. Vattalia visited the island, it concluded in a report that the form of taxation and tithe collection was the reason that triggered the uprising; the committee suggested abolishing the oppressive tithe and substituting it with indirect taxes on imported and exported goods. The government responded immediately to the recommendations of the Vattalia committee and abolished the tithe in 1803, ending the riots, murders and burning of properties in the country. The island's powerful families were convinced to end their decades-old feuds and allow the Septinsular Republic to impose its centralizing authority. Tranquillity returned to the island, and the tithe was abolished for good in 1820 on all islands except Kythera, where it remained until 1825.[17]

Merchants participated in the political process as a separate group in the new politics of the land.[18] With the arrival of the Republican French, some merchants felt powerful enough to claim a role in the political sphere and exchange their economic power with political representation and participation. In a period of turmoil (1799–1802) merchants were granted political recognition, as is indicated by their inclusion in the municipal council of Corfu, established during the Republican French rule.[19] In 1802 the regent of Corfu, G. Sicuro, appointed Stefano Paramithioti as 'Capo e Procuratore del Corpo Merantile' (Chief and Procurator of the Mercantile Body),[20] an appointment that reflects the wealth and importance of Paramithioti among other merchants and shows the ability of merchants to organize as a distinct commercial association. In 1809 a similar initiative was called *Compagnia Jonia* and was approved by Karouzos, president of the Senate.[21] The institutionalization of commerce by merchants and their formation as an interest group predated the emergence of the liberal Ionian bourgeoisie in the nineteenth century.

In 1802 the Senate of the Septinsular Republic issued a decree in Greek, Italian and French that shows the perceptions of the authorities about society and social classes in particular, calling on 'inhabitants of all classes and orders of the islands' to restore order. Moncenigo, the representative of Russian interests and effective governor of the islands, wrote this document that reflects his personal views but also his perceptions of Ionian society. In December 1802 the 'double list' of candidates for electing the senators was introduced for the first time; it remained until the 1840s as a way of ensuring that preferred deputies were elected. In 1803 Moncenigo announced to the Ionian people the need to form a government and enhance political power through a new institution: the four-member Collegio Politico, the executive of the state.[22] The decree declared the hereditary right to political participation, the last time politics were determined in such a premodern fashion. Peace was restored on the ground when the Russian army quelled the last pockets of violence near the city at the village of Potamos and further south in Lefkimi. The government expressed in an announcement its gratitude to the Russian army for 'the arrest of the criminals and insurgents of the Land, and for destroying the bond of Anarchy and Disorder'.[23]

In 1803 there was a change of guard in power. When Theotokis, power broker between different authorities (French, Russian, and the local families) died, Komoutos, a noble from Zante, took his place as president of the Septinsular Republic. For the Senate to convene in Corfu with legitimacy, other islands and especially Zante had to recognize the authority of the Corfu council. Another sign of submission to centralized authority and one of the first duties of the Senate and the Russian commissioner, Moncenigo, was fiscal consolidation, especially raising revenue to cover expenses for the army. Financial administration of the period October 1802 to December 1803 yielded 226,992 talers while expenses stood at 220,745, leaving a meagre 6,427 talers. At the same time the state commission for finance estimated that 300,000 talers had to be spent to cover the needs of the state, of which 228,000 was for the needs of the Russian army and 14,000 for the Ionian army, leaving very little for the other needs of the fledgling state. One of the first resolutions of the assembly was the formation of a militia recruited from all classes of Ionians. This was a novelty since wealthy Ionians could buy off forced labour (which is what militia service was) during Venetian times. Some assembly deputies put up a strong resistance, claiming that military obligation should only burden peasants and not city residents, but they were a minority, and a resolution for the formation of a 1,200-strong militia passed in the Ionian Assembly.[24] Albanian irregulars served as the militia both during the Septinsular Republic and under French occupation (1807–14), showing no preference or loyalty other than to their paymaster.

The presence and role of a small group of Ionian statesmen made the transition from one foreign rule to another less challenging and antagonistic than it would have been otherwise. Theotokis, together with Efstathios Valaoritis (the uncle of the later famous poet and deputy to the Ionian Assembly) were among the small group of Ionians who stood at the helm during the transition years between 1797 until 1815. Valaoritis was held in such esteem by the French officials that he was appointed president of the Senate in 1809; judged as untrustworthy by the first British administration of Commissioner Maitland, he was suspected of plotting against the protectorate in the Lefkada uprising of 1819. The political career of his son, Spyridon, was also successful; he served as deputy and senator, and after unification he became minister of foreign affairs, minister of finance, president of the Parliament and ambassador in London.[25] The poet's father, Ioannis, however, was a successful and adventurous if not risky merchant, breaking the British blockade of Genoa and later of Corfu. It was only later in life that he also entered politics and represented Lefkada until 1856. These political families, with their knowledge and experience in government, were crucial in the transition from one form of state to another, and for Ionian governmentality as it matured during the years of the Ionian State.

Fertile Associations and the Roots of Ionian Governmentality

During the 'transitional' period of 1797–1814 some Ionians developed their ability to govern but they also created a public sphere through associations of knowledge. Ionian governmentality meant rationality in government through measurement, calculation and the application of results for the promotion of the wealth and security of the population. In the seventeenth and eighteenth centuries Ionian intellectuals created associations for the promotion of knowledge that emerged outside the structures of political power; in the nineteenth century intellectuals, politicians and other liberals combined their local knowledge with imported ideas and government practices borrowed from French and especially British colonial rule. Over time these circles of knowledge developed into groups of intellectuals aiming to formulate public policy.

Literary associations created a collective identity among Ionian intellectuals who became political outside the confines of the old bastion of politics, the Governing Council. Ionian intellectuals following their studies in Italian and other European universities brought ideas, knowledge and experience. This tradition laid the foundations for the emergence of Ionian voluntary and literary societies during the nineteenth century. In Italian cities the *academia* (associations of scholars) and the *casino* (meeting places for leisure, gambling and occasionally business) were predominant forms of social life and sites of sociability.[26] In Corfu this tradition goes back to the seventeenth century; in 1656 the 'Academy' (degli Assicurati) was founded by thirty doctors, lawyers, literary figures and poets, and lasted until in 1716.[27] Most members of these associations were graduates of the University of Padova, doctors of medicine and law, Orthodox as well as Roman Catholic.[28] The 'Academics' were praised by travellers Spoon and Wheeler, who noted the international recognition of the group and publicized the erudition of some distinguished members such as Nikolaos Voulgaris, a member of the elite Corfu family.[29] These were the roots of an Ionian Enlightenment that focused less on philosophy and language and more on the practical, as in applied science, medicine, legal thought and, from the early nineteenth century onwards, its application in government. The glow of this Enlightenment revealed several intellectuals in medicine and politics, and an interest in improving the capabilities of the Ionian economy and, by implication, the well-being of Ionians and the fortunes of their state.

Corfu was undoubtedly the hub of this intellectual–social world. The group of the 'Fertili' was more specialized than the 'Assicurati', and aimed at improving agricultural production. The Fertili was founded in 1676 by Augoustino Capello and met until at least 1678. In the eighteenth century, in 1734, a new academy, of the Περιπλανώμενοι ('Wanderers'), members of Corfu's aristocratic families, continued the enquiries, intellectual pursuits and tradition of collective organization, and discussed mostly theological issues.[30] These meetings promoted a common worldview outside the standard seat of political power and created a space where debate was possible, especially among those who were excluded from the city's Council of 150.[31] Towards the end of Venetian rule, De Zorzi, governor of Kefalonia, mobilized some of the island's aristocrats and founded an 'Agronomical Academy' in 1791 and endowed it with 150 ducats per year. The intellectual pursuits of this academy, besides poetry and other literary fields, included the economic development of the island of Kefalonia through modernizing agriculture.[32] The 'doctor-philosopher' Francisco Zulatti devised the constitution of the academy, stating explicitly the aim of development and growth of agricultural production, which included the draining of marshes and the improvement of cultivation (of grapes), aims that continued to attract interest during the British period and elicited greater intervention of state officials and a clearer institutional mandate.

This form of collective agency promoted independent thinking, experimentation with new forms of knowledge and its dissemination to a wider public (of the same class) aimed at improving the state of the Ionian economy. Such associational activity acquired political dimensions; in the eighteenth century one of the criteria for inclusion in the Corfu and Zante political body was a university degree, an academic title that completed the other 'qualifications' of aristocratic ('noble') descent and state employment.[33] These institutions were essentially social and to some extent political clubs of readers – learning societies, promoting useful knowledge and other intellectual pursuits. The Republican French period unleashed the forces of political radicalism among the more progressive Ionians and (temporarily) abolished the aristocratic regime. The associations of scholars were central in this radicalization. In 1797 'political societies of public civil education' were founded, one in Corfu and one in Kefalonia, where 'patriotic' speeches were heard; the content and agenda of these meetings was social and therefore political, according to an Ionian historian: 'the most courageous and provocative republicans socialized there, those who vehemently wanted to accelerate social reforms and improvements'; among those early radicals were 'the most wise and liberal islanders and French'.[34] The society had its doors open to the people after its meetings. There were interesting and innovative things happening in Ionian cities during 1797–98. Some of the first radicals were promoting social reforms and with the opening of the doors of the political societies a public space was opening too. Social reforms stopped abruptly, however, when Count Moncenigo, the Russian plenipotentiary, took over as head of the government under the protection of the Russian army in 1799.

In the first years of the nineteenth century, Ionian intellectuals participated actively in the political life of their islands, as these passed under the aristocratic rule of the Ottoman-Russian protectorate of the Ionian Republic (1800–1807). Francisco Zullatti, founder of the Agronomical Society in Kefalonia, was the secretary of the commission that proposed the reforms of the 1803 constitution. The meetings of the Agronomical Society stopped when public order broke down in Kefalonia but continued in 1811 when, under Governor De Bosset, the society contributed to the reconstruction of agriculture; the same year the French founded the Agricultural and Industrial Commission in Corfu showing the colonial developmental projects by both British and French officials. These initiatives intended to address issues of agricultural production, and were influenced by similar progressive ideas of French and Italian intellectuals whom Ionians met during their studies and later corresponded with.

Medicine was a fertile field for the germination of modern ideas of social organization. Ionian doctors formulated and implemented health policies based on liberal ideas of social organization. Health and living conditions both in the ports and in the country varied from unsanitary to atrocious. Malaria, typhus and dysentery were common and endemic due to the unhealthy and infected water (particularly in city wells) but also due to improper food preservation. Illnesses spread among the most vulnerable, including children, but deaths – because undocumented – are very hard to estimate. The French army brought a new approach to governance. Among the French military staff that came to the islands was the Italian doctor and historian Carlo Botta (1766–1837), who joined the Napoleonic army in Italy and wrote the first natural and medical history of Corfu, while stationed there for a year.[35] Botta's book is the first systematic study of how the natural environment affects health, and is also an important source for living conditions in the late eighteenth century. The book had quite an impact on the intellectual life of the islands, since many Ionian and British writers referred to it for descriptions of the environment and the climatic conditions, already since 1815 when Emmanuel Theotokis published his 'Memoirs on the Ionian Islands'.[36] When the Russian army arrived in 1799, Ionian doctors often took a leading role because of their expertise in the modernizing project of trying to improve health conditions. These men came from aristocratic Corfu families who assumed more political roles together with their medical expertise. In Kefalonia, doctor Marinos Valsamakis served as a judge, doctor Ioannis Krasas as a member of the High Police and the State Security Committee, and doctor Stamatelos Petritsis as a member of the executive council of the island, the so-called 'Presidency'.³⁷ Most famous of all, Ioannis Kapodistrias also studied and practised medicine before going into administration as minister of the Septinsular Republic.

Ionian doctors promoted their own group organization, the Collegio Medico, a medical association founded in Corfu in 1802 with the initiative of the young Ioannis Kapodistrias after his studies in Padua. Kapodistrias completed his training in state affairs and administration in 1803, when he became the general director of the executive power under Count Moncenigo, the Russian plenipotentiary. Kapodistrias was rewarded for his exceptional performance in 1803 as extraordinary commissioner sent to maintain peace on all the islands where uprisings had broken out, and he was also appointed secretary of state for foreign affairs and trade.³⁸ Among the duties and mission of the medical association was the examination and appointment of doctors and surgeons before granting a licence to practice their profession. M. Lesseps, the French imperial commissioner, granted to the Collegio the authority to consult on health and sanitation issues, inoculation, births, and children's health.³⁹ This was the first professional organization of the Ionian Islands and it included a Jewish doctor, Lazaro Mordo.⁴⁰ The Collegio Medico and the Ionian Academy were the two most important associations for the spread of useful knowledge; they were also the first bodies of Ionian experts in the fields of medicine and public policy. In 1805 the Collegio Medico promoted the inoculation of the population against smallpox on all the islands; its members met monthly and formed sanitary committees that supervised public health, a practice that continued during the years of the Ionian State.⁴¹ The French initiative for the inoculation of the population and the improvement of public health, although introduced for the French troops, extended to the rest of the islands' population. Inoculation began in Kefalonia in 1806, and in 1810 French Imperial Commissioner Bessieres appointed the Central Inoculation Committee in Corfu. These initiatives extended to the country as well as the city for the first time; three doctors were appointed, targeting not only disease and illnesses but also the superstition of the country's residents, vulnerable to quacks who more often caused deaths than found cures. The committee and their work promoted the modernizing principle of a patronizing state that aimed to 'civilize' the populations under its control, just like the French army did in many other colonized lands; this was after all a common pattern of the European colonial governmentality project in the nineteenth century, and continued during the period of British rule with more initiatives from doctors in the Ionian State. During the French occupation of 1807–14 the Collegio formed public health committees of Ionian doctors. The institution of the 'doctor for the poor' was created to offer consultation to the poor and visit twice a day a dispensary where the doctor saw patients; there was even a provision that obliged the doctor to visit patients in cases of emergency, day or night.[42]

The Ionian Academy, founded in 1808, was the culmination of previous voluntary associations of knowledge but sanctioned by the French colonial administration.[43] The academy was more than a learning society because it prioritized 'the perfection of agriculture, manufacture, commerce, the increase of public and private wealth in the islands and the promotion of science … and the progress of letters'.[44] To realize these goals one of the first initiatives of the academy was to gather statistical information for the islands and record the resources and the productive capabilities of the population. Stylianos Vlassopoulos published his book 'Statistical-Historical Information on Corfu', focusing on one of the first tasks of governmentality, the need to measure and classify populations in order to govern them more efficiently.[45] Vlassopoulos offered a policy-making report that is distinct from previous documents created by Venetian or Ionian officials. Born into a noble family, Vlassopoulos like many members of his class studied theology and law at the University of Padua. When he returned to Corfu he served in the highest echelons of the administration as *Syndico* until Venetian rule ended in 1797. In 1801 Vlassopoulos was one of the members of the Onoranda Deputazione, or the Honourable Deputation, the committee formed to represent all classes in Corfu and alleviate social and political conflicts; in the years that followed he served in the Septinsular Republic government, and under French occupation, in one of the highest offices, as Amministratore del Governo. Vlassopoulos's motive, as he said, in writing his 'Statistical-Historical News' was his membership of the Ionian Academy. The academy became the new institution of knowledge that used modern approaches to knowledge, such as data collection and quantification for the study of living conditions and the development of the economy of the islands. This first statistical recording of Corfu confirms that living conditions at the beginning of the nineteenth century (most likely in 1803) for the large majority of the rural population were wretched. Swamps bred infectious diseases, mainly malaria, and people died in significant numbers due to the absence of doctors, and because of people 'who were not even barbers' but dared to pretend they could help people; as a result 'they killed more people than nature would if left alone'.[46] Vlassopoulos, aware of the problem that the country folk faced, stressed how important the order of the French commissioner was in 1810 to appoint three doctors for the rural areas and provision them with the necessary and appropriate medicine, outlawing the activities of quacks. Doctors, law graduates and other intellectuals, encouraged by the modernizing aspects of French rule, formulated and shaped Ionian governmentality in the field of medicine through the academy and its research and policy initiatives.

Other forms of knowledge besides medicine included discussing modern methods of measurement and calculation explicitly aimed at reaching useful conclusions about how to develop the island's economy as well as pursuing more noble aims. Every week members of the academy offered classes in physics, chemistry, botany, political economy, law and mathematics. Correspondents with European associations of learning reveal the ambitions and the intellectual networks of members. The academy, a French–Ionian initiative, functioned until 1815, and was resurrected in 1825 when the Ionian University was established. The projects, designed by the academy to improve the economy of the island, continued in the 1840s with the Agronomic Society, with branches on all the islands, which promoted the draining of marshes, the cultivation of new crops (tomatoes) and the expansion of viniculture, all important for economic development.[47] Vlassopoulos's legacy was already important in the 1820s when the measurement of agricultural production and the classification of the Ionian population in economic sectors – 'agriculture', 'manufacture' and 'commerce' – was introduced, the result of the colonial practice of measurement and calculation, and of equally important Ionian initiatives. The institutional organization and the collection of information on the economy and the population of the islands was part of the systematic use of knowledge on the individual and the territory. Despite these practices that provided fertile ground, the construction of colonial governmentality had in fact begun soon after the British occupied the Ionian Islands during the Napoleonic wars.

The French also introduced in Corfu one of the most important tools for an efficient governmentality in a modern state, the printing press. The first publications in the Ionian Islands were government newspapers and pamphlets. This is how print culture came to the islands, first in Corfu and then in 1809 in Zante, when the British occupied the island. The 'government printing office' as it was named was one of the first in the region until the 1830s when Muhammad Ali opened a similar government newspaper in Cairo and in Crete, and Greek newspapers were published in Athens.[48] In Corfu several newspapers were published during the period: *Monitore Ionio* 1803–11 and *Gazzetta Urbana* from 1802 onwards, *L'anno* and the literary magazines *L'Ape* and *Mercurio Literario*. Thirty years later, Moustoxidis expressed his concern and opposition to the British protectorate, took his views to London and the colonial secretary, who was forced to respond and receive a special report on his views by Commissioner Douglas. The publication of newspapers and the emergence of a 'public opinion' through the press for the first time in the early nineteenth century created a tradition of publishing political views, generating interest among the public and a culture of dialogue; this culture resonated in the late 1840s when a vibrant and influential Ionian public sphere and a public opinion emerged with several newspapers that continued after the islands became part of Greece, but lacked the purpose of critique towards British rule and the Ionian State.

From Occupation to Protection

Between 1800 and 1814 British domination expanded to distant parts of the globe and created an 'Anglo-Mediterranean order'; this period marks the beginnings of 'Britain's modern engagement with Hellenic affairs'.[49] Ionian societies experienced the burst of modernity for the first time during the first French occupation by the Republic French (1797–99) and the occupation of Corfu by the Imperial-Napoleonic French in 1807–14. During the Napoleonic wars British military expansion in the Mediterranean resembled the conquest of a string of fortifications and islands in the Indian Ocean. The islands of Reunion, the Seychelles and Diego Garcia passed under French rule in 1803 when Napoleon supported the revival of slavery and gained the backing of the local elite. In 1810 a British fleet, with ten thousand sepoys embarked, sailed from India and took over the islands. Sepoys were an established force for British imperial expeditions in South Africa in 1795, in Egypt in 1801 and in Ceylon in 1803.[50] Around the same time a similar takeover took place in the Ionian Sea. In 1809 the British ('Anglo-Corsican') fleet carried hundreds of Corsicans, Sicilians and Maltese who manned the ships and fought on behalf of the British crown in the Mediterranean. A fleet with sailors from Mediterranean acquisitions fought and conquered the southern Ionian Islands in 1809 and 1810. Mauritius and the Seychelles were captured in similar fashion, and the Seychelles were turned into prison islands; their connection to the British colonial Mediterranean lasted until 1956 when the Cypriot leader Archbishop Makarios was exiled there for a year. The abrupt transfer from French to British control of tens of islands and regions from Asia and the Indian Ocean to the Mediterranean and the Caribbean marked the post-Napoleonic shift in the global balance of power. No less significant was the experience of colonial administrators in these early years of British global hegemony; the first commissioner of the Ionian Islands, Thomas Maitland, negotiated with Toussaint l'Ouvertoure, the leader of the Haitian Revolution, the treaty that agreed the withdrawal of British forces from Haiti, and he served as governor of Ceylon and Malta before taking command of the Mediterranean fleet and settling in his newly built palace in Corfu. Maitland followed the typical circuit of colonial officials during and immediately after the wars against Napoleonic France.

Even before the British takeover of the Ionian Islands, the French imperial sway suspended political rights to self-administration that had been granted during the Septinsular Republic. French rule lasted seven years in Corfu and less than three in Zante and Kefalonia. Economic problems, such as inability to import wheat, bred discontent with the French, while the British blockade disrupted severely the Corfu oil trade. As a result, the price of oil plummeted, currants served as animal food and wheat imports stopped, while the prices of all imported products on the islands soared.[51] This crisis caused many Ionians to rethink their allegiance to the French.

Other developments in the region increased the strategic importance of the Ionian Islands during the Napoleonic Wars. British Consul and merchant Spyridon Foresti in Zante convinced the War Office that good relations with Ali Pasha were necessary; Foresti also reassured his superiors that the people of Zante would welcome a British invasion, a recommendation that encouraged British plans to seize the islands from the French in 1809–10. British ships could secure a base and work together with Ali Pasha on the mainland, but they would also prevent the French from transforming the islands into a strong fortress that would offer advantages in their struggle with Austria. Officials in London were so determined to invade and occupy the islands that they rejected the advice of the military commanders in the Mediterranean not to do so. The War Office was too keen to extend its bases in the region, combine with the Sicily forces and prevent the French from gaining a stronghold.[52] British plans also took into account calls among Christians in the Morea for involvement and offers of protection, but quickly the option to take over the Ionian archipelago emerged as the preferred one, and seventeen hundred troops captured Zante in October 1809.

British officers promised Ionians that this was the dawn of a new era now that the years of oppressive French rule were over.

Brigadier-General Oswald and Captain Spranger announced to the people of Kefalonia in 1809:

> We present ourselves to you, inhabitants of Cephalonia – not as invaders, with views of conquest, but as allies, who hold forth to you the advantages of British protection, in the freedom and extension of your commerce, and in the general prosperity of your island. Contrast these obvious advantages with the privations you have laboured under since you were passed over from the yoke of Russia to that of France, and deprived, at one blow, of your independence as a nation, and your rights of freedom as men. We demand from you no exertions but such as are necessary for your own liberation – no other aid than what reciprocal advantage requires.

The Ionians needed little more convincing. However Oswald also clarified the limits of freedom bestowed on Ionians: 'Hostility, whether shown in acts of opposition to us, or in aid to the enemy, must, of course be repressed'.[53] Oswald proclaimed the arrival of a new liberal spirit, promising 'protection and redress of wrongs, liberty of conscience, and personal freedom and security'.[54] These words remained in the realm of political rhetoric, given the authoritarian rule of Thomas Maitland that followed shortly.

Charles de Bosset, governor of Kefalonia and military commander on the islands during the British occupation, took local conditions seriously and translated them into policy; a few years later, in 1816, he wrote how British rule could face strong resistance just as other foreign powers had in the past. De Bosset's views show a profound understanding of Ionian intentions despite the short time he had spent in Kefalonia, and reveal the principles that could have determined alternative British policies and governance in the Ionian Islands. De Bosset believed that British rule should consider the resources of the islands and the character, superstitions and interests of Ionians. He thought that the British task was to make Ionians feel attached to the protecting power, which in turn would have to increase their prosperity. Ionians had suffered under Venetian rule and governance that was corrupt and immoral. In the twenty years of 'revolution' that followed the end of Venetian domination, the situation had become worse. There was potential, especially for younger Ionians, to develop their abilities and use their education under an Enlightenment government. This younger generation, educated and potentially loyal to the British Empire, had to be the target group of the government, which would appoint Ionians to public office. To this end, schools and the eradication of superstition, which prevailed among the clergy and the people, were a priority and this is precisely what many reformist Ionians thought in the 1830s and

1840s. De Bosset also took into account the 'natural and moral condition' of Ionians. Approximately two hundred thousand people, he argued, were divided unequally on each island. The interests, resources and character of the islands and their inhabitants presented serious differences that British colonial officials had to take into account. Before devising the constitutional charter, Maitland had to consider the political factionalism of elites on each island, the animosity between the aristocrats of Zante, Corfu and Kefalonia.[55] No mention is made of social groups such as villagers, tenants, or the urban poor of different islands; de Bosset believed that the elites of each island had much more to lose from a reconfiguration of economic, social and ultimately political relations on the islands than other groups of Ionians, and British rule had to come to terms with the elite groups first.

De Bosset noted that many aristocrats supported France or Russia, where their sons had been educated, had adopted the ideas prevalent there and had served as military officers or civil servants. These two countries rivalling Britain offered opportunities to Ionians to increase their wealth and prestige, acquire experience in the international political scene and use it in Ionian politics. De Bosset probably had Ioannis Kapodistrias and his exceptionally illustrious career in mind, a career that started as minister in the Russian Foreign Office, continued with his appointment as the first governor of Greece in 1827 and ended tragically with his assassination in 1831. Count Moncenigo, from Zante, whose role during the Septinsular Republic was equally important, served as minister in the Court of Turin, and Count Loverdo from Kefalonia was a general in the French army. These were only some of the Ionians who served foreign powers and came back to the Ionian Islands to offer their services and expertise in government. During the period of the Ionian State, high commissioners faced the dilemma of whether to appoint British officials and substitute Ionians, or use Ionians and tempt them with higher salaries. British commissioners secured the consent of Ionians by maintaining some in public office with salaries that overburdened the state budget; no commissioner, however, adopted de Bosset's suggestions to open British army and civil service positions to Ionians, but instead used Ionians for the Ionian State since their training and experience qualified them for the posts. It seemed and probably was a wise choice – at least until the next generation of Ionian liberals challenged the state that had made them, by seeking to either reform it or abolish it.

On 6 February 1816, in a manner less cautious than de Bosset's account, *The Times* reported that the Ionian Islands would form a republic, 'liberated' from French 'tyranny' and protected from 'rapacious neighbours'. The news, we are told, generated quite a sensation, much optimism and hopes that independence would spread from the Ionian Islands to the Greek peninsula. The author attributed the Ionian achievement to Count Capo d'Istria (Kapodistria) of Corfu for his decisive action to place the islands under British protection:

> The first news of the re-establishment of the Republic of the Ionian Islands was received here with a joy that is not to be described. The happy consequences that [this] will have for us are beyond all calculation. Delivered from the vexations of our neighbours, everywhere protected by the triumphant flag of Great Britain against the rapine of the corsairs, our vessels will cover the Adriatic and the Mediterranean, and bring us abundance and encouragement to industry, whilst our valuable productions ensure us a return, when once they can be sent without obstacle to all parts. Closely united by a common constitution given us by England, the blessings of freedom, prosperity and industry must soon elevate the inhabitants of this young state to a higher degree of intellectual and moral cultivation, which may extend from hence over the whole continent of Greece. A place of refuge for every Greek, who desires to enjoy in peace the property he has acquired abroad, or to withdraw himself from the oppression of the Turks increasing in power and population, we shall be proud to display to Southern Europe the example and fruits of political and religious toleration, and thus to form a link of the chain to embrace the nations of the north and of the south, and bring them near to each other. We should merit the reproach of the blackest ingratitude, if, with those encouraging prospects of futurity, we did not recall with profound regard him to whom we chiefly owe them; who led the eyes of mighty monarchs to look favourably upon us; who, inspired by ardent old Greek patriotism, employed all the powers of eloquence, all the perseverance of virtue, to obtain for us an independence of which we will show ourselves worthy; who, amidst the din of arms, in the confined occupation of the headquarters, in the splendour of courts and entertainments, amidst the most important labours of the Vienna Congress, never lost sight of the little island which gave him birth ... We speak of our countryman and friend, Count Capo d' Istria.[56]

The piece evokes the exuberance and aspirations about the long-term consequences of Ionian 'independence' for the 'whole continent of Greece'; in 1816 Greece of course was a cultural concept for few, a geographical entity for some and an imaginary national project for others. There were different historical alternatives before the outbreak of the Greek rebellion in 1821, which changed dramatically and decisively the historical trajectory of the Greek state. In the extract above an important phrase is the 're-establishment of the Republic', a political project probably unthinkable in most places in post-Napoleonic Europe; a republic, even under the protection of Great Britain, similar to the Russian protection of the Septinsular Republic, was the first Greek State. A few years later, after a long and revolutionary struggle and civil war among the insurgents, the Greek Republic (1828–31) and later Kingdom (1832) were created under the supervision and 'protection' of not one but all three of the great powers that had ruled the Ionian Islands. The first test, however, for British colonial authority in the Ionian Islands came from a shrewd and lethal enemy: the plague.

Fighting the Plague: The 'Strong Hand and Unnerved Power of Government'

On the evening of 15 December 1815, authorities in Corfu received a letter from the Justice of Peace in the Lefkimi district in the south of the island, reporting that an illness of considerable concern had appeared in the village of Marathias. Commander James Campbell called military doctor James Tully and formed a commission to investigate and report on the illness. Although the distance from Corfu town was only twenty miles, the commission travelled by ship and reached the affected area the following day. Doctors found that a remittent fever had been raging for a month, killing thirteen of the fifty residents of Marathias. The commission discovered that superstition had gripped the residents; they believed than an evil spirit of a man who had been murdered in the village a few months before was responsible for the deaths, and they had tried to scare it away with prayers and litanies. All victims had been struck by fever in the evening or during the night after returning from their fields; they all died as if they had been strangled or whipped by an invisible hand. For the residents of Marathias the evil spirit tortured the damned all night until their last breath and then moved on to the house of another unsuspecting victim.[57] When Tully, the British military doctor, officers and soldiers arrived at the village, they were shocked by people's superstition and their deplorable condition. Remittent fevers appeared every year in the autumn; the marshland around the village and the unusually hot autumn weather, with little rain and a constant southerly wind, intensified symptoms. Tully and his officers, noting the unhealthy living conditions, suggested that the causes of the illness were in the village; what concerned them was its transmission and its force. The doctors and soldiers offered any help they could, and advised villagers to stay clean and above all to avoid contact with each other.

The account of Tully, a military surgeon and director of the Sanitary Commission of the Ionian Islands in 1815, encapsulates several challenges the British faced a short period after they took over Corfu; the plague outbreak revealed to the new rulers that there were isolated communities extremely difficult to reach by land, as there were no roads and only old paths connecting them with each other and the capital Corfu. Most villagers lived in poverty, suffered illnesses and were gripped by superstition that could kill them, as the plague outbreak in Marathias shows. How the British authorities and their Ionian counterparts handled the challenge shows how determined they were to govern and also how Ionians reacted to their new masters.

The Ionian Islands, similar to many other regions in the Mediterranean, the Ottoman Empire and the Italian peninsula, suffered frequent plague outbreaks; to prevent them the Venetian administration created a system of quarantine stations in all the major ports of its empire, the lazzareto.[58] The islet located outside the port of Corfu that locals still call Lazareto could only partially protect the island from the transmission of disease. During the British blockade of Corfu in the last period of French occupation (1807–14) contraband trade and the smuggling of goods from the mainland opposite flourished; goods from areas ravaged by plague could also slip onto the island away from officials in the customs house. When Tully and his team diagnosed the plague they implemented measures with decisive response in a moment of crisis, the first crisis since Maitland took over the administration of the islands.

European armies tackled the plague for the first time in 1798 when Napoleon landed in Egypt. Thomas Maitland, governor of Malta and soon to become commander of the Mediterranean fleet and the first high commissioner of the Ionian Islands, visited Napoleon in 1814 on the island of Elba where he was imprisoned, and discussed with Bonaparte how to confront the disease. Napoleon informed Maitland that segregation – by force if necessary – of the population into healthy and sick was the best if not the only measure against it.[59] Maitland and Tully knew, because of the 1813 plague outbreak in Malta where they had both served before their appointment in Corfu, that they could not hesitate. Tackling the disease became more systematic, included observation and the application of tried practices as in every modern state. This challenge would be much harder to overcome if Ionian doctors and officials had not been trained in combating disease and organizing the population in times of emergency. Reports leave no doubt about the severe impact of the disease in Corfu:

> Extract of a letter from Malta, Jan. 9 [1816]: 'By the latest advices from Corfu, we are informed that an epidemic disease prevails there, and is described as a typhus fever; but its being attended with buboes, carbuncles, and petechiae convinces me it is the plague; and I understand our

governor and our medical men are of the same opinion. I am fully persuaded such measures will be adopted as to arrest its progress, which is easily effected by cutting off all communication between the inhabitants'.⁶⁰

Despite strong preventive measures, reports from villages neighbouring Marathias talked about similar symptoms, evidence that the disease had spread. The presence of many local doctors eased the task for the British medical officer; Tully admits his staff lacked practical experience in fighting the plague, but possessed impressive theoretical knowledge. The doctors from Corfu followed his orders diligently, visited patients regularly (twice a day) and organized camps where they quarantined the sick and prohibited them from communicating with healthy residents who also checked regularly for any symptoms.⁶¹ Despite all these measures the plague continued to spread even if at a lower speed; in some villages it even showed signs of abating. By April the plague had ebbed according to *The Times*:

> Extract of a letter from Zante, 4th of April, 1816: 'We quitted Corfu just a week ago. I am happy to inform you that the plague appears to be completely subdued in that island, as no new cases have appeared in the villages within the infected district for upwards a fortnight, according to the last reports from Dr Broadfoot, who is left in charge of the medical department there; and but a very few cases have appeared during that period in the suspected camps, so that it may be hoped that it will shortly be eradicated from the island'.⁶²

The plague killed 375 people, and many more would have died if the army deployed in the region had not enforced a strict isolation system. The disease could have reached Corfu and become impossible to control. The example of Malta, where cholera in the early 1820s damaged the island's flourishing international trade, provides the alternative scenario.⁶³

Tully was thorough, systematic and successful in tracing every case to understand how the disease had spread. On some occasions he took extraordinary measures; in Melikia he locked residents in their homes every night. Despite all precautions there were setbacks; when people refused to stay in on Easter night and went to church on 20 April, the plague spread. Tully was indefatigable and detected the original case; he questioned village notables, talked to relatives, visited patients, and collected all evidence available. He finally discovered the origin of the disease and the first victim but also culprit who brought the plague to Corfu: when Spyrakis, a resident of Perivoli, smuggled goods from the mainland opposite, he condemned himself and hundreds of others to a slow and painful death.⁶⁴

In June 1816, when Tully was confident that the situation in Corfu was under control, he went to Kefalonia to investigate symptoms of a similar nature. The causes of the outbreak there were much clearer than in Corfu. Wheat production in Kefalonia, as on most islands, sufficed for three to four months; people often migrated for the harvest season to the mainland where they received payment in kind. When they returned, the authorities quarantined them for seven days, under surveillance by health officials. Antonis Ventouratos was returning from Arta, in the Ottoman region of Epirus, a few days after the plague had appeared there; Ventouratos and his companions found the bodies of two Turks on the road and stripped them of their belongings. When they reached the port of Agia Efthymia in Kefalonia they were quarantined for a week, according to regulations. On the sixth day Ventouratos got ill but his companions convinced him to say nothing so that they would avoid detention for much longer. Ventouratos managed to conceal his condition from the authorities and his cousin helped him to get to their village of Comitato, where he died the same day. Doctor Metaxas, who examined the body, failed to report any cause for concern despite his reputation and training. Only when the disease had killed nine people did the village notables write a letter to the authorities in Argostoli with their concerns. A team of doctors arrived from Argostoli to find that several people had died. The worrying reports reached the government in Corfu on the morning of 20 June, stating that eight people had died the previous night; the response was immediate and followed the same pattern as Corfu: 'On the afternoon of the same day, a detachment of military arrived from headquarters, three public officers, deputed by the department of health, accompanying them, who were charged with the general superintendence of the infected village and vested with supreme power'.[65]

When the next day Commander Maitland reached Kefalonia, he learned about the plague outbreak and ordered Tully to go to Comitato immediately. Tully found a loosely imposed cordon and the villagers terrorized. He first arranged and oversaw the cleaning of the village, imposed a strict quarantine and set up camp for the whole operation on the shore of the village of St Pantaleone. His report was grim; the whole island was under threat and 'nothing but the immediate adoption of the most decisive and energetic measures can avert the propagation of this dire malady (if it be not already propagated) throughout the island'.[66] Tully oversaw the transfer of patients to the camp on the beach, ensured that soldiers would watch out not to touch the infected, recorded how helpful his experience from Corfu a few weeks before had been, and asked his assistant in Corfu, a Doctor Bormelli, to join him in Kefalonia.

Despite reports about the disobedient and 'savage' character of the people, Tully found them cooperative in following his orders. He explained to people in every house he visited why he wanted them to leave their houses and be detained in a camp. This public relations campaign worked and there were no incidents of disobedience, maybe because the army and militia were present. People saw the houses of the sick burn but at least they understood why. Existing roads were in bad condition and the large population of the village compromised the effort to stop the disease from spreading; Comitato was not like Marathias, where only fifty people lived, but a village of seven hundred people. The villagers were even more destitute than those of Lefkimi in south Corfu, and were 'a horrid mess', living in a mountainous area with little land for cultivation: 'They are truly wretched in every sense of the term, and it is altogether a horrible country, nothing to be seen but mountain overhanging mountain, rocky and almost inaccessible; no vegetation nor even a bush to shade us from a vertical sun'.[67]

How did people live in such dire conditions? Mostly, by herding sheep and goats – which incidentally caused Tully great concern since animals could also transmit the disease. In an extraordinary demonstration of efficiency, Tully assigned flocks to designated areas with fixed boundaries, nominated keepers and ordered the village primates to make sure that flocks did not mix. Within nine days and after all these measures of quarantine to people and animals alike, 360 people of the village under various degrees of suspicion and under the strictest discipline were ordered daily to 'plunge into the sea, without regard to age or sex, and all of their susceptible effects having also been daily immersed in sea water, for the space of two hours, and subsequently exposed to the heat of the sun, the thermometer in the shade on the beach standing at noon at 88 [degrees]'.[68] The scenes must have been extraordinary, and reflected the gravity of the situation.

Just like during the Corfu plague, doctors from Kefalonia contributed the most. On 9 July Tully reported to Count Rivarola, 'a person fitted for his duty from his long experience in matters of plague, and whose exertions during the existence of that malady in Malta were both conspicuous and successful'. Maitland invested the Count with supreme powers over the health departments of Kefalonia, Zante and Ithaca. Not everyone in Comitato, however, responded rationally to Tully's orders; 'Priest Gabraele' buried his own son in his kitchen instead of informing the authorities that a member of his family had fallen ill. It was only when the priest himself fell ill that he confessed to what he had done. Despite the casualties, however, just like in Corfu, Tully and his team managed to contain the disease in Comitato. Quarantine, isolation, constant surveillance and control confirmed the tactics developed in Corfu in the previous months and in Malta before that. From that time on the British-controlled Ionian State returned to its previous and equally important role of trying to impose quarantine on people and goods arriving on the islands; that would have been one of the biggest challenges to local and central administration in the years of British rule. During this first period of British military rule, however, and before the facade of independence granted by the constitutional charter of 1817, the authorities had successfully faced their first serious challenge on the islands; but this was to be only the first of many; as Tully wrote: 'Under such dangerous emergencies as those we have been recording, the strong hand and unnerved power of Government must be interposed, or the evil rapidly dilates itself'.[69] For the first time Ionians experienced the strong hand of a government, only this time it was 'for their own good', a central claim in all governmentality projects. Systematic investigation and drastic measures, the recording of the disease and its symptoms, causes and ways of transmission – but especially the response of the authorities – was a prelude to what would follow during the period of British rule.

In July 1817, a year after the plague had ended, a procession took place in Corfu to thank the patron saint, Spyridon, on the anniversary of the 'liberation from the plague'. Various processions were held in the district of Lefkimi as well. In Corfu, Adam, the acting commissioner during Maitland's absence, the 'civil and military authorities' and a large part of the population followed the procession. During these early days of British rule the government ordered an annual pension of sixty tallers to the families of four village leaders – Pietro Catechi, Spiridione Lengiti, Giovanni Temponera and Atanasio Lacca – who perished trying to stem the spread of the disease. These were some of the people at the forefront of the battle to tackle the plague, and their families were the first to receive state benefits.[70] The British army, with the help of Ionian doctors and officials, implemented a strict policy of sanitary precaution, demonstrating the building of a strong central administration. The British-Ionian administration took measures to alleviate the economic consequences of the disease, allowing inhabitants of the villages stricken by the plague to get an extension in paying their loans, assuming that their harvest had been destroyed, in an early example of welfare provisions for those hard hit.[71] This was the first of several challenges that British rule faced during the early days of the colonial state. The personal involvement of officials such as Tully was not exceptional but the norm; the role of Maitland, similarly, sealed the first crucial years of the British protectorate.

Notes

1. Markou Theotoki, *O Ioannis Kapodistrias en Kefallinia kai e staseis aftis en etesi 1800, 1801, 1802. Istorikai simioseis eksaxthise ek ton eggrafon tou archeiou tis Eptanisou Politeias*. Corfu, 1889, 2.
2. The celebrations included the planting of the liberty tree during the welcoming of the French in Corfu and the burning of the *Libro d' Oro*, the Golden Book with names of the Nobility of each island. E. Koukou, *Istoria ton Eptanison apo to 1791 mechri tin Anglokratia* [The History of the Ionian Islands from 1797 until English Rule]. Athens, 1999, 3rd edition, 47; N. Karapidakis, 'Departement de Corfu, 1798: Les troubles', in Tassos Anastassiadis and Nathalie Claire (eds), *Society, Politics and State Formation in Southeastern Europe during the 19th Century*. Athens: Alpha Bank Historical Archives, 2011, 235–54.
3. Andreas Andreadis, *I Eptanisiaki Dimosia Oikonomia kata tin periodon 1797–1814*, Athens: Karavias 1936, 22–30.
4. Dror Ze'evi, 'Back to Napoleon? Thoughts on the Beginning of the Modern Era in the Middle East', *Mediterranean Historical Review* 19(1) (2004): 73–94.
5. H. Bjelovucic, *The Ragusan Republic: Victim of Napoleon and its own Conservatism*. Leiden: Brill, 1970. The merchant city-state of Ragusa – present-day Dubrovnik – stayed out of warfare and used all its diplomatic shrewdness to excel in commerce and shipping. Despite its motto, 'Libertas', Ragusa remained a tributary state and enjoyed Venetian protection until the fourteenth century, Hungarian suzerainty until the mid sixteenth century, and manoeuvred between autonomy and dependence on Ottoman sultans and the Austrian throne until its fall to Napoleon's France in 1808.
6. Bjelovucic, *The Ragusan Republic*, 77. J. McKnight, 'Admiral Ushakov and the Ionian Republic: The Genesis of Russia's First Balkan Satellite'. Thesis dissertation, University of Wisconsin-Madison, 1965.
7. Peter Mackridge, 'Venise après Venise: official languages in the Ionian Islands, 1797–1864'. *Byzantine and Modern Greek Studies* Vol. 38 (1) (2014): 68–90.
8. Peter Mackridge, *Language and National Identity*, 39. The Greek version calls the citizens of the Septinsular Republic 'Hellenes'.
9. Aliki Nikiforou, *Syntagmatika Keimena ton Ionion Nison*. Athens: Idryma tis Voulis ton Ellinon, 2008.
10. Constitution of 1800.
11. I. Konidaris, 'I thesi ton thriskeftikon koinotiton sta syntagmata tis Eptanisou Politeias (1800–1807)', *Eptanisos Politeia (1800–1807)*, Praktika Synedriou, Argostoli: Etaireia Kefalliniakon Istorikon Erevnon, 2003, 47–56.
12. G. Mavrogiannis, *Istoria ton Ionion Nison*. Vol B. Athens, 1889, 90–91.
13. G.I. Dellis, 'Ta anthopina dikaiomata sto Syntagma (Katastasin) tis "Eptanisou Politeias" tou 1803. Epidraseis ton ideon tou evropaikou diafotismou sti thespisi tous', in *Eptanisos Politeia (1800–1807): to proto aneksartito elliniko kratos*, Kerkyra: G.A.K. – Archeia Nomou Kerkyras, 2001, 57–77.

14 A. Mazarakis, *Viografiai ton endokson andron tis nisou Kefallinias*. Venice, 1843 (Athens: N. Karavias, 1999), 295–306.
15 *The Times*, 20 October 1800, p. 2, col. c.
16 G. Mavrogiannis, *Istoria ton Ionion Nison*. Vol B, 57.
17 A. Andreadis, *Peri tis Oikonomikis Dioikiseos*, vol. A, Athens: Karavias, 1914, 178–84.
18 N. Moschonas, 'Ta Ionian Nisia kata tin periodo 1797–1821', in *Istoria tou Ellinikou Ethnous*, vol. 11. Athens: Ekdotiki Athinon, 1978, 396.
19 Ibid.
20 T. Papadopoulos, *Ioniki Vivliografia. 16ος–19ος aionas. Vol. B,1851–1880*. Athens, 2000, 126.
21 Ibid., 166.
22 Ibid., 129–30.
23 Ibid., 136.
24 G. Mavrogiannis, *Istoria ton Ionion Nison*. Vol B, 98–99.
25 G. Savvidis and N. Kykourgou (eds), *Aristotelis Valaoritis. Vios, Epistoles kai Politika Keimena*, v. A. Athens: Ikaros, 1980, 21.
26 D. Caglioti, 'Voluntary Societies and Urban Elites in Nineteenth-Century Naples', in Graeme Morton, Boudien de Vries and R.J. Morris (eds), *Civil Society, Associaitons and Urban Places: Class, Nation and Culture in Nineteenth-Century Europe*. Aldershot: Ashgate, 2006, 39–53.
27 E. Yotopoulou-Sisilianou, 'I Eptanisiaki paideia sta chronia tis ksenokratias', *Kerkyraika Chronika* XV, 1970, 101–21.
28 E. Lountzis, *Peri tis politikis katastaseos tis Eptanisou epi Eneton*. En Athinais: X. Nikolaou Filadelfeos, 1856, 249.
29 P. Tzavara, *Scholeia kai daskaloi sti venetokratoumeni Kerkyra (16os–18os ai.)*. Athens: Stamouli, 2003, 296–97.
30 P. Chiotis, *Istorika Apomnimonevmata Eptanisou*, vol. 6. Zakynhtos, 1887, 218–19.
31 N. Karapidakis, 'Apo ton koinotismo stin politiki: koinoniologia ton dianoumenon kai ton anthropon tis politikis drasis ston eptanisiako choro (teli tou 18ou aiona arches tou 19ou)', in A. Nikiforou (ed.), *Eptanisos Politeia (1800–1807): ta meizona istorika zitimata*. Kerkyra: G.A.K – Archeia Nomou Kerkyras, 2001, 33–41.
32 Papadia-Lala, *O thesmos ton astikon koinotiton ston elliniko choro kata tin period tis venetokratias (13ος–18ος aionas). Mia synthetiki proseggisi*. Venice: Elliniko Institouto Vyzantinon kai Metavyzantinon Spoudon, No. 24, 2004, 421.
33 Karapidakis, 'Apo ton koinotismo stin politiki', 33–41; D. Arvanitakis, 'I aftoviografia tis Martinegkou: i rogmes tis siopis kai I pollaples diastaseis tou kosmou' [The Autobiography of Martinengou: The Ruptures of Silence and the Multiple Dimensions of the World], *Ta Istorika* 22(43) (2005): 397–420.
34 S. Loukatos, *I Eptanisiaki politiki scholi ton Rizospaston*. Argostoli, 2009, 75.
35 C. Botta, *Storia Naturale e medica deli Isola di Corfu*. Milan, 1798; J. Fiore, 'Carlo Botta: An Italian Historian of the American Revolution', *Italica* 28(3) (1951): 155–71.
36 Em. Theotoky, *Details sur Corfou*. Corfu, 1826, 13.

37 G. Pentogalos, *Giatroi kai Iatriki tis Kefalonias sta chronia ton ksenon kyriarchion (1500–1864)*. Thessaloniki: University Studio Press, 2004.
38 W. Kaldis, *John Capodistrias and the Modern Greek State*. Madison: University of Wisconsin, 1963, 4–5.
39 S. Vlassopoulos, *Statistikai – Istorikai peri Kerkyras Eidiseis*. Kerkyraika Chronika, Vol. 21, (1822) 1977.
40 There were also the religious-based occupational organizations called fraternities, but these were skill-related and comprised lower- and middle-class artisans and craftsmen as well as labourers.
41 Chiotis, *Istorika Apomnimonvmata Eptanisou*, 220–21, 229–30.
42 Corfu Archives, ANK, Avvocato dei Poveri, F. 3, doc. No. 3884 / 14-2-1837.
43 Chiotis, *Istorika Apomnimonvmata Eptanisou*, 230–31.
44 Vlassopoulos, *Statistikai*; Joyce, *The Rule of Freedom*, 13.
45 Vlassopoulos, *Statistikai*, 81–82.
46 Ibid., 37.
47 Chiotis, *Istorika Apomnimonvmata Eptanisou*, 237.
48 S. Gekas and P. Krokidas, 'Public Health in Crete under the Rule of Mehmed Ali in the 1830s', *Egypt / Monde Arab* 4(3) (2007): 35–54. The French also brought a press to Missolonghi in the 1820s during the revolution; it can be seen today in the Historical and Ethnological Society Museum in Athens.
49 Holland, *Blue-Water Empire*, 19.
50 R. Gott, *Britain's Empire: Resistance, Repression and Revolt*. London and New York: Verso, 2011, 188.
51 L. Zamit, *Oi Maltezoi stin Kerkyra kais ton eyrytero mesogeiako choro. Synthikes pou tous odigisan se metanastefsi*. Kerkyra: Etaireia Kerkyraikon Spoudon, 1995, 18.
52 W. Wrigley, *The Diplomatic Significance of Ionian Neutrality, 1821–1831*. London: Peter Lang, 1988, 53–54.
53 F. MacGachen, *The Ionian Islands: A Sketch of their Past History, with Reference to their Position under our Protectorate*. London, 1859, 10.
54 V. Kirkwall, *Four Years in the Ionian Islands. Their Political and Social Condition*. Vol. 2. London, 1864, 71; Koukou, *Istoria ton Eptanison*, 91.
55 Charles de Bosset, *Parga and the Ionian Islands; a refutation of the mis-statement of the quarterly review and of Lieut.-Gen. Sir Thomas Maitland on the subject; with a report of the trial between that officer and the author*. London, 1821.
56 *The Times*, 6 February 1816.
57 J.D. Tully, *The History of the Plague, as It Has Lately Appeared in the Islands of Malta, Gozo, Corfu, Cephalonia, & c. Detailing Important Facts, Illustrative of the Specific Contagion of that Disease, with Particulars of the Means Adopted for Its Eradication*. London, 1821, 87–88 and 125.
58 K. Konstantinidou, 'To kako odevei erpontas'. *Oi limoi tis panolis sta Ionia Nisia (17os-18os ai.)*. Venice: Hellenic Institute of Byzantine and Post Byzantine Studies, 2007.
59 H. Christmas, *George Augustus Frederick Fitzclarence, The Literary Gazette: A Weekly Journal of Literature, Science, and the Fine Arts*, Volume 5. London: H. Colburn, 1821, 355.
60 *The Times*, 12 February 1816.

61 Kostis claims that Tully was arrogant claiming that people in the Ionian Islands were not 'civilized' enough to protect themselves from the scourge of plague (Kostis, *Ston Kairo tis Panolis* p. 257), but it is fairer to say that his account was class-specific, since Tully praises the training of Ionian doctors and their role in combating the plague.
62 *The Times*, 1 May 1816.
63 Bayly, *Imperial Meridian*, 240.
64 Tully, *History of the Plague*, 142–43.
65 Ibid., 161.
66 Ibid., 167.
67 Ibid., 189.
68 Ibid., 193.
69 Ibid., 147.
70 *Gazzetta Jonia*, 2 August 1817.
71 Senate Resolution of 11 November 1818, Anagnostiki Etairia Library, Corfu.

 Chapter 2

BUILDING THE COLONIAL STATE

During the nineteenth century, British colonial authorities faced the issue of keeping public order in the colonies.[1] Governors administered vast territories and dealt with local issues through a combination of general rules and principles from the Colonial Office, but also by using a lot of experimentation and flexibility in adjusting to local conditions. Distance from London, measuring in some cases thousands of miles, meant that decisions could not wait for weeks until letters to the Colonial Office had been read, and orders dispatched and received. When Maitland served as governor of Ceylon and took as one of his first tasks to save the Treasury £200,000 he only received one mail with a note from the undersecretary for the colonies; to answer every despatch sent by every colonial officer would have been an impossible task.[2] In 1825 communication between Corfu and the Colonial Office (which was officially established as a separate department in 1831) became more regular with the organization of the Ionian post office; even then communication with London still took four to six weeks. Until Corfu was connected to the telegraph system in the 1850s, it was not uncommon for high commissioners in the Ionian Islands to decide first, and inform the Colonial Office later. The volume of communication was simply extraordinary, making it difficult to handle; letters that arrived at the Colonial Office on 11 March 1823 included dispatches of several months from 'Ceylon, Mauritius, Cape of Good Hope, Gibraltar, Malta, the Barbary States and the Ionian Isles'.[3] After all, officials in London were interested primarily in two things: uninterrupted and secure commercial operations, and keeping public order; on some occasions, such as on the outbreak of the Greek war of independence, colonial officials were also interested on how to avoid a diplomatic incident, first with the Ottoman Empire and then with the erratic Greek Kingdom after its establishment in 1830.

The Ionian State built a bureaucracy that continued the legacy of previous administrations but introduced a more systematic communication between the central government in Corfu and the local governments of other islands, as well as the communication of the commissioner with the Colonial Office, one of the main functions of a modern state. Correspondence between the commissioner in Corfu and the resident governors of the islands was frequent and detailed, and formed part of a surveillance system; this was established mainly for international affairs that became volatile during the Greek war of independence in the 1820s and for suppressing any opposition to the protectorate. Internal communication was necessary for the function of many other government offices such as the hated High Police, established by the French and directed by the high commissioner himself. The police maintained the right to arrest and expel individuals without trial, a practice followed also in the 1840s and 1850s by hardliner Ward against radical unionists.

The Other United States, or the Elephant and the Maggot

> When we consider that the American United States contain twelve millions of people; the Ionian united states one hundred and ninety thousand; the one a continent, the other (all the islands united) about half the size of Yorkshire; the annual revenue of the one about six millions (I suppose, for I do not know exactly), the other one hundred and forty thousand pounds, that is to say, inferior to the income of some English noblemen; when we consider these things, it may be truly said, that the Lord High Commissioner of the Ionian united states can have no claim to a salary equal to that given to the President of the United States of America.[4]

Colonel Charles James Napier, resident of Kefalonia, was the most outspoken critic of the British-Ionian administration and compared the two states, 'although one is but a miniature of the other. It is said that a cheese maggot placed in a solar microscope appears like an elephant, and about the same proportion exists between the United States of America and the Ionian Islands; yet the salaries of their rulers are on a par!' Napier had quite a few things to say about the quality and cost of British administration, especially in Kefalonia where he served as the resident governor for nearly a decade and wrote extensively about it in his treatise, *The Colonies. Treating of their Value Generally – of the Ionian Islands in Particular*:

> By a reference to the sketch (Plate No. 1) we shall see that, like the Bermudas, the Ionian Islands possess a *central position*, being surrounded by countries undergoing great political changes, in which changes England right or wrong, will interfere; with which countries she drives a considerable traffic, and among which she oftentimes has waged, and

may again wage war. We see that the Ionian Islands are midway between England and the Persian Gulf; are two-thirds of the way to the Red Sea: they are conveniently situated to communicate with all parts of the Levant: they block up the mouth of the Adriatic Sea. *Constantinople, Smyrna, Alexandria, Tripoli, Tunis, Malta, Sicily, Naples, Leghorn, Genoa, Ancona, Venice, Trieste,* form a belt of great towns around them, at no very unequal distances; a steam-boat could go from the Ionian Islands to any one of these great commercial cities in about sixty or eighty hours: in short, a steamer from the islands can reach large cities in *Asia*, in *Europe*, or in *Africa*, within a few hours' time. They are central to these three continents and they bear strongly upon the lines of the Mediterranean commerce.[5]

This demonstration of the geopolitical as well as commercial value of the Ionian Islands runs throughout the first part of Colonel Napier's book *The Colonies*. He continues by arguing the prospects of developing the trade to the Indian subcontinent via the Middle East rather than round the Cape, a trip which he considers more costly as well as more time consuming. Napier's account is perhaps one of the most interesting and revealing. His views on the position of the Ionian Islands in the British Empire project derive partly from his great love for the people of the islands and a strong intimacy he developed during his term as Resident of Kefalonia, and partly from his personal animosity with High Commissioner Frederick Adam, who ultimately managed to replace Napier, something that Napier never forgave. *The Colonies*, published in 1833, begins with a classification of the colonies into three categories, demonstrating the potential profits for a country if it is "properly governed". The first class of colonies were those 'important from their extent of territory and rich productions, such as the East and West Indies'; the second class 'those important in war and in commerce, but which in consequence of the small size are not productive of wealth, such as Malta, Gibraltar and Bermuda'; the third class, in which for Napier the Ionian Islands belonged, 'have an extent of territory and population united to a political and commercial importance, that by good government, may become productive of wealth and power to Great Britain; such are the Canadas, the Cape of Good Hope, and the Ionian Islands'. This contemporary classification of colonies is obviously a very different one from the current historiographical one, which has always studied the Ionian Islands together with the other Mediterranean possessions, Malta and Gibraltar.

The Russian-Ottoman protectorate of the Septinsular Republic, created during the Napoleonic wars when a long-term solution for the Ionian Islands seemed too complicated, served as a blueprint for the

Ionian State under British protection, the preferred arrangement in the Congress of Vienna in 1814; this choice, by famous and informed Ionians like Kapodistrias who supported the idea of the protectorate, shows the continuities in a tradition of regional state formation. The Ionian Republic was re-established as the 'United States of the Ionian Islands' with the Treaty of Paris on 5 November 1815. The constitutional ambiguities of the articles, however, created an anomalous state; according to the first article the islands were to form 'one, sole, free and independent state, under the name of the United States of the Ionian Islands'. The second article placed the islands 'under the immediate and exclusive protection' of the king of Britain. The third article gave to the states 'the power to regulate their interior organization' but 'with the approbation of the protecting power',[6] only to add to the confusion. These ambiguities transformed gradually into contradictions that were never resolved and prevented the islands from assimilating to the British colonial structure. The Treaty of Paris also stipulated that the first lord high commissioner had to devise a constitutional charter that would be ratified by the king of Great Britain. The framing of this charter was largely influenced by the character and experience of Thomas Maitland, then governor of the Mediterranean Fleet and Malta, who justified to his superiors his actions to concentrate all powers to the seat of the high commissioner in the following way:

> I was in possession of very few books touching the subject and the whole of the document now transmitted to England has been made more with a view to the general ideas stated by your Lordship to me in England, and the general view of the characters of these people than to any precedent we can look at, or any constitution we can have recourse to… They are not in that state of society that fits them either for a free constitution, or for being left to themselves under any government of any kind.[7]

This no man's land condition of political maturity of Ionians was Maitland's excuse for imposing an autocratic rule; the lack of any similar 'precedents' was more a pretext than a legitimate reason for designating all powers to the office of high commissioner. The immaturity of Ionians was a recurrent theme in British discourse on how best to rule this corner of their constantly expanding empire. From the early days of the protectorate, British views and perceptions of Ionians and their loyalties were quite hazy, but British priorities and imperial plans were unclouded. The following extract from parliamentary debates is revealing:

> Mr Leslie Foster was convinced that in the new arrangement the interests and tastes of the islands were best consulted. National independence

was not their desire. They had tried that during the French revolution. He quite agreed as to the interesting character of the natives, who were the only ascendants of the ancient Greeks that had not passed under the Turkish yoke ... The inhabitants knew that Turkish ambition aimed at the islands, and that they could not preserve themselves by a parchment treaty. They disliked Russia and they detested French as protectors; and England appeared as their most salutary protector ... They were a peculiar people, and if properly governed would be most attached subjects of the British empire. Corfu was one of the strongest places in the world; but he hoped the islands would not be managed on a military principle, though troops in each isle might be necessary. It should be rendered evident to the people that in civil affairs they governed themselves, and they would then prove the most valuable acquisition, securing us a strong port in the Levant, preventing any other power from raising its standard in the Morea, making us the arbiters of that part of Europe, and giving us the power at the mouth of the Adriatic Gulph. He thought no arrangement possible which could be better that what had been concluded.[8]

The story of the Ionian protectorate is largely the disillusionment and frustration of many colonial officials and members of parliament with those 'peculiar people' that never really became 'most attached subjects to the British Empire'.

The 'Unites States of the Ionian Islands' maintained the federal state character of the Septinsular Republic. This was explicitly stated by Colonial Secretary Bathurst:

> You will direct your Attention to the Civil Habits and religious Opinions of the Inhabitants, rather than to abstract Theories of Government, or a partial Consideration of that Constitution, under which we have grown and prospered. And, for this purpose, you will select a Council (in number not exceeding fifteen) consisting of the principal Inhabitants who are most distinguished for their Probity, Experience and discretion. You will charge them with preparing a form of a Constitutional Charter which will be submitted for the consideration of a Legislative Assembly to be convoked by you for that special purpose. This Assembly must consist of a number not exceeding forty, including the Council, who shall form an integral part of it, and in order to obviate all objections, you will cause the assembly to be elected in the manner in which the Assembly was elected in the Year 1803.[9]

The Colonial Office gave direct orders to Commissioner Maitland to play down any expectations the Ionians might have developed when it came to representative government, and knew these orders would resonate well with the commissioner. What is most interesting and revealing is that Bathurst realized that the British authority could not ignore the precedent of the form of rule developed during the

Septinsular Republic, and in particular the constitution of 1803. It was equally inevitable – indeed desirable – that the 'principal inhabitants' (i.e. those already in power) would have to be employed in government to ensure a smooth transition.

The political identity of the state was liberal in the sense that citizens as individuals enjoyed certain constitutional freedoms under the protection of the British monarch, but in practice the British commissioners allowed very few liberties. This system of autocracy, unchanged but not unchallenged for three decades, is typical of the political institutions, the most prominent instrument of British rule according to Peter Burroughs, 'designed for communities whose populations seemed unsuited to elective Assemblies: alien Europeans in Quebec (before 1791), Malta, the Cape, and Mauritius'.[10] The case of the Ionian State under British protection sheds some light on the history of colonial possessions in their transformation from occupied territories to state entities with representative government. The Ionian Islands formed a colonial state only to an extent, according to the definition that in a colonial situation political sovereignty has been seized by a foreign political power and the indigenous population is treated by the conquering state as fundamentally inferior (e.g. as barbarians, savages, heathens, an inferior race, a stagnant civilization, or denizens of a 'failed state').[11] While Ionians were not treated as equals, they were responsible for their affairs (within limits), and on some occasions the aristocracy impressed the British with their education and cosmopolitanism.[12] They were considered immature and permanently unfit for government. Capodistria considered the Treaty of Paris the best possible fate for his fellow Ionians. Maitland bypassed the constitutional obligations of the treaty and devised with his aides the charter of 1817. To justify an absolutist and autocratic rule, Maitland and other British officials and writers used the analogy of the immature and childlike Ionians. This was the 'rule of colonial difference', according to which there were stages of political development and maturity before people reached a modern and progressive phase.[13] Plans for the expansion of the empire were sometimes drawn from readings of ancient history and the expansion and rise of the Athenian and Roman empires. These scholarly constructed aspirations and schemes for empire building can be found in the writings of Leckie, a Scottish planter with estates in Sicily, who argued for the indispensable character of an insular empire across the Mediterranean, which would be 'britannised' and would maintain the expansion of the empire eastwards, unlike the Roman Empire's stagnation and inevitable, according to Leckie, decline.[14]

The priorities, principles and intentions of Maitland are inscribed in the 1817 constitutional charter.[15] The separation into an executive (the 'Senate') and the legislative (the 'Ionian Assembly') became important as the basis for reform, but was practically meaningless since all power rested ultimately with the high commissioner. The appointment of regents, who had to be Ionians, and residents (British military officers) on each island, the appointment of local councils and the election of representatives (following a double list drafted by the commissioner), were the main characteristics of the new system of government. This structure ignored British pledges of independence when they 'liberated' the islands from French occupation. Future commissioners reserved the right to observe and control the daily activities of the Senate. The compulsory presence and intermediation of the secretary of the commissioner – his right-hand man – for the approval of all laws and acts of government ensured that the commissioner controlled the legislative as well. His right to prorogue the assembly complemented the authoritarian powers of the commissioner. The appointment of judges by the Senate and the commissioner's role in the Supreme Court led to further confusion over the limits to his powers; if that was not enough, martial law was declared for long periods on the islands following an insurrection and other real or perceived threats to social order, such as the revolution of 1821.

The 1817 constitution granted all power to the high commissioner, who controlled extensively the police, the courts, all offices of government as well as the High Police, a secret police force entirely accountable to him with powers to arrest, imprison and exile individuals without trial. British governments controlled foreign relations on behalf of the Ionian State, signed treaties with foreign powers and controlled the military, which comprised a strong British garrison of over three thousand soldiers stationed in Corfu. This clause secured the status of British protection for Ionian subjects who benefited significantly abroad, especially those settled and trading in the Ottoman Empire. British officials held the most important posts: the treasurer general, the principal secretaries, the residents on each of the six islands (except Corfu) and the members of the Supreme Judicial Bench. The Senate was divided into three departments, the General, the Political and the Financial, and consisted of five members and a president, the head of state. Legislation often passed as Atti di Governo (Acts of Government) when the assembly was in recess. The Senate (indirectly therefore the high commissioner) approved the civil list (the payment of all state employees), controlled exclusively all expenditure, and nominated local officials such as the regents of each island. The assembly consisted of forty members and a president; twenty-nine were elected from a double list of candidates and eleven selected ex officio – these were the senators and the regents from the previous five-year term of the Ionian Parliament.

Below this federal government, local governments for each of the seven islands made them – technically at least – a federation of individual states, hence the 'United States of the Ionian Islands'. The municipal council on each island consisted of five members, nominated by the regent and picked among the ten most successful candidates in the elections. Despite this 'devolution' of political power the system of governance left the initiative as well as the final word to the high commissioner, who nominated and controlled the president and the Senate, and everyone else from there further down the state hierarchy; no legislation passed by the Senate was valid without his consent, and all appointments by the Senate or the regents had to be approved by him. This structure made real devolution a fallacy but the bureaucracy that was created allowed both for regulation on the part of the state as well as for intervention and participation on the part of the people. The system of petitions to the central and local governments of each island reveal the range of issues that Ionians submitted regardless of whether they were educated or illiterate (in which case they submitted by proxy of a lawyer or a literate representative).

The commissioner approved all legislation including the Acts of Government passed by the Senate when the assembly was not sitting or had been prorogued. British judges – together with the high commissioner – held supreme judicial power and received high wages; the aim was to prevent the corruption and bribery that had prevailed during the Venetian years and which fair-minded British and progressive-thinking Ionians found disgusting and unacceptable. The president of the Senate received £1,400 per annum, a senator £700, a regent £400 and the assembly members £108 each, all extraordinary sums for a small state and its economy that placed severe pressures on the federal budget.[16] The most outrageous of all was the amount Maitland received: £5,000 as governor of Malta, £3,500 as commander-in-chief in the Mediterranean, £1,000 as lord high commissioner, and a £1,000 pension as governor of Ceylon on top of other allowances that secured him £13,000 a year. This sum provoked ironic comments in both Britain and the Ionian Islands, voiced in the House of Commons by Joseph Hume among others who called it 'a most moderate computation' and others arguing that the highest paid official of the United States of the Ionian Islands received proportionally more money than the President of the United States of America, an opinion that Napier shared as well.[17]

The regime that Maitland planted with the Ionian Charter incorporated institutions from previous regimes, the Septinsular Republic and the period of the French occupation. The Ionian State was a conservative colonial invention, infused by Maitland's own prejudices and experience in colonial administration. In his Proclamation to the Ionian People on 19 November 1816, soon after taking over, Maitland stated his ideas and plans for the administration of the islands: 'His Excellency does not have a doubt to reveal that he is informed that some contemplated about His Excellency that he intends to make modernisation to the order of things of these States. But this thing is equally distant from both his beliefs and his duty, to his Monarch on the one hand and to the People of this State, on the other'.[18]

Maitland's declaration that he wished to avoid radical changes in Ionian society and institutions that contradicted his beliefs, the duty to his monarch as well as his obligations to the Ionian people, deflated any expectations that liberal Ionians had cultivated after the arrival of the British on the islands; on the contrary, the 'first classes of political society', those willing to negotiate with the new power and who saw in Maitland the opportunity to build a strong state, were enthusiastic. These were the people whom Hume, in a speech in 1821, called the people 'always ready to worship the rising sun'.[19] Their willingness to support British rule and Maitland personally (though not all of them did) is hardly surprising; after the 'chaos' and 'civil war' of the early nineteenth century and the French and British occupation, the elite families of Corfu, Zante and Kefalonia longed for a period of order and stability, provided they could keep their property and privileges. After the losses during the Napoleonic wars and the Corfu blockade, merchants rushed to welcome the new governor of the islands, and organized a lavish dinner in his honour. The 'Ionian Newspaper' in June 1816 wrote: 'Whereas the traders need to feel more than anyone else the benefits to Trade from the Protection of Great Britain strived to show to our Apostle, Magnanimous Protector their hope and gratitude towards him, together with the rest of the inhabitants'. Nineteen merchants organized a dinner for 120 guests. The gates of the city opened to welcome villagers, for the first time lifting the quarantine that the British army had imposed to stop the plague outbreak in the south of the island. This was the first ceremonial demonstration of British imperial sway and power. A *giostra*, a re-enactment of the medieval equestrian competition, followed and completed the celebrations; both English and Corfiote riders took part, and Angelos Mastrakas won the prize, a sword that Maitland awarded, with the phrase 'Maitland, Reviver of Corfiotes' inscribed on it.[20] The prize expressed the gratitude of the

Corfu elite, not of Ionians as a whole. In the evening a ball and dinner offered by Maitland at the palace ended the first ceremonial display of British power in Corfu. Although his manners may have disgusted, estranged or disappointed many 'elegant Ionians',[21] for the merchants of Corfu who organized the dinner, Maitland was quite welcome.

Despite the narrative of the British reform 'mission' in the Ionian Islands, a report from 1809 on the political and general condition of the islands and on the judicial system is much more neutral – if not positive and hopeful – than later accounts, which referred to the 'character' of Ionians that had been affected by the corruption that prevailed during the Venetian years.[22] The decline of Venice and by implication of the islands was, according to British sources, to blame for the violent character of Ionians and the lack of credibility of the judiciary and other state institutions. Maitland, a smart and authoritarian man, quickly realized that the 'anarchy' and the 'civil war' of the early years of the nineteenth century was essentially a 'class war'.[23] In the British colonial mind a state under the rule of law was synonymous with a strong state, and law reform became the cornerstone of policies of most high commissioners. These policies aimed at protecting the 'people' from Ionian politicians and landowners, who – Maitland believed – only had their personal fortunes in mind. Installing new morals in society and politics, a form of citizenship worthy of British standards, required the rule of law and order that only British authority could impose. The construction of the image of Ionians as corrupt, violent and ungovernable prevailed, especially in the first years of British protection, only to reappear in its last years, when the islands became ungovernable indeed, even if for entirely different reasons: a decade of economic and social crisis and the demand for union of the Ionian Islands with the Greek Kingdom. The image of the decadent, corrupt and untrustworthy 'childlike' Ionians was a fine pretext for imposing an absolutist state as a protectorate that would essentially function as a colony.

The first official ceremony of the British representative and the new Ionian establishment after the granting of the new constitutional charter was held on 29 December 1818. The soldiers raised the flag of the new state in the citadel, and the archbishop blessed the dignitaries, the lord high commissioner and the appointed Legislative Assembly at the Cathedral of St Michael. At one o'clock, 'more than thousand people were treated to a feast of beef, lamb, plenty of bread, wine'. The high commissioner threw a 'magnificent ball with dinner for more than 500 persons' in his palace, in the great hall that was especially illuminated.[24] The first government of the Ionian State was to the extent possible representative of different islands of the new, federal state:

Baron Emmanuel Theotoky as president, and the senators Cavaliere Stamo Calichiopulo of Corfu, Conte Niccolo Anino of Kefalonia, Conte Demetrio Foscardi of Zante, Sign Felice Zambellly of Santa Maura, and Doctor Basilio Zavo of Ithaki. These were hardly 'men of the people' but loyal, promising members of their respective island's elites who offered their support to the new regime and their new masters.

As part of the charm offensive, Maitland ordered the pardon and release of several convicts held in the Corfu prison for minor as well as more serious crimes. Niccolo Angiolo Bondi from Corfu, sentenced for theft to five years in public works, saw his term reduced to two years; Annetta Jaxa from the island Lissa (present day Vis in Croatia), sentenced to two years in prison by the criminal court for adultery, was released from prison; in total, thirty-four imprisoned Ionians, plus some natives of Suli (Epirus) and one from Candia (Crete) were released. This demonstration of magnanimity, however, did not mean that the new state and its governor would be soft on crime; a few months before, in September 1817, Emmanuel Valassi had been found guilty of robberies and was executed, while Ioannis Spigger was publicly humiliated and imprisoned after being found guilty of embellishment.[25]

British policy in the Ionian Islands and Maitland's rule faced severe criticisms in Parliament by Hume and other radical MPs. Maitland's constitution of 1817 was basically considered a travesty – or rather, as Henry Bennet, Hume's associate called it, a 'mere mockery, a trick, a juggle; high sounding, and pompous indeed; something to the ear; a little to the eyes, but in fact – in substance – nothing'.[26] Several arguments in the British Parliament found fertile ground in the Ionian Assembly and among Ionian liberals, who expressed many of the concerns that British parliamentarians had first voiced. Several of the criticisms, however, about practices of the British-Ionian administration were misleading; Bennet castigated Maitland for barring Ionians from civil service, preferring and privileging foreigners, but the truth was that the overwhelming majority of posts and therefore responsibility for managing the Ionian State were filled by locals, with the exception of the few top officials.

In 1821 not only Maitland but colonial officials also adopted the discourse of paternalism and argued that the recent turbulent history of the Ionian Islands did not qualify them for enjoying 'perfect liberty'.[27] Others supported Maitland as well, revealing the divisive effect of the Ionian issue in the British Parliament. When Castlereagh intervened he reminded MPs that the islands were not a colony and so could not be ruled by a constitution offered by Britain, a rhetorical and institutional formality used to avoid the challenges to British rule that Ionians and British could raise. Maitland imposed a centralizing state and gave extraordinary powers to the post of high commissioner, but at the same time he was shrewd and far-sighted enough to understand recent Ionian political history. After two decades of instability, social conflicts that caused anarchy on most islands, and successive occupations by other imperial powers, the British administration and Maitland wanted stable governance; 'tranquillity' as the stated aim is the word that appears quite often in the colonial archive and in the records of the British Parliament. It was the landowning families who were experienced in local politics and administration through their participation in the islands' councils. These were the dominant and hegemonic groups in Ionian societies, and they shared the same goals as Maitland, namely order and stability. Rather than a radical break in the history of the islands, the British takeover and the formation of the Ionian State represent a continuation of the previous political order under the overwhelming authority of Great Britain. The real turning point would come later, first in the 1820s with the outbreak and outcome of the Greek Revolution, and then in the 1840s and 1850s with the rise of reformism, liberalism and outright hostility to the British regime of the Ionian protectorate.

Disarmament: A Local Uprising, the Greek War of Independence and the Impossible Neutrality

One of the first accounts of a local military force in the Ionian Islands comes from 1563 in Kythera, where a militia of 150 men controlled a population of about three thousand, aiding the small Venetian force stationed there. On the same island the leaders of the militia (*capo di squadra*) intervened in times of crisis; when famine struck in 1667–73 the leaders asked the governor of the islands for help and food, which they received.[28] This was typical of all islands throughout the Venetian period. Arms remained common, partly as a result of the uprisings in the country and the need to have a militia for fear of Ottoman invasion. Disarming the population to control the country was always a challenge but when Venetian governors tried to restrict and control guns they failed, as the several resolutions during the Venetian period show.[29] It was at the turn of the century that public order broke down on almost all of the islands. Uprisings between 1799 and 1802 spun out of control, and the central government of Corfu ordered the captains of the militia and other forces to assert their newly acquired authority and impose control in the country.[30]

British army officers were quick to realize how tense class relations were on the islands. In 1812 the Kefalonia Council resisted the idea of Governor De Bosset to construct a bridge across the lagoon that would link the capital with the opposite shore. They were afraid, they argued, that the villagers of Dilinata, Faraklata, Omalos and Pyrgi could attack the town, as they had done in the past.[31] Despite these objections the bridge was built; the obelisk dedicated to the Swiss officer of the British army who governed the island for a few years reminds us today of the first public work in the Ionian Islands under British rule. The attitude of powerful families in Kefalonia towards British military occupation ranged from tacit support to outright enthusiasm and servility; the uprisings on all the islands in the early nineteenth century shaped the decision making and policy of British governors and first commissioner Maitland. The Kefalonia Council members were afraid that the rebellion of the country folk against the French occupation and the city's elite could be repeated; De Bosset was able to 'quell the civil conflicts and animosities, and pacify villagers and burghers' as Ionians admitted.[32]

Controlling the country's often-rebellious population in a long history of Ionian insubordination to authority was high on the agenda of Maitland and his staff. The number one issue that Maitland and also his successor Commander Frederick Adam were concerned with was disarmament, as an indispensable step to control the country's population. This was no mean task; an uprising, caused by what locals considered excessive taxation and by the much more famous and destabilizing Greek war of independence, defined the policy of British commissioners on public order; Ionian realities convinced Maitland, and Adam after him, as well as their superiors in the Colonial Office, that they had to disarm the population to prevent the possibility of armed rebellion and resistance, and avoid a diplomatic embarrassment between Britain and the Ottoman Empire. The system they built followed the structure of the previous period. In Corfu the island was divided into four large districts and eight smaller ones, responsible in total for ninety-four villages. Depending on the village population's size, the government appointed notables (*vecchiardi*) and police officers (*contestabili*), armed and principally responsible for keeping order and enforcing the law. Constables respectively informed central police authorities in the cities about what was happening in the country. The country folk traditionally formed armed bands, protecting the shores and hunting down fugitives and bandits.[33] This system became more sophisticated during the British period, with an extensive and intensive control of the 'country' as the stated aim, and the hierarchy designed with the resident of each island at the top and the director of police, the notables and the constables in each village below him. Notables needed the trust of the director of police but often lacked the trust of their fellow villagers, who did not hesitate to request the substitution of notables who did not even know how to write or read, skills necessary for services such as issuing poverty certificates to those in need.

Village notables were responsible for public order and the management of the country's population but served also as the assessors of the annual harvest, appointed by the courts and paid in kind from the produce they estimated; this arrangement left ample room for corruption and made it harder for producers to escape the vicious circle of indebtedness and bankruptcy.[34] The British forces attempted to control the islands with a militia, similar to the 'Greek regiment' of Zante during the period of British occupation in 1809–16. In 1819 military commander and second High Commissioner Adam designed the Ionian militia according to similar security forces arrangements under previous regimes. This plan required recording every male over 18 years old in Corfu, dividing them in three categories: those single and between 18 and 35 years old; those married and between 18 and 35 years old; and men, both single and married, between 35 and 50 years old. It was estimated that a force of 500 older (over 35) and 1,200 younger (under 35) men was considered adequate for keeping order in the country.[35] The hierarchy followed the military pattern of dividing the force in companies, with captains, lieutenants and corporals. The force would have changed considerably the balance of power and the penetration of colonial rule into the daily lives of Ionians, transforming Corfu and the other islands into a garrison state, similar to the one developed in India and elsewhere in the empire.[36] Once the Greek Revolution broke out in 1821, the plan to form a militia was abandoned, probably because the existence of a large armed population potentially hostile to the Ionian government was considered to be a high risk.

Disarming the population was a crucial step of the British authorities in their determination to control a rebellious population; martial law was imposed on several occasions, testing and transgressing the limits of the constitutional mandate of the high commissioner; Maitland imposed martial law for the first time in 1819 in Lefkada and, following the outbreak of the Greek Revolution, again in 1821 in Zante and 1822 in Corfu, part of the strategy of enforcing strict regulations on bearing arms.[37] All individuals, both Ionians and foreigners, were obliged to get permission from the police – and to explain whether they needed their gun for hunting or for protecting and guarding their home and property – in order to receive an annual licence for the price of four shillings, another source of revenue for the state. The *Government Gazette* published the names and residency of each licence holder annually. This law aimed to control the country's population (where arms were abundant) and to keep public order with fines of twenty-five shillings to those who broke the law. These regulations applied to all islands and were considered necessary, especially after the two events that tested the limits and effectiveness of British Ionian governmentality: the uprising of Lefkada in 1819 and the outbreak of the Greek Revolution in 1821.

Resisting Taxation

The first major challenge to British authority after the 1816 plague came in 1819 from the island of Lefkada ('Sta Maura' contemporaries called it). The armed rebellion of 1819 revealed British attitudes towards acts of violence that could jeopardize the internal stability of the state, and explains the criminal code provisions for national security drafted in the early 1820s. In 1818 the central government in Corfu decided to construct a canal between Lefkada and the opposite shores. The project would be financed mainly by a new local tax on wine and oil exports. Rumours about taxes on everything – doors, windows, weddings (including sex with the bride on the first night), funerals and births – caused outrage among the villagers; absurd rumours that the British would tax sex irritated men, who were exceptionally proud about their masculinity and highly resistant to any invasion of their privacy. In Lefkada, unlike the other islands, land was divided into many small freeholds and not held by a few large landed proprietors; and the new tax outraged the farmers of the island as well.[38]

Other reports, however, did not leave any doubts about the real causes of the insurgence, which were not tax on sex but good old tax on agricultural incomes. Joseph Hume, in his intervention in the British Parliament during the discussion of the Ionian State affairs, insisted that the heavy taxation was the principal cause of the uprising.[39] Taxation had become more burdensome as the new administration needed funds. Even in London eyebrows were raised about the extraordinary expenses for the new palace of the lord high commissioner. Maitland complained that he could not find a decent residence in Corfu and preferred not to stay in the Venetian governor's building in the old fortress but to erect a palace worthy of British rule. The decision without any debate, let alone concern from the assembly was taken in November 1818; earlier, in April 1818, the Battalion of Saints Michael and George had been established in Great Britain as the Order of the Ionian Islands. Architect George Whitmore took over the supervision and construction of the building in Corfu, as well as the design of Upper and Lower Square, and the Cistern of Maitland, as it was called, in Upper Square. The building was the personal project of Maitland and incurred significant costs on the Ionian budget since limestone was transported from Malta, and wood from Italy. The fifty engineer soldiers who were sent from Britain dug the foundations on 23 April 1819 – Saint George's Day – and the official inauguration took place on the same day four years later, when the commissioner moved into his new residency. According to Whitmore, the palace cost in total £45,000,[40] which was an extraordinary sum for the size of the Ionian State budget, and about a third of its annual revenue – in a good year.

All this had to be paid for with extra taxes. The salaries of senators and the assembly were a concern, but it was the absolute control of Maitland and especially his tax hike that provoked the Lefkada uprising. Note the uneasiness of a British author towards the fairly new possessions and the loyalty of their people; as *The Times* reported:

> In addition to the ordinary sources of revenue, the Government daily resort to new taxes. In September last, an impost was laid on the flocks and herds, which are very numerous in the parts of Santa Maura, Cephalonia and Zante. The experiment of this financial measure having been made on the first of these islands, the country-people remonstrated with the local authorities; but before redress could be obtained, an insurrection began in the village of Sfachiotes, and soon spread through the rest of the island; the people opposed the collectors of customs, whose chief, Sig. Siciliano, was killed. Military force having been sent from the garrison, the insurgents of the 3d inst. proceeded towards the city. Major Stovin, the British Commandant, with part of the garrison took up a position on the hill that commands the main road, to protect the town; and on the approach of the insurgents a regular action took place, in which it is said 13 men were killed, and several wounded on both sides. Major Stovin, having retired with his detachment to the fortress, in order to secure it, the country-people entered the town, and assailed and burnt the houses of those persons who were known to have supported the new tax. Sir Tho. Maitland, being absent from the islands when the news of the affair reached Corfu, Sir Fre. Adam sent 350 men with artillery to Santa Maura. This reinforcement not proving sufficient, a second was sent in haste, and hopes are entertained that with its assistance the insurrection will be quelled. There are some apprehensions that the same spirit may manifest itself in other islands, particularly in Zante and Cephalonia, the inhabitants of which may make a stand in their mountains for a long time. In that case our situation would become very critical, as the British forces are at present hardly adequate to the garrison duty of this and other fortified places in the island: and in consequence of the existing system of administration in this country, the majority of the natives cannot be depended on.[41]

The same newspaper had reported a few days earlier that there were five or six thousand men in Lefkada capable of arms, and women 'who are very active'.[42] Such anxieties about armed men *and* women reveal British perceptions at the time, and explain why such acts of rebellion were crushed often at great human cost and without any consideration of the image of the British army or empire during those early days of the protectorate.

The response of the British troops to the threat set the tone for future reactions to armed disruptions of public order. The entire population was ordered to surrender their guns and ammunition; martial law was declared the day after the troops arrived, and remained in force until 20 May 1820, eight months after the rebellion was crushed. Most of the insurgents were accused of treason and court-martialled. Some escaped to the opposite shores, but four people were executed and their bodies were tarred and hanged, scarring collective memory with the fate awaiting those who rebelled.[43] Thirty years later the merchants of the island who urged Commissioner Ward to complete the work of his predecessor promoted the opening of the canal that would save ships the trip around the island. In their petition, fifty-six merchants, proprietors and other 'residents' of Lefkada asked for the completion of the work and the improvement of the road network around the port, which had become dangerous.[44] In the 1850s merchants could negotiate much better with the Ionian State authorities than armed peasants had done in 1819. The violent crushing of the rebellion contrasted with the British benevolence during the 1816 plague in Corfu, but not with the stark and immediate response of Maitland's regime to the presumed 'conspiracy' that Ionian politicians were plotting against him, which led to Flamburiari, a senator who 'was thrown in a dungeon at Zante, because he had signed a petition to his Britannic majesty, complaining of the arbitrary conduct of Sir T. Maitland'.[45] Both responses however were facets of the colonial modernity that British rule introduced on the islands; military practices were used to combat disease and save lives, while military force was used to suppress rebellion. The brutal response of the British forces in Lefkada is probably another reason why the people of that island were among the first to help the Greek Revolution in 1821 and rallied behind the cause to unify the Ionian and Greek states, making Lefkada one of the most 'anti-British' islands of the Ionian Sea.

Maitland's views reflected the principles of the Colonial and Foreign Office, which opposed nationalist movements, especially in nations under British influence.[46] The outbreak of the Greek Revolution in March 1821 posed a major challenge to the delicate balancing act of

British colonial rule over the islands' population, and unsettled the order that Maitland, Adam and their administration together with Ionians were trying to keep. The policy of the Ionian State of strict neutrality and the response of the British administration make better sense within the context of British policy in the region in the early nineteenth century, which had been determined by developments before the outbreak of the revolution.

The Russian-Ottoman alliance of 1800 that created the protectorate of the Septinsular Republic was tested when the War Office asked Ali Pasha to recruit native mercenaries for the British army and station them in Corfu. The Russians objected, wary that the presence of Muslim irregulars would incite turmoil among the pious inhabitants of the island, and prohibited Ali from interfering with Ionian affairs, essentially blocking any British involvement. When the Ottoman fleet mutinied in 1799 in Corfu there was violence between locals and Turkish crews. To retaliate, Ali Pasha attacked the Souliotes in Epirus and prepared to invade Santa Maura and Parga. The Albanian ruler did not allow two thousand native mercenaries to join the Greek Light Infantry led by Captain Richard Church, a future hero of the Greek Revolution. The British sent William Martin Leake, an artillery officer and a famous author of his travels, with munitions, both in 1805 and again in 1809, a cargo of thirty-five canons as payment for the services of Ali to the British in their struggle with the French for control of the region. The British occupation of the Ionian Islands between 1809 and 1814, and the initially cautious if not hostile attitude to the Greek war of independence, were a continuation of this policy of tentative short-term alliances with strong regional rulers like Ali; when the British negotiated directly with the local power holder, Ali Pasha, they were less concerned about the fate of the Ottoman Empire's central authority and more about their long-term interests in the region.[47]

Britain's Royal Navy captured easily the southern Ionian Islands between October 1809 and June 1810. Local irregulars who served as mercenaries quickly changed sides, abandoning the French and joining the units under the command of British officers. Locals gave the British an enthusiastic welcome, hoping that Ionian independence would be restored, especially when, in Zante, Oswald, commander of the British forces, raised the flag of the Septinsular Republic together with the Union Jack. Ionians soon discovered that this was a propaganda scam and a common pattern emerged; every time there was a change of regime and occupying force, some Ionians cheered, but disillusionment invariably followed enthusiasm. Many locals were positive towards the

British presence because they did not wish another Russian–Ottoman alliance and had never quite accepted French occupation; Ionians in Zante were eager to restore trade, and their profits, under British protection. Oswald liked the idea of the locals paying for the British protection and defence, because he intended to improve the strategic capabilities of Ionian harbours and to train Christian Albanian mercenaries to serve under British command, following the model established in both Corsica and Calabria. This plan required the presence of Major Church, who trained a large group of future Greek insurgents, who included one of the later heroes of the Greek Revolution, Theodoros Kolokotronis. Church and Kolokotronis worked together during the revolution and in the period after independence. Foresti announced to Foreign Secretary Canning that locals were quite pleased with the British presence, and that the council of the island had requested that the British government formally annexes them.[48] In the meantime British relations with Ali Pasha remained close, and improved when the Albanian ruler provided timber and corn in exchange for support and munitions from the British forces, negotiating directly with them, without the intermediation of the sultan.

In March 1821, however, when the Greek Revolution broke out in the Peloponnese, High Commissioner Maitland had very specific concerns; the uprising of 1819 in Lefkada had stressed the importance of keeping public order in the country. As if the domestic balance of power was not precarious enough, in the spring of 1821 the Greek Revolution became a headache for the cool-headed Maitland and the 'friendly to the Ottoman sultan' British Empire. News about the outbreak of the Greek Revolution against the Ottoman Empire in March 1821 spread in the Ionian Islands like a wildfire.[49] The insurgency had been forthcoming ever since Kolokotronis sailed from Zante with just his four trusted comrades to Kardamili in Mani in January 1821, although rumours in the Morea talked about Kolokotronis bringing four thousand fighters with him. The Ionian government could, in theory, demonstrate its sympathy with the insurgents demanding their freedom, but at the same time acknowledge the right of the Ottoman Empire to crush the rebellion. Despite a declaration of strict neutrality by the Ionian State in June 1821, many Ionians joined the revolutionaries on the mainland. Ionians, protected by Britain, claimed to represent Britain in their war effort, embarrassing and potentially damaging British–Ottoman relations. The government's response left no doubts when it ordered Ionians to return otherwise their property would be confiscated; and two ship owners from Kefalonia were declared pirates for fighting with the Ionian State flag.[50]

The crucial role and contribution of Ionians to the revolution is fairly well known but historians have not considered its consequences for Ionian State policy. Merchant captains from the island of Ithaki were among the first to join the secret revolutionary organization Filiki Etaireia (the 'Society of Friends') in 1814, which organized the Greek insurrection. Some volunteers from Ithaki were present in the first uprising of the war of independence, the failed Danube campaign in February 1821 under the leadership of Alexandros Ipsilantis, while the small island of Kalamos in the Ionian Sea offered refuge to hundreds in 1821,[51] and became a place for Greek captains to hide and recuperate during the revolution – all evidence of the inability of the Ionian State to enforce neutrality within its island borders. The most important connection in the history of the islands and the Greek Revolution was the appointment of the first governor of Greece in 1828, Ioannis Kapodistrias, of Corfu, who first learned the art and science of government as a minister of the Septinsular Republic, before serving as minister in the Foreign Office of the Russian emperor. In 1821, Andreas Metaxas, from Kefalonia, was one of the most prominent Ionians to gather around two hundred men and cross to Roumeli to fight; he survived both the battles and the in-fighting among Greek factions, and was appointed the first prime minister in 1843 after the constitutional *pronunciamento* that checked the absolutist rule of King Otto.

The geopolitical importance of the Ionians Islands adjusted British policy in the 1820s to the developments of the Greek war of independence. Uprisings in the area of Naples in Italy in the early 1820s and the battles in Epirus and Morea in 1821–22 forced Maitland to take extraordinary measures to maintain the always elusive 'perfect tranquillity' on the islands. Ionians joined the war of independence and Gordon, a British officer with a regiment of Greek-Albanian troops in Zante, was openly pro-Greek, embarrassing Ionian neutrality. Maitland could understand the enthusiasm that gripped many Ionians since they were 'in favour of the insurgents, who were of the same religious persuasion with themselves, with similar habits, language, and manners', but he expected Ionians to obey state policy and enforce a strict neutrality. For Maitland, participation of Ionians in the war highlighted the conflict between nationality and citizenship; citizenship had to prevail and Ionians had to follow the government's orders for neutrality. For all his brutal character Maitland's point was quite sophisticated, and tapped on a central debate in the history of nationalism.

The islands closer to the mainland presented a more immediate threat to the policy of neutrality. The enthusiasm many Ionians felt for the revolution presented the British, and Maitland personally, with an international relations problem and a stark choice on how to react. Some Parga refugees crossed to Epirus and tried to recapture their city, failing bitterly, and Maitland declared that they would not be welcome back in Corfu after 'their rapacious campaign'.[52] Many Zantiotes crossed to the Morea to fight, and Maitland declared martial law in the Ionian Islands, one of several times martial law was imposed prior to 1864, and he decided to disarm the population. When a boat with Muslim refugees tried to dock in Zante and get provisions, some Zantiones were outraged and sought revenge for atrocities against Christians in the Ottoman Empire. A small group of twenty British soldiers with an officer were present to ensure that the ship would abide by the quarantine regulations but also receive much-needed supplies. The bystanders, some of them armed, attacked the soldiers, killing one and wounding the officer, forcing the rest to retreat and wait for reinforcements. Similar atrocities occurred in Cerigo (Kythera), when Muslim refugees from Monemvasia on their way to Crete were slaughtered on the shore; the British resident was unaware of it for three days.[53]

For Maitland, the Zante incident was a premeditated armed uprising and not a spontaneous act, since Ionians had attacked and killed British soldiers. Maitland declared martial law for the second time in two years, and in his speech explained the reasons why he decided to disarm the population and punish those responsible for the crime. The real issue for the commissioner was the extensive presence of firearms and their widespread use to solve disputes, which was leading to hundreds of murders every year. Maitland argued that since piracy was no longer a threat thanks to the British protection of the islands, people did not need to possess arms; instead, Ionians were using them to solve minor disputes and personal feuds with disastrous results, which was preventing Ionians from becoming civilized. Maitland announced that arms possession would be limited to those receiving a licence from the police, so that the law could be enforced, order kept, and crime and murder rates lowered. Using the incident in Zante as an excuse to control arms possession, Maitland thus reduced the ability of Ionians to challenge British rule with armed rebellions. The case of the Lefkada (Sta Maura) uprising must have been in Maitland's mind. His speech revealed the real dimensions and intentions of Ionian 'neutrality'; keeping Ionians neutral in the conflict between the revolutionaries in the Morea and the Ottoman army was an issue of international relations. According to British foreign policy, the Ionian State would remain neutral; by declaring neutrality, however, Maitland recognized early and indirectly – on behalf of the British Empire – the belligerent parts. He served his own purposes, and used neutrality to impose a more efficient social control that would prevent anti-government uprisings in the future.

When violence against Muslim refugees and Ottoman soldiers erupted on the islands of Zante and Cerigo in 1821, Maitland was worried that similar rebellions could break out and destabilize the state with uprisings that could challenge or at least embarrass British rule. Violence against any of the belligerent parties, especially refugees, threatened domestic tranquillity, and violated the strict neutrality of the Ionian State, under British protection.[54] For both Maitland and his successor Frederick Adam, the threat of rebellion on the islands was real, and the Zante incident highlighted the danger. Adam requested additional forces to be ready for deployment in Ionian waters, 'to preserve the tranquillity of those states', assert British naval superiority, and protect Britain's possessions against the 'irritable fancies and feelings of a Greek population'.[55] Travellers to Corfu were well aware of the communication between Ionians and the insurgents in Morea, Rumeli and Epirus; government agents intercepted letters and suppressed all intelligence from these lands. Many Greeks from other places were present on the islands, armed and ready to cross to the mainland once they felt they were safe, but their presence was destabilizing the Ionian State. The decision to disarm the population was part of an overall security operation by the British forces on the islands, as officers informed a traveller: 'The English in Corfu told me that these measures, on the least commotion would be followed by the general disarming of the islanders; which they considered the more necessary, as these people are all excellent marksmen, and so expert in climbing and jumping on their mountain and rocks, that they would be almost a match for English riflemen'.[56] The riotous troupes found the experience of serving in the Ionian Islands debilitating and resorted frequently to drunken and disorderly behaviour,[57] and their relations with locals is mostly told through these stories of conflict, while the stories of daily interaction are almost entirely absent from most historical accounts.

Adam, commissioner in the making, realized the urgent need to control the population and the threat that the Greek Revolution posed for social tranquillity on the islands. Revolution in the Morea, Roumeli and the Aegean, the imposition of neutrality and the threat of disorder on the islands led to a stricter and more controlling Ionian State, suspicious of its citizens. Beyond the rather futile attempt to insulate the islands from the heat wave of the Greek Revolution, the Ionian State government gained on at least one account; many Ionians were happy to leave the islands, surfing on the revolutionary wave of nationalism and ridding Ionian State authorities of their troublesome behaviour (many of them, however, returned to the islands). On the other hand the pretext and reality of the revolution offered the government an opportunity to introduce measures to discipline, control and punish the population if they overstepped the boundaries of neutrality that the Ionian government had placed.

Miscommunication between the Ionian government and the Admiralty, who had clearly underestimated the complexity of the situation, at least in the first few months after the revolution and not before neutrality had been violated, also played a role. Enforcing neutrality was directly linked to preventing an internal rebellion, which was easier said than done, especially in the pirate-infested waters of the Ionian Sea. The Colonial Office and British officials in the islands considered the problem so acute that in 1823 the British agreed to form a treaty with the insurgents and recognize them officially, to control and if possible prevent acts of piracy in Ionian waters. The change of policy was not only due to pragmatism but also chance; in 1822 Canning succeeded Castlereagh, and British policy turned in favour of the revolutionary movements in the Ottoman and Hapsburg empires, which Canning saw as destabilizing and potentially beneficial for British policy.[58]

Disarming the Revolutionaries in Greece

The disarmament and effective control of the population by the Ionian State present a stark contrast with the case of the post-revolution Greek Kingdom. The ability of the state to enforce order is one of the markers of modernity and relates to the question of whether and to what extent post-revolution Greece was a modern state.[59] When the conflict between conservative and modernizing groups erupted after the outbreak of the revolution, Westernizing intellectuals won the upper hand even if only on paper and form rather than substance. In 1824, Lord Byron, while staying in a village in Kefalonia at a critical moment of the revolution, negotiated a loan with British bankers in London and chose to support financially and therefore politically Mavrokordatos, one of the 'heterochthones' or foreign-born, instead of Mavromichalis, the Morea notable. The 'autochthonous' or indigenous elite groups and warlords, however, still maintained armed bands under their control for several years after the revolution.

The disruption of public order by popular rebellions, and reluctance to centralization and paying taxes lasted for decades. The origins of this long-lasting disruption date to the period of the Greek Revolution, especially during its most violent years of civil war. When the Troizina

Assembly convened in 1827, Greek insurgents were drifting between factions and individuals vying for power and control. The success of the revolution was hanging by a thread; Ibrahim Pasha, son of Mehmet Ali of Egypt, was ravaging the Peloponnese, and the assembly provided much-needed momentum. On 27 March 1827, Lord Cochrane was elected supreme commander of all Greek naval forces, and on 2 April, Richard Church was appointed commander in chief of all land forces. Greeks surrendered their military and civil leadership to British officers, an event with political consequences that would soon affect the negotiations of the British, Russian and French governments with the sultan. The next day the assembly elected John Kapodistrias to be governor of Greece for a seven-year period. Kolokotronis and Karaiskakis, the military commanders of Morea and Rumeli respectively, were the main supporters of Kapodistrias and influenced the decision. Kolokotronis managed to quiet the concerns of the islanders, especially Hydra, who also supported British presence in Greece and were keen to secure commercial gains in the post-revolution order but were sceptical of the Russian-trained Ionian Kapodistria. Similarly, Stratford Canning agreed despite his own reservations: 'Capodistrias was a Greek of the Ionian Islands, but still a Greek. The Greeks had need of a foreigner to direct their counsels, first for overruling their internal factions, and secondly for linking their courses of operations with established practice of Europe. Count Capodistrias was to all appearances the only foreign statesman whose qualities and circumstances at all corresponded with these conditions'.[60] This logic prevailed during Kapodistria's period as well as during the first years of King Otto's rule.

The conflicts and the intervention of Ibrahim Pasha of Egypt with his army and navy in 1825 would have ended the Greek war of independence and would have classified it is a violent, long-lasting insurrection that certainly challenged, but ultimately failed to dismember, the Ottoman Empire at the southern tip of the Balkan peninsula; instead the revolution has gone down in history as the first insurrection in the Balkans that led to an independent Greek State. Reality was a lot less romantic however; poverty, destruction, and a lack of opportunity and security prevented the population from returning to a normal life for years. War was still being waged in many parts of the country that had no settled borders. The challenge that Capodistrias took on when he arrived in Greece in January 1828 was how to establish a strong executive power and organize a central government, and therefore succeed, where everyone else had failed during the war, in commanding the respect and trust of various factions and introducing institutional reforms that would be acceptable to those below him, such as Cochrane and Church, who abused the power vested in them. Collection of taxes was difficult because provincial authorities did not cooperate; misappropriation and embezzlement was common. The notables could dispense public funds as they wished, since they were unaccountable. The country was militarily fragmented, economically destitute and in a state of disunity verging on collapse. In the late 1820s, differences with the Ionian State could not have been more striking. How the two states developed and to what extent they converged over the thirty-five years that followed are key questions that can explain the historical trajectory and the beginnings of the Greek State.

Otto became king of Greece in 1832 at the age of fifteen; too young to take over, a regency was appointed by King Ludwig, Otto's father, consisting of Von Armansberg, Heideck and von Maurer. The first decree of the regency did not mention the constitution or democratic representation, and declared Otto the God-appointed king of Greece. Von Armansberg was close to British influence and was appointed head of the regency, while Maurer was responsible for education and religious issues. The regency, between 1832 and 1835, produced a system of administration – sometimes called the 'Bavarian Protectorate',[61] demonstrating the similarities with the British Protectorate – and was mostly the work of von Maurer. The regency found a political world highly divided according to territorial rivalries and self-styled parties or rather factions, according to the influence of Britain, France and Russia. Similarly to the challenges that Maitland faced, the Bavarian regency had to address two related issues: the widespread violence and insecurity, especially in the rural areas; and the survival of the population, who needed a stable income from the land that had remained uncultivated during the war. For this reason the treaty of 1832 arranged for a foreign army of European soldiers to arrive in Greece and disband the irregular troops. One of the early laws prohibited carrying weapons without a permit and introduced passports for travel from one district of the new country to another. The army was organized around the Bavarian force, and was based on principles of discipline and official hierarchy, and a police force was designed.[62]

The presence of an armed population, however, was much more difficult to control in Greece than among the relatively unruly and armed Ionians. The formation of a strong army trained by the Bavarians tried to integrate the fighters of the war of independence, provide employment and cajole them into supporting the new authority. Unlike in post-revolution Greece, in the Ionian Islands there was a successful campaign of disarmament precisely as a result of the revolution. The outbreak of the war of independence in 1821 changed the plans of the Ionian State for an Ionian militia, and the idea was quickly abandoned as too dangerous and rather unnecessary. The organization of an efficient police force and a strong army garrison of a few thousand men in Corfu and a few hundred on the other main islands was considered – and indeed was – sufficient for keeping public order and defending the islands from attack, that in the post-Napoleonic wars era did not seem imminent. There were other consequences; during this period, especially towards the end, gun crime but also knife fights and murders were significantly reduced, as Ionian men chose the court over the dagger, and Ionian women chose slander suits over street fights.[63] The presence of a strong police force and prohibition on the possession of firearms was part of introducing a new civic order. It was after the outbreak of the Greek Revolution that Maitland declared martial law on the islands. He calculated (overestimating) that 130,000 Ionians with firearms could easily overcome his 3,500 British soldiers, and so decided to disarm the population on threats of severe punishment, and to only rearm Ionians who were registered and under the command of his officers, one island at a time. This plan he executed with success, beginning from Zante, the island closest to Morea and the site of violence against Muslim refugees of the war in October 1821. This policy, one of the most effective and long-lasting of Maitland's term as high commissioner, remained in place until the end of the protectorate. The ability of the Ionian State to disarm the population and impose control within its territory contrasts with the failure of the post-revolution governments of the Greek Kingdom. In 1823, shortly before his death, Maitland could claim convincingly that a British-controlled territory remained tranquil even though it was situated right next to a war zone. Having controlled gun possession among Ionians, the Ionian State embarked decisively on the other important project of colonial governmentality – to 'civilize' as well as to rule through the force of law.

Notes

1. For an account of the British Empire from the perspective of the colonized that brings to light little-known and revisits well-known cases of colonialist violence, see Gott, *Britain's Empire*.
2. Manning, *British Colonial Government*, 488.
3. D. Young, *The Colonial Office in the Early Nineteenth Century*. London: Longmans, 1961, 27.
4. C. Napier, *The Colonies. Treating of their Value Generally, of the Ionian Islands in Particular: The Importance of the Latter in War and Commerce*. London: T. & W. Boone, 1833, 156.

5   Napier, *The Colonies*.
6   M. Pratt, *Britain's Greek Empire*. London: Rex Collings, 1978, 106–8.
7   Maitland to Bathurst, 6 May 1817, CO 136/186, P.R.O.
8   Parliamentary Proceedings, *The Times*, 22 May 1816.
9   Earl Bathurst to Sir Thomas Maitland (L.H.C.), 29 August 1816, CO 136/187, NA, PRO.
10 P. Burroughs, 'Imperial Institutions and the Government of the Empire', in Andrew Porter and Roger Louis (eds), *The Oxford History of the British Empire. Vol. III, The Nineteenth Century*. Oxford: Oxford University Press, 1999, 185.
11 G. Steinmenz, 'The Colonial State as a Social Field: Ethnographic Capital and Native Plocit in the German Overseas Empire before 1914', *American Sociological Review* 73 (2008): 589–612.
12 Gallant, *Experiencing Dominion*, 33.
13 P. Chatterjee, *The Nation and its Fragments*. Princeton: Princeton University Press, 1993; T. Metcalf, *Ideologies of the Raj*. Cambridge: Cambridge University Press, 1995, 6.
14 Bayly, *Imperial Meridian*.
15 E. Kalliga, 'To Syntagma tou Maitland gia ta Eptanisa (1817). Ionies katavoles kai vretanikoi stochoi', *Istor* 3 (1991): 93–120.
16 Pratt, *Britain's Greek Empire*, 106–8.
17 Hansard T.C., Parliamentary debates, New Series, VII, 14 May 1822, p. 567, in M. Paschalidi, 'Constructing Ionian Identities: The Ionian Islands in British Official Discourses, 1815–1864'. Doctoral thesis, University College London, 2010, 94.
18 *Ionian Newspaper*, No. 89, 28 November 1816.
19 Hansard T.C., Parliamentary debates, New Series, 7 June 1821, Vol. 5, 1130.
20 *Ionian Newspaper*, No. 77, 27 June 1816.
21 E. Calligas, 'The "Rizospastai" (Radical-Unionists): Politics and Nationalism in the British Protectorate of the Ionian Islands, 1815–1864'. Ph.D. dissertation, London School of Ecoomics, 1994, 29.
22 BL Manuscripts, Add. 43217, ff. 238b–239.
23 Maitland to Bathurst, 27 February 1816, CO 136/5.
24 *Gazzetta Jonia*, 3 January 1818.
25 E. Moschonas, *Agnosta kai spania Monofylla Syllogis N. Karavia 1797–1863*. Athens: Vivliopoleio Karavia, 1967, 14.
26 Paschalidi, 'Constructing Ionian Identities', 114.
27 Ibid., 116.
28 I. Psara, 'Peina sta Kythera (1666–1673)', *Praktika E Panioniou Synedriou*, vol. 1, Argostoli, 1989, 139–51.
29 Conscription and forced labour and service was the main reason for the uprising of the Zante middle class; see D. Arvanitakis, *To rebelio ton popolaron (1628). Koinonikes antitheseis stin poli tis Zakynthou*. Athens: ELIA, 2001.
30 Papadopoulos, Thomas. *Ioniki Vivliografia. 16ος-19ος aionas. Vol. B, 1851–1880*. Athens, 2000, 109.
31 M.-P. Solomos, *Geniki Dimosionomia tis Kefallinias. Etos syntheseos 1859*. Athens, 1996, 65.

32 Chiotis, *Istorika Apomnimonevmata*, Vol. 6, 221.
33 Ermannos Lountzis, *Peri tis politikis katastaseos tis Eptanisou epi Eneton*. En Athinais, 1856, 253.
34 Angelo-Dionysis Demponos, *I Peitharchiki Prostasia. Apo tous Agones tou laou tis Kefalonias*. Argostoli, Dimos Argostoliou, 1985, 109.
35 Ektelestiki Astynomia 22, υποφ. 22 Ι.ΑΚ.
36 D. Peers, *Between Mars and Mammon: Colonial Armies and the Garrison State in Early Nineteenth-Century India*. London, 1995.
37 Act 41, 1st Parliament, 27 April 1822.
38 Henry Jervis-White Jervis, *History of the Island of Corfu and of the Republic of the Ionian Islands*. London: Colburn, 1852, 214.
39 Hansard T.C., Parliamentary Debates, Vol. 5, 7 June 1821, 1134.
40 Iordanis Dimakopoulos, 'To Anktoro ton Agion Michael kai Georgiou', in Ennio Concina and Aliki Nikiforou-Testone (eds), *Kerkyra: Istoria, Astiki Zoi kai Architektoniki 14os–19os ai*. Kerkyra, 1994, 105–11.
41 *The Times*, 20 November 1819.
42 *The Times*, 8 December 1819.
43 Calligas, 'The Rizospastai'.
44 CO 136/787, N.A.
45 Hansard T.C., Parliamentary Debates, Vol. 5, 7 June 1821, 1130.
46 Paschalidi, 'Constructing Ionian Identities', 78.
47 Wrigley, *The Diplomatic Significance*, 48–50.
48 Ibid., 55–57.
49 Paschalidi, 'Constructing Ionian Identities', 130.
50 Jervis, *History of the Island of Corfu*, 218.
51 K. Mponi, 'I symvoli tis Ithakis kai tou Kalamou eis to yper aneksartisias agona tou ethnous', *Praktika Tritou Panioniou Synedriou*, 23–29 Spetemvriou 1965, Vol. I, Athens, 1967, 240–45.
52 Substance of Sir Thomas Maitland's Address to the Legislative Assembly of the Ionian Islands, 4 March 1822, London, 1822, 6.
53 Jervis, *History of the Island of Corfu*, 219.
54 Wrigley, *The Diplomatic Significance*, 113–14.
55 Adam to Bathurst, 26 June 1821, CO 136/1085.
56 C. Muller, *Journey through Greece and the Ionian Islands, in June, July and August*. London, 1821, 70.
57 Wrigley, *The Diplomatic Significance of Ionian Neutrality*, 102–03
58 Koliopoulos and Veremis, *Modern Greece*, 24.
59 K. Kostis, *Ta kakomathimena paidia tis Istorias. I diamorfosi tou neoellinikou kratous 18os–21os aionas*. Athens: Polis, 2013.
60 Kaldis, *John Capodistrias and the Modern Greek State*, 36–38.
61 J. Mavrogordato, *Modern Greece: A Chronicle and a Survey 1800–1931*. London: Macmillan & Co, 1931.
62 W. McGrew, *Land and Revolution in Modern Greece, 1800–1881: The Transition in the Tenure and Exploitation of Land from Ottoman Rule to Independence*. Kent, OH: Kent State University Press, 1985, 98.
63 Gallant, *Experiencing Dominion*.

 Chapter 3

Law, Colonialism and State Formation

A ruling class 'manages' to inscribe its power over subaltern classes through the law as well as though other forms of subordination.[1] Law is considered 'the cutting edge of colonialism',[2] and part of the 'civilizing mission'; not only for Africa and India, where law played a central but ambiguous role in establishing control in many colonial situations,[3] but also for British possessions in the Mediterranean. Empires erased or absorbed existing plural legal systems and substituted them with a procrustean 'state-dominated legal order', to control those subordinated.[4] Law, the courts and the police introduced a new political order and imposed a new culture.[5] This chapter reveals the discourse over the role of colonial governance that shaped the thinking of colonial governors, and shows how British officials transferred practices learned from previous colonial experience to achieve legitimacy during this formative period of British rule in the Mediterranean. The construction of an efficient bureaucracy and a 'state-dominated legal order' was successful due to the transfer of ideas on law reform from Malta and Ceylon (present-day Sri Lanka) to the Ionian Islands, but also because it incorporated the experience of Ionians from previous forms of rule in the islands.

This chapter shows the ways in which the tenacious class structure of the Ionian Islands under British rule 'produced' the institutional and in particular legal framework that is so important in any process of state formation. Law reform was among the priorities of many colonial powers in search of legitimacy, as was an efficient bureaucratic administration and ordering practices for the control of the population. In the Ionian protectorate the project of legitimization failed when nationalism and the radical unionists prevailed, but the construction of an efficient even if expensive bureaucracy was quite successful. The extended powers that high commissioners enjoyed led to governing practices that would have been hard to introduce in Britain, even though a civil society had been in place there since the eighteenth century.[6] Maitland based his ideas about legal reform and governance on his previous experience as a colonial administrator, and saw similarities between the 'tribes' of Ceylon, Maltese society and the Ionian Islands, where Maitland ended his British colonial career; British officials drew comparisons between Ionians and other subjects of the empire, and portrayed Ionians as the 'Mediterranean Irish'.[7] His opinion on crucial issues such as criminal justice and a state based on the rule of law is evident in a number of declarations, regulations and speeches to the judiciary of Malta between 1813 and 1816, as well as in his declarations to Ionians after 1817. During and especially after the Napoleonic wars the Ionian Islands experienced the application of rational principles, social engineering and the substitution of the 'rule of law in place of the rule of men', as one historian called it.[8]

The colonial state in parts of the empire such as India was founded on conflicting views about political economy that oscillated between demands for immediate profits and liberal principles of rule; some historians have argued against views that speak of the overwhelming power of existing Indian institutions and practices in the formation of the colonial state.[9] Colonialism in the Ionian Islands was only to an extent a radical break with the past and previous forms of rule, and entailed many new characteristics that gave a new meaning to what Ionians called *xenokratia*, or xenocracy. The modernizing regimes of French and British colonialism coincided with the rise of the distinctive domain of European modernity, the bourgeois public sphere and civil society.[10] In early modern Europe, 'a new form of political rationality combined two seemingly contradictory modalities of power: one, totalizing and centralizing, the other individualizing and normalizing'.[11] During the period of British rule, the domain of the 'social' and civil society did not emerge in opposition to the state. The end of Venetian rule in 1797 forced the Ionian political elite to abandon their mainly managerial role and assume a governing and decision-making role. The political rationality of government – Foucault's 'governmentality' – requires a distinction between sovereignty and government, and between discipline and government. It was during the Septinsular Republic that some independence – even if truncated – was achieved, and Ionians for the first time acquired experience in running a state under Russian–Ottoman military supervision and later under French and British colonial rule before they participated in the Ionian State. This independence remained predominantly in the field of institutions, and law in particular – the field of expertise for many Ionians; it was here that the battle for decolonization and the end of xenocracy was fought, since for radical-unionist Ionians the constitution of 1817 was not only unjust, it was also illegal.

The impact of changes in law by colonial regimes is one of the most contested issues in debates on colonialism, development and the formation of the colonial state.¹² Changes in law to promote an efficient landownership system and policies to redistribute revenues raised from agricultural production and exports, derived from modern notions of state administration. This was not, however, the product of colonial rule but a process of modernization that drew on the colonial encounter and tapped into the legal expertise of Ionians and their training in law reform from the period of the Septinsular Republic. Decades before the indigenous modernization under colonialism in South Asia, Ionians promoted their own modernity using their education skills, and their experience of French rule, Russian protection and finally British colonialism. In the Ionian Islands legal reform and the codification of laws, and the organization and function of justice, preoccupied many colonial governors (high commissioners) who made it their personal project. Commercial legislation facilitated the founding of joint-stock companies and allowed participation in the novel economic activity of shareholding in insurance companies and banks. It was partly these institutions that changed economic and social attitudes and contributed to the making of the Ionian bourgeoisie, credited by some with a Weberian modernizing spirit that defined the Ionian private and public sector.¹³ Changes in law were integral to the making of the British-Ionian colonial state. At the same time, law and the rights of Ionians under British rule became a field of conflict, resistance and negotiation, but also one of opportunity for Ionians who were considered British subjects when they found themselves abroad and in need of British protection.¹⁴

British colonial rule in the Ionian Islands took the form of a protectorate – created by the Treaty of Paris in 1815 – and promoted a modernization process. British colonial officials transferred ideas and projects from other colonial possessions as part of their mission to serve the British Empire project. Court records leave little doubt that during this fifty-year period Ionian men and women changed their attitudes towards crime, the law and the courts through a reformed criminal justice system.¹⁵ Civil and commercial justice under Venetian rule was organized with a number of courts, at which Venetian governors presided as supreme judges on each island. At the end of the seventeenth century, courts of peace in Zante (1675) and Corfu (1692) had consisted of citizens who administered their own affairs as well as those of other classes, leaving room for corruption and vindictive justice based on personal interests and feuds. The administration of justice was basic and unfair; public prosecutors and fair proceedings were non-existent, and the accused were tried in Italian, a language that Ionians who lived in the country and the urban poor could not understand without the help of an interpreter appointed by the council. This perversion of justice continued until the implementation of Greek language in the courts in the 1850s (although it had been proclaimed in the constitutional charter and decided by Commissioner Nugent in the 1830s).[16] The basic source of injustice and inefficiency, however, was the absence of a code of laws; instead justice was administered following customary law and a series of centuries-old statutes (of assize), the decrees by Venetian governors of the island and the Venetian legislation.

In 1797, Venice was taken over by the French republican forces and the Ionian Islands followed the fate. When the French arrived in Corfu they implemented the first reforms in the administration of justice and organized civil and criminal courts while reform accelerated during the period of the Septinsular Republic (1800–1807), the autonomous state under Russian protection and Ottoman suzerainty. The Imperial French (1807–14) introduced for the first time a 'juridical imperialism' that spread under the influence of Napoleonic France.[17] During the period of British occupation (1809–15) the British also maintained the existing court system but soon devised plans to change it as it was considered unacceptable. In 1809–10 the British took over the southern Ionian Islands; Governor Cambell reported from Zante that civil and criminal justice did not operate for the protection of rights and freedoms of the people, and the same held for Kefalonia. The intervention of local notables in the administration of justice was outrageous, especially for solving their own internal differences. Court decisions were mostly vindictive, pitting the interests of one family against another, and among families seeking to influence or directly control judges. Corruption continued to be rife even if crime was less widespread after the British takeover. To address the issue of corruption, Campbell suggested placing the administration of justice under British authority and modifying significantly the old Venetian penal code.[18]

Maitland sought to break with the corrupt Venetian past, especially in the administration of justice. Civil and commercial justice under Venetian rule was organized with a number of courts, and Venetian governors served as supreme judges on each island. The basic source of injustice and inefficiency however was the absence of a code of laws. Venetian governors administered justice according to customary law and decrees and the Venetian legislation, where appropriate.[19] State formation and the administration of justice advanced during the Republican French, who implemented the first reforms and organized civil and criminal courts; reform accelerated during the period of the Septinsular Republic. The Imperial French did not alter the internal administration of the islands, which under French rule were moulding and converging into a unified administrative region. In the field of justice, however, the French introduced for the first time a 'juridical imperialism' that spread under the influence of Napoleonic France.[20]

For many colonial administrators the difference between them and the peoples they ruled was essentially one of 'character'. The argument has been made about Victorians, who praised what they considered the main aspects of character: 'industry, energy, self-help and self-discipline, thrift, honesty, integrity, devotion to duty, and manliness in the face of difficulty'.[21] These characteristics formed part of the discourse of colonial officials long before Victorian times and reflected an ethic considered necessary for economic success and social advancement in Britain and, by implication, in colonies, dependencies and other regions that had already fallen under direct or indirect British clout by the early nineteenth century. Such principles determined the rationality of many colonial governors and officials during their term in the Ionian State. Maitland often compared the Ionian Islands with Malta, and saw both regions as part of the same geopolitical space that was important for British commercial and strategic interests. At the same time there were 'social evils'; the vendetta, violence and murder dominated 'national character' and mentalities in both Malta and the Ionian Islands, and had to be tackled by codifying the civil and criminal law and the operation of a supreme court, as well as reform of the police and the criminal justice system.[22] Maitland's mission was to use institutions to change the 'character' of people under his control – a no mean task.

Arguments about the unsystematic character of the British Empire aside, the imperial project was probably more coherent than previously thought.[23] This coherence was more the result of the circuit of colonial administrators than of some grand design emanating from London. Maitland and other colonial officials after him transplanted ideas about colonial rule from their previous experience. The leeway Maitland was given by the Treaty of Paris to introduce a constitution allowed him to use the experience from his terms as governor of Ceylon and Malta freely. Personalities played a role; the rude and arrogant character of Maitland and his authoritarian style earned him the nickname King Tom,[24] while for decades after the British army left, mothers disciplined their children by telling them that *Maitilas* would come and take them if they misbehaved. Maitland used extensively the Maltese constitutional template for drafting the constitutional charter and appointed Joseph Nicholas Zamit, who had also drafted the Malta constitution. Zamit had helped Maitland to carry out the reform of the Law Courts in Malta and served in Corfu as one of the judges of the High Court, a post reserved only for British in the Ionian Islands. When the British government in 1818 instituted the Order of St Michael and St George, Zamit was nominated as one of the first members and commander of the new order. One of Maitland's most trusted men, Zamit advised Maitland until the death of the latter (in 1823) on matters important for his role as high commissioner of the Ionian Islands, such as the administration of justice.[25] In his early days, Maitland did not trust Ionians, despite the training in law that several of them had received in some of the best Italian universities. It was those Ionians, however, who manned most positions in the administration of justice, except the top ones, which were reserved for British judges. Maitland not only used extensively his experience from Ceylon and Malta to draft the constitutional charter of the 'United States of the Ionian Islands', he also prioritized the British Supreme Court judges, who received higher pay than their Ionian counterparts and they too often experimented with Ionian legislation; but the general direction of codifying legislation and controlling the appointment of judges in each island to ensure their compliance with British-Ionian government remained intact.

Maitland's main source of inspiration however for the Ionian justice system drew on the constitution of 1803; this, Maitland argued, had remained idle despite its virtues, because of the French occupation and rule after 1807, which abolished the truncated independence of the Septinsular Republic. The 1803 constitution had established a civic as opposed to a feudal aristocracy, that was based on property, wealth and education; it introduced the rights of man and citizen, and provisioned that the language of the state was Greek, although it was written in Italian: *'lingua nazionale greca volgare'*, clearly identifying the everyday language spoken on the islands as a national language.[26] Maitland declared that he would rule with 'wisdom in Legislation and Experience' – both personal experience, which Maitland had gained during his career as colonial administrator, and his experience of the rule of law on the islands. The colonial officer formulated many of his ideas during his term as governor of Malta; these views echo a mixture of British and continental jurisprudence of the late eighteenth and early nineteenth century.

What transpires from the correspondence with the Colonial Office concerning Malta, and by implication the Ionian Islands, is Bathurst's instructions not to create a rupture with the past legal tradition or their major administrative structures such the judicial system, but rather to provide security for them and their property – a recurrent promise to Ionians too throughout the protectorate's life:

> You may consider yourself authorised to intimate in a private manner to the principal individuals in Malta that, while His Majesty's Government

thus publicly mark the incorporation of Malta with the dominions of the British Crown, it is not their intention to destroy the laws which at present exist in the Island, or to make any other changes in the establishment and practice of the courts of justice than such as appear necessary to keep pace with the improved condition of the inhabitants, and as may effectually give to His Majesty's Maltese subjects the fullest security in their persons and property.[27]

Thomas Maitland and his colonial experience deserves special attention. As in Ceylon, 'King Tom's rule' was characterized by respect for native interests combined at the same time with contempt for local notables who he asserted were harmful to their own country, and a demand for efficiency from his officials. For Malta he had devised plans for a commercial court and a gradual reorganization of the courts, which until then had conducted their proceedings in Italian, exactly like Ionian courts. He encouraged the use of English instead of Italian in the town and the Arabic in the country, but presumably with little success at least as far as the latter is concerned. Similarly also to the Ionian Islands, an English barrister, titled the king's assessor, advised the governor, except the two supreme judges who on the islands were British.

The rationale in Maitland's discourse reveals a much more sophisticated understanding and use of recent Ionian history, and the ability to pollinate one colonial possession with reforms implemented in another (from Ceylon and Malta to the Ionian Islands). In 1839 when Ionian liberal Mustoxidi submitted a memorandum to the Colonial Office proposing constitutional reform, he also praised the virtues of the 1803 constitution. For Mustoxidi, Ionian political independence was enshrined in the 1803 constitution but went back to the period of Venetian rule and therefore could not be scaled back in the nineteenth century; Mustoxidi argued that the 1803 constitution introduced 'more liberal and equitable principles' than the British-designed constitution of 1817.[28] As he stated in an address to the legal authorities of Malta: 'The great principle upon which ... the Government of these Islands should be conducted is that there should be a complete separation between the executive, the legislative and the judicial authorities'.[29] These were inherent contradictions in an attempt to maintain a facade of liberal governance that essentially abolished any independence of the judiciary from the executive. Maitland announced the independence of judges from the executive authority and established their permanency in their positions, only to dismiss the measure in the following paragraph by declaring that under specific circumstances he maintained the right to suspend a judge from his place and change convictions that carried the death penalty, postponing the independence of the judiciary. His effort to reconcile these two contradictory statements by arguing that 'there [he] execute[s] merely a judicial function, totally separate and distinct from either the Executive or Legislative Authority vested in [his] hands', merely reveals his anxiety to reconcile a liberal facade with an autocratic spirit.

The authority judges should enjoy was a thorny issue that Maitland tried to tackle. In Malta, just like in the Ionian Islands, the judicial system was influenced by the legal tradition as it had developed since the early modern period. One of the most important aspects of this tradition was that the judge's duty was not merely to enforce the law but to interpret it as well.[30] This tradition contrasted with the British perception of a judge's role, which held that a judge was an impartial arbiter regulating the affairs between the two parties involved according to written law or precedent. In his address to the judicial authorities, Maitland argued that he would eradicate the assumption that the judge should have the power to question the applicability of the law in hand. According to him 'it is [the judge's] duty merely to execute that law, be it good, bad or indifferent'.[31] Maitland stated in an address to the legal authorities of Malta that he would form the government of the Ionian Islands with a complete separation between the executive, the legislative and the judicial authorities. He announced the independence of judges from the executive authority and established their permanency in their positions, only to dismiss the measure in the following paragraph by declaring that under specific circumstances he maintained the right to suspend a judge from his place and to change convictions that carried the death penalty, postponing the independence of the judiciary.

For Maitland, Malta and the Ionian Islands lacked well-established civil societies. He ignored even the guidelines set by the colonial secretary on the legal reforms in Malta, and followed his personal agenda.[32] These views and practices reflect the peculiarity of colonial condition that provided colonial governors the opportunity to exercise absolute power; such were the conditions that created the Ionian Protectorate, where all power remained in the hands of the high commissioner. Maitland sought to break with the previous Venetian regime, contrasting it with the brave new reformed world he was building for Ionians, and set as his priority to maintain order and protect people from crime.[33] He drew a comparison between the jury system, as it operated in Britain, and the extended powers that judges enjoyed in continental Europe (including Malta and the Ionian Islands). As Maitland did not trust Ionians, he believed that trial by jury was a system suitable for 'civilized societies' only.[34] In Corfu, the representative of British power avoided experimenting with the jury system, postponing it for another day, by which time Ionians would presumably have matured into political subjects.

Only a few years before, however, during his term as governor of Ceylon, Maitland had introduced trial by jury in the 1810 charter of justice, for the practical purposes of relieving the supreme court of its responsibility and making trial by one judge more acceptable. The premise was that if each member of the political community could play a role in the administration of justice it would be more difficult for legal and social elites to exercise control over the social life of a community. When Maitland was sent to Ceylon in 1802, part of his mission was to fix the finances of the efficient but expensive government that Dundas and North had set up on the island, and to end the pointless war with the king of Kandy.[35] Maitland strongly opposed the introduction of trial by jury in Malta and later in the Ionian Islands, because – in his opinion – the inhabitants of Malta were not yet politically mature enough for such a reform. In any case, Maitland was also being impractical; when he recommended trial by jury, he was following the tradition of English criminal law, whereas Dutch colonial rule of the island had introduced the laws of Holland, and there was scarcely a trace of original Singhalese laws remaining when an English judge tried to codify native law. Maitland had found in Ceylon a judicial establishment that included a supreme court consisting of two English judges, who the governor joined in cases of appeal, blurring the separation of judicial and executive powers. This arrangement explains many of the institutions that Maitland decided for Ionians and for the independent Ionian State.[36] In tune with practices of absolutist governments, Maitland was not interested in promoting a separation of powers, a civil society, freedom of speech and the press, to avoid opposition and criticisms of the government; wisely perhaps, since the newspaper became the most forceful weapon of opposition to the Ionian government in the 1840s and 1850s. As a result of Maitland's progressive policies to favour British settlers and employees in Ceylon in the 1830s, juries served as particular instruments of colonial conduct.[37]

Police and the Criminal Justice System

Police, as an instrument of colonial hegemony, are critical in understanding the function of colonial power. British colonial officers and state-builders with legal expertise and political capital exercised power in the Ionian Islands much earlier than in other colonial settings, such as India, where British civilizing efforts began in the 1830s through the imposition of control systems, and used very different discipline and control technologies imported from Europe.[38]

Maitland was successful in laying the foundations of Ionian colonial governmentality because he kept in place but also transformed mechanisms he found from the period of the Septinsular Republic. One of them was the institution of police; no modern state could be efficient and assertive without a well-organized, disciplined and loyal police force. For Maitland, Adam and other colonial officials, police administration was crucial to maintaining law and order on the island states.

The Ionian State continued practices developed under Venetian and French rule, and assigned to police authorities the role of regulating and controlling a range of economic and social activities, the labour market, the population in the country, and especially the political activities and attitudes of Ionians towards the regime but also towards the Greek war of independence, as well as the revolutionary movements in Italy. The French upgraded and reorganized the police and social control mechanisms inherited from the Venetian period during their period of occupation (1807–14), especially in Corfu. In 1811, the French administration merged the various police forces, the High Police and the Municipal Police, into a General Commissariat de Police; interestingly, one of the first activities of the new force was the recording of the natural movement of the population (births, deaths, arrivals, departures) – more a research task than a police mandate.[39]

In March 1818 the first act of the first Parliament of the Ionian State established the three police forces: the High Police, the Executive Police and the Court Police. Building a modern colonial state involved creating a strong police force and a surveillance system to support it. The 'Act that Regulates the Police of the United States of the Ionian Islands' was indispensable for the organization of the criminal justice system and one of the foundations of Ionian governmentality. Police under British rule integrated existing institutions and practices that were based on modern social technologies of surveillance and control, which the Ionian State used and exercised often with very little restraint, especially against political opponents of the regime. An efficient and sophisticated network and bureaucracy was put in place; police recorded information on the conduct of individuals when someone applied for employment in the civil service, and informed other departments when Ionians petitioned for a grievance. British and Ionian officials created a police organization that expanded to all islands and set up a system of surveillance to follow Ionians – or other nationals – suspected of subversive activity against the protectorate or other similar-minded regimes, such as the Habsburg in Italy in the 1830s and 1840s. The Executive and High Police were very active after the formation of radical, anti-protectorate groups, in Kefalonia in particular. There was also the Civil Police (Polizia Civile Municipale), authorized to oversee daily (and nightly) activities of Ionians.[40] High and Executive Police followed directly the orders of the commissioner and the residents of the islands, and placed under surveillance any activity deemed subversive, imprisoning and sometimes sending into exile any Ionians who became more vocal against the regime of protection.[41]

The 'resident' – always appointed by the high commissioner – presided over the local council just as the commissioner in Corfu oversaw the Senate (the executive of the Ionian State). This privilege gave each commissioner powerful tools to control local governments exploiting the balance of power between 'feudal chiefs' and their 'slaves' on each island. Depending on the character of the resident, the powers he held were very significant; when Colonel Napier arrived in Kefalonia the island was under martial law, which practically meant that he was the sole judge in all criminal and correctional cases. When martial law was lifted, Napier was surprised that many of the 'labouring class, or, as they are there termed the "infamous class" (the very expression exhibits the state of society!)' begged him to remain in power instead of regular courts. Such pressure justified and legitimized Napier's own rule, the pleas of the country folk to defend them against the abuse of justice perpetrated by those who served as judges and were relatives of the island's elite.

Maitland having realized the extent of French reforms on the Ionian justice system followed the basic articles of the 1803 constitution and introduced or rather kept in place three types of court; the courts of first instance, the criminal courts and the commercial courts, but also courts of appeal.[42] Maitland also approved the reopening of courts of peace in rural areas country that were first introduced by the French but were then ignored in the following years during the Septinsular Republic and the Imperial French.[43] The Supreme Court was called the Supreme Council of Justice of the United States of the Ionian Islands (Supremo Consiglio di Giustizia) but followed the principles introduced by the constitution of 1803.[44] Matiland copied the name of the Supreme Court from Malta, and the court tried cases of perversion of justice and cases of public servants who were not British.[45] The provision in the 1817 constitution of the increased jurisdiction of the Supreme Court in which two judges were British reveals the scepticism of the British (and Maitland personally) towards local judges. The most important task assigned to the Supreme Court was the drafting of new codes, civil and criminal, which was already in the 1803 constitution but had not progressed at all. The commissioner maintained control over the Supreme Court as well, since he could not only appoint the two British judges in the name of the British monarch but also appoint the two Ionians elected by the Senate and approved by the commissioner. If this was not controlling enough, the commissioner also sat ex officio as extraordinary member to the Supreme Court Council.

The Parliament in 1823 introduced regulations for the functioning of courts, continuing the work done in the previous year, celebrating the achievement of having tried since the previous November more than 120 cases in the criminal court of Corfu, and leaving none pending – quite an achievement. Having eliminated the backlog the state turned its attention to the court of appeal. Two prestigious Ionians, Angelos Chalikiopoulos and Andreas Moustoxidis, were members of the first session, which sat three days a week.[46] In May 1823 the Senate authorized the Supreme Council of Justice to submit to the executive suggestions for the improvement or abolishment of existing laws, and the introduction of new ones. The rationale of the act acknowledges that the few years experience of the operation of the courts under British rule proved that existing laws were in may parts 'obscure and defective', and called for the formation of codes. Until that work was complete the law suggested that in cases of absence of laws, judges should suggest laws to the supreme council to recommend to the executive power.[47]

The reform of the criminal justice system and the project of governmentality in the Ionian Islands would have been incomplete without the reorganization of the prisons. In May 1820 the law on the foundation of new prisons 'in the United States of the Ionian Islands' followed reports of various regents of the different islands that noted the 'generally harsh conditions of imprisonment', the material state of the islands and the 'inability to adjust'.[48] The Ionian State achieved a more effective mechanism of control with the necessary infrastructure that updated a pre-Banthamite philosophy of rule, and gradually caught up with developments in Europe. The essence of colonial liberal governmentality is precisely this imposition of a new, 'modern' system of control and regulation, such as the prison system that was based on humanitarian and utilitarian grounds. This project was part of the overall plan to build courts ('Palaces of Justice') with prisons in the basement. The penal code completed the legal edifice of prisons, houses of discipline and houses of correction,[49] but the overall aim of codifying legislation was to elevate Ionians to the status of 'civilized' nations.

'Civilizing' through Legal Codes

The legal systems of British, Dutch and French colonialism evolved from a system of fragmented legal principles that coexisted in the laws of colonial states to a more hierarchical model of legal pluralism as it was shaped by the colonial power and absorbed other juridical forms.[50] Colonial states became a fertile arena for such legislative experiments. The extensive powers that colonial administrators enjoyed allowed them to introduce legal reforms that would have been opposed in Britain, where a civil society had already existed since the eighteenth century.[51] Codification of law in the colonies was the result of a dialectic relation between theoretical principles and empirical observation. Even in India where fervent utilitarians were driving law reform, perceptions of the 'native' character and culture was crucial to the drafting of the criminal code. Codifying criminal law was a continuous process of cross-fertilization among colonies. The Gold Coast criminal code followed codes already in force in India and St Lucia; the Northern Nigeria criminal code was based on the Queensland code; and the codes of Kenya, Uganda, Tanganyika and Nyasaland were all modelled on the Nigerian code.[52]

Hybrid legal systems developed in the Mediterranean under British and French colonial and imperial rule much earlier. In the Ionians Islands, one of the first colonial places where laws were codified, British commissioners took intro consideration local conditions in Corfu, Kefalonia and Zante, as well as the existing legal framework, especially in commerce. The Septinsular Republic had been drafting commercial regulations since 1805, following examples of other states or regions with the autonomy to legislate on commerce, such as the island of Hydra, also important for Greek shipping. British and Ionian legal 'experts' dictated the principles and rules of the new legal order. The transformation of 'men of honour' to 'men of law' took decades, and it was only after changes in attitude to male violence, and above all to a more controlling state that inscribed heavier penalties, that Ionians were gradually convinced to choose the courts from the dagger and the bullet.[53] Law reform and codification became a priority of British commissioners; although the task was completed in 1839 and was approved in 1841,[54] drafts of the civil, criminal and commercial codes had been discussed extensively in the Ionian government and the Colonial Office since the early 1820s. The codification of laws was considered so important that it was inscribed in the constitutional charter (art. VII), and commissioners followed with their commitment to introducing legal codes.

Successive high commissioners set the codification of legislation as one of their highest priorities, and gave speeches to the Ionian Assembly pledging a new ethos and practices; Maitland had alerted the assembly since its first sittings to the need to construct legal codes.[55] It was a matter of the 'highest importance and in the interests of all to form a system of laws'.[56] Maitland's priorities were the internal stability of the state, the 'civilizing' of Ionian society and the uninterrupted course of its economic life, and especially commerce. Documents produced by British colonial officials and travellers' accounts show that despite the different scope and nature of these texts (memoirs, travelogues, political treatises, public speeches, etc.), two recurrent issues informed the discourse: the corruption of the Venetian authorities and the necessity to introduce legal reform and render 'natives' eligible to rule themselves at some indeterminate point in the future.[57] This corrupt system of justice, allegedly, resulted in the people's propensity to violence and their limited trust in judicial institutions; the codification of law was promoted as an instrumental measure for protecting 'the people' from themselves and distilling a new ethos in Ionian society. The urgency of Maitland to introduce a penal code echoed a delegate from Kefalonia, Daniel Coidan, in the session of 1 December 1817. Coidan stressed the 'infinite defects of Venetian criminal laws', but the assembly only followed his advice after Maitland had recommended the formation of a commission to complete the organization of justice and the criminal procedure.[58] It was only in 1825, however, that the Parliament adopted the act that specified the complete revision of the penal code; still little happened, other than the proposition by Frederick Adam urging the assembly to complete its task.[59]

Ionian lawyers played an important role in this reformed criminal justice system. Training in law had traditionally been the qualification for acquiring social status and political rights since the constitution of 1803. State building accelerated in the 1820s, with further organization of the courts, the police and the state archives, but especially with the regulation of professional groups, lawyers and assistant attorneys, who lacked a degree in law but possessed adequate and accredited court practice. These interest groups together with notaries remained indispensable for an efficient bureaucracy. This was the first time that Ionian jurists as 'experts' took on the task to codify the islands' chaotic legal system. These were some of the reforms during Frederick Adam's term as commissioner. Unlike the constitutional charter that was drafted by Zamit, the trusted Maltese assistant of Maitland, the committee for the codification of laws consisted of lawyers Chalikiopoulos Mantzaros from Corfu, Dionisios Flambouriaris from Zante, Focas Cosmetatos from Kefalonia, Kontas from Lefkada, and Karouzos, the secretary of the Ionian Academy and the English secretary to the Senate.[60] The team reflects the federal character of the state but also the power of the political class and the aristocratic families, a result of their negotiation and compliance with British colonial officials. Panagis 'Marinos' Salomon, for example, another statesman from Kefalonia, published in Bologna in 1822 the *Progetto di codice commerciale e di navigazione per gli Stati Uniti delle Isole Ionie* [Project for a code on commerce and navigation of the United States of the Ionian Islands], which he dedicated to the Ionian government; Salomon also published a treatise on commercial failure, *Sui fallimenti e bancarotte* [On bankruptcies], and an essay for the improvement of agriculture, *Esposizione sulle cause politiche-economiche che si oppongono ai progressi dell' agricultura nelle Isole Ionie* [Essay on the political-economic causes that hinder the progress of agriculture on the Ionian Islands] also in Bologna in 1825.[61] Ionians were not short of ideas on commerce, and agricultural reform played a central role in drafting the legislation to achieve the stated goals, on which both liberal Ionians and many commissioners agreed.

Ionian governments introduced various codes in drafts and in amendments between 1830 and 1851. The civil code was approved in 1830 and the penal code in 1835, both written in Italian. In 1841 the penal and the civil codes were reformed and the commercial code was approved, incorporating various previous acts and regulations in operation in Ionian trade; the penal code was reformed twice more, in 1844 and 1851, completing the codification of laws in the Ionian States.[62] British colonial administration of the Ionian Islands drafted a criminal code for the first time in 1823. The proposed code included a mixture of liberal and conservative ideas as seen in the approach to the death penalty. On the one hand the code aimed at restricting the application of capital punishment to crimes against life and against the security of the state. On the other hand, in cases where the death penalty was deemed necessary it was applied according to medieval and early modern practices. Article 29 leaves no room for interpretation and states that: 'The punishment of death shall be executed by day, by hanging the culprit by the neck with a rope, on the gallows, and in a public place in the island in which the criminal court shall have pronounced sentence'.[63] Modern and premodern elements bundled together; the judicial procedure had to be transparent and the act of punishment remained public.[64] The code only sanctioned what had been common practice in the islands ever since they fell under British rule; in 1815, Anzoletos Paparatos and Efstathios Aggelopoulos from Zante were condemned to death for money forgery; the doomed were paraded and executed, and the executioner burned their tools at the time of their death, throwing into the sea what remained.[65] Public punishment was aimed at making an example of criminals while maintaining its performative character, but also breaking with Venetian legal tradition. Nevertheless, this break with the past was not definite. Under the criminal code, punishment remained a spectacle since the condemned were still executed in public. The fifth article stated that 'persons condemned to death should, in their way to the place of the execution, be dressed in black, with a black vale [sic] which will cover their face and carry a sign that will indicate their position'.[66] Corporeal punishments were rarely included in the criminal code draft.[67] The code clearly prioritized penalties that included the physical confinement of the condemned (e.g. imprisonment, exile) over fines or other non-corporeal punishments. The British-Ionian state, however, reacted brutally when the army suppressed armed rebellions, as was the case in Lefkada in 1819 but especially in Kefalonia in 1848 and 1849. The hangings, public floggings, and burning of houses that followed the armed rebellions caused outrage around Europe and shocked Ionians, reminding them of the consequences of martial law; these reactions tilted the Ionian mood against British and Ionian state officials.

The changes introduced in the criminal code reflected humanitarian ideals that by that time were becoming popular in Britain.[68] By the beginning of the nineteenth century there were over two hundred capital offences in Great Britain, more than in any other European country.[69] The practice received the support of the majority of the public, famous jurists (Coke, Blackstone and Stephen), and church leaders. The first recorded dissent in the British Parliament against public executions occurred in 1819.[70] The 1832 Reform Act repealed capital punishment for stealing up to the value of five pounds, and for horse, sheep and cattle stealing,[71] and only in 1867 did executions stop being a spectacle in public places.[72] Resistance against the abolition or even the restriction of the application of capital punishment was strong, but until the 1830s it was not unusual for a minor to be hanged.[73] It is interesting that liberal colonial officials introduced a degree of leniency in the application of capital punishment in the criminal codes of the colonies. In India, just like the in the Ionian Islands, the 1837 draft of the criminal code stipulated that capital punishment will be inflicted 'only in cases where either murder or the highest offence against the State has being committed', effectively being much more lenient than in Britain.[74]

Lord Nugent, the commissioner from 1832 to 1835, highlighted three major changes in the new criminal code, and all three related to the correctional methods employed. Confiscation of properties of felons condemned to death or hard labour for life was abolished, only to return in the 1840s; death punishment was reserved only for those crimes that resulted in the loss of human life and for high treason. The main idea behind the replacement of imprisonment with fines was to assist ex-convicts after their release. Nugent argued that the sentence to replace the death penalty would be 'a sentence little less severe, namely, that of perpetual hard labour, and separation from all intercourse with their fellow men for the remainder of their lives, leaving to them in future nothing of life but a mere existence – a hard existence – a constant memorial of their guilt and of the justice of their punishment'.[75] Nugent and the British authorities believed that they had found a modern way to punish more effectively, by extending the duration of the punishment and reducing its severity.

This became clear in the penal code, when it was finalized in 1841; the code introduced the novel concept of correction that aimed at moral improvement through labour during the period of confinement in prison. It is interesting that similar principles were not introduced in the Italian penal code until 1889.[76] The law even provisioned for the release of those jailed for life after twenty-five years, provided they had demonstrated good conduct and had been 'corrected'. British colonial officials noticed the shortcomings and grey areas of this first penal code, but it was the Ionian Assembly that finally completed the task that had lingered for almost fifteen years. In 1834 Lord Nugent, a fervent liberal, presented to the Legislative Assembly a second draft; in the speech delivered before the Legislative Assembly on 9 August 1834, Nugent described the general principles on which the new criminal code of the United States of the Ionian Islands should rest. The distinction between his liberal views and Maitland's authoritarian attitude is evident. Nugent's liberalism however was conditional: 'all laws, abstractly considered, are evils, not only as restrictions to liberty, but also because, by the natural imperfection of all human Governments, they may become the means of occasional injustice. Every law should therefore be adopted only as the less of two evils'.[77] According to this philosophical pessimism, Nugent, instead of clearly stating the goals that were to be achieved through the imposition of a new criminal code, chose to refer to the 'evils' that British jurists tried to avoid when drafting the code, namely obscurity and superfluity.

Nugent and his aides went to great lengths to legislate issues of state security. A staggering 149 articles, almost one-fifth of Nugent's code, aimed at safeguarding the internal security of the state, a more concrete legal block compared to the first draft of the code. The code provided a detailed index of virtually all the known offences that could be committed against the state, emphasizing the nuanced distinctions between different types of offences, and providing the minimum and maximum penalties for each offence. The painstaking efforts of the legal architects of the code to pin down every possible threat against internal security, plus the severity of the punishment that attacks against the state carried, reveals the will of the legislators to safeguard the internal stability of the state. The authors of the code legislated against the outbreak of civil war that might ensue: (1) among the populations of the Ionian Islands ('*fra le popolazioni degli stati uniti*'); (2) among the people of the same population ('*fra le persone che compongono una popolazione*'); (3) among different classes of inhabitants ('*fra differenti classi degli abitanti*'); or (4) against one class ('contro una classe'). The provisions for possible threats against the internal stability of the state show the conflict between 'different classes' that posed a potential threat to the internal stability of the state. British and Ionian officials and legislators, were aware of the power relations in Ionian society that in the past had led to uprisings, especially in the rural areas, and had challenged the rule of urban elites and the 'internal stability' of the state. Under British rule the danger had to be avoided, and the law became the principal instrument to implement stability and order; in this sense law reform and codification advanced Ionian governmentality.

The administration of justice remained a concern of high commissioners, who introduced or suggested changes in the local jurisdiction of the judges on different islands to prevent interfering in the administration of justice, on the role of the 'House of Senators', their election and the period for which elected, their salaries and their duties;[78] most thorny was the issue of proroguing the assembly, a right exercised by commissioners with little concern for the perception of the protectorate or the adverse effect it had – very different from the one intended, which was to govern the islands as smoothly as possible. By the time British-Ionian colonial administration had designed and implemented the legal framework for Ionians, the Ionian State had started measuring them.

Notes

1. N. Poulantzas, *Keimena. Marxism, Dikaio, Kratos*. Athens: Nisos, 2009, 50.
2. M. Chanock, 'Making Customary Law: Men, Women and Courts in Colonial Northern Rhodesia', in M. Wright and M. Hay (eds), *African Women and the Law*. Boston: African Studies Centre, Boston University, 1982.

3   P. Fitzpatrick, 'Custom as Imperialism', in J.M. Abun-Nasr and U. Spellenbert (eds), *Law and Identity in Africa*. Beitrage auf Afrikaforschung, 1 (1990): 15–30.
4   L. Benton, 'Law and Colonial Cultures: Jurisdictional Politics and the Formation of the Colonial State', *Comparative Studies in Society and History* 41(3) (2000): 563–88.
5   S. Merry, 'Law and Colonialism. Review Essay', *Law & Society Review* 25(4) (1991): 889–922.
6   E. Kolsky, 'Codification and the Rule of Colonial Difference: Criminal Procedure in British India', *Law and History Review* 23(3) (2005): 632–33.
7   Gallant, *Experiencing Dominion*.
8   M. Misra, 'Colonial Officers and Gentlemen: The British Empire and the Globalization of Tradition', *Journal of Global History* 3 (2008): 147.
9   S. Sen, 'Liberal Empire and Illiberal Trade: The Political Economy of "Responsible Government" in Early British India', in Kathleen Wilson (ed.), *A New Imperial History. Culture, Identity and Modernity in Britain and the Empire 1660–1840*. Cambridge: Cambridge University Press, 2004, 136–54.
10 J. Habermas, *The Structural Transformation of the Public Sphere*. Cambridge, MA: MIT Press, 1989.
11 Scott, 'Colonial Governmentality'.
12 L. Benton, *Law and Colonial Cultures. Legal Regimes in World History, 1400–1800*. Cambridge: Cambridge University Press, 2001.
13 E. Prontzas, 'Oikonomikes epidoseis tou 19ou aiona stin Eptaniso'. Praktika *I enosi tis Eptanisou stin Ellada*, vol. I. Athens: Akadimia Athinon, 2005, 531–44
14 S. Gekas, 'Colonial Migrants and the Making of a British Mediterranean', *European Review of History – Revue Europeenne d' histoire* 19(1) (2012): 75–92; A. Seymour, 'How to Work the System and Thrive: Ionians and Pseudo-Ionians in the Levant, 1815–1964', in Anthony Hirst and Patrick Sammon (eds), *The Ionian Islands: Aspects of their History and Culture*. Cambridge: Cambridge Scholars Publishing, 2014, 75–105.
15 T. Gallant, 'Women, Crime and the Courts in the Ionian Islands during the Nineteenth Century', *Historein* 11 (2011): 138–56, 138–56; Idem, 'Honor, Masculinity, and Ritual Knife-Fighting in Nineteenth Century Greece', *American Historical Review* 105(2) (2000): 359–82; Idem, 'When "Men of Honor" Met "Men of Law": Violence, the Unwritten Law and Modern Justice', in Efi Avdela, Shani d'Cruze and Judith Rowbotham (eds), *Crime, Violence and the Modern State, 1780–2000*. London: Edwin Mellen, 2010, 69–92.
16 P. Mackridge, 'Venise après Venise: official languages in the Ionian Islands, 1797–1864'. *Byzantine and Modern Greek Studies* Vol. 38 (1) (2014): 68–90.
17 S. Solimano, 'I Francesi e le Isole Ionie. Imperialismo Giuridico in difficolta spunti per un approfondimento', in S. Vinciguerrra (ed.), *Codice Penale degli Stati Uniti delle Isole Jonie (1841)*, CEDAM Padova, 2008, XXV–LIV.
18 M. Stavrinou, 'Stoicheia tis dimosias zois sta notia Eptanisa, symfona me anekdoti anaphora tou antistratigou James Campbell (1813)', *Kerkyraika Chronika*, vol. XXVI. Kerkyra, 1982, 109.

19 Lountzis, *Peri tis politikis katastaseos tis Eptanisou epi Eneton*, 229, 235.
20 Solimano, 'I Francesi e le Isole Ionie'.
21 P. Cain, 'Character and Imperialism: The British Financial Administration of Egypt, 1878–1914', *Journal of Imperial and Commonwealth History* 34 (2006): 178.
22 Maitland to Bathurst, 1 March 1817, CO 136/7.
23 Misra, 'Colonial Officers and Gentlemen'.
24 W. Dixon, *The Colonial Administrations of Sir Thomas Maitland*. London: Longmans, 1939, 107.
25 H. Cosmetatos, *The Roads of Cefalonia*. Argostoli: Corgialenios Library, 1995, 47.
26 M. Dendias, 'Symvoli is tin meletin tou Ionikou Syntagmatos tou 1803. O thesmos ton eforon', *3 Panionio Synedrio*. Athens, 1967, 58–64.
27 F. Madden and D. Fieldhouse (eds), *Imperial Reconstruction, 1763–1840: The Evolution of Alternative Systems of Colonial Government*. New York and London: Greenwood, 1987, 712.
28 British Parliamentary Papers, XLVIII (401): 'Memorial of Cavaliere Mustoxidi', 1840.
29 CO 136/1241, TNA.
30 A. Mazzacane, 'Law and Jurists in the Formation of the Modern State in Italy', *The Journal of Modern History* 67 (1995): S62–S73.
31 CO 136/1241, p. 8.
32 CO 158/24, Maitland to Bunbury, 20 June 1813; CO 158/24, Maitland to Bathurst, 2 April 1814; CO 159/4, Bathurst to Maitland, 5 July 1814; WO 6/124, f. 70, Bunbury to Maitland, 17 June 1813, reprinted in Dixon, 'The Colonial Administrations of Sir Thomas Maitland', 147.
33 Address to the Legislative Assembly, 1820, Manuscripts, British Library, Add. 47290 f 222.
34 CO 136/1241, p. 12–13, TNA.
35 Manning, *British Colonial Government*, 447.
36 Ibid., 455.
37 Scott, 'Colonial Governmentality', 191–220.
38 D. Arnold, *Police Power and Colonial Rule. Madras 1859–1947*. New Delhi: Oxford University Press, 1986; A. Gupta, *Crime and Police in India (Up to 1861)*. Agra: Sahitya Bhavan, 1974; A. Gupta, *The Police in British India, 1861–1947*. New Delhi: Concept, 1979; P. Griffiths, *To Guard my People: The History of the Indian Police*. London: Ernest Benn, 1971; S. Sen, 'Uncertain Dominance: The Colonial State and its Contradictions (with notes on the history of early British India)', *Nepantla: Views from South* 3(2) (2002): 391–406; A. Yang, *Crime and Criminality in British India*. Tucson: University of Arizona Press, 1985; A. Yang, 'Disciplining "Natives": Prison and Prisoners in Early Nineteenth-Century India. South Asia', *Journal of South Asian Studies* 10(2) (1987): 29–45.
39 G. Bokos, *Ta monofylla tou kerkyraikou tyografeiou kata tin periodo tis gallikis kyriarchias sta Eptanisa (1797–1799, 1807–1814)*. Kerkyra: Ionio Panepistimio, 1998, 227, 232, 244.

40   G. Moschopoulos, *O Thesmos tis Astynomias sta Eptanisa. Ta kefalliniaka archeia tis Ektelestikis Astynomias (1815–1864)*. Argostoli: G.A.K. Archeion Nomou Kefalonias, 1997, 7–11.
41   H. Zervos-Iakovatos, *I epi tis Agglikis Prostasias Eptanisios Politeia kai ta kommata*. Athens, 1969.
42   Nikiforou, *Syntagmatika Keimena ton Ionion Nison*, 619.
43   Ibid.
44   Ibid.
45   For the Supreme Council of Justice in Malta, see Dixon, 'The Colonial Administrations of Sir Thomas Maitland', 150. In March 1817, Maitland informed Bathurst, the colonial secretary, that he would introduce the supreme council in the Ionian Islands following its successful operation in Malta, CO 412/207.
46   No. VI, First Session of the Second Parliament, 22 March 1823.
47   No. XII, First Session of the Second Parliament, 20 May 1823.
48   Act No. 3 of the First Parliament (26 May 1820).
49   Act No. 17 of the 8th Parliament, 11/23 May 1840.
50   Benton, 'Colonial Law and Cultural Difference'.
51   Kolsky, 'Codification and the Rule of Colonial Difference', 632–33.
52   H. Morris, 'A History of the Adoption of Codes of Criminal Law and Procedure in the British Colonial Africa, 1876–1935', *Journal of African Law* 18(1) (1974): 22–23.
53   Gallant, 'When "Men of Honour" Met "Men of Law"'; Gallant, 'Women, Crime and the Courts'.
54   IIGG, No. 469, 9/21 December 1839.
55   *Ionian Islands Government Gazette*, 4 May 1817.
56   Le tre costituzioni (1800, 1803, 1817) delle sette isole Jonie ed i relativi documenti con l' aggiunta dei due progetti di costituzione del 1802 e 1806 e delle modificazioni e riforme alla costituzione del 1817. Corfu, 1849, 153.
57   J. Davy, *Notes and Observations on the Ionian Islands and Malta*, Vol. II. London, 1842, 146–47; G. Bowen, 'Ionian Administration', *Quarterly Review*, xci (Sept. 1852), 321; W. Goodison, *Historical and Topographical Essay upon the Islands of Corfu, Leucadia, Cephalonia, Ithaca, and Zante*. London, 1822, 203; T. Kendrick, *The Ionian Islands*. London, 1822, 245.
58   1st Parliament, Verbali dell' Assemblea Legislativa, 22 April 1819.
59   Act No. XVIII, Corfu, 1825.
60   P. Chiotis, *Istoria tou Ioniou Kratous apo tis systaseos autou mechri enoseos (1815–1864)*, Vol. B. Corfu, 1878, 12–13.
61   Salomon, Marino. *La statistica generale dell' isola di Cefalonia. Una delle sette componenti lo stato politico Jonio sotto la denominazione di Stati Uniti delle Isole Jonie*. Corfu: "Jonia", 1859; Athens, 1996, 9.
62   J. DuPont, *The Common Law Abroad: Constitutional and Legal Legacy of the British Empire*. Littleton, CO: Rothman Publications, 2001, 791.
63   CO 136/206.
64   M. Foucault, *Discipline and Punish: The Birth of the Prison*. New York: Pantheon, 1977, 32–69.
65   IIGG, No. 58, 2 November 1815.

66 CO 136/206.
67 The practice of public flogging remained in use even after the imposition of the code, which implies that colonial officials did not always follow the formal procedure in their efforts to enforce order
68 R. Follet, *Evangelicalism, Penal Theory, and the Politics of Penal Law Reform in England, 1808–1830*. Basingstoke: Palgrave, 2001.
69 S. Gupta, *Capital Punishment in India*. New Delhi: Deep & Deep Publications, 1986, 28.
70 D. Cooper, 'Public Executions in Victorian England: A Reform Adrift', in William Thesing, *Executions and the British Experience from the Seventeenth to the Twentieth Century: A Collection of Essays*. London: McFarland, 1990, 149.
71 B. Block and J. Hostettler, *Hanging in the Balance: A History of the Abolition of Capital Punishment in Britain*. Sherfiel Gables: Waterside Press, 1997, 87.
72 V. Gatrell, *The Hanging Tree: Execution and the English People, 1770–1868*. Oxford: Oxford University Press, 1994, 23.
73 Gupta, *Capital Punishment in India*, 27; Block and Hostettler, *Hanging in the Balance*, 22–23.
74 Reprinted in Gupta, *Capital Punishment in India*, 24.
75 CO 136/206.
76 S. Vinciguerra, *Codice Penale Degli Stati Uniti Delle Isole Jonie*. Padova: CEDAM, 2008, cxiv.
77 CO 136/206. V Parlamento, b. 139, Verbali del Senato, 6 June 1835.
78 T. Papadopoulos, *Bibliographie Ionienne. 16ος-19ος aionas. Vol. B´1851–1880*, no. 3474. Athens, 2000, 21.

 Chapter 4

Colonial Knowledge and the Making of Ionian Governmentality

'Statistics': The Science of the State

British colonialism involved more than formal or informal political influence, imposing the rule of law and opening access to markets while taking into account military considerations; one of its main thrusts and overall projects was the desire to control natural and human resources. As a result, 'the form and content of the knowledge that was produced out of and enabled resource exploitation, commerce, conquest and colonisation' has moved centre stage among historians of the British Empire.[1] The British imperial project for the Ionian Islands rested on military and geopolitical priorities, but once the British took over the islands they had to rule approximately 220,000 people. Infrastructure works, such as roads, bridges, lighthouses (the first built in 1822 in Corfu) and administrative buildings were part of the developmental project many colonial governors and modernizing Ionians promoted. Raising the living standards of the Ionian population, what contemporaries called 'progress', however, depended on the finances of the Ionian government; these determined its ability to carry out public works and thus improve living conditions on the islands. Sources such as the Blue Books of Statistics, collected by the British authorities for colonial administration purposes, documents of the Ionian State bureaucracy and accounts of Ionians and British contemporaries reveal a colonial modernity that found fertile ground among the educated Ionians who followed the logic of accountability, transparency and found innovative expression of interests in the public sphere, but also through collective petitions.

After 1827, population registers were constructed annually for the Blue Books of Statistics. This collection of knowledge formed the backbone of colonial policy in the Ionian Islands and in the empire as a whole. The 'Blue Books' were compiled in all colonies of the British Empire with the aim to provide imperial officials with the knowledge that they considered important for optimal government. These books recorded population, revenue, trade, shipping, currency, public works, legislation, civil servants, enumeration of schools, prisons, hospitals and lunatic asylums, in an impressive attempt to impose colonial uniformity on vastly different societies. These series were published and evaluated by the Parliament and were intended to provide an imperial compass; British commissioners took into account the wealth of information to be found in the registers. Sometimes with accuracy and sometimes in approximation, officers collected information about the population and the economy of colonies as well as of other areas such as the protectorate of the Ionian Islands, even if it was only for measurement and recording purposes.

Venetians had compiled 'cadastral' sources for centuries, but the Venetian *Proveditore*, or governor, never used these sources to achieve the sophisticated level of colonial governance of nineteenth-century colonial rule. Ionians quickly adopted measurement and the detailed record keeping of population, land, production, climate, customs and geography in a fine example of local governmentality.[2] Later in the nineteenth century, colonial statistics informed Parliament and shaped colonial policy. Statistics were part of a technology of domination, and as such developed in most colonial regimes, especially in India; they were one of the 'investigative modalities' that were crucial to the operation of colonial power, together with the historiographical, the observational/travel, the survey, the enumerative, the museological and surveillance.[3] In the Ionian Islands one could add to these modalities the juridical, given the importance that all commissioners gave to the introduction of codes and the modernization of legislation in Ionian societies.

Commissioner Maitland and his successor, Commander Adam, used whatever colonial knowledge was available to them when they took over the Ionian Islands; they succeeded in overcoming the challenges of plague, the arrival of a refugee population from Parga and the regions where the Greek Revolution had broken out, and an armed rebellion that was crushed in Lefkada. Colonial governmentality in the Ionian Islands was, however, a much wider project that included collection and application of colonial knowledge generated in the Ionian Islands or transferred from and to other parts of the empire. Maitland brought to the Mediterranean his experience from Ceylon and other 'tropical' colonies, and Napier, who became governor of India at the peak of his career, acquired experience while serving in Kefalonia, the colonial appointment he wrote extensively about. Napier, Resident of Kefalonia in the 1820s, used the knowledge he had gained from the 'experiment' in Bermuda to keep soldiers employed in road construction; working in the sun was healthier than being unemployed and more prone to illness.⁴ Some colonial governors, such as Napier and Maitland, were able to use the experience gathered form one colonial appointment to another, often 'experimenting' as they wrote with all kinds of colonial knowledge. Colonial modernity in the Ionian Islands, however, was very much the result of Ionians who founded philanthropic and literary associations and societies, joint-stock companies and especially who ran the Ionian State administration; the printed press and the formation of political parties realized the liberal project and shaped the Ionian public sphere. Governmentality encapsulates a modern form of power that focused on 'population', a new social and economic entity that emerged in Europe between the sixteenth and the nineteenth centuries. The ability to rule transformed into a 'scientific' approach to government, aimed at the wealth and security of the 'population', and emerging as a new category of social and public policy discourse. People could be 'objectively' quantified and therefore measured through new forms of knowledge such as political economy;⁵ to know how to measure was to control.

Collection of information on the economy and the population of the islands systematized knowledge on the individual and the territory. The 'archaeology' of this tradition, the origins of systematic information gathering, goes back to medieval times; the first archive in Corfu dates from 1336, and in Zante from 1485, while in Kythera government documents have been archived since 1530, and in Kefalonia since 1588;⁶ the dates represent the bureaucratic organization of local authorities to conform to the requirements of Venetian colonial administration. Over time these archives became depositories of historical knowledge, a quality they maintain to this day. Travellers, foreign officials and historians have used these record offices to write histories of the islands, while the tradition of the Ionian archivist-librarian-historian continues to the present. The collection of statistical information was part of this production of knowledge that besides ensuring future historical research facilitated efficient colonial governance. Venetians compiled 'cadastral' sources for centuries but were interested in how many Ionians could be drafted to defend their island and Venetian interests in the Mediterranean. However, no Venetian *Proveditore* used these sources to achieve the sophisticated level of nineteenth-century colonial governance, to use population as a resource for economic development at an empire-wide level. Colonial statistics informed Parliament and shaped colonial policy, and were part of a technology of domination that most colonial regimes developed.⁷

Colonial knowledge was produced according to British principles of classification and order. In the Ionian Islands associations of learning that dated to Venetian times, legal experts and social and political reformers were equally important in shaping Ionian governmentality before the arrival of British officers and their mentality. Ionian modernity and liberal governmentality had begun during the French occupation and was as much a local project as it was a product of French and subsequently British colonial modernity. Colonial officials, foreign and local merchants and intellectuals, journalists and politicians promoted a modernization of local society that fixed institutions, categories and identities, creating new hierarchies and in the process inevitably excluding some Ionians in order to benefit others. On the other hand, state institutions and practices that shaped governmentality in Ionian cities complemented private initiatives of a civil society. The collection of statistics in the Ionian State and the dissemination of numerical information and knowledge were embedded in the colonial discourse of modernity that many Ionians had adopted since the early nineteenth century; the French administration opened the Ionian Academy in 1808, founded by Ionian intellectuals, to compile the first 'statistical' register of Corfu following the principle that only populations that are known and identified can be governed properly.[8] The academy commissioned the first statistical recording and scientific project of measurement of population in Corfu, a turning point in the history of Ionian and Greek governmentality. By the time the British took over the Ionian Islands the making of a modern bureaucratic Greek State under colonial paternalism – and partly because of it – was well under way; Ionian Greeks were perfectly able to adjust to the requirements of British colonialism and organize in collaboration with British officials the Ionian State. The previous administrative tradition certainly played a big role in shaping state capacity, which was based not only on personal experience but also on key texts. The works that bridged Venetian governing practices of data collection and British-Ionian colonial statistics were the *Scoglio Statistico dell' Isola di Cephalonia ed osservazioni relative*, published in 1810, the 'historical statistical' account of the city and island of Zante by P. Mercati,[9] (*Saggio Storico Statistico della Citta et Isola di Zante*, Zante 1811), and the 'statistical historical' account of Corfu by Stylianos Vlassopoulos, commissioned by the Ionian Academy in 1808 under French rule, and published in 1822.[10] These 'statistical accounts' were inspired by the first scientific report during the French republican rule by Carlo Botta, who joined the Napoleonic army in Italy and wrote the first 'natural and medical history of Corfu', where he stayed for a year in 1798–99.[11] Local knowledge and information aimed to improve agricultural productivity, a central aim of high commissioners, Ionian governments and liberal politicians. The books of Mercati and Vlassopoulo became standard references for works produced during the period of the protectorate, such as archaeological travel literature dealing with the history, 'customs' of Ionian society as contemporaries understood it, and they predated the Montgomery statistical account.

A statistical tabulation of people and the economy on 'inhabitants, professions, arts and trades, edifices and machines, waters, marine, animals and productions' was published by Napier in 1825, 'composed by the municipal officer in the year 1823', as the front page mentions, 'by order of the President C.J. Napier and Dr Pandasin Caridi'. Napier noted that he did not have much confidence in their accuracy 'but they are probably as correct as most tables of this nature are'; five magistrates were employed in forming the tables.[12] This statistical recording does not conform yet to the aggregation imposed by the Colonial Office after 1826, and is therefore much more useful for a more detailed study of people, their trades and the economy of the island overall.

The creation and use of statistics are key in understanding colonial rule, and inform central debates on colonial governmentality for settler colonies, the tropics and South Asia,[13] but not for European and Mediterranean lands such as the Ionian Islands. The collection and publication of colonial statistics in the 1820s improved the techniques of domination and rule in the Ionian State. The classification of the Ionian population into the three economic sectors – 'agriculture', 'manufacture' and 'commerce' – became the colonial practice of measuring population and pigeonholed the tens of occupations and diverse forms of employment into these three sectors. This was the moment when Ionian bureaucracy produced an 'economic' sphere to improve the efficiency of rule. In the collection of colonial statistics a process of abstraction was inevitable. The sources created by local officials differ significantly from the documents elaborated according to the guidelines of the Colonial Office. In 1818, one of the first tasks of the newly created Executive Police was the registration of all shopkeepers, traders, merchants, brokers, manufacturers and pharmacists of Corfu; the list shows hundreds of individuals and tens of occupational titles.[14] A few years later, most of them were classified in the generic category 'commerce' and some in 'manufacture', which referred to the whole island, not just the city. According to British colonial governmentality, collection of statistics for the more efficient management of the population strengthened state administration and improved – in theory at least – the quality and efficiency of rule. The logic of colonial administration and the scale on which population was recorded distinguishes Ionian State statistics from the previous Venetian registers but also

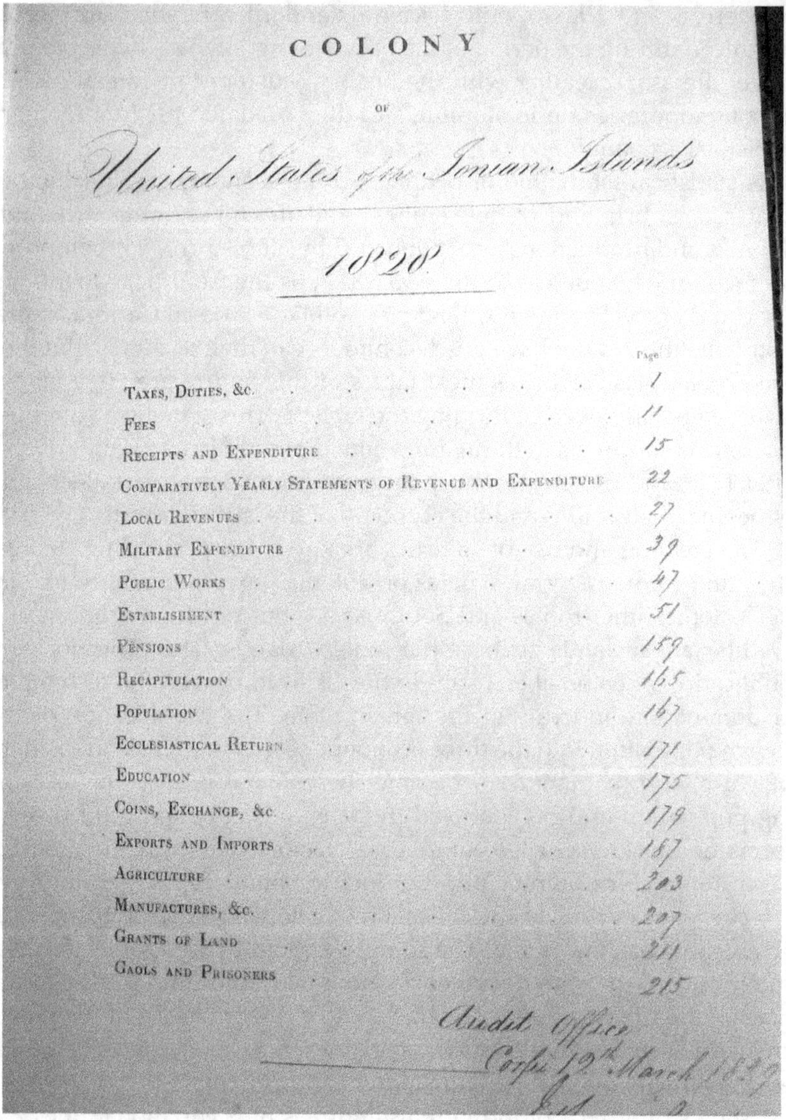

COLONY

OF

United States of the Ionian Islands

1828

	Page
Taxes, Duties, &c.	1
Fees	11
Receipts and Expenditure	15
Comparatively Yearly Statements of Revenue and Expenditure	22
Local Revenues	27
Military Expenditure	39
Public Works	47
Establishment	51
Pensions	159
Recapitulation	165
Population	167
Ecclesiastical Return	171
Education	175
Coins, Exchange, &c.	179
Exports and Imports	187
Agriculture	203
Manufactures, &c.	207
Grants of Land	211
Gaols and Prisoners	215

Audit Office
Corfu 19th March 1829

Figure 4.1 First page of the 'Blue Books of Statistics', 1828.

from its co-temporal Greek Kingdom and other neighbouring states, which borrowed state data collection techniques from French administrative practices. British colonial statistics divided people according to economic sectors, but also measured and produced tables of prisoners, paupers, monies, imports and exports, just like for any other part of the empire. In the 1820s, British colonial administration integrated the

Ionian Islands into its structures and patterns of information gathering; by then, Ionians had already developed their own notion and practices of governmentality.

The Colonial Office improved the methods of information gathering when a select committee recommended changes to the office's practices in the 1820s. One of them was the publication of the Blue Books that made information on the colonies available to other departments of the London government, aiming to solve a perennial problem at the heart of government's decision-making process that concerned the colonies. The challenges that the select committee faced were colonial accounting and the information colonies provided regarding money and accounts, but also the difficulty of gathering adequate and complete information and timely returns of the Blue Books. These problems continued to concern the Colonial Office well into the 1830s; nevertheless, the changes introduced amounted to an information revolution.[15] Colonial governance moulded economies and societies that varied widely into the model the Colonial Office had designed for the administration of the colonies. The collection of Ionian colonial statistics followed these changes in the Colonial Office practices of gathering data. The Ionian government sent annual statistical registers recording production, commerce, incomes and vital statistics, as well as a series of other figures. The most comprehensive registers of colonial statistics were collected as the Blue Books of Statistics for the period 1821–63; annual reports by the high commissioner of the Ionian Islands to the Colonial Office accompanied the Blue Book for each year (only for the period 1843–62)[16] and the parliamentary reports, distilled from the Blue Books for the periods 1833–42 and 1850–63.

The British colonial authorities classified the Ionian population in a manner compatible with other colonies for reasons of uniformity; the only tables that Ionian State officials did not fill in were the ones reporting the number of 'Whites', 'Free Slaves' and 'Blacks', since for the British the Ionians were definitely white (although unfit for self-rule) and there were no plantations or slave owners. These sources provided in-depth knowledge of distant lands and people, and were supposed to improve significantly the capacity of the Colonial Office and the British forces around the world to govern and rule. Sometimes painstakingly and often in approximation, officers collected information about the population, exports, imports, the civil lists of people employed in colonies but also in 'grey areas' such as the protectorate of the Ionian Islands. The Ionian Islands were classified for administrative purposes together with other Mediterranean 'colonies' such as Gibraltar and Malta, but frequently compared to 'tropical' colonies, for accounts that aimed to improve the health of the troops stationed there. By 1824 the office was receiving more despatches from the Ionian Islands than Malta: in 1816, 142 letters comprising 1,016 pages were received from Corfu, whereas only 63 letters of 74 pages were despatched; in 1824, 225 letters of 2,160 pages were received while 193 letters of only 300 pages were sent.[17] In their first years as a protectorate the 'United States of the Ionian Islands' had been left almost entirely in the hands of Maitland and Adam, who nevertheless sent long reports to their superiors in London.

British-Ionian government officials advanced the methodology and quality of the information they collected as they followed classifications that applied to all colonies and served the needs of the British colonial administration. British officials calculated people, production and trade – the 'population' and the 'economy' – and included a wealth of other information on currencies, weights and measures, for the Ionian Islands, just like they did for all colonies; Ionian economies and societies were a world away from those in the Caribbean, dominions in Canada or Heligoland. British colonial officials bypassed local idiosyncrasies in the name of efficient administration. This process culminated in India, where a mine of information was produced by the famous Indian Civil Service, a model of colonial administration over a vast territory with a population of hundreds of millions.

By the 1830s and 1840s, the Ionian State could already claim a well-organised, if not always functional, civil service. The governing principle introduced a new set of rules on how to administer natural resources, and classified population as a resource for the first time. The transition from earlier, premodern forms of rule was a smooth one because several Ionian politicians in the early years of the protectorate and the fundamental institutions of landownership remained in place until 1825 and the abolition of feudalism: the abolition of the feudal restrictions in landownership was considered a 'development of progress, which will advance the economy and prosperity of the state and of private persons'.[18] The new forms of knowledge and power were central for the Ionian colonial state to gain legitimacy. When forms of achieving legitimacy and discipline became oppressive to a level that was not acceptable by the most advanced – radical – Ionians, the colonial state's contradictions and its relationship with the colonized reached breaking point. For several decades, however, producing colonial knowledge, measurement and classifications developed independently from, and predated, the politics of union. The culture of numbers extended beyond the Ionian State's administrative and courts system to the publication of subscriptions of funds and numbers of shares in joint-stock companies, the names of shareholders, the revenues of the Ionian State, and the quarterly reviews of the savings banks and the Ionian Bank.

The information explosion from the 1830s onwards and the compilation of colonial statistics introduced a novel form of governance. Ionian State officials compiled lists of vital and other statistics that were then computed at the Colonial Office; despite their obvious limitations in terms of accuracy and design of categories to classify people, they demonstrate the shifts and trends in the Ionian population and economy, and reveal crucial aspects of state – that is bureaucracy – building. Commissioners submitted reports to the Colonial Office in which they often talk about inaccurate population numbers, because many Ionians, especially from the southern islands, migrated to Greece for the harvest season or were travelling at sea. These seasonal migrants numbered a few thousand and so the difference in the figures could be substantial; this therefore obliges us to look at them as trends, not 'facts'. The population data in the Blue Books shows a significant increase of population in forty years, reaching 228,264 in 1863 from 175,902 in 1824. There were 46,725 more Ionians living on the islands in 1841 than there had been in 1824, an impressive increase of 26.6 per cent, and 52,362 more by 1863, a few months before the integration of the islands with the Greek Kingdom. The fastest rate of growth occurred in the early 1830s, when the population increased by 17 per cent. This rate of growth reduced to between 0.83 and 1.7 per cent in the period 1836–41.[19] It was only in the 1850s that the Ionian population declined at an overall rate of –0.98 per cent, but this was even more during the years 1851 and 1856. The Crimean War deprived Ionians of the abundant grain provisions from the Black Sea that they had previously enjoyed; a local economic crisis raged from the late 1840s on all the islands, coupled with an outbreak of cholera in Corfu and Kefalonia; and the disease of the vines in Zante and Kefalonia significantly harmed the currant production – all of these factors together cost human lives and forced emigration, both seasonal and more permanent.

Some comparable works on the demographic history of nineteenth-century Greece[20] allow us to draw a larger picture for 'Greece'.[21] Table 4.2 shows the five-year average for all islands. By comparison, Greece in the 1860s had five-year averages of 0.80 (1865) and 0.69 (1870).

The population increased on all islands except Paxos, and especially in Kythera; Kefalonia and Zante also demonstrate a population surplus by the end of the period, while the number of people that lived in Corfu barely changed from its births/deaths equilibrium. Islands with high mortality (Sta Maura, Zante) also show high fertility although we do not know the rate of infant mortality to estimate more accurately

Table 4.1 Ionian Islands population, exempting foreigners.

Source: Ithakisios, 'I ekseliksi ton vasikon dimografikon charaktiristikon', 475–530.

Island	1824	1831	1841	1851	1861	1863
Corfu	44,351	51,287	66,158	70,885	63,649	64,974
Kefalonia	53,090	53,286	62,156	69,684	73,867	70,948
Zante	36,715	34,303	39,752	39,103	39,455	39,329
Lefkada	17,213	17,797	17,386	18,679	20,659	20,842
Ithaki	8,747	9,213	10,358	11,194	11,820	11,950
Kythera	10,515	8,488	9,496	12,655	14,226	14,605
Paxoi	5,271	4,755	5,193	5,128	4,993	5,616
Total	175,902	179,129	210,499	227,328	228,669	228,264

Table 4.2 Ionian Islands natural movement, 5-year averages.

Source: Ionian Islands Blue Books of Statistics, CO 136/1392–1426, TNA.

	Ithaki	Sta Maura (Lefkada)	Corfu	Kefalonia	Zante	Paxoi	Kythera
1828–32	0.57	–0.1	0.9	0.84	–0.91	0.32	1.35
1833–37	1.02	0.03	0.92	1.05	–0.16	0.5	1.27
1838–42	0.78	0.63	0.31	0.97	0.18	0.04	1.3
1843–47	0.79	0.93	0.54	1.24	0.44	–0.11	1.27
1848–52	0.62	0.47	0.32	0.65	0.35	0.29	1.01
1853–57	0.42	0.06	0.33	0.28	–0.7	–0.49	0.88
1858–62	0.7	0.63	0.93	0.68	1.41	0.12	1.1

population growth; high fertility rates on all islands (with the exception of Paxos), above 3 per cent in Zante, coexisted with high mortality rates, prevalent during times of disease, such as the 1850s. Corfu's population increased until 1851 at a rate of 2.8 per cent but dropped significantly in the 1850s, and picked up again in the early 1860s. In Kefalonia the population increased in the 1830s and 1840s, but dropped sharply in the 1860s. The population in Zante also increased in the 1830s and remained stubbornly stable for the next thirty years, reflecting perhaps the seasonal migration for agricultural work to the Greek Kingdom. Ithaki stands out because of the long-term absence of men who sailed as far as the Black Sea to trade grain; however, population increased at a rate of 0.55 to 1.2 per cent.[22] The population in Kythera decreased by more than two thousand people (a rate of 2.75 per cent) in the 1820s, a drop that relates to the war of independence in the Morea and the devastation caused by Ibrahim in the region, which affected the livelihoods of the population and the life of the island. From the 1840s until 1864, the population increased significantly, notwithstanding the emigration of people from Kythera, which even changed the traditional family and household structures on the island;[23] local conditions, including migration, significantly affected population trends on each island.

British colonial statistics also measured population density, data that writers of accounts on the Ionian Islands replicated with interest. Corfu was the most densely populated, with 264 per square mile, and Zante a close second (252 per square mile). Ithaki and Paxoi were also densely populated, while Kythera and Lefkada were not. In Corfu the country areas could sustain a larger population because there was no great emigration wave, except to the city, where opportunities for work are documented in sources from the 1830s.[24] Population density incited people to migrate, at least during the harvest season; when the islands and the Greek Kingdom united, Ionians – especially from the southern islands – settled in sparsely populated areas of the western Peloponnese, where conditions were ideal for the cultivation of currants, in which many Ionians were experienced.[25]

More people were born, survived and raised in the Ionian Islands in the 1860s than in the 1820s; the most impressive changes occurred in the first twenty years of the protectorate. These people lived in hundreds of villages and a few ports, and by the end of the period they numbered almost a quarter of a million. Ionians cultivated more land and more of them worked in agriculture and commerce, while fewer stayed in handicraft manufacturing activities. These factors weighed heavily on the islands' economies and societies, especially from the 1840s onwards. The climate, according to one study of the 1830s, was 'nearly tropical', which explained the remittent and intermittent fevers occurring frequently, and in 1833 they formed nearly two-fifths of the total admissions into the hospitals of the town. The total number of people with diseases who were admitted to hospitals in the 1820s, the first years of British rule, was 15,191, of which 3,300 were common fevers and 1,400 remittent fevers. Dysentery was the next most important disease in military hospitals, and diarrhoea also occurred frequently among British soldiers.[26] By the time cholera broke out in Corfu and Kefalonia in 1855–56, population density had reached 350 per square mile and continued to rise until the disease outbreaks which killed nearly five hundred people in Corfu alone and hundreds in Kefalonia and Zante. When the 'proto-industrial' sector of Zante, and Corfu's rural household manufacture in cotton spinning and cloth making declined, the profitability of currants in the 1820s led more people into agriculture; when crisis hit in the 1840s they moved to ports in search of employment or simply alms, and many emigrated elsewhere in the Mediterranean. The robust maritime commercial economy of Ithaki and Kefalonia in the Black Sea grain trade eased population pressures and brought much-needed 'invisible' income, remittances and cash earned outside the Ionian Islands, but probably spent in them. Fertility among the islands' population was at its highest in the late 1820s and early 1830s; it remained significantly high but declined gradually in the 1840s and 1850s. Mortality decreased steadily for the period 1828–51 and the population increased, as Ionian cities benefited from the arrival of immigrants who traded or worked as artisans. Only in the 1850s did mortality increase, due to the cholera outbreaks and malnutrition, which affected many more Ionians than in the previous decades. The year 1855 was the only time when deaths surpassed births in the history of the protectorate.[27] The generally low death rate is also explained by another factor: the significant infrastructure projects that the Ionian State promoted during the first two decades of the protectorate, when state finances allowed commissioners and the government to carry out such works. In turn, the ability of the Ionian State to improve living conditions depended on the revenues collected from the commercial economy, which was transformed during the period of the protectorate; Ionian officials and 'statisticians', but also the many British writers of the period, recorded these changes, noting the commercial as well as strategic potential and importance of the islands.

Cultivated land remained about a half of all available land in Corfu in 1839;[28] peasants could work on specific plots of land with the right to plant and cultivate whatever they wished on a fifth of the land, while the rest was cultivated according to the requirements of the landowner. The tax paid depended on production costs, namely if the landlord provided all material (tools, seeds, etc.) except labour he received two-thirds of the crop. On the islands that produced currants the growers' only option was to sell their produce to the landowner or give the olives to mills owned and controlled by landowners, with an additional 10 per cent tax. Relations of production became probably more cumbersome during the period of British rule;[29] tenants were able to hold possession of land in perpetuity but with little potential or drive for improving agricultural productivity. Landowners on the other hand, knowing that they would definitely receive a portion of the produce otherwise more debts would be incurred on their tenants, had even less incentive to improve productivity.

The semi-feudal and semi-colonial conditions in agriculture, the Venetian-old dependency on cash crops exported and grain imported continued unabated during the period of British rule. This dependence compromised whatever steps towards modernization were taken, because central authorities and Ionian officials were unable or unwilling to implement the agricultural reforms they designed. More Ionians turned to agricultural and to some extent to commercial activities, especially in the currants production and export sectors of Ionian ports that became profitable in the 1820s. In the Greek Kingdom on the other hand, changes in the institutions of landownership strengthened small-scale property holders, especially in the war-ravaged Peloponnese.[30] Ionian governments oscillated and remained unable or unwilling to change landownership and landholding but also credit relations; the initially significant but unfinished and incomplete changes in the education system, and the practically abandoned public works after the 1840s, were also crucial and explain why more and more Ionians abandoned whatever support they gave to the protectorate. Despite reforms high commissioners promoted in the legal system, political and economic institutional changes failed to win any long-term support from Ionians.

The failure to change landownership relations and improve opportunities for the majority of agricultural producers depended also on conditions on the various islands. In Corfu the biennial oil production kept small landholders and tenants insecure. Ionian economies were already integrated with international markets for agricultural goods, currants, olive oil and grain. Imports of manufactured goods crowded out domestic manufactures and the small textiles handicraft manufacture from regional markets, assuming that they could expand given limitations of capital. The number of people who were employed in agriculture and shipping increased towards the end of the period, while Ionians employed in 'manufacture' all increased until 1861. By 1863, however, there was a significant drop in the numbers and percentages of all Ionians employed. According to the colonial statistics, the Ionian population was not only increasing but was also becoming younger. Population registers distinguish between male, female and 'alien' in the working population (those registered employed) of the islands, but did not include female or child labour in any of the sectors despite women and children contributing to the family income. Of all seven islands, Ithaki had the largest working population registered and was able to maintain its non-working population better.

The profitability of the currants crops and the olive groves for most of the period and the 'deindustrialization' that the islands' economy experienced indicates why Ionians in most islands 'moved' into agriculture in ever-increasing numbers. In 1858 in Corfu (Table 4.3) approximately 30 per cent of the total population – the estimated working population recorded, which obviously did not include women and children – was

Table 4.3 Ionian Islands working population, according to sector.

Source: Ithakisisios, 'I ekseliksi ton vasikon dimografikon charaktiristikon', 492.

Year	Total population	Working population	Working population according to sector						% of working to total population
			Agriculture	%	Manufacture	%	Commerce	%	
1828	181,192	55,350	41,236	22.7	9,308	5.2	4,806	2.6	30.5
1831	179,674	48,127	38,877	21.6	5,793	3.2	3,457	1.9	26.7
1836	193,041	51,234	41,042	21.2	5,829	3.0	4,363	2.3	26.5
1841	210,499	58,316	45,240	21.5	8,112	3.8	5,054	2.4	27.7
1846	216,682	65,163	50,220	23.2	8,749	4.0	6,194	2.8	30.0
1851	227,328	62,791	49,083	21.6	7,590	3.3	6,118	2.7	27.6
1856	218,402	63,425	49,191	22.5	7,760	3.5	6,474	3.0	29.0
1861	228,669	66,909	51,262	22.5	8,365	3.6	7,282	3.1	29.2
1863	228,264	58,940	44,748	19.6	7,136	3.1	7,056	3.1	25.8

registered as belonging to one of the three sectors, a percentage that declined towards the end of the period, making it more difficult for those employed to sustain the rest of the population. The 'dependant' population reached as much as 70 or even 80 per cent in Sta Maura (Lefkada). The profitability of vineyards for raisins on the southern islands was the other reason many more Ionians moved to agriculture, making the Ionian and Greek economies more similar and therefore integration after 1864 easier, predating the boom in the national currant cultivation that continued until 1893. Ithaki was the island with the lowest number of people employed in agriculture, showing an increase of just 10 per cent at the end of the period. The most impressive transformation took place in Zante, where fewer than 70 per cent had been agricultural labourers in 1828, but more than 90 per cent were by the end of the period, a change that is undoubtedly linked to the profitability of currants and a 'smooth deindustrialization', with people abandoning textile production. The agricultural population increased slightly in Kefalonia and Sta Maura. By far the highest increase can be seen in Zante and Corfu, showing the profitability (or the anticipated profits) of the currant and olive crops respectively. The turn to agriculture accelerated in the 1830s and 1840s, the 'critical' decades for the Ionian economy. The working population registered under 'commerce' increased steadily, while the percentage of the 'working' to the 'total' population fluctuated, but declined again in the early 1860s. These results raise concerns about the validity of the data, especially since for several islands the numbers remained the same for several decades.

The number of people employed in agriculture increased in Corfu until the early 1850s when an economic crisis, cholera and the Crimean War affected agricultural production and trade. The needs of Corfu, the Ionian capital, reflect to some extent why many of its residents were employed in 'commerce' and 'manufacture'. The restructuring of the Ionian economy was the result of economic policies and changes in the international economy to facilitate British colonial interests. The economic policy of the Ionian State changed the fortunes of each island according to the individual island's productive capabilities, but also according to the needs and choices of the each island's population within the limits imposed by the social relations of production.

The people of Kefalonia classified in the category 'manufacture' were artisans, craftsmen and workers in pottery, textiles, and barrel making for olives, currants and shipbuilding; in Kefalonia the number of those employed in 'manufacture' increased both in percentage terms (from 12 to 16 per cent) as well as in actual numbers. Commercial activity in Kefalonia declined rapidly in the 1830s, but recovered and increased steadily. In 1810, when the British occupied Zante, the percentage of people employed in 'manufacture' was probably higher than 25 per cent. In the first extensive census of the island under British rule, in 1811, the occupations of more than 4,000 people were recorded; 1,260 (many of them women) were employed in cloth manufacture, production and distribution (spinning, weaving and 'tailoring'), while 750, or 24 per cent, of those recorded were cotton spinners – an impressively high number by many standards.[31] By the late 1850s, Zante had less than a third of its people employed in manufacture compared to 1827, when information had been collected for the first time. After the 1820s the economy of Zante 'deindustrialized' and people moved to agriculture since they found currant production much more profitable than cotton spinning or rope making; from 8,200 people in 1828 (or 25 per cent of the population) the number of people in 'manufacture' it plunged to 5,500, although all sectors measured fewer people. 'Manufacture' in Zante meant principally cotton spinning; in Corfu soap making employed fewer people at the end of the period than at the beginning, and 'commerce' included an impressive variety of occupations, incomes, and cycles of business that get lost in the mass of colonial statistics. In Corfu the number of people in 'manufacture' dropped substantially from 20 per cent of the working population to just over 9 per cent within ten years, a trend that started in the 1830s. Both Corfu and Zante therefore 'deindustrialized' significantly, with more people shifting to agriculture than commerce. On the contrary, the percentage of the working population of Kythera employed in manufacture increased substantially, especially in the last ten years of British rule.

In Ithaki, systematic recording stopped in 1843, preventing any safe conclusions or even estimates on the numbers of people employed in the different sectors. People in Ithaki earned their income in 'commerce' as sailors and merchant captains in very significant numbers throughout the period (above 30 per cent); it was Kefalonia, however, that provided up to 4,200 men in shipping by 1860,[32] an extraordinary number not just for the island but for the whole Ionian State. The number of people employed in 'commerce' was high in proportion to the number who lived in Ithaki, and were mainly employed in shipping. In this case the number of those employed in 'commerce' reflects the significant role of shipping for the island's economy and population. This had even been remarked on earlier in the century by Leake, a British officer travelling in the region, who noticed the extraordinary number of people employed in shipping relative to the size of the island's population. Ithaki was already developing the famous sector that peaked during the Ionian phase of Greek-owned shipping (1870s–1910s).[33]

Refugees, Foreigners, Immigrants: Passports and Surveillance in the Ionian State

The issue of citizenship and nationality emerged for the first time during the Septinsular Republic when statesmen Moncenigo and Kapodistrias assigned the High Police with the authority to grant passports only to those that deserved it, as the regulation ordered. Foreigners had been recorded in the Ionian Islands before, but in the early nineteenth century such recordings became more systematic and consistent, and reflected the policy considerations of the Napoleonic and post-Napoleonic Wars regimes. The Commission of High Police that was set up on 7 July 1805 announced that within five days all foreigners would be traced and recorded, with the assistance of hotel and other property owners in and around the city and its suburbs. The same decree ordered all foreigners to register with the authorities within eight days; such obligations burdened Ionians who moved within the limits of the state as well, for example from one island to the other.[34] The High Police acted in this case as the powerful executive arm of a strong Ionian State under a climate of suspicion and tension that was never too far away for the High Police and its superiors – the president in this case, and the high commissioner later. This practice of surveillance, however, was introduced for the first time and it was considered so indispensable that it lasted until the end of British rule. Subsequent decrees by the Imperial French in 1807 and the General Police concerned the movement of foreigners and their obligation to carry travel documents; this is the point in time when the passport was invented as a crucial tool of public administration, and the Ionian State was among the first state entities to introduce such a practice. To confuse historians, however, Ionian authorities considered 'foreigners' (*forestiero*) to be not only the citizens of other states but also Ionians who travelled within the state, for example from Corfu to Kefalonia.

Surveillance, however, did not prevent the ever-expanding commercial networks, in which Ionians were intrinsically involved. Studies of commercial networks and merchant houses have revealed abundant records that document business activities and enable historians to write individual stories of merchant families and communities.[35] The Mediterranean has emerged as a place of interest for historians researching migration and community networks, and the role of state policies.[36] In the nineteenth century migration was just one of the three levels at which the British Mediterranean connected the people who fell under the clout of British imperialism. The first was the 'top' level of British administration and colonial control; the second level of connection was the exchange of goods between British-ruled or British-influenced Mediterranean ports (in colonies or independent states); and the third level of connection was the mobility of people around Mediterranean ports. Merchants, sailors, masons and other craftsmen, as well as itinerant and seasonal migrant women working as prostitutes, moved and settled around Mediterranean ports, and their neglected Mediterranean stories have only recently been acknowledged.[37]

In the British Mediterranean, in Malta and the Ionian Islands, migration began in 1815, soon after the inclusion of the Ionian Islands in the British sphere of influence. The first colonial migrants from Malta to Corfu arrived when Sir Thomas Maitland brought them over to build the Palace of St Michael and St George between 1818 and 1824; sailors from Naples, Corsica and Sicily formed the first fleet of the Ionian State, and many became naturalized Ionian citizens. Employed by the British Royal Navy during the Napoleonic Wars, they arrived in Corfu with the British fleet in 1814; it was known as the 'Anglo-Sicilian' fleet, since it included Sicilians, Corsicans, Napolitans, Genovese, Calabrians and Maltese.[38] But most foreigners who settled in Corfu were not Catholics from the Italian peninsula or Malta but from Parga in Epirus, the old Venetian possession. Migration from other parts of the Venetian Empire had always enriched the social, economic and cultural-educational life of Ionian cities; but in the nineteenth century the overwhelming number of immigrants belonged to the already large lower class of the urban poor, with significant implications for urban identities and the policies of the Ionian State towards the newcomers, and state practices for the regulation of immigration and citizenship.

British rule brought opportunities and employment for most Ionians. Foreigners from other British 'possessions' migrated and negotiated the colonial encounter in various and more complex ways than the usual collaboration/resistance dichotomy suggests. This type of migration has received scant attention from historians and social scientists, and is a novel way of looking at the emergence of Mediterranean identities during the period of Mediterranean colonization. Migrants from Britain did not settle in Mediterranean colonies and outposts. Migration did, however, take place within British colonies and other areas under British rule, even if not comparable but similar to the indentured labour in other parts of the British Empire. The first Maltese arrived in Corfu as stone masons for the building of fortifications and the Palace of St Michael and St George.[39] The main group of immigrants, however, were the refugees from Parga, whose story created a sensation in the British Parliament, among the British public and in the Greek national psyche as a story of Muslim brutality; most importantly, it forced the

Ionian State to accept them and it dragged Ionian affairs closer to developments on the mainland.

The Parga Refugees

In 1818, High Commissioner Maitland and the British Empire ceded Parga to Ali Pasha. The decision reflected the priorities of British imperial policy towards the Ottoman Empire. After the dissolution of the Venetian Republic, Parga followed the fortunes of Corfu; in March 1814 a few months before the French surrendered Corfu to Commander Campbell, the town's leaders surrendered Parga to the British flag, only to receive a very lukewarm protection until their fate was decided in international deliberations between Britain and the Ottoman Empire.[40] When British officer Campbell occupied Corfu in 1814 his takeover included Parga almost by default. No provisions were made for Parga in the Paris Treaty of 1815 that established the Ionian Protectorate, and it is unknown whether the decision to abandon Parga was made by the Colonial Office in 1815. There are claims that the sultan negotiated the purchase of Parga with the British ambassador in Istanbul in 1817.[41] It is more likely that a combination of diplomatic pragmatism, ignorance and indifference towards Parga determined the fate of its people and affected the history of Corfu.[42] The 'incident' of Parga moved European artists and made the small town of Epirus famous because of the tragedy that its people faced. The publicity raised awareness of Muslim-Ottoman cruelty towards Christians at a time before the outbreak of the revolution. Francesco Hayez and Cherubino Cornienti painted *Refugees of Parga* and Apollodore Callet the painting *The Boarding of People from Parga*. A number of poems and other literary works were also produced, inspired by the Parga exodus, with the most famous being the work of Ugo Foscolo, entitled 'Narrative of Events Illustrating the Fortunes and Cession of Parga'.[43] The people of Parga were forced to accept the agreement that determined their livelihoods. Maitland sent de Bosset, the experienced commander of Kefalonia, with three hundred soldiers to keep order and prevent an armed resistance to the deal the British government had struck with Ali Pasha. Disputes over the amount of compensation soon emerged. The notables of Parga estimated their wealth at 200,000 pounds, a very large amount for the time, while Ali Pasha though the claims were far too high. Corfu assessors put wealth up to 2,300,000 tallers, compared to the Ali Pasha officials at merely 1,025,700; after several negotiations that dragged on for months until June 1819, Maitland decided that the city would pass to the hands of

Ali Pasha at only 142,425 pounds or 660,000 tallers. The issue generated debate in the British Parliament and became a 'party question', with both Tories and Whigs 'publishing their own version, each of which lay equally remote from the truth'.[44] For months, parliamentary debates, newspaper articles, pamphlets and books preoccupied the British public.

The case of Parga forced Ionian State authorities to define citizenship in the Ionian Islands. The Ionian State passed its naturalization law early on in 1820 to accommodate the approximately three thousand refugees from Parga.[45] One of the most important laws of the Ionian Assembly at the time was the act that gave Parga refugees the status of citizen (*diritto di cittadinanza*) as long as they registered with the authorities of the island and provided a birth certificate showing that they had been born in Parga.[46] The settlement of the Parga refugees put severe pressures on housing in the suburb and affected living conditions, even though British versions of the story claimed that the economy of Corfu benefited from the industrious Parga refugees. The Ionian government formed a committee to distribute payments as compensation to the refugees. In June 1819 the committee noted the 'remarkable behaviour of some of the evicted Pargeioi' who protested against the evaluations of two committee members and the inability of the refugees to solve their differences and come forward to state their claims. They were warned that failure to declare their objections to the evaluations of each property and the amount of compensation would force the committee to set compensation prices irrevocably.[47] Frustrated with the refugees, the government committee gave them a ten-day deadline to solve their internal disagreements and state their claims. In early 1821 the Executive Police registered the first of the Parga refugees, and recorded 743 families living in Mandouki.[48]

Nearly twenty years after the refugees settled in Corfu, living conditions for many Parganiotes had barely improved. In 1837 their representatives filed a petition to Commissioner Douglas begging to remain in the government barracks where they had lived since 1819. The priests who signed the petition first declared that the people of Parga lived in Mandouki in absolute poverty and often resorted to begging to earn a living.[49] Other Parga refugees, like Pietro Stanello, who lived in Mandouchio and their families requested permission to settle in Greece after communicating with the Greek consul in Corfu. Zervo, the inspector of the Executive Police, reported on the conduct of the refugees and informed that they had not been naturalized subjects of the Ionian states.[50] Parga refugees were still facing problems in the 1850s; in 1852 the 'community of Parginoi' through their representatives, a committee of seven residents of Mandouki, petitioned Commissioner Ward for compensation and they stated their belief to the efforts of both the commissioner and the British ambassador in Constantinople. The letter that forty-two Parginoi signed describes how many of their compatriots 'have been condemned in the most destitute condition to the utmost poverty'. Still, the petition 'celebrates the glorious day of 10/22 March 1814 because all the people and the land, protected by the glorious nation, enjoys significant improvement and progress; which the Parginoi have been deprived of all these years, however they do not despair'. The petition wished the best to the Queen and the 'whole English nation', and reminded their recipient of their hope that one day they would return to their ancestral land. Some Parga refugees such as Konstantinos Vasilas did not need any assistance from the state or his fellow citizens from Parga or Corfu. Vasilas moved to Corfu with his family, some capital and an established network of business connections in the Adriatic ports of Trieste, Ancon and Venice. His nephew, Xenofon Vasilas, became president of the Corfu Exchange in 1856 and the director of an insurance company of Corfu. The Vasilas family and especially the two brothers were members of the Corfu elite that was growing in the first half of the nineteenth century, partly because of the new profitable business of property owning and renting, as well as trade.

Immigrants and the State

In an era of increasing mobility as more and more travellers arrived in the Eastern Mediterranean with Corfu as one of their first stops en route to the 'Orient', political refugees from Italy arrived in the 1820s onwards. Ionians (or foreigners living in the islands) also travelled, for commercial, educational (primarily) or even political purposes. The arrival of steamships facilitated travel and communication, and inaugurated the era of (not yet mass) tourism. During the period of political turmoil in the Italian peninsula the need for surveillance increased and the measures were taken drastically. Until 1836 foreigners and permanent residents born abroad were included in the general population, while between 1837 and 1863 they were recorded in a separate category. Corfu, as the seat of government, attracted most foreigners from the 1830s onwards, accounting for up to 80 per cent of the total foreign population, and up to 15 per cent of the total island population in the period 1828–63.[51] Between the 1830s and 1860s the entries of naturalized subjects in the official newspaper of the Ionian State show that the status of the islands as a British protectorate and the port of Corfu encouraged foreigners to ask for and obtain Ionian nationality. Naturalization figures show the number of immigrants to the Ionian Islands; the right to British protection that Ionian citizens enjoyed became a pull factor, especially for immigrants from the mainland opposite. The Maltese were already colonial subjects and settled easier in Corfu. The proximity of the island to Epirus and Italy explains the origin of most foreigners asking for Ionian citizenship: 39 per cent of naturalized Ionians came from Epirus and 15 per cent from southern Italy, Campagna and Sicily; in addition, 28 per cent came from the Ionian Islands and petitioned to obtain Ionian citizenship. Approximately 75 per cent of these declared Corfu as their political domicile, and 33 per cent were merchants.[52] A steady increase of naturalizations throughout the 1850s and a sharp decline in the early 1860s reflect the foreseeable unification of the islands with Greece, which would make naturalization less attractive.[53] Throughout the period most immigrants were merchants or professionals.

Ionian authorities regulated mobility and migration, seasonal, from the islands to the mainland opposite, as well as immigration to Corfu and the other islands by means of the annual registers but especially by issuing passports.[54] Most passports in the period 1800–1870 were issued to Ionians (47.21 per cent); passports to Ottoman citizens, practically the Greek Orthodox of the Epirus region, to facilitate their travel to the Ionian Islands come second (15.07 per cent). Several British (11.7 per cent of passports) travelled from and to the islands, while Maltese also show increased mobility (9.34 per cent of the travelling documents), most likely to their native island. Six per cent of documents were issued for travellers from the Italian states and the Greek Kingdom. Other countries' citizens represent the rest of the documents: Austria 3.18 per cent, and the rest from France, German states, Belgium, Sweden, Norway, United States of America, Spain and the Netherlands. In total 14,160 people (75.3 per cent men, 16.03 per cent women and 8.6 per cent children) were recorded during the whole period. Passports were issued by the police under the orders of the Ionian government to regulate illegal mobility at a time when such administrative practice did not exist in neighbouring states; these passports provided Ionians with the protection they needed, and were used extensively when trading or travelling abroad.[55]

In 1826 about three hundred Maltese settled in Kefalonia in what was designed to be an agricultural colony. The project was part of Governor Napier's attempt to reform agriculture and improve production by introducing modern farming techniques.[56] When he arrived he found 'agriculture at the lowest pitch; [he] saw land (uncultivated) in abundance, men idle, and food imported'. To this end he established a colony of three hundred Maltese in 1827, but the plan failed despondently:

> The whole scheme was baffled, by an intrigue at Malta, entered into for the purpose of getting rid of their superannuated paupers and inconvenient characters ... after trying in vain for two years to make them cultivate the ground, the local Government of Cefalonia was obliged to stop the issue of rations to these people ... and instantly the Maltese spread over the island, begging for food.[57]

The attempt failed after two years and was not repeated; the Maltese were ex-convicts and other 'undesirables', and could not have made much difference in agricultural production. The Maltese who left from the failed Kefalonia agricultural colony project settled in Corfu in 1832 and 'regenerated' the Catholic population of Corfu. In the 1830s there were around 4,000 Roman Catholics, of whom 2,500 were foreigners, most of them Maltese.[58] This mobility is to a large extent an outcome of the colonial experience. Employment in the Ionian State was a significant pull factor for the Maltese, Sicilians, Corsicans and later Epirotes (Christian Greeks from the mainland opposite) to settle in Corfu. Maltese continued to migrate within the British Mediterranean, following the occupation of Cyprus.[59] In the mid 1830s up to 70 per cent of all immigrants came to Corfu, enriching the diversity of the city; they came from Malta, Epirus and Italy, especially the south, and these population movements significantly affected marital behaviour since the majority of them were male and many of them married and settled in Corfu.[60]

Table 4.4 shows a significant reduction in the number of foreigners between 1830 and 1832, which might be related to the method of data collection, and/or to the changing economic conditions during those years. Registration of foreigners, most of them merchants, became more systematic under Imperial French rule, and this continued during the period of the Ionian State. Migrants from the Ottoman mainland contributed to the diversity of the port of Corfu that all travellers and writers talked about when arriving in Corfu. Registers from Corfu in 1812 and 1818 indicate migration patterns and commercial specialization. In these sources the *negozianti* (wholesale merchants) are clearly distinguished from the *mercanti* (retailers) and the *bottegai* (shopkeepers).[61] In 1818 the police registered all those keeping a store, a tavern, or a food place, plus anyone selling goods, indicating the amounts that they were required to pay; the register recorded hundreds of individuals, many of

Table 4.4 Corfu population (1830–32).

Source: Prontzas and Anoyatis-Pelé, *Kerkyra 1830–1832*, Table II.4, 425; Table II.7, 427–30.

	1830				1831				1832			
	Men	Women	Foreigners	Total	Men	Women	Foreigners	Total	Men	Women	Foreigners	Total
City	7.646	6.595	4.605	18.846	7.963	6.755	3.524	18.242	7.906	6.888	3.395	18.189
Suburbs	3.791	3.321	2.614	9.726	4.001	3.341	2.386	9.728	4.051	3.374	2.412	9.837
Villages	19.418	16.541	1.029	28.572	19.842	16.897	1.056	27.970	20.341	17.372	957	28.026
Total	30.855	26.457	8.248	65.560	31.806	26.993	6.966	65.765	32.298	27.634	6.764	66.696

them with foreign names. Merchants from Bordeaux and England, and the Chiot firm of Theodoro Ralli and Company, one of the most famous commercial houses, lived in Corfu. When in 1819 the British Crown sold the town of Parga on the mainland opposite the port to a regional Ottoman notable, Ali Pasha, the refugees that came to Corfu reinforced existing commercial networks in the Adriatic and the Ottoman Empire. In later years the ethnic diversity of the merchant group was enriched by immigrants from Epirus, other areas of the Ottoman Empire, the Italian states, Malta, Britain, Holland and even Switzerland.[62] During the period of British rule, European merchants settled in Corfu and established their own firms to act as agents for shipping companies and engage in trade, auctions and the provision of luxury goods and services (such as discounting bills) for the port's elite of British officers, foreign and local merchants and travellers. The founding of the Ionian Bank in 1840 further incorporated the Ionian ports into an imperial business network.[63] Foreign merchants involved in the import of British manufactured and colonial goods, and in the export of currants (in Kefalonia, Zante and Patras), also served as consuls for various states with regional commercial and trading interests. From the 1850s onwards, when Corfu, Patras, Syros and later Piraeus were linked with other ports in the Mediterranean with the expansion of steamship lines, foreign and local merchants also acted as commercial agents for these companies. Overlapping roles and commercial specialization were inherent characteristics of merchant groups in all port cities, Greek and elsewhere in the Mediterranean.

Migrants from the southern Ionian Islands moved to Patras in the late eighteenth century and again after 1828, following the revival of the currant trade and seasonal labour. Similarly merchants who settled in Corfu and Zante came from the mainland (the Peloponnese).[64] Long-established commercial networks between Patras and the Ionian Islands developed further in the nineteenth century; the Ionian Islands and Patras were to some extent integrated economically both by the transfer of capital (in the marine insurance sector, for example) and by currant exporters operating from the islands of Kefalonia and Zante, as well as Patras.[65] There was significant emigration from Kythera, for example; in the 1830s the British resident reported that about five hundred people migrated seasonally to Crete and the Peloponnese.[66]

During the period of British rule many merchants, among other immigrants to Corfu, became naturalized Ionian subjects.[67] The privileged status of the Ionian Islands as a British protectorate and the location and commercial prospects of Corfu as an important Adriatic port induced migrant merchants to become Ionian nationals. The proximity of the island to Epirus and southern Italy explains the origin of most 'foreigners' who requested and received Ionian citizenship. Approximately three-quarters of those petitioning for Ionian citizenship registered Corfu as their political domicile, and a third of immigrants with a recorded occupation were merchants. Naturalization petitions increased steadily throughout the 1850s and declined sharply in the early 1860s, reflecting the unification course of the islands with Greece after 1862.[68] As contemporaries noted, several important merchants of olive oil were Jewish.[69] When in 1864 the islands united with Greece and adopted the constitution of 1865, which enfranchised all males above the age of twenty-one, 40 per cent of the Jews recorded in the electoral list were merchants, confirming the religious diversity of Corfu's mercantile class.[70] Data on migration provide a useful starting point for the demographic characteristics of port cities and the profile of merchant communities, especially the 'management' of immigrant groups by state authorities in these ports cities.[71] The Ionian State built the capacity to record and control those who travelled to and from the islands as part of a security exercise and surveillance, an exercise consistent with the overall bureaucratic organization of state authority. Merchants needed more attention, however, as they formed a very strong interest group that promoted its interests in complementary but also conflicting ways with the Ionian government.

Notes

1. T. Ballantyne, 'Colonial Knowledge', in Sarah Stockwell (ed.), *The British Empire: Themes and Perspectives*. London: Blackwell, 2008.
2. One such example is the book by Emmanuel Theotoky, *Details Sur Corfou*.
3. Cohn, *Colonialism and its Forms of Knowledge*.
4. Napier, *Memoir on the Roads of Cefalonia*, London, 1826, 66–67.
5. S. Gunn, 'From Hegemony to Governmentality: Changing Conceptions of Power in Social History', *Journal of Social History* 39(3) (2006): 705–20.
6. P. Chiotis, *Istorika Apomnomonevmata Eptanisou*, Vol 6, 1887, 260.
7. Pels, 'The Anthropology of Colonialism'.
8. Joyce, *The Rule of Freedom*, 13.
9. P. Mercati, *Saggio Storico Statistico della Citta et Isola di Zante*, Zante 1811, published in J. Davy, *Notes and Observations*, Vol. II, Chap. 2, London, 1842.
10. Vlassopoulos, *Statistikai – Istorikai peri Kerkyras Eidiseis*.
11. Botta, *Storia Naturale e medica*.
12. Napier, *Memoir on the Roads of Cefalonia*, 92–93.
13. Cohn, *Colonialism and its forms of knowledge*.

14 Register of pharmacists, shopkeepers and manufacturers, subject to taxation for the daily cleaning of streets (according to the Senate resolution 3 September 1818), Reading Society, Monofylla, 28 October 1818, V-8.
15 Z. Laidlow, *Colonial Connections 1815–1845: Patronage, the Information Revolution and Colonial Government*. Manchester: Manchester University Press, 2005, 182.
16 Paximadopoulou-Stavrinou, *Politeiografika Ionion Nison*.
17 Young, *The Colonial Office*, 249, 283; and from page 247: 'The word colony … is rather a convenient administrative distinction, which usually, but not always, indicates a territory administered by an official responsible to the Secretary of State for the Colonies'.
18 *The Times* 22 July 1825 (page 2, col e).
19 D. Ithakisios, 'I ekseliksi ton vasikon dimografikon charaktiristikon tou plithismou tis Eptanisou kata tin period tis Agglikis Prostasias kai ti methenotiki period 1815–1864–1900', *Epistimoniko Synedrio Praktika*, vol. A. Athens: Vouli ton Ellinon – Akadimia Athinon, 2005, 475–530.
20 For significant contributions that concern the islands of the Aegean, Mykonos and Syros, and its capital Ermoupolis, see V. Hionidou, 'The Demographic System of a Mediterranean Island: Mykonos, Greece, 1859–1959', *International Journal of Population Geography* 1 (1995): 125–46; V. Hionidou, 'Nineteenth-Century Urban Greek Households: The Case of Hermoupolis, 1861–1879', *Continuity and Change* 14(3) (1999): 403–27.
21 V. Hionidou, 'Dimographia'[Demography], in K. Kostis and S. Petmezas (eds), in *I anaptyxi tis ellinikis oikonomias kata ton 19o aiona (1830–1914)* [The development of the Greek economy during the nineteenth-century]. Athens: Alexandreia, 2006.
22 Ithakisios, 'I ekseliksi ton vasikon dimografikon charaktiristikon', 483.
23 V. Hionidou, 'From Modernity to Tradition: Households on Kythera in the Early Nineteenth Century', in Silvia Sovic, Pat Thane and Pier Paolo Viazzo (eds), *The History of Families and Households: Comparative European Dimensions*. Leiden and Boston: Brill, 2016, 47–68.
24 E. Prontzas and D. Anoyatis-Pele. *Kerkyra 1830–1832. Metaksi Feoydarchias kai apoikiokratias*. Thessaloniki: University Studio Press, 2002.
25 A. Fragkiadis, 'Agrotiki oikonomia kai ekswteriko emporio', in K. Kostis and S. Petmezas (eds), *I anaptyksi tis ellinikis oikonomias kata ton 19o aiona (1830–1914)*. Athens: Alexandreia, 2006, 153–74.
26 R.M. Martin, *History of the British Possessions in the Mediterranean*. London: W. Nicol, 1837, 323.
27 Ithakisios, 'I ekseliksi ton vasikon dimografikon charaktiristikon', 498.
28 William Henry Smith, *The Mediterranean: A Memoir Physical, Historical, and Nautical*. London, 1854, 102.
29 Gallant, *Modern Greece*, 95.
30 K. Kostis and S. Petmezas (eds), *I anaptyksi tis ellinikis oikonomias to 19o aiona*. Athens: Alexandreia, 2006, 27.
31 Mercati, *Saggio Storico Statistico*, Chapter 2.
32 P. Kapetanakis, *I pontoporos emporiki naftilia ton Eptanison* tin epochi tis Vretanikis katochis kai prostasias kai I Kefalliniaki yperochi (1809/1815–1864)'. Ph.D., Ionian University, 2009, 327–28.

33 G. Harlaftis, 'To emporonaftiliako dikyto ton Ellinon tis Diasporas kai I anaptyksi tis ellinikis naftilias ton 19o aiona: 1830-1860', *Mnemon* (15), 1993: 69–127.
34 A.N.K., A.I.G., Eptanisos Politeia, F. 473, subf. 3 and passports, A.N.K., F. 2.
35 I. Baghdiantz, G. Harlaftis and I. Minoglou (eds), *Diaspora Entrepreneurial Networks: Four Centuries of History*. New York, 2005; M. Chatziioanou, *Oikogeneiaki Stratigiki kai Emporikos Antagwnismos. O Oikos Gerousi ton 19o aiona*. Athens: MIET, 2003 (and other works).
36 J. Clancy-Smith, *Mediterraneans: North Africa and Europe in an Age of Migration, c. 1800–1900*. Berkeley: University of California Press, 2011.
37 T. Gallant, 'Tales from the Dark Side: Transnational Migration, the Underworld and the "other" Greeks of the Diaspora', in Dimitris Tziovas (ed.), *Greek Diaspora and Migration since 1700: Society, Politics and Culture*. Aldershot: Ashgate, 2009, 17–30.
38 Chiotis, *Isotira tou Ioniou Kratous*, 19
39 Zamit, *Oi Maltezoi stin Kerkyra*, 76–117.
40 Proceedings in Parga, and the Ionian Islands, *The Quarterly Review*, 1820; 23, 45, 116.
41 I. Vervitsiotou, *Ekthesis ton gegonoton osa synevisan prin kai meta tin paracho-risin tis Pargas. Syggrama ekdothen en Parisiois Gallisti kata to 1820 etos nyn the metafrasthen ypo Ioannou Vervitsiotou*. En Kerkyra, 1851, 25.
42 It is interesting that British Foreign Minister Castlereagh thought that Parga was an island; Jervis, *A History of the Island of Corfu*, 207.
43 P. Cochran, *Byron's Romantic Politics: the Problem of Metahistory*. Cambridge: Cambridge Scholars Publishing, 2011, 210.
44 Jervis, *A History of the Island of Corfu*, 210–11.
45 Jervis notes they were about 2,700; Jervis, *History of the Island of Corfu*, 209.
46 Atto di Parlamento, No XIV, Seconda Sessione, Primo Parlamento, 22/05/1819, (Korgialeneios Library), Argostoli, Kefalonia.
47 E.A. 849, Subfolder 27, Notification, 30.06.1819.
48 *Catalogo degli Parghi abitanti a Manduchio*, E.A. 22, υποφ. 44, 25/02/1821.
49 Petition 95, CO 136/661, N.A.
50 Petition 185, CO 136/661.
51 Eftychia Kosmatou, 'La population des Iles Ioniennes XVIIIème-XIXème siècle', Ph.D. Dissertation, Université de Paris I, Paris 2000.
52 Ionian State Acts of Parliament and *Ionian Islands Government Gazette*, 1840–1963, National Archives, London, and Reading Society Library, Corfu.
53 Of the eighty-nine merchants naturalized, forty-nine (or 55 per cent) asked for political domicile in Corfu, while thirty-eight (or 42 per cent) asked for domicile in Zante. *Ionian Islands Government Gazette*, 1840–1963, National Archives, London, and Reading Society Library, Corfu.
54 A. Nikiforou, *Ta diavatiria tou 19ou aiona ton archeion tis Kerkyras (1800–1870)*. Kerkyra: G.A.K. Archeia Nomou Kerkyras, 2003.
55 Zamit, *Oi Maltezoi stin Kerkyra*.
56 Napier, *The Colonies*, 260.
57 Ibid., 241, 255.
58 E.A. (Executive Police), 1719, 1 /91, I.A.K.

59 Gail Hook, 'Mr. Fenech's Colony: Maltese Immigration in British Cyprus, 1878 to 1950', *Journal of Cyprus Studies* 13 (2007): 27–51.
60 C. Nikolaou, 'I oikonomiki sygkyria stis gamilies symperifores. Oi katholikoi stin Kerkyra (1815–1864)', in Aliki Nikiforou (ed.), *Θ' Panionio Synedrio, Praktika vol. A*. Paxoi: Eaireia Paxinon Meleton, 2014, 333–57.
61 Istoriko Arheio Kerkyras (IAK), Town Population Register, 1812–1814, Executive, Police 1319; and Register of Corfu Merchants, Corfu 1818, Ionian State 232a. For a good definition of the terms *negozianti, mercanti* and *bottegai*, see Olga Katsiardi-Hering, *The Greek Merchant Colony of Trieste, 1750–1830*. 2 vols. Athens, 1986, II, 393–408 (in Greek).
62 A. Mousson, *Ein Besuch auf Korfu und Cefalonien im September 1858*. Zurich, 1859 (Greek translation). Athens: Istoritis, 1995, 41.
63 P. Cottrell, *The Ionian Bank: An Imperial Institution, 1839–1864*. Athens: Alpha Bank Historical Archives, 2007.
64 N. Bakounakis, *Patra. Mia elliniki protevousa ton 19o aiona*. Athens: Kastaniotis, 1995, 72–73.
65 For the history of Greek-owned shipping and the 'Chiot' and 'Ionian' phases of this development, see G. Harlaftis, *A History of Greek-Owned Shipping: The Making of an International Tramp Fleet, 1830 to the Present Day*. London: Routledge, 1996.
66 Hionidou, 'From Modernity to Tradition', 54.
67 From the early 1840s onwards, the *Gazette*, the official newspaper of the Ionian state, published all naturalizations. The information includes the petitioner's name, place of origin, occupation (in most cases) and place of domicile.
68 The concentration of naturalized merchants in Corfu and Zante was striking: forty-nine (or 55 per cent) of the eighty-nine merchants naturalized, asked for political domicile in Corfu, while thirty-eight (or 42 per cent) named Zante. That 97 per cent requested domicile in these two towns shows the indifference of the immigrant merchants to the towns of Argostoli and Lixuri in Kefalonia; *Ionian Islands Government Gazette* (IIGG), 1840–1963.
69 D. Ansted, *The Ionian Islands in the Year 1863*, London, 1863, 14; for the history of the Jews in Corfu, see S. Gekas, 'The Port Jews of Corfu and the "Blood Libel" of 1891: A Tale of Many Centuries and of One Event', *Jewish Culture and History* 7(1–2) (2004): 171–96.
70 The number of Jews in the retail trade included mostly peddlers (60 of 113), while the shopkeepers were basically sellers of wines and spirits. A high proportion of the Jewish craftsmen were tailors (127 of 194).
71 S. Gekas and M. Grenet, 'Trade, Politics and City Space(s) in Mediterranean Ports', in Carola Hein (ed.), *Port Cities: Dynamic Landscapes and Global Networks*. London: Routledge, 2011, 89–103.

 Chapter 5

'A TRUE AND HATEFUL MONOPOLY'
Merchants and the State

The Ionian Commercial Economy

A central issue in debates about the colonial states is the 'contradictory structure of colonial economies';[1] this dimension is even more important in the case of the Ionian Islands, whose political status was by definition ambivalent, and its economy suffered all the disadvantages and enjoyed none of the advantages of a colony, as one British official had commented – this was a rather unfair comment since Ionians were protected when trading or travelling abroad. The ambiguous state of Ionian independence manifested itself most vividly, however, in the political economy of the Ionian State. Responding to the call by Cooper and Stoler for a more complex engagement with colonial institutions and the work that colonial states do beyond the political aspects of decision making on the economy, this chapter looks at the categories of inclusion and exclusion in the labour economies. 'Labour' and 'trade' were not entities with fixed meanings across time and space in the British Empire but can serve as key concepts in understanding the political economy of colonialism in the Ionian Islands. It is more productive and historically accurate to focus on the forms of power that specific institutions projected and reproduced, in the 'field' of economy as much as anywhere else.

Research on the economic history of the British Empire has focused more on the balance sheet of empire, the costs and benefits of imperial projects for European nations, but less on the costs and benefits for the colonized.[2] Population, resources, and distance from and access to markets seem to have determined the potential of each economy in the 'periphery' to participate in a globalizing economy between the 1840s and 1950s.[3] The Ionian Islands were part of the 'periphery' and for about fifty years experienced Britain's economic expansion and political clout. While the crops produced and exported remained the same even if markets changed, other sectors showed unprecedented dynamism; long-distance shipping, banking and insurance appeared for the first time and in more sophisticated ways than in the Greek Kingdom after its establishment in 1830.

British formal and informal empire involved commercial penetration and political influence, a policy that meant 'trade with informal control or trade with rule where necessary', especially in areas such as Latin America and the Ottoman Empire,[4] a 'model' that is considered more appropriate for the 'white colonies'.[5] The colonial-style system of governance in the Ionian State successfully integrated existing political structures, and transformed the political culture of state administration. The Ionian Islands became the testing ground for British commercial and political expansion during the nineteenth century. British-manufactured goods first appeared on the islands in large volume during the period of the Napoleonic Wars, when the British navy seized three of the islands and replaced the French as 'protectors' of the islands.[6] After the establishment of the Ionian State a regional economy in shipping, commerce and increasingly seasonal agricultural migration integrated the Ionian Sea economy to the imperial network. The British-Ionian state as well as the post-union administration under the Greek Kingdom failed to stem the centuries-old social conflict between town and country, and between the landed gentry and the landless peasants and tenants who worked the land; this failure or unwillingness of British commissioners and Ionian State officials became clear when a conflict simmered and erupted during and after the 1865 elections. A market economy was emerging, supported by usurious capital 'dissolving social relations among farmers as well as among the relics of feudalism'.[7] The Ionian Islands, however, were only partially a market economy, and post-feudal sclerotic institutions held Ionian economies back, and most Ionians in a state of poverty.

The Ionian Islands Balance of Trade

During the earlier period of the Ionian State trade contracted, in the late 1820s, late 1830s and early 1840s. During the latter period of British rule, Ionian ports experienced extraordinary trade growth. The volume of imports and exports increased in an impressive way, especially during the period 1840–64. The total value of trade was around 1 to 1.4 million pounds for the first period of modest commercial activity but jumped to more than 2 million pounds by the end of the protectorate.[8] The surge was mainly due to the increasing role of transit trade. The Ionian State balance of trade shows the deficit between imports and exports, which was only partly funded by the income of some Ionians from shipping, clandestine trade and their payment in kind during their seasonal work in the grain harvest on the mainland

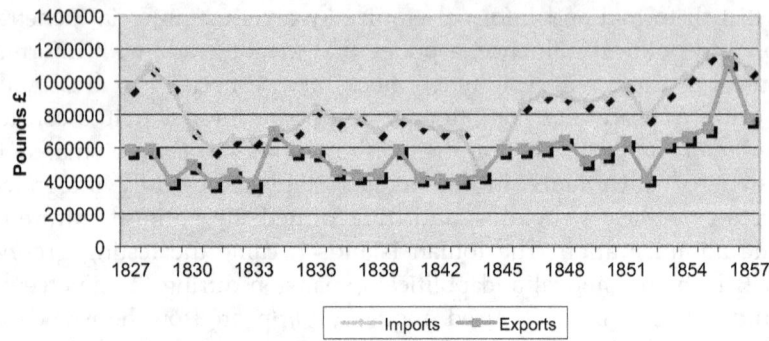

Figure 5.1 Ionian State Imports–Exports, 1827–57.
Source: Ionian Islands Blue Books of Statistics, CO 136/1392–1426, TNA.

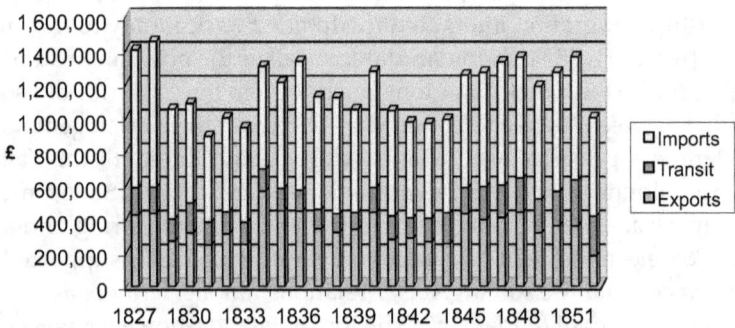

Figure 5.2 Total value of imports, exports and transit trade.
Source: Ionian Islands Blue Books of Statistics, CO 136/1392–1426, TNA.

opposite. The Ionian trade balance, and by implication the Ionian fiscal condition (since there was only indirect taxation and port duties), was constantly in deficit.

The role of Corfu as a transit port explains the growth of trade overall in the total number of imports and exports in Ionian statistics. Until 1840 transit trade was a relatively small percentage compared to the total value of traded goods, around 15 per cent. After 1849 the growth is impressive, and by 1863 transit trade reached 44 per cent of the value of all traded goods.[9] The deficit in the balance of trade and the absurd taxation regime between each island – since the islands constituted, at least in theory, individual states – form the two basic deficiencies and ultimately failures of the Ionian State public finances.[10] The trend of both exports and imports, improved only in the late 1850s following the destruction of the currant crop in the early 1850s and the Crimean War in the mid-1850s.

The increasing importance of the transit trade was noted by commissioners early on, and is confirmed by the Blue Books. The currant trade represented the largest percentage of exports in the 1830s and in the years 1845–47; it was surpassed by goods in transit through Ionian ports, mainly Corfu and to a lesser extent Zante. The percentage of transit exports increased steadily from the early 1840s onwards, rocketed in the late 1850s to more than 70 per cent of total exports, and fell again in the early 1860s but was still as high as 63 and 55 per cent of all exports. The transit data primarily concern Corfu and Zante ports, where goods were stored before being sent to the mainland, Patras, southern Italy, and other areas as far as the Black Sea, from where grain was carried back to the islands. The goods that transited through the port of Corfu were primarily British-manufactured goods and grain, going on opposite directions. The role of Corfu port throughout the period can be discerned through the above data. The rise in goods exported signifies the increasing role of the port as an entrepôt for conveying goods to neighbouring markets. British commercial interests included the grain trade in transit from the Black Sea, the currants exported from the southern Ionian Islands and the import of British-manufactured goods for re-export to neighbouring markets. The fluctuations and any risks for merchants associated with international trade were offset by their large profits from producers who ultimately bore the cost of high taxation on the agricultural goods. The olive oil and currants exports from the Ionian State continued to bring in revenues for the government, and this sector holds the key in understanding the formation of the Ionian State colonial economy; the reversal of revenues and the deteriorating state of Ionian finances in turn determined the public works policy and the attitude of middle- and lower-class Ionians towards British-Ionian state authority.

Olive Oil and the Export Economy

By the late eighteenth and early nineteenth century, a few well-connected Christian and Jewish merchants controlled the olive oil trade in Corfu through connections with Venetian merchants and deterred any ambitious newcomers.[11] The British blockade during the French occupation (1807–14) harmed the olive trade and reduced the income of thousands of Corfu families, which practically abandoned olive cultivation by 1816. The inherent volatility and the biennial nature of the crop explain the intense fluctuations in the volume and value of olive oil exported from the Ionian Islands, mainly produced in Corfu and Paxos. There were still markets for olive oil after the 'decline and fall' of Venice, especially during the industrial revolution, when olive oil was used as a lubricant for machines; demand for olive oil on the islands was constant as it was used extensively to illuminate the households and towns of the islands. In the 1830s, in favourable years, olive oil yielded nearly ten million gallons and significant revenues for the government.[12] However, there was plenty of room for improvement of productivity in the pressing of olives; the first attempts to mechanize oil extraction with a steam engine took place in 1835.[13] The fruit was left to fall to the ground, a practice that Ansted, writing in the 1860s, found particularly hard to understand when compared to practices of olive picking elsewhere in the Mediterranean; Ansted estimated that a lot less was exported legally and a lot more was smuggled out of the country.[14] People suffered price fluctuations but not everyone suffered in the same way:

> It must not be supposed that all the country people are thus poor. There are some whose houses though apparently little different in the exterior, are really much more commodious, and are far better furnished. As a contrast to the hovel just described, I was taken into the house of a respectable small farmer, one who farmed a certain tract of olive grove, vineyard and arable land, partly his own, partly paying a rent, either in money or kind.[15]

This form of rural economy, multicropping olives, vines and cereal, maximized economic security but reduced productivity; it was the price to pay for landholders locked in unproductive and small landholdings.[16]

The failure of the olive harvest in 1837, 1846, 1851 and 1857 added to the volatility of the cash crop, but towards the end of the period

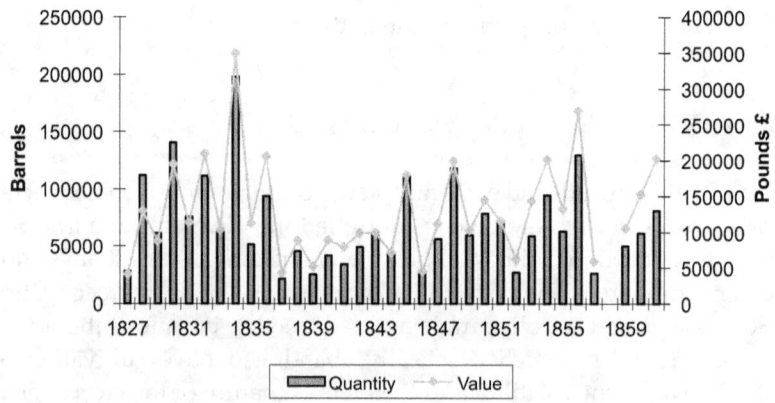

Figure 5.3 Value of olive oil exports.
Source: Ionian Islands Blue Books of Statistics, CO 136/1392–1426, TNA.

olive oil still represented half of all exports. The export value of olive oil increased gradually but only slightly. Prices increased substantially in 1858, and increased a further 25 per cent in 1860. The quantities produced did not follow the price increase. Olive cultivators in Corfu were in a much better position to maintain a living standard than the cultivators of vines on the southern islands, who gradually faced problems of overproduction and lower prices due to a highly elastic demand. By contrast, olive oil could find good prices in distant markets and guaranteed a much better income for the villagers of Corfu, which partly explains their different attitude towards the British and Ionian State authorities, especially in the cities, where the presence of the army and police was strong. There were hardly any food riots or rebellions, such as those that had occurred on the southern islands, especially Kefalonia, in the late 1840s and early 1850s. Production continued to increase after the Ionian Islands became a part of Greece, with the crop of 1887 exceeding all the crops of the British period except the ones of 1834 and 1858.[17]

A few years after Corfu became part of the Greek Kingdom a report confirms the 'state of agriculture, which as a science must be considered as still in its infancy'. Attempts to establish model farms failed; and agricultural schools were too poorly attended to make a lasting and broad impact. With great Victorian flare the author of the article considered it also a matter of 'taste':

> A taste for agricultural improvements, or for improvements of any sort, involving a change in old-established routine, does not exist among any class of the population. The class of proprietors who ought to be the foremost to show a good example were content to depend for their subsistence on the often precarious produce of their vines and olives, eked out perchance by salaries derived from public employments, of which under the British protectorate they enjoyed an almost exclusive monopoly.[18]

Indolence, supposedly, continued to be endemic because of the malaria that festered in marshlands, ravaged the country's population and prevented the cultivation of wheat. Despite its orientalist tone, the article essentially echoes the failure of British-Ionian administration to implement any long-lasting changes on Ionian agriculture or the fortunes of the island's population after decades of British rule.

Currant Fortunes

More important than olive oil for Ionian revenues were currants, the type of raisins cultivated in the islands since the sixteenth century. Currants gradually became an essential ingredient to puddings and cakes, and were glorified by Charles Dickens in his novel *A Christmas Carol* as a symbol of middle-class affluence.[19] Currant consumption in Britain increased steadily during the period, reflecting the general consumption trend of sweets and stimulants, as the latter became popular among all social classes. For all their faults, however, one should not blame the British-Ionian administration for not trying, and in fact they made several attempts to improve cultivation methods. Napier, the local governor (resident) of Kefalonia, devoted several chapters of his book to the state of agriculture on the islands and his attempts to improve it; he was so impressed by his own ideas about a local 'yeoman' labour being the solution to agricultural inefficiency, not only around the empire but especially closer to home, that he even theorized about it in his book *Colonisation*, arguing that the best way to avoid famine in England and Ireland was to break up the large estates into small ones and create a 'yeomanry'; it was not Napier, however, who sought to create a 'commercial peasantry'.[20] Nugent's efforts in the 1830s to relieve Ionians from debt went much further. By the time the islands were about to join Greece, in the early 1860s, the value of Ionian currants exported primarily to Britain was decreasing, despite the increasing amount of currants being exported; this period predated the collapse of the currants prices in the 1880s and 1890s, and the first emigration wave from the Peloponnese to the United States.

The substantial contradiction that appeared in the currants trade – a trade based on landholding conditions that were extremely dated and unproductive, on the one hand, but at the same time, after the 1840s, a trade that was channelled through the increasingly sophisticated and demanding (in terms of capital) system of distribution and financing of the Ionian Bank – was never resolved. Given that the two primarily currant-producing regions were islands, Zante and Kefalonia, there was

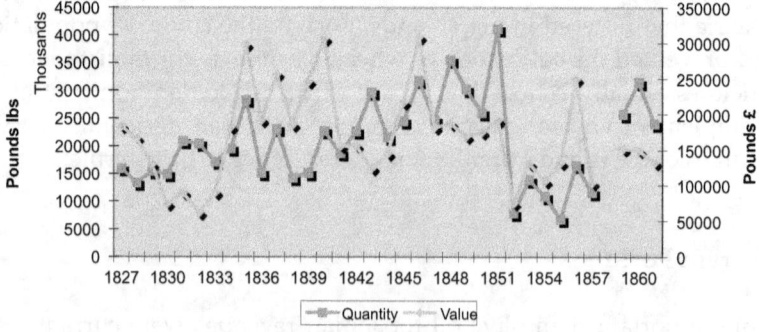

Figure 5.4 Exports of currants in quantity and value.
Source: Ionian Islands Blue Books of Statistics, CO 136/1392–1426, TNA.

a limit to the production that could be achieved; more people moved into agriculture, especially on those islands, not for strictly economic reasons but basically when the revolution took hold in the Peloponnese and currants production there practically stopped.

The 1820s was a turning point for the currant-exporting Ionian Islands. When the Greek war of independence broke out, hostilities prevented the cultivation of the precious fruit in the north-western Peloponnese, and so Kefalonia and Zante currants were the only ones in the market. The boom in the currant trade during the 1820s can only be compared with the overproduction of the years 1870–90 in Greece, the 'golden age' of Greek currants that followed the destruction of French vineyards, and the currants exports became the principal source of revenue for the Greek State.[21] The duties paid for the export of currants (18.5 per cent) were the principal source of revenue for the Ionian government long before the Greek State became addicted to currants. Currants exports ranged between 45 and 55 per cent of the total exports of the Ionian State, while olive oil exports (mainly from Corfu and some small quantities from the island of Paxos) ranged from a minimum of 18 per cent in 1827 to 45 per cent in 1848. High commissioners asked for a reduction in the import duty on currants in Great Britain. The

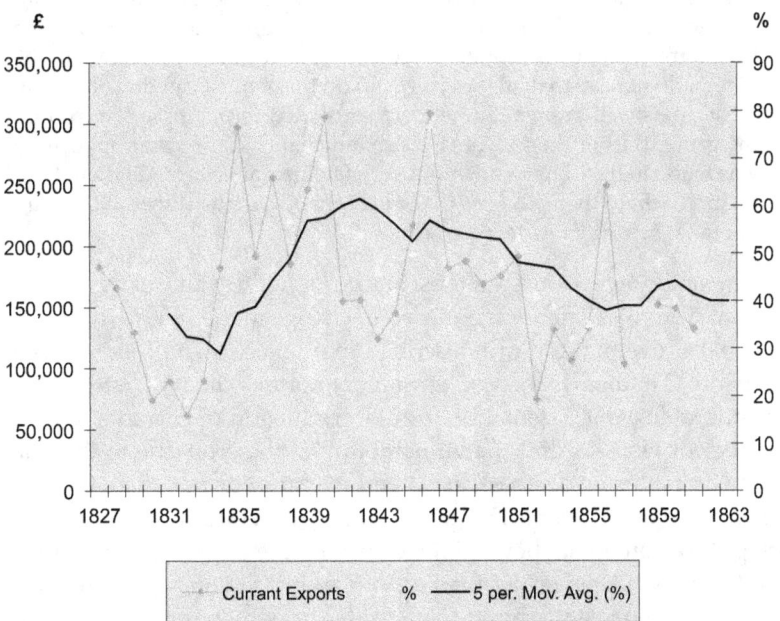

Figure 5.5 Currants exports, 1827–63, amount and percentage of total exports.
Source: Ionian Islands Blue Books of Statistics, CO 136/1392–1426, TNA.

extremely high export tariff of 19.5 per cent was intended to increase the revenue of the Ionian State – which, however, remained in deficit.

The passolina, or *uva passa* (dried grapes) as locals called it, required constant care throughout the year until the fruit became ripe. After vintage the grapes were exposed to the sun for a fortnight and then they were stored and eventually shipped. During the drying stage a mere shower could destroy entire quantities of the harvest and condemn producers to a year of further indebtedness and impoverishment. When dry, currants were carried in bags to warehouses (*serragli*), owned by landowners or merchants, for storage. Warehouse owners issued receipts for the amount of currants producers deposited, receipts that could be negotiated and circulated as money. This transaction was not always fair, and relations between the owners of warehouses (*serraglianti*, who stored the fruit until it was sold and exported) and producers were complex. Napier, resident of Kefalonia, described in a short story how he envisaged the transaction between the *serraglianti*, a group around which there is very little information so far, and the producers of currants. Napier investigated the practices that surrounded the transaction, and noted:

> Another fraud is practised: a merchant and a *seragliante* make their written agreement for a false price; this is entered at the custom house, but privately, the merchant pays more than the sum stated in the written legal agreement; the proprietor receiving only the sum mentioned in the latter. I do not say that all the *seraglianti* do this, but all can do it, and that most do, is well known. Some merchants tried to purchase the fruit on the ground, from the peasants: these merchants know what opposition was made to this. They know that very few peasants dare sell them their fruit; in debt to their *seragliante*, the peasants would be ruined if they did not take their currants to his *seraglia*.[22]

Currant growers suffered most at the marketing stage of the crop; this is what Commissioner Nugent tried to change in the 1830s. The adversities that growers faced are described in a letter to *The Times* by 'T.H.', probably Thomas Hancock, currant exporter. Hancock stressed the considerable capital demands for the production of currants, the large number of workers and the vulnerability of the crop due to the uncertainty that the vine disease caused and the unpredictable rain that could destroy the whole crop: 'The grower must, therefore, look to a remunerating price somewhat beyond the common rate of profit on agricultural capital'.[23] John Davy, chief medical officer in Kefalonia for seven years, travelled extensively around the islands and left an important memoir; he asked Thomas Hancock, one of the currant exporters from Zante and Patras, and associate of Barff & Co, to write a statement on the currant produce and trade.²⁴ Mr Hancock states that by the early 1820s, when the Greek war of independence was ravaging Morea, all cultivation was suspended. Currants on the islands were sold for up to 96 Spanish dollars per hundredweight (100 pounds), dropping to 60 dollars (or 37 shillings) by 1826. By that year, according to Mr Hancock, the growers of Kefalonia had extended their plantations. Prices started declining, and by 1831–32 Morea currants had returned to the market and prices on the islands were as low as 16 dollars (or 10s 6d) per hundredweight. The rapid fall is also attributed to the import duty in England, which was up to 44s 4d per hundredweight. Mr Hancock argued that the 50 per cent reduction of this to 22s 2d per hundredweight, achieved in 1834, was to be attributed to the 'very strenuous exertions by the Lord High Commissioner and the merchants in London engaged in the trade'. Hancock was one of the merchants pressing for the duty reduction. Production during a fruitful season in Greece and the Ionian Islands could reach up to 18,000 or even 20,000 tones, which was far too much for consumption in Britain alone. Napier, the resident of Kefalonia, recorded that from 1821 the war of independence 'threw the whole trade into the hands of the islanders, and the price mounted up from 13 dollars to 100 dollars per hundredweight, the produce likewise increased in quantity from 4 millions to 11 millions of pounds weight'.²⁵ High duties and vulnerable crops gradually suppressed prices, even if there was a boom in the currant trade in the 1820s. This interval, however, was not enough to alter the conditions under which the growers were getting credit for the expensive-to-cultivate currant plantations. English merchants and commercial agents who conducted their own business on the islands were also in charge of the Morea, exporting currants.²⁶ Exporters, aided by small-scale traders in the country, provided money and goods, especially grain, for the farmers' needs. As a guarantee they bought the next year's produce, getting the small capital they were lending, plus the interest of 18–24 per cent, in kind. The growers were obliged to give all their crop to a merchant at an already fixed price, thus enabling the merchant to sell at a far greater price than the one at which he had bought the fruit.

The currants trade was the first field of conflict between merchants and the state; the English and some Ionian merchants who exported currants from the islands were the clear winners. Nugent, high commissioner in the early 1830s, was concerned about the grievances of growers, locked as they were in highly disadvantageous trading conditions. In his letter to the Colonial Office, Nugent explains his measures for improving the growers' place in the currant production and export chain. Nugent recommended to the Parliament in London a large reduction in the export duty on currants, and introduced a loan to growers from a sum of £35,000 on security of the produce.[27] As T.H. reports in his letter to *The Times*:

> In his necessities the grower was forced to have recourse to borrowing the money requisite beforehand for the expensive annual cultivation of the currant. The English merchants residing in Zante and Cephalonia, and other monied individuals, found it advantageous to advance money at 8 and 10 per cent, bespeaking frequently, as a condition the whole anticipated produce at an exceedingly low rate: and this practice became so general, as very much to govern the market, and consequently, the less needy grower was obliged to content himself with the same price, now become a general one.[28]

The most important and innovative part of the plan was to create a public fund to advance money as government-backed loans. Nugent sensed that the 'compensation' for the state revenue that would inevitably come from the reduction of duties, could only be achieved if growers entered the market competition on equal terms with the merchants, without depending on them for cash. Nugent stated that his intention was to break down the 'monopoly in a manner consistent also with every principle of free trade' and to 'arm the poorer party with capital to enter the market on equal terms with the other'; in the 1830s this was a lofty ambition, not just in the Ionian Islands but everywhere else. Nugent intended to strike a balance in the currants market and change the practices that had persisted on the islands according to the 'principles of free trade' that his country had first taught the world. This was the first time a British commissioner had attempted to introduce fairer if not more free trade practices to the islands' economies. Nugent envisioned modern market practices for local growers, where pre-existing debts, other forms of economic and social subordination or even fear would give way to competition on 'equal' terms between producers and merchants. The bill Napier introduced to the Ionian Parliament – important for British commercial interests – found its way into *The Times*, where it was published in full and with the obligatory commentary. The Executive approved the Act of Government in 1833 titled 'for the prevention of monopoly, and the regulation of deposits and sales on currants': 'For the purpose of destroying the monopoly which up to this time has been practiced [sic] in currants (the principal produce of these states), to the great loss of the proprietors of these islands'. The law required depositaries to present government officials of each island where currants were cultivated with a book recording the exact quantity of currants stored before 15 October each year and send the price of currants to the central government for publication in the *Ionian*

Gazette.²⁹ The same issue of *The Times* published an aggressive letter accompanying the translation of the bill, which argued that Nugent was 'unfit' for the post of high commissioner of the Ionian Islands because he did not represent British – that is mercantile – interests. The audacity of the letter is extraordinary; but the document informs us on how British commercial policy shaped the Ionian economy and the finances of the Ionian State:

> The trade in currants barely pays a freight. When it is considered that England consumes upwards of 8,000 tons of currants from the Ionian Islands, this act, so hostile to British commerce, is a very ungracious return for our custom and our protection. Its effect on the Ionian Islands will be very prejudicial to their interests. Not a merchant will attempt to trade under these restrictions; and with such a rival near the islands as in the Morea, producing 3,500 tons of finer fruit, this bill will act as a direct bounty to the Greeks, who have the good sense to leave their trade free. To relieve the currant proprietors Lord Nugent has lowered the export duty from 60 to 18%; but he has more than doubled the import duty on many articles and nearly trebled it on British colonial produce. Rum pays 2s per gallon, coffee 12s per 100lb, sugar 12s to 15s. Lord Nugent is a liberal but his measures are at variance with that character. He is totally unfit for his present post.

Such intervention in Ionian and British colonial policy came directly from the lobbying of English merchants in the Ionian Islands who exported currants and of the importers of British (colonial) goods to the Ionian states. A few weeks later the 'seat of the Ionian Government' published in the same newspaper a reply letter, stressing that its opinions were strictly authentic. The letter argued that the law generated enthusiasm in the assembly, because it addressed a burning issue for the people of Ithaca and especially Kefalonia and Zante, the subject of many previous petitions. Refuting the claims in the previous letter and pitting the interests of Ionian growers against English merchants, the writer argued that since 1829 Ionian raisins had been charged excessively, with 44s per 100 pounds, while raisins from British colonies paid 10s, and from foreign countries 20s. 'Extreme injustice and partiality' as a result meant that 'people of the Islands felt that G.B. [Great Britain] considered them as colonial possessions only when it suited her political convenience, and that in her financial agreements they were treated more as a conquered country'. It was this unfavourable policy towards Ionian currants that stifled prices, and the consequences were soon felt on the islands. Prices depreciated and many noble and previously even affluent families on the southern islands were reduced to poverty. The previous years the market price for currants on the islands had been as high as 30s. per hundredweight (and this is certainly very much within the mark), in 1832 it had fallen below 8s. The counter proposal was to streamline all duties at 18.5 per cent on the value of all goods exported from the islands – oil, valonia, soap and currants. These difficulties led to a situation where 'in the Isles of Zante and Cephalonia the culture of the plant was sensibly and visibly diminishing'. The author (T.H.) praised the action of the government to raise the fund through the establishment of local banks for granting 'under certain circumstances' loans at 6 per cent to cultivators, and to 'emancipate them from the thraldom in which the monied speculators and their own necessities held them'. However, unless the duty of 44 shillings was reduced to 10 or 12 shillings, little would change.[30]

This crisis of the Ionian economy in the 1830s explains Nugent's intervention in the currants market. Several English merchants went bankrupt because of the fluctuations in the price, and cargoes remained unsold for months.[31] Merchants exporting both from the Peloponnese and the Ionian Islands (Zante and Kefalonia) were less affected, because a bad harvest year on the islands could be balanced by a good year in the Peloponnese. The volatility of production and the reduction of revenues harmed Ionian State finances since its income derived solely from the export and import duties. Currant merchants, local and British, were so powerful that they challenged Nugent's plan to rid growers from the usurious bonds and cut the nets spun to the Ionian countryside to promote and essentially protect and subsidize the production and trade of currants, against the principles of free trade.

The commercial policy of the Ionian State did not affect only the currants trade. British and Ionian importers enjoyed a favourable customs tariff, which enabled them to import British industrial products at a tax rate of 2 to 7 per cent. The islands operated within a taxation system that imposed tariffs on trade between the islands (each island was a State, hence the official name 'United States of the Ionian Islands') and exporters paid the import duty in England, where the majority of the currants were exported to; this is why the reduction in tariffs was on the agenda of successive commissioners. Seaton started promoting a reduction in import duties to the Colonial Office in his 1844 report for the Blue Book of 1843:

> Some advantages have been derived from the reform which has been effected in the Quarantine System and Sanitary Tariffs, and both having been reduced to the lowest possible scale compatible with efficiency. The political position in which these Islands are placed, which will not admit of their enjoying the advantage of Colonies, but the reduction of the

Currant Duties notified this year by the Protecting Power, will probably greatly extend the sale of their Staple Products.³²

The political status of the islands as a protectorate entailed few economic privileges and certainly none of the advantages afforded to any colony, as Commissioner Douglas noted in the 1830s. For the British Treasury, the Ionian Islands were an independent state with which Britain had commercial relations and to which favourable terms were exceptionally allowed, due to their status as a protectorate; but when diplomacy called, similar and even more privileges were granted to the Greek Kingdom, until the rupture in good relations with Britain during the Crimean War (1853–56). For most of the time and certainly on the issue of import duties for Ionian agricultural products in Britain, the Ionian Islands economy and society were caught in a semi-colonial trap that closed in as decades went by.

The vine disease of 1851 had grave consequences for the Ionian Islands as well as Greece. This was one of the factors that changed the production capabilities and the revenues of the Ionian State, and from then on the ability of the state to spend more than the salaries and pensions on education, public works and improving Ionian living standards. Foreign markets were equally important; while Zante and Kefalonia currants were shipped to English ports until the end of the British protectorate, later in the nineteenth century another competitive distribution and trading network emerged in Amsterdam and Rotterdam, and as a result Kefalonian currants went to the Netherlands.

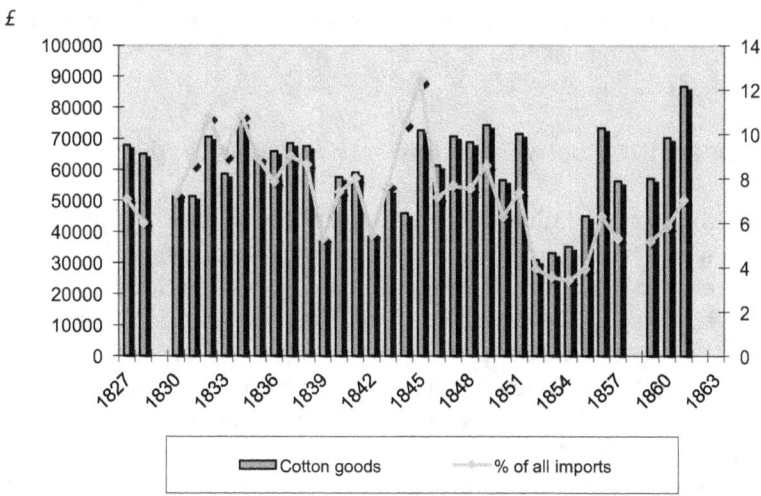

Figure 5.6 Value of cotton imports and percentage of total imports.
Source: Ionian Islands Blue Books of Statistics, CO 136/1392–1426, TNA.

The recession of the last quarter of the nineteenth century reduced demands even further.[33]

During the period of British rule, however, Britain was by far the main trading partner of the small islands state. The 1861 imports records show the needs of the people on the islands, including of course the British garrison, officers and other foreigners with money to spend on the expensive imported goods. The extraordinary value of £188,760 pounds worth of cottons and cotton yarn comprised more than 63 per cent of the total imports that year from Britain, with woollen goods and coals in a distant second and third, at £17,800 and £16,300 respectively. By 1860s cotton goods were being imported in large quantities in Corfu and were then distributed to other markets, as one British observer noted, and in any case it was impossible for Ionian markets to purchase all these goods.[34] The value of cotton goods imports more than tripled after 1833, and reached £58,709 pounds in the late 1850s.[35] The balance of trade remained in deficit, as the Ionian treasury export records for the years 1856–61 show.

If the export of currants and olive oil was important for the economic survival of the tenant farmers and state revenues, grain was equally important. All islands, especially the densely populated ones, imported considerable quantities, with Corfu importing more for the extra needs of the British garrison. Merchants trading grain carried the second largest volume of trade after the currant merchants of Zante and Kefalonia, and were important not only for the revenues of the Ionian State but especially for the survival of the population and the formation of the Ionian liberal bourgeoisie, as for some merchants trade became a matter of ideology as well as profit.

Grain Politics: Between Monopoly and Free Trade

The provision of grain in sufficient quantities to keep people fed and content has been among the most important tasks of regimes across time, even more so in the grain-deficient Ionian Islands. Merchants were among the most vocal groups to send petitions to local and central governments supporting their interests. During the Venetian period, local authorities privileged grain importers and bakers, and allowed the guild of bakers to control the preparation and especially the price of bread.[36] For the first few decades of the Ionian State, high commissioners and the Ionian government regulated and moderated the supply of sufficient wheat for the islands, but merchants lobbied for the application of the principle of free trade, which, as they reminded the government, Great Britain had first taught the world. From Venetian times to the nineteenth century, there had been transformations in the political economy of Ionian governments, and in the agricultural production and export of commodities, but especially in the relationship between state and merchants. As the centre of gravity shifted from Venice to London, Ionian merchants adapted to the changing conditions and entered the profitable Black Sea markets with dynamism. Merchants took an active role in the formation of the Ionian State and evoked liberal principles to support their free trade demands. The debate that broke out in Corfu during the 1830s and 1840s reveals the advanced knowledge and understanding of free trade principles that Ionian merchants were putting forward to the Ionian State, and that won the argument of the day.

High Commissioner Thomas Maitland was aware of the ideas of Adam Smith on the economics of the empire and free trade that propelled a colonial liberal ideology and drove British imperial expansion. When people in Corfu faced starvation Maitland abolished the government's corn monopoly, but the few grain importers forced up the price of bread: 'whatever Adam Smith may say on this subject, I cannot support his doctrines to the extent of starving a whole population'.[37] The level of independence that the British rulers of the islands could exercise (especially in times and matters of urgency), depended on their character, but remained within the general pattern of the management of the empire, which, in such a vast entity with long distances between the metropolis and the colonies, had to allow for personal initiative, agendas and ambitions.[38]

The 'freedom' of the right to trade grain became a contested issue from the beginning of the protectorate; despite the occasional liberal inclinations of high commissioners and their administration, needs in times of scarcity made intervention necessary. This ambivalence of the state towards the issue – sometimes granting freedom to trade but at other times enforcing a monopoly and restricting trade – represents a fine example of cases in which the interests of the state coincided, contrasted or coalesced with the interests of grain importers. The extensive cultivation of olive groves in Corfu and currants in Kefalonia and Zante meant that local grain production did not suffice for more than three months even on these large islands with more land for cultivation than the smaller ones. Ionians and the state bought the grain necessary for the rest of the year with profits generated from the cash crops. The first law of the Ionian states to ensure grain supply was passed in April 1819, reflecting the concerns of the government, which the following year also regulated the taxes on grain imported to Kefalonia.

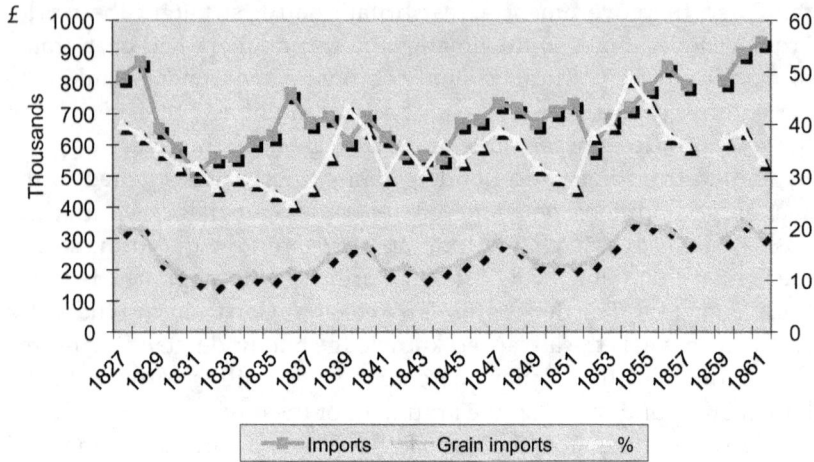

Figure 5.7 Value of grain and total imports and percentage of grain imports.
Source: Ionian Islands Blue Books of Statistics, CO 136/1392–1426, TNA.

Overall grain imports represented between 40 and 45 per cent of the total imports of the Ionian State in the years from 1827 to 1855.[39]

Wheat shortage was a problem on all islands, and grain imports from Zante and Kefalonia to Corfu or from Corfu to other islands was common. In 1828, Kefalonia experienced such a situation and asked for a large supply of corn from Corfu.[40] The question of whether the state should maintain a form of monopoly, which contradicted the spirit of the times but safeguarded the population against famine or allow the market to regulate the price of grain and bread, was never resolved because the Ionian government and several high commissioners oscillated between the two views. Ionian merchants, specializing in the import and re-export of wheat, articulated and pursued their interests collectively and managed to influence state policy. Merchants put forward arguments about the prosperity of their country, which would result from a policy favourable to commerce and in tandem with the rest of the 'civilized' world.

In March 1833, High Commissioner Nugent removed the tariff on grain and other cereals in an attempt to reform commerce and agriculture. Free trade of grain and flour was allowed in Corfu, 'as in the other islands', and time was 'allowed for the grain administration to sell the remaining grain'.[41] This in effect left the capital of the state without provisions, and in August 1834 the government decided to appoint a grain committee to regulate wheat prices. The municipal council appointed five committee members, two of whom were public functionaries and three were heads of 'distinguished' families of wholesale grain merchants. This committee set grain prices according to price fluctuations in foreign markets, and argued that the previously 'free' (unregulated) grain market had neither brought the price down nor improved grain quality; most significantly it had left Corfu exposed to the interests of speculators. The scepticism on free trade practices is evident in the decision of the grain committee to keep a stock of grain in the stores for emergency needs.

In April 1836, under Commissioner Douglas, a new Act of Government regulated foodstuffs and the price of bread while allowing the free sale of meat and fish. The decision was based upon previous experience, which proved that tariffs imposed on foodstuffs not only increased their market price but also encouraged smuggling and left many citizens unable to buy food at reasonable prices. In 1837 the government worried about the scarcity of wheat and decided to 'guard' the state against it. The 'experience' of the few years that trade was restricted was of 'greatest benefit' to the population and ensured the supply of wheat throughout the state. The Act of Parliament prohibited grain merchants from trading grain in transit and created a depot of wheat 'in sufficient quantity for the usual consumption of the Island (Corfu) and for supplying any accidental and momentaneous wants of the other islands of the state'. The municipal council of Corfu was responsible for the administration of the depot.[42]

The imposition of monopoly in the grain market faced stark and orchestrated opposition. In 1836 and 1837 'citizens of Corfu' sent two petitions to the lord high commissioner, indexed (wrongly) as 'Sundry Cephaloniots. Praying that the Monopoly may be taken off Grain'.[43] In the second petition, dated 24 March, the same citizens of Corfu painted a bleak picture that they argued emerged after the imposition of monopoly by the government and the Grain Administration.[44] The petitioners expressed their conviction based on the 'right of everyone to trade wheat freely', and requested a return to the previous regime, which gave more jobs to port workers; similarly they suggested that the commissioner should dismiss the Grain Administration, claiming that it had not brought the price of bread down or improved the quality of bread, and nor had the 'monopoly', as they explicitly call it, extended commerce or encouraged mobility of capital. The merchants of Corfu noted that the policy of free trade of wheat applied in Zante and Kefalonia, and asked for 'equal' treatment in Corfu. To legitimize their request the petitioners claimed they expressed the destitute and the poorest of Corfu, who would also benefit from the 'freedom to trade'. Sixty-two 'citizens of Corfu' signed the petition, the first of them a priest, followed by several grain merchants, two doctors, and other members of the island's 'people'.

By the early 1840s, Ionian merchants debated publicly issues of political economy, and petitioned to the supreme authority of the islands and representative of British power to convince the Ionian government that intervention in the grain market was not desirable and perhaps not even acceptable by Great Britain. High commissioners acknowledged publicly in the Ionian Assembly the importance of the grain trade: 'The duty upon the importation of Grain, falling equally upon Ionians and foreigners, residing within the State, not only is scarcely felt, but affords a certain branch of Public Revenue, and at the same time encourages the cultivation of this most essential article'.[45] The 'freedom to trade grain' had become a public matter. Reopening the debate put pressure on the government in Corfu to abolish restrictions on the grain market; in November 1841 Corfu merchants petitioned the high commissioner again for allowing an unregulated grain market.[46] Their arguments were based on previous experience from the period 1816–18, when merchants claimed that freedom to import grain greatly benefited the commerce of the states, and the island of Corfu in particular, but also the prosperity of the country as a whole. The treasurer general of the Ionian state, Woodhouse, in a letter to the high commissioner accompanying the petition, refuted the allegations of the merchants, arguing that the price had increased dramatically during the two-year period, besides the constant danger of a shortage of grain.[47] No one was lying; arguments were not mutually exclusive but simply partial. During the period 1816–18, prices increased and the islands were sufficiently provisioned with grain. Woodhouse concluded that grain merchants had earned a lot already from the amount of grain that was being imported 'transit' through the port of Corfu, and re-exported to neighbouring areas. Ionian merchants clashed with the state officials on grain trade, following the example of the British currant merchants, and were able to impose their opinion and will.

In June 1842, when the Corfu government succumbed and abolished the Grain Administration, supplies of grain in the Corfu depots dropped. Mackenzie was fiscally prudent and quite popular as commissioner; a 'student of economics',[48] Mackenzie realized that he had to accept the offer of the 'most important and prestigious merchants of Cephalonia' who promised to have ready for supply 30,000 kg of wheat, ready to be delivered on three months notice.[49] The official state newspaper praised the Kefalonia merchants for their donation, as it gave merchants in Corfu enough time to import the necessary quantities. The Kefalonia merchants offered to have the supply ready for the needs of

Corfu in exchange for a return to the free trade regime; this was serious lobbying and bargaining indeed, that took advantage of the needs for bread in Corfu. Fourteen merchants of Kefalonia signed the letter with their offer and promise to have the quantity ready on 3 months' notice.

The debate turned public when the state newspaper published two articles on the issue.[50] The first article defended the work of the Grain Administration and the need to safeguard the population from famine. The author of the second article, most likely a merchant, not only accused the Grain Administration of a 'true monopoly ... and a great deal more hateful', but also criticized them for buying less expensive and less nutritious 'Turkish grain' rather than the grain from the Black Sea. The author was well versed in the relatively new 'science' of political economy, and cited J.B. Say and his example of Paris in 1817–18 to stress the parallel with Corfu, arguing that neither place benefited from monopoly of grain, nor did people buy bread at a cheaper price. He also rejected an essential argument of the Grain Administration supporters, that of protection of the public against a famine in times of scarcity, by saying that 'Smith has shown that the interest of the merchant speculator of the wheat in the inside, and the interest of the mass of the people, although apparently opposite, are precisely the same in the years of the more great famine (Lib. IV. Cap. 5)'.[51] The author praised the connections of wheat importers with Black Sea ports, stressing the guaranteed provision of wheat and combining a theoretical knowledge and arguments with the practical experience of a business-savvy grain trade merchant. The international networks that Ionians had established could secure provisions at home in the grain-starved Ionian markets.

The official reply of a government official to the powerful arguments of the grain merchant 'declared' 'the two following truths: 1. The Government sincerely wishes to see the wheat trade as prosperous as possible. 2. That, without any doubt, if scarcity of wheat did happen again, as happened to all the islands a few days ago, the Government will hurry to fulfil its first duty to the people, to form the Grain Administration anew, with its benevolent and truly paternal aim, which first dictated its establishment'. The article concluded that a major misunderstanding had occurred between the government's intentions towards free trade and the merchant's response by writing the article. The government never intended to abolish free trade in support of a monopoly:

> We, according to all economists recognise in monopoly the two characteristics: A. The concentration in a few hands of any commercial sector. B. The abuse of this concentration for a hated profit. The one

who argues the opposite having as only aim to disagree with us, limits his idea of monopoly and does not let it escape from the sphere of etymology. Therefore, while we cannot, honestly speaking, call the Grain Administration a monopoly, since it is an establishment for the benefit of the people, the respondent, based on etymology, does not only call it thus for the concentration and labours to present it as hated, but also fails to find in it the second and more essential characteristic of the monopoly.[52]

Merchants lobbied for issues that concerned their own as well as the common good, including that of producers; one such issue was the reduction of import tariffs on Ionian goods in England, and merchants requested the intervention of the commissioner to his superiors in London. In 1844 more than fifty petitioners from Zante requested a reduction of the import duty to the same level as the duty on South African wine, which, they claimed, was taxed less and as a result their island's excellent wine was disadvantaged. The destruction of the crop in 1840 led to 'sad results' and forced the commissioner to send monthly subsidies in aid of the farmers.[53]

Merchants in Kefalonia developed an even stronger argument and convinced the Ionian government to support the grain trade. In 1845 'merchants and ship owners of Kefallinia' thanked the high commissioner in the *Ionian Gazette* for having the prudence to strike an agreement with Russia so that Ionian vessels could continue to trade grain from the Black Sea ports without the extremely high duty of 50 per cent applying to all vessels carrying the Ionian flag; the merchants also thanked the Queen, head of the protective power, in a rare manifestation of loyalty to the British Crown. This public appreciation shows an acknowledgement and a satisfaction that the Ionian State had protected their interests in exchange for such declarations of loyalty and gratitude from the twenty-five merchants and shipowners who signed the thanking letter:

> To the owners of vessels and to the merchants of this island remains only to raise their feeble voice to express their strong gratitude, because in all cases, as in the present one, so much the Protective Nation has shown interest in the Ionian Islands. Your Excellency may accept pleasantly the expression of their feeling and order to render it public through the Ionian press.[54]

Differences of interpretation notwithstanding, merchants supporting a free grain trade argued for the abolition of the grain committee even more aggressively in petitions written in the 1850s, although fewer merchants signed; only grain merchants could mobilize for such an issue during the crisis of the 1850s. Merchants and other Ionians committed to free trade practices and ideas following principles of political economy were aware of social conditions and recognized the importance of regular and adequate grain supplies for social stability and peace. Merchants were also informed about fluctuations in grain prices on international markets during the Crimean War of 1853–56. In September 1853, in an extraordinary sitting in the presence of the high commissioner, the government, showing prudence, discussed whether any and what measures should be taken to prevent a shortage of wheat in the following winter. In the initial statements, the senators acknowledged

> the happy influence which the freedom of Trade has exercised upon the resources of the Country. However well managed the Government Monopoly may have been, the average Price of grain has not been higher, since it was abolished, while a great impulse has been given to commercial enterprise. In all Islands, the amount of Capital, and shipping employed in Trade, has increased; Agencies have been established, correspondence opened ... On the other hand, the old Government Agencies, for the purchase of Corn, are broken up ... and the Senate feels that by interfering, in any way, with private enterprise, it would only cripple the operations of Trade, without any substantial benefit to the community.[55]

By the 1850s it was clear that the tide had turned. Ionian governments rarely expressed such strong commitment to the principles of free trade. The impositions or not of free trade involved the whole economy, the whole 'community' of the Ionian Islands. The senators, though, felt obliged to clarify their position and intentions to the grain merchants, offering their account of the state of the grain markets on the islands and beyond during the turbulent time of the Crimean War:

> The Senate considers in like manner, that if Merchants be not allowed to export freely, what they have freely introduced, and to carry it, if they can, to a better Market, Ship-owners will avoid Ionian ports; and instead of becoming, as they ought to be, under the safeguard of British Protection, the natural Depots of Corn for the neighbouring continent, the Islands will be left to trust to such precarious supplies, as chance or necessity may bring amongst them. The Senate therefore, wishes the merchants of the seven Islands to understand, that the Government pledges itself, most distinctly, and solemnly not to interfere with these operations; upon all these grounds think it expedient that one general system should be adopted; that, that system should be perfect Freedom of Trade, without any attempt on the part of the Authorities to control the operations of Merchants ... The Senate, nevertheless, conceives that it has, still, another duty to perform, in a matter affecting the general subsistence. Trade, in the Islands, is carried on, upon a small scale. Capital is in a few hands. There is little competition. Almost all the Ionian Houses, engaged in the Corn Trade, have their correspondents in Odessa, or Tanganrock; and

few have established relations with other Markets. It might, therefore, happen in the present state of Eastern affairs, that, in spite of every effort, a temporary suspension of Commercial Transactions may occur; Vessels may be detained by natural causes, or by Political events; and from the small quantity of grain usually in Store, one or more of the Islands may be reduced to a state of actual famine.[56]

The recurrent fear of starvation and famine that could result from a war loomed large in the 1850s. The government created a grain fund of 30,000 kg for emergency cases of 'absolute necessity', promising not to interfere with the free trade of grain. Cavalier Jerostathi as president, Signore Elia Vassilachi and A. Dendrino managed the fund and were responsible for policy recommendations to the government and the grain storage. Other islands were subject to the same rules: no intervention in the free market of grain, except in cases of absolute necessity.

The Crimean War made the circumstances of absolute necessity very real. In March 1854, when the ports of the Black Sea and the Sea of Azoff closed, the government prohibited all grain exports, whether imported for consumption or in transit.[57] In 1845 commercial decline had been prevented with the treaty between the Ionian State and the Russian Empire; nine years later though, suspension of free trade on the islands was indispensable if a famine was to be avoided. In June 1854, nine merchants and firms, among them Rallis & Mavroyiannis, Fels & Co., Dimas, Kandonis & Seremetis, G. Marketis & Sons and J. Courage, protested and petitioned the high commissioner in Greek and English 'praying that private individuals may be allowed to purchase and sell grain'.[58] The opening paragraphs of the petition paint an almost idyllic world of free grain trade, where prices are moderate, the quality superior, 200,000 tallers have been put into circulation, bakers and merchants of the 'second class' are doing lucrative business, and practically everyone shares the profits from the purchase and resale of grain in the port of Corfu. The merchants stated diplomatically that their aim was not to criticize the government, which had been forced to 'return to the archaic principle of monopoly' to safeguard the livelihood of its citizens, but to remind them about 'the most vital and precious of industrial liberties', the free grain market. The merchants requested the abolition of monopoly in order to 'avoid the total devastation of many industrial classes and small merchants', and challenged the government to take all necessary measures to 'protect all social classes' without 'destroying totally free competition, which is the soul of industry and the most natural, just and beneficial means for compromising the conflicting interests of producers, consumers and merchants'. This is what the petitioners called their 'spirit'. The petition ended by providing the example of the Kingdom of Naples, and suggesting that the Grain Administration continues its work while allowing for the sale and purchase of grain by individuals. During this period grain merchants intervened in issues of economic policy, promoting their interests under a facade of welfare considerations, and widening their appeal by claiming to represent national interests.

Pressure on the government gained momentum the following year. More merchants petitioned in April 1855, beginning again with a bold statement on the principle of free trade: 'The Protective Power has given to the world the glorious example of the complete and honest application of the principles of freedom of trade, which theory and practice have elevated to unquestionable axiom'.[59] The petition outlined the disadvantageous effects of the 'monopoly' of the Grain Administration. 'Peasants and the class of the poor' were left facing starvation while merchants could not employ the capital they had so arduously and industriously collected. The time had come for the government to suspend restrictions on the grain trade simply by following the merchants' detailed plan for the absorption of the grain quantities by the market without prejudicing the work of the Grain Administration and without loss to the public chest. The grain merchants signing the petition were: Dimas, Kandonis & Seremetis, Cavalier Ioannis Kefalas, N. Lambros, Ralli & Mavroyiani, Nikolaos Paschalis, the firm P. Kremydi, D. Damiris, Fels & Co., Chr. Kremydis, Kapotzari Bros, G. Topalis and G. Manetas. All were well-established merchants, taking the initiative to stir state economic policy towards their interests, emphasizing their long experience in the grain trade.

Ideas about free trade emerged on smaller islands too; in spring 1855 several merchants of Cerigo (Kythera) petitioned for the removal of prohibitions to export oil. In their petition there are impressive arguments on free trade, defending the principle on behalf of the people. Petitioners argued there was little other source of income, following the crisis of the winter 1855 and the shortage of money making it difficult to buy even basic goods. The arguments are very similar to the ones of Corfu merchants: the government's 'commitment' to free trade and the benefits that derived for all people.[60] These petitions show the widespread use of arguments of free trade to promote business interests of grain merchants and claw back the traditional and centuries-old state protection of grain provision in the Ionian Islands. This gradual takeover of the grain market by merchants, who on the one hand untangled from state obligations and on the other realigned with state authorities, is mainly explained by the dominant place of Ionians in the Black Sea grain trade.

Ionian Shipping and the Age of Steam

The citizens of the Ionian State and the vessels carrying the Ionian flag enjoyed British status, the main advantage of protection.[61] This Ionian 'narrow-sea economy' extended from the Ionian Islands in the southern Adriatic to the Ottoman regions in western Greece and the Peloponnese. The Ionian State economic policy towards British imports was particularly favourable; the opening of Corfu as a free port in 1825 facilitated foreign and especially British trade. Ionian economies transformed when large quantities of more competitive British-made cotton goods were shipped to Corfu and from there to neighbouring ports.[62] Wholesale traders, the *negozianti*, and a whole fleet of small boats distributed British-manufactured goods to smaller ports in the region and further south to Patras. In the 1820s, Napier identified the prospects that the Ionian economy offered to British goods, especially after the end of the Greek Revolution; note the basic condition that Napier thought should exist:

> If our protection was well administered, we should find the islands afford a good market for our manufactures; ... the islanders (particularly the Cefalonians) drive a considerable retail trade: for example, a vessel is freighted thus – the owner, the master, the sailors, and all their friends, contribute in money or goods and when the vessel is loaded with a variety of articles, away she sails, a floating shop, directing her course to all places where the master and crew think a demand may be found for any portion of their cargo. If this vessel is large, she goes to Constantinople, to the Black Sea, to Smyrna, to Alexandria, to the coast of Italy &c.; and if small, she runs up a thousand little creeks, and trafficks with the villages on the Greek and Dalmatian coasts: in this way an extensive traffic is carried on. When Greece is able to form a regular government, a great increase will take place in the demands for all the luxuries of life, and English commodities will, by their excellence, beat others out of the market, if the prices of the English goods can, by reduced taxation, be so lowered as to give our superior workmanship a fair competition; in that case, whenever a large English ship arrives at the Islands, the small speculators would club their cash, purchase its cargo, and away they would go in smaller vessels into the various ports and villages on the costs of the neighbouring states, under protection of the British flag, without which these vessels neither feel safe, nor could they show the enterprise they do. The importance attached to the English flag in these islands is exceedingly great, and besides its positive advantages, there exists among the Greeks a great admiration of the British navy.[63]

Ionian merchant captains continued to trade with the Dalmatian and Albanian coasts, with Epirus and the south-western coasts of Greece as a result of the rise in imports of British-made goods.⁶⁴ The government allowed a freer market of grain because of the need to provision the Ionian Islands adequately with grain, but mainly because of the connections and the commercial interests of Kefalonia merchants in the Black Sea grain trade. During the second and third decades of the nineteenth century Greek merchants in Odessa, Taganrog and other Black Sea ports dominated the grain trade. Ionian merchants were prominent among other Greeks in the often-called Anglo-Russian and Mediterranean grain trade.⁶⁵ Around the turn of the nineteenth century (and especially after the 1776 Russian–Ottoman treaty) merchants from Kefalonia and Ithaca, usually with little experience or capital, looked for better business prospects in the Black Sea, taking advantage of the privileged status of their vessels' flag that British protection provided and the business opportunities that the increase of the grain trade opened.⁶⁶ These merchant captains used their status as Orthodox Christians to operate in the Russian Black Sea ports and plugged into the loose business organization of these areas that lacked banks and credit networks. By 1834 there were 150 Greeks in the port of Galatsi, 105 of them being Ionians, while 34 Ionians had founded merchant houses in Vraila, the other large port of the Black Sea.⁶⁷

Ionian ports and their shipping sectors played a vital role in the expanding commercial economy of the islands during the nineteenth century.⁶⁸ The number of Kefalonian ships impressed contemporaries, who talked about 300 vessels of large and smaller tonnage.⁶⁹ The actual tonnage of Ionian ships grew from 21,600 tons in 1820 to almost 56,500 tons in 1860, a more than 160 per cent increase (or from 221 to almost 400 seagoing merchant ships); so contemporary observers were not that off the mark. What is more impressive is the number of people from the island of Kefalonia employed in shipping, estimated to have increased threefold from 1810 to 1860.⁷⁰ The Vallianos family from Kefalonia are early representatives of the Ionian phase of Greek shipping 'tycoons', whose activities show the volume and impact of the firm's trading activities.⁷¹ Born in 1808, Marinos Vallianos, the eldest of three brothers, settled in Tangarok, where in partnership with Avgerinos, another merchant, he established himself as a principal trader and one of the first Greek of the 'diaspora' to combine trade and shipping in a single commercial activity.⁷² Vallianos bought large quantities of grain during the Crimean War at a very low price, and sold them at a very large profit after the end of the war. After opening a house in Istanbul in 1849, his range of activities expanded to London in 1858 and Marseilles in 1869,⁷³ making in fact a very atypical Ionian merchant shipowner since he hardly ever traded in the Ionian Islands, although he never forgot his native land; his statue dominates the main square of the city of Argostoli, a token of appreciation for his donations to the island.

Less wealthy and less connected Ionians involved in the grain trade employed simple business methods such as joint venture.[74] These methods aimed at securing profit with the least risk possible. Due to the profitability of the grain trade, the image of the rags-to-riches captain, merchant of grain, is perhaps not far from the truth, as the several examples of the Greeks in the Black Sea, who started in the manner described by Davy, demonstrate. 'Wandering' in the Mediterranean until the necessary capital is raised and then travelling up to Livorno until the cargo is sold, was the answer to the lack of credit that the anonymity of these merchants entailed. Without the surname of a Ralli or a Rodocanachi, or at least not working for one of these houses, meant that other business practices had to be employed to solve network limitations and lack of information. In 1838, a merchant-ship owner from Ithaca travelled to Odessa, where he bought grain from another merchant (also from Ithaca and stationed there), and tried to guess the price at which he would be able to sell by the number of Ionian vessels in the port of Odessa. Returning to the islands, where his connections lay, he travelled from port to port trying to sell the cargo at the best available price.[75]

A substantial commercial network developed between merchants of Kefalonia and Ithaca, who travelled to the Black Sea to buy wheat and sold it around the Mediterranean – in Trieste, Livorno, and even in some cases London. By the early 1840s merchants in Corfu were importing grain as agents of the principal grain trade houses of Ralli, Rodocanachi, Scaramanga and Avgerinos, as Corfu served as a depot for the storage of grain from the Black Sea and served British commercial and military interests.[76] These houses placed agents in all the principal ports of the Mediterranean, and Corfu was a link in the chain of the grain trade between east and west. There is a clear association and parallel between Corfu port and another *porto franco* (free port) of the time and with very similar characteristics, Livorno, where the grain trade was extremely significant for the port's and the grain merchants' prosperity.[77]

Grain trade was only one of the issues that mobilized merchants to act collectively. In 1837, Filippo Lavrano, Costantino Gerostathi, Costantino Mostra, Tamvaco & Micrulachi, Pietro Economos, Spiridon Dima & Candoni and Forte & Yarak petitioned for the introduction of more bills of exchange into circulation.[78] Without a bank, it was the government that controlled and recorded the circulation of paper money on the islands. Merchants addressed a specific and acute problem and requested the government to act as a banker and to withdraw from the market the silver dollars that were less valuable than pounds. Before the establishment of the Ionian Bank and the issuing of banknotes, money circulation was an object of negotiation. The Treasury in London directed monetary policy of the Ionian State and shipped silver pound coins from Britain after its officials had decided how many dollars they would receive in advance. Such problems were significantly reduced with the opening of the Ionian Bank, the first modern financial institution on the islands, and the circulation of banknotes, but also with the operation of several insurance banks in the 1840s and 1850s that discounted bills of exchange, facilitating trade and exchange. Closely related to the circulation of money and the availability of credit was communications between the islands and other Mediterranean ports, as the age of steam had come to the Ionian Islands and Ionians were quick to appreciate it.

The British administration created an impressive maritime connectivity between the Ionian Islands and other ports as part of an overall reorganization of administrative functions. When Campbell took over in Zante he stressed the need to organize education, combat crime and disorder, and reform the postal service. The ability of the state to send and receive information reliably, and with security for those transferring it, is one of the most crucial and foundational functions of a state.[79] The British in Zakynthos were quick to re-establish communication with Malta, and published the regulation in March 1813, appointing Demetrios Zervos as the director to oversee the communication of the island (and the wider region) with the well-known Maltese packets. The network included the main Adriatic ports, Malta, the ports of the Peloponnese and Western Rumeli. When the following year the British took over Corfu, the headquarters of the postal service moved to Corfu together with the printing press that the British had brought from Malta to Zante. It is clear that for Campbell, and the four Ionians who assisted him, the Post Office was integrated together with the printing press and the Executive Police in an attempt to control information and the dissemination of news, as well as the movement of people. In 1819 the islands were connected to Great Britain through Malta once a month, and with Trieste more regularly, at a cost to the Ionian State of 12,000 pounds annually. In 1826 steam technology was introduced for the first time in the region with the purchase of the steamboat 'Frederick Adam', connecting the Ionian Islands weekly and streamlining communications and the regular exchange of correspondence as well as goods and people. In the following year, 1827, the postal service became a monopoly and tariffs for letters and parcels were introduced. In 1833 the Ionian government renamed the steamboat 'Adam' to 'Eptanisos', and connected it with a number of sailing boats to the regions of the newly independent Greek Kingdom. It was then, in the mid-1830s, that communication between Patras, Corfu and Trieste, but also Zante and Otranto, across the channel to Italy became more regular. Gradually, the Austrian Lloyd steamboat company delivered the mail, while the government responded to calls by merchants for a more convenient schedule to receive their correspondence and to have adequate time to reply and send their letters. The agreement between Lloyd and the Ionian government in 1853 advanced communications even further, connecting Ionian ports more regularly with Greek and other European ports, but also with ports further east that were served by the line Trieste–Smyrna in 1857. In 1859 the first Ionian stamps were printed, and by 1861 the Corfu postal service was handling tens of thousands of letters for the rest of the Ionian Islands and the neighbouring areas.[80]

Communication between the Ionian Islands and London improved significantly when, in 1830, the British Admiralty started a mail service from Falmouth to Corfu. In 1831 the trip from England to Corfu, stopping at Cadiz, Gibraltar and Malta, took twenty-nine days.[81] In the mid-1830s the paddle steamer took seventeen days to reach Malta from Falmouth, and another five days to Corfu; ships waited eight days to collect mail from Athens and returned to Malta and then on to England.[82] The first Ionian steamers arrived in Ionian waters in 1825 and served the Ionian State and its administration, operating as passenger boats. It is striking and a sign of regional integration (and disintegration) that in the nineteenth century Ionians could travel more frequently and regularly form one island to another than one can do today. The Greek Kingdom, on the contrary, did not acquire any steamboats until 1853 when the Greek Steam Navigation Company ordered the steamer *Othon* in England.[83] The first Ionian steamboat cost £25,000 and Commissioner Nugent was enthusiastic about the boat travelling to Ancona and connecting the islands with Italy and the rest of Europe. In his report to the Colonial Office in 1833, Nugent stressed the benefits for the Ionian protectorate when several travellers started arriving in the 1820s: businessmen started trading in the newly founded Kingdom of Greece, and above all the advanced internal communication of the Ionian State, crucial for the administration of each island. The boat was running at a profit, and Nugent's report proposed employing another boat for even better communication and more efficient administration.[84] In 1833 the steamboat operation brought in revenues of £2,867 compared to expenses of £2,188 and most profits came from the passengers' tickets. More importantly than the profits the connection of the islands to Corfu increased the capacity of the Ionian State to rule efficiently and firmly, while offering a modern service to those travelling in the Ionian Sea. The steamboat (and another sailing boat) travelled three times a month to Paxos, Leukada, Kefalonia, Zakynthos and Patras in the Greek Kingdom, and once a month to Ancona. The second boat arrived in Corfu in 1836 and served the Ionian administration for at least twenty years without competition, and at a profit until the arrival of the Austrian Lloyd steamboat company in the 1850s. The Ionian connection of steamers was so important that the Greek Kingdom was totally dependent upon it until at least the 1850s; all communication with Athens travelled to and from Europe through the Ionian Islands.

The Ionian State provided merchants with the means to communicate and trade more efficiently. Ionian merchants responded promptly through petitions to the central administration; in 1837 Tamvaco & Micrulachi, Spiridion Dima & Candoni, Ralli & Mavrogianni, Costantino Mostra, Nicolo Damiri, Candos, Costantino Baldas and others petitioned for the Ionian steamer 'Eptanisos' to take and receive mail to and from Venice. These merchants saw in steam travel the potential for extending their business with more frequent communication with Venice and Trieste. The arguments in the petitions reveal the priorities of merchants, who argued for the need to improve port infrastructure and commercial facilities, to increase the circulation of money and enable the discounting of bills of exchange, and to develop frequent communication services and networks within the Ionian States. At the time, the Ionian government held a monopoly over the areas of economic activity, banking and communications.

In 1844 merchants and bankers expressed their concern about the absence of regular and frequent communication between Corfu and the rest of the islands. The two Ionian steamers that departed from Corfu and called at the other islands carried mail once every ten days. When one of the ships was out of order and docked for repairs, communication was even less frequent since the remaining ship only toured twice a month. Besides those regular trips, communication depended on small trading boats, and was subject to delays and adverse weather. Communication between the islands was not only the concern of merchants and 'bankers': 'very great inconvenience arises from the delay to which letters from England and other parts of Europe, America are subjected from the same cause'. Even with regular Lloyd's boats calling on Corfu, letters did not make it on time to the southern islands 'where much of the trade with the country is carried on'. The petition presented a solution: 'The remedy would be found in making use of the services of the Packets belonging to the Company called "Lloyd Austriaco" in Trieste'. Petitioners were well informed and had acted after receiving Lloyd's commitment: 'Your memorialists are authorised to state that this company would be ready and willing to contract with the Ionian Government to perform the service for all the Ionian Islands on fare and moderate terms. Your Memorialists believe that in employing the boats of the said Company, a great saving of expense would result to the Ionian Government'. Kettlewell, the secretary of the Ionian Bank in Corfu, signed the petition – unfortunately the only banker whose signature is legible. Lloyd's packets travelled to Patras, but bypassed the southern Ionian Islands to the detriment of those islands' trade and to the disappointment of the 'memorialists'. For the first time the Ionian Bank board members and the firm Ralli & Mavrogianni offered the outsourcing of communication services to a private company and argued for the need to integrate further the islands to a frequent communications, information and exchange network. For the Ionian Bank board members, as well as commercial houses in the Ionian Islands, a regular and reliable information network clearly could not rely on the Ionian State services.[85]

For several years after Austrian Lloyd established a line between Trieste and the Levant, calling at Corfu, nothing happened to connect the other Ionian Islands to the steamers network. In 1849, however, 'Ionian, British, and Foreign Merchants, Proprietors and other residents in the islands of Zante and Cephalonia' petitioned the Colonial Office in stronger language than before for the 'immediate and uninterrupted communication' of their islands with the port of Trieste.[86] The export of currants to Trieste and the commercial correspondence by merchants in the grain trade, made the frequent communication for the merchants and 'proprietors' of the islands imperative. The delays not only impeded trade but inflicted serious losses to merchants because remittances of specie (coins) from England and the Continent through Trieste were subjected to 'heavy and extra expenses of transhipment at Corfu'. The last paragraph of the petition encapsulates the incentives, ideology and commercial expectations of merchants from the State:

> Your Memorialists having thus represented the grievances under which they labor at a period when free trade and uninterrupted communication are so universally and advantageously advocated throughout the World, and when all Protection even to the abolition of the British navigation Laws is on the point of being removed, venture to hope that a free communication may henceforward be permitted to take place between the Islands of Zante and Cephalonia, Trieste, and the Levant, by the aforesaid

Austrian Lloyds Steamers, or by those of any other Nation or description that may offer.

The 109 signatures and the argument on free trade are impressive. The anticipated opening of the steamer communications market is evident and the petitioners are keen on obtaining the endorsement of the authorities to an extension of the privileges of Austrian Lloyd to other steamer lines. In the 1850s, competition intensified as these privileges extended to a number of other companies for which merchants in Corfu acted as commercial agents. The 109 merchants and proprietors who signed strived to connect their islands with international trade routes. The petition bypassed the lord high commissioner and addressed Earl Grey, secretary for the colonies – a significant upgrade of lobbying that indicates increased confidence. Petitioning British secretaries was an extremely thorny issue after Mustoxidi submitted a petition to Colonial Secretary Russell in person, and broke with tradition. The petitioners explained the situation in detail, and signed as 'Ionian, British and Foreign Merchants, Proprietors and other residents of the islands'. They petitioned for a better communication of the islands through Trieste and 'between the islands, Patras, Athens, Constantinople, the Black Sea, the Levant and Egypt on the one hand and the Continent of Europe and England on the other', and describe how they suffered both commercially and 'materially'. The cause of their suffering as they informed the secretary of the colonies was that there had been communication by Lloyd of Trieste, which had served the island of Corfu for years, but they had 'been prevented' from linking Zante and Kefalonia with the communications network.

Peter Clarke, the currant exporter from Zante, signed first, and Lindsey, manager of the Ionian Bank branch at Zante, signed last. The powerful politician and supporter of the 1821 revolution, Candiano Roma, signed in Italian as *possidente* (proprietor) and three more signed proprietor in Greek, κτηματίας. Twenty-three Zantiotes signed in Italian as proprietor, at the beginning of the petition, indicating that the petition probably originated from them as they are all on the first page of the list. Forty-four people signed from Kefalonia, most of them merchants, with the last one being the Ionian Bank manager Saunders, which shows the unequivocal support of the Ionian Bank in both Kefalonia and Zante. Unlike Zante, only three people from Kefalonia signed as *possidente*; landowners in Zante were more interested in establishing better communication and markets for their currants. Most signatures are in Italian, reflecting either the preference or the sole ability of the majority of the merchants to write and conduct business in Italian.

The issue of commercial correspondence was essential for the merchants of Zante and Kefalonia, islands with substantial currant exporting trade. The merchants lobbied the Ionian government on behalf of the Lloyds company to transfer their letters for more efficient business transactions. The supporters of the Lloyds company ended up getting embroiled in the politics of the protectorate. A few months later the newspaper of the Reformist Party brought the issue to their front page.[87] According to the article, 'several years ago' the Lloyds asked for the entrustment of the islands' communication, a proposal that was rejected due to the terms proposed. In turn, the company asked that its ships be granted at least the privileges that other companies enjoyed in Corfu, which were considered as warships and were exempted from certain duties, obviously a loss to Ionian revenue. Several years later the same merchants wrote to the colonial secretary and he in turn ordered the Ionian State to grant Lloyds the privileges that would ensure regular and frequent communication between the southern Ionian Islands, Corfu and other ports. Communication was not established, however, for business reasons:

> How come the Lloyds steamers are not travelling around the rest of the islands? Needless to say that this is not in the interest of the company. This Company is a commercial one and intends to profit. It cannot hope to any profit if the competition of the Ionian steamers does not stop, and if monopoly is not established.

According to the *Patris* newspaper the government faced a dilemma, to either relinquish steamship communication to Lloyds, lose control over prices and fire the people employed in the state steamers, or deny privileging the Austrian company and continue as before. There was clearly a competition between Corfu merchants and merchants of the other two commercially important islands, who asked for equal treatment and support for their business interests. In the case of such competition the Ionian government faced the challenge of allowing a monopoly to be established by Lloyds. This monopoly lasted only for a few years. Towards the end of the 1850s and in the early 1860s more steamer companies entered the competition and expected the same privileges as Lloyds, and used merchants in Corfu as their commercial agents. Merchants, bankers and landowners engaged in the export trade exercised whatever leverage they had to convince Ionian State commissioners to serve their interests; in doing so they also shaped Ionian politics towards a fine balance between what was promoted as local interests, the interests of the protecting power and the particular group and class interests of the merchants and other petitioners.

A Brave New Business World

Ionian merchants, intellectuals, professionals and some landowners created mechanisms that advanced cooperation through social and business networks. This process was part of the emergence of institutions of urban governance that included municipal councils, sanitary committees, philanthropic associations and commercial organizations. Commercial and philanthropic associations, the Exchange and the Chamber of Commerce, and also new forms of business organization such as joint-stock companies, created and sustained business networks in international trade but also advanced the cohesion of the Ionian bourgeoisie. Through commercial mechanisms, merchants as an organized body acquired greater power by negotiating directly with the government. These were also sites of socialization; the Exchange and Chamber of Commerce became places where businessmen and government officials could interact.

The Exchange in Corfu was founded in 1843 and the Chamber of Commerce in 1851. The *Borsa*, as Ionians called the Exchange, facilitated commercial and social interactions; merchants and 'proprietors' met in the Exchange, read foreign newspapers and socialized. The 'Society of Merchants', a group of local and foreign merchants dating from 1838, founded the Corfu Exchange; the *Government Gazette* heralded the event as one 'following the example of the most eminent metropoles of Europe', one among many 'establishments that signal the advanced pace of civilisation'. The newspaper congratulated the society for 'supplying themselves with abundant well-known newspapers of the most noble nations, not only to expand their commercial relationships but also to enrich and enlighten their knowledge, through this medium making our condition even better'.[88] In Corfu, merchants and landowners were invited to subscribe to the Exchange by paying an annual contribution. This was the first time an 'official group' of merchants negotiated with the government, as opposed to the guild called the 'Body of Merchants' (*Corpo di Negozianti*),[89] which in 1802 had appointed a single merchant as the representative of the 'merchant body' (*corpo mercantile*).

The liberal reforms of Commissioner Seaton offered the opportunity to different groups to promote their agenda outside the Legislative Assembly. The first group that became organized as a body with elected representatives was the merchants of each island. In Corfu the establishment of the Chamber of Commerce, the main commercial mechanism, created serious fractions among the merchants of the island. On the other islands, the organization of merchants into an elected body was less problematic. In November 1851, just after the resolution of the Senate that established the chamber was published in the *Gazette*, S. Inglessi, a prominent merchant of Corfu and among the founders of an insurance company, wrote a petition representing forty-two merchants of Corfu, expressing their dissatisfaction with the recent establishment of the Chamber of Commerce.[90] Their grievance was not targeted against the body as such, but instead protested that the government had appointed the chamber as the natural heir of the *Borsa*, the Exchange that challenged the legitimacy of the assumption that the older Exchange represented the commercial community of Corfu. New hierarchies emerged among merchants with the biennial publication in the state newspaper of the list containing the 'official' group of merchants.

The interests of Ionian merchants converged in the field of credit relations but occasionally clashed in the field of marine insurance that was part of the banking boom in the Ionian Islands. The Ionian Commercial Code, once in effect in the 1840s, regulated the provision of credit more strictly but also created new hierarchies among merchants. All those practising commerce were obliged to keep accounts for the settlement of disputes in the commercial courts. Before the implementation of the code, contemporaries claimed that even wholesale merchants failed to keep their books 'properly', although this was how a merchant debtor could be declared insolvent. Cases of insolvency and bankruptcy show that creditors enjoyed stronger protection after the introduction of the commercial code since they could control credit networks, claim outstanding debts through legal procedures, and declare debtors insolvent or bankrupt.[91] Merchant creditors determined the dominant code of business ethics by defining the key virtues and vices of contemporary business practice and asserted their authority over debtors in Ionian towns, where negotiations over credit still involved a face-to-face process and the complexities of bureaucratic societies were only beginning to emerge. While ethnicity and religion remained important criteria for advancing credit, there are no cases that show these factors influenced the decision of creditors to declare someone insolvent or bankrupt, whether they were Jews or Christians, locals or foreigners settled in Corfu or the other ports of the islands.

Merchants who controlled credit networks played an increasingly important role in regulating the settlement of commercial debts through their involvement in the judicial process and the commercial courts.[92] In 1856, 'several merchants of Corfu' petitioned the state for a greater role in upholding and implementing existing commercial law.[93] The petition was successful and in August 1857 the 'Law Respecting the Appointment of Assessors in the Sittings of the Commercial Courts and Tribunals' was enacted. Merchant creditors, elected by the chamber in the judicial process of debt settlement, served as assessors in cases where they had personal business interests. One of the most powerful merchants in the Ionian Islands and a naturalized Ionian, Ernest Toole, a currant exporter and manager of the Kefalonia branch of the Ionian Bank, was elected to the post of assessor. As the economic crisis on the islands deepened in the late 1840s and early 1850s, the Ionian Bank became increasingly involved in the liquidation of land for the debts of landowners and tenant farmers. Toole was involved in the process of declaring merchants and other borrowers of the bank insolvent and trying to reclaim part of the collateral. Jewish merchants were excluded, and in an attempt to redress this injustice eight Jewish merchants petitioned the high commissioner to be admitted to appear before the commercial court as assessors.[94] The petition – a rare piece of evidence of the self-perception of Jewish merchants vis-à-vis other Corfu traders – was successful.

One of the most dynamic business sectors of the Ionian economy, and one that connected credit and shipping, was marine insurance. It is also one of the least explored sectors of the Greek economy in the nineteenth century, although it has been identified as an organic sector of capital accumulation and investment.[95] The development of the insurance sector illuminates the early orientation of the Greek economy towards services, namely commerce, banking and shipping, a central issue in Greek economic history. In the Ionian Islands marine insurance companies proliferated between the 1840s and 1860s; this new form of business organization used established networks, between the Ionian Islands and Venice, Trieste or Livorno on the one hand and the Black Sea ports such as Odessa and Taganrog on the other. Joint-stock companies established in those ports attracted capital and fuelled the lucrative nature of the insurance sector. Merchant investors spread business risk by investing relatively small amounts in more than one company.[96] This know-how was transferred to Ionian ports when conditions were ripe, the legal framework was there and capital was available in the Ionian State. In Livorno, Greek merchants were equally entrepreneurial in the insurance sector, following the rise of the Tuscan free port after the defeat of Napoleon; Greeks contributed to the founding of an insurance company in 1817.[97] In 1806 the first marine insurance company was founded in Odessa with Greek–Russian investment, reflecting the rapid rise of the grain trade in the Black Sea.[98]

In Ermoupoli the development of insurance companies followed the growth of the port's activity during the period 1829–46 and shows the parallel trajectories of Greek and Ionian insurance sectors. The two most important companies of Ermoupoli, the 'Ellinikon Asfalistikon Catastima' (Greek Insurance Establishment) and 'Filemporiki' were founded in 1829–30. Twenty years later there were seven insurance companies operating under tough competition from companies in Istanbul and around the Black Sea. By the late 1850s the period of growth for the port of Ermoupoli was over, although decline lasted longer than it has been assumed.[99] In Patras the development of the insurance sector is linked to the rise of the currant trade and the profits arising from it. Six companies were established between 1849 and 1858, providing insurance against the risks from travelling at sea but also against fire.[100] In the Ionian Islands, the development of a vibrant insurance sector reflects the growing shipping sector of the Ionian economy, especially on the islands of Kefalonia and Ithaki. Between 1841 and 1863 eight insurance companies were founded on the islands of Corfu (2), Kefalonia (3), Zante (1) and Ithaca (2). The expansion of insurance companies in the Ionian Islands coincided with the rapid rise of the grain trade and with the role of Corfu as a port for conveying goods to neighbouring markets. In the early nineteenth century, merchants from Kefalonia and Ithaki decided to look for better business prospects in the Black Sea, settled in the ports and benefited from the rapid rise of the grain trade.[101]

Towards the end of the 1850s there were moves towards integration of the insurance sector and the emergence of a 'national' insurance market between Ionian and Greek companies. In 1857, when the fate of the Ionian Islands had not yet been decided, the plan of the Colonial Office to incorporate the islands of Corfu and Paxos as colonies and cede the rest of the Ionian Islands leaked to the press, accelerating developments on the issue of union. In the same year the shareholders of insurance companies in Corfu were contemplating merging with insurance companies in Greece. Twenty-eight percent of the shareholders in these companies come from or were based in Corfu, while sixty-five percent resided in Patras, the centre of the companies.[102]

The Greek consul in Corfu informed his superiors in Athens that merchants involved in Greek and Ionian insurance were thinking of merging their companies into one named 'Greek Insurance'; the idea was so novel that the consul requested advice from the government on 'whether such a union is possible'.[103]

Such enquiries reflected existing partnerships through established as well as new networks between Ionians and Greek companies; in 1858 there were 71 shareholders from Corfu and 60 from Kefalonia who owned shares of the Greek Steam Navigation company, based in

Ermoupoli, and the first major state enterprise, a 'national champion', that failed to deliver.[104] Merchant investors from Corfu and Patras also supported jointly the founding of the 'Elliniki Atmoplooia' [Greek Steam Navigation Company] in Patras, which did not go ahead.[105] The concentration of capital in these companies and the geographical and business networks that coincided between Corfu and Patras can be seen by the fact that 28 per cent of the shareholders in these companies came from or were based in Corfu, while 65 per cent resided in Patras, the centre of the companies. The Ionian Islands and Patras marine insurance companies shared capital, investors and expertise while in the currant-exporting islands, firms such as Toole and Barff & Hancock operated from the islands of Kefalonia and Zante as well as from Patras. This older network provided much available capital for the investment to the insurance companies and shipping. This was the beginning of a national insurance market with the extensive investment of Ionian capital in Ermoupoli and Patras, and indicates an insider's knowledge of business opportunities among merchants and investors not only in the two Greek ports and in Corfu.

The presence of Ionian investors in the Elliniki Atmoplooia, for example, both at its initial unsuccessful launch in Patras in 1853 and at Ermoupoli in 1857, when the company started operating, demonstrates how local business interests and national sentiment overlapped. Still, it is difficult to unveil the key factors, which determined contemporary investment strategies and business decisions. Scaltsounis, a well-known figure and author of books on commerce and business, Ionian politics and the business world, tried to create an Ionian bank under the auspices of the National Bank of Greece. He was also the founder of the insurance bank 'Arhangelos' in 1854, and a principal share-holder in more than one company (in 1868, for example, he owned 100 of the 379 shares in the 'Odysseus' company). The plan entailed the establishment of a competitor to the British-administered bank and was designed to attract the number of merchants required by Ionian law as subscribers of the necessary capital. While the first attempt failed, a more organized move to establish a bank in 1864 – a few days before the union with Greece – earned the support of more than eighty merchants and landed proprietors in Corfu. Paramithiotis, the agent of the National Bank of Greece in Corfu, proved more efficient than Scaltsounis; the timing of the plan, once union had been decided, influenced business strategies and the response of Corfu merchants to the new bank.[106]

Shipping and investment in the Ionian Islands, Syros and Patras became mechanisms through which new groups emerged in Ionian and

Greek cities. The urban societies of Corfu, Kefalonia, Patras and Syros – there was hardly such a dynamic business class as yet in Piraeus, let alone Athens – grasped business opportunities in the development of shipping and commerce, showing a new mentality. While hoarding was the only form of 'saving' before modern credit institutions, in the brave new business world there were new investment opportunities: the calculation of risk and the measurement of value in paper (shares and notes and not only coins). The new professions and social roles of directors and treasurers, the annual general meetings, the publication of the profits and performance of each company in the local newspapers, and, most importantly, the publication of the names of the shareholders, directors and owners, following the spirit of accountability, indicate the new social and economic practice of investment in a modern economic behaviour.

Small shareholders responded to the opportunities presented by increasing shipping activity, the accumulation of capital and the legal framework, the three factors that explain the 'age of insurance' in the Greek economy between the 1840s and 1860s. Participation in the insurance companies secured an income not only for the principal merchant or the ship master, but also for the physician, the notary, the judge, the lawyer, as well as, in some rare cases, for the teacher and the priest or their wives and daughters. In the 1850s, groups of Ionians and other Greeks subscribed to insurance companies and to the bourgeois values of accumulation, calculation and the readiness to take risks while anticipating profits. This new business culture and social attitude to risk and profit could not mask the poverty and hardship that most Ionians still experienced in the 1840s and 1850s.

Notes

1 F. Cooper and A. Stoler, *Tensions of Empire: Colonial Cultures in a Bourgeois World*. Berkeley: University of California Press, 18–19.
2 See, for example, P. O'Brien, 'The Costs and Benefits of British Imperialism, 1846–1914', *Past and Present* 120 (1988): 163–200; and the reply by Kennedy in P. O' Brien, 'European Economic Development: The Contribution of the Periphery', *Economic History Review*, 2nd Series, 35(1) (1982): 1–18; on institutions and colonial rule, see D. Acemoglu, S. Johnson and J. Robinson, 'Institutions as the Fundamental Cause of Long-Run Growth', in P. Aghion and S. Durlauf (eds), *Handbook of Economic Growth*. Amsterdam: Elsevier EB, 2005, 385–472; and D. Acemoglu, S. Johnson and J. Robinson, 'The Colonial Origins of Comparative Development: An Empirical Investigation', *American Economic Review* 91 (2001): 1369–401

3 P. O'Brien, 'Colonies in a Globalizing Economy, 1815–1948', GEHN Working Paper No. 08/04, London School of Economics.
4 Gallagher and Robinson, 'The Imperialism of Free Trade'.
5 M. Lynn, 'British Policy, Trade, and Informal Empire in the Mid-Nineteenth Century', in A. Porter, *The Oxford History of the British Empire*. Vol. 3, The Nineteenth Century. Oxford: Oxford University Press, 1999, 101–21.
6 J. Williams, *British Commercial Policy and Trade Expansion, 1750–1850*. Oxford: Clarendon Press, 1972, 413–14. The policy first applied in 1809 was to bring British goods from Malta instead of Venice.
7 S. Asdrachas, 'Feoudaliki prosodos kai gaioprosodos stin Kerkyra tin epochi tis Venetikis kyriarchias', in S. Asdrachas, *Oikonomia kai Nootropies*. Athens: Ermis, 1988, 57–76, 60; Prontzas and Anoyatis-Pele, *Kerkyra 1830–1832*.
8 N. Koskinas, 'Emporoi kai emporiko diktyo ton Ionion Nison, 1815–1864', Praktika Θ´ Panioniou Synedriou, Paxoi 26–30 May 2010, vols A´-B´, Aliki Nikiforou (ed.), Παξοί, Εταιρεία Παξινών Μελετών, 2014, 411–440.
9 Ionian Islands Blue Books of Statistics, CO 136/1392–1426, TNA.
10 A. Andreadis, *I Enosis tis Eptanisou kai I dioikisis tis Prostasias*. Athens, 1907, 13–15.
11 Guillaume de Vaudoncourt, *Memoirs on the Ionian Islands, Considered in a Commercial, Political and Military Point of View*. London, 1816, 424.
12 Martin, *History of the British Possessions*, 324.
13 'The quantity of oil that two expert labourers can express in a day is estimated at ten or twelve jars of rather more than four gallons each. Sir Edward Baynes informed me, in September 1835, that he was then sending out to Corfu a steam-engine with hydraulic presses, for the squeezing of the olives and with four pair of stones attached for the grinding of corn' – Martin, *History of the British Possessions*, 352.
14 Ansted, *The Ionian Islands*, 50–52.
15 Ibid., 63–64.
16 T. Gallant, *The Edinburgh History of the Greeks, 1768 to 1913: The Long Nineteenth Century*. Edinburgh: Edinburgh University Press, 2015, 245.
17 Andreadis, *Peri tis oikonomikis dioikiseos tis Eptanisou*, 1914 Vol. B, 15.
18 *Journal of the Society of Arts*, 26 April 1878, 480.
19 Bakounakis, *Patra*, 144–45.
20 Bayly, *Imperial Meridian*, 157.
21 V. Patronis, 'Stafida kai agrotiki metarrithmisi', in T. Sakellaropoulos (ed.), *Neoelliniki Koinonia. Istorikes kai Kritikes Proseggiseis*. Athens: Kritiki, 1993, 61.
22 Napier, *The Colonies*.
23 Letter to the editor, *The Times*, 30 August 1833, p. 3, col. b.
24 Davy, *Notes and Observations*, 91–95.
25 Napier, *The Colonies*, 338.
26 Patronis, 'Stafida kai agrotiki metarrythmisi', 78.
27 Nugent to Stanley, Corfu, 16 September 1833.
28 *The Times*, 30 August 1833, p. 3, col. b.
29 *The Times*, 1 July 1833.

30 *The Times*, 30 August 1833.
31 Papageorgiou, 'Dimografika kai Oikonomika Megethi sta Agglokratoumena Eptanisa (1824–1826), me vasi to aporrito arheio tou Vatikanou', *Praktika E' Panioniou Synedriou*. Athens, 1986, 83–94.
32 Despatches, No. 59, 1844, CO 136/122, T.N.A.
33 Kalafatis, 'Paragogi kai emporia stafidas'.
34 Ansted, *The Ionian Islands*, 472.
35 Davy, *Notes and Observations*, 59.
36 F. Karlafti-Mouratidi, *I techni tou psomiou sti venetokratoumeni Kerkyra: to sitari, oi choroi, oi anthropoid*. Athens: Poreia, 2009.
37 Maitland to William A' Court, 23 November 1818, C.O. 136/1107, P.R.O.
38 Burroughs, 'Imperial Institutions and the Government of the Empire', 176.
39 Ionian Islands Blue Books for the years 1827–1863, CO 136/1.
40 Kirkwall, *Four Years in the Ionian Islands*, Vol. 2, 123.
41 *Ionian Islands Government Gazette* (IIGG), No. 119, 30 March 1833.
42 Act LIX, Fourth Session, Fifth Parliament, 10 April 1837.
43 Register of Petitions 1837–1841, CO 136/1041, P.R.O.
44 Petition 31, CO 136/661, P.R.O.
45 IIGG, 8 March 1841.
46 Petition 367, 18 November 1841, CO 136/695, P.R.O.
47 'Notes on the Petition presented by the Merchants of Corfu to His Excellency the Lord High Commissioner, in relation to the Trade of Wheat', 30 November 1841, Petition 367, CO 136/695, P.R.O.
48 Kirkwall, *Four Years in the Ionian Islands*, Vol. 2, 158–59.
49 IIGG, No. 598, 30 May 1842.
50 The article appeared in No. 673 of the IIGG. Unfortunately a mistake led to the number 573 of the year 1842 being inserted in the volume that contains the issues of the newspaper for the year 1843, instead of 673.
51 IIGG, No. 676, 27 November 1843.
52 Ibid.
53 18 March 1844, CO 136/122, P.R.O.
54 IIGG, No. 46, 3 November 1845.
55 IIGG, No. 93, 26 September 1853.
56 IIGG, No. 93, 26 September 1853.
57 IIGG, No. 116, 6 March 1854.
58 Petition 105, CO 136/832, P.R.O.
59 Petition 97, CO 136/841, P.R.O.
60 Petition No. 56, 1855, CO 136/841, N.A.
61 *The Times*, 1 December 1815.
62 J. Chircop, 'The British Imperial Network in the Mediterranean 1800–1870: A Study of Regional Fragmentation and Imperial Integration'. Unpublished Ph.D. thesis, University of Essex, 1997, 71.
63 Napier, *The Colonies*, 15.
64 In 1857 the Greek consul in Corfu was writing in his report to Athens that 'the majority of textiles are re-exported in Epirus, Patras and Messolongi'. Ionian Senate file, Royal Greek Consulate, Document 2842, 1, IAK.

65 The Anglo-Russian grain trade was largely carried out by Greek firms with offices in London, such as the Rallis, Rodocanachis and Scaramagas merchant firms; S. Chapman, *Merchant Enterprise in Britain: From the Industrial Revolution to World War I*. Cambridge: Cambridge University Press, 1992, 246.
66 These 'golden years' of commerce started after Russia occupied the southern territories around the Black Sea and welcomed foreign merchants, among them many Greeks; see Kardasis, *Ellines Omogeneis sti Notia Rossia*. The corn laws in Britain did not allow free import of grain until 1846, when they were abolished to support British agricultural production. S. Fairlie, 'The Corn Laws and British Wheat Production, 1829–76', *Economic History Review* XXII (April 1969): 88–116.
67 V. Kardasis, *Apo tou istiou eis ton atmon, Elliniki Emporiki Naftilia 1858–1914*. Athens: MIET, 1993, 116–17.
68 P. Kapetanakis, 'The Ionian State in the "British" Nineteenth Century, 1814–1864: From Adriatic Isolation to Atlantic Integration', *International Journal of Maritime History* XXII(1) (2010): 163–84. While increased shipping activity obviously benefited some Ionians, the argument that shipping contributed to the well-being of the Ionian population is a gross generalization.
69 Davy, *Notes and Observations*, 63–64.
70 Kapetanakis, 'Shipping and Trade in a British semicolony: the Case of the United States of the Ionian Islands (1815–1864)' *Cahiers de la Méditerranée* 85, 2012, 269-283, URL : http://cdlm.revues.org/6770, 269–83.
71 Harlaftis, *History of Greek-Owned Shipping*, chapter 3.
72 V. Kardasis, *Ellines Omogeneis sti Notia Rossia 1775–1861*. Athens: Alexandreia, 1998.
73 Harlaftis, 'From Diaspora Traders to Shipping Tycoons: The Vagliano Bros'.
74 'The manner in which it is conducted is in every way rude and primitive. Each ship employed commonly belongs to its captain and 2 or 3 other proprietors; and as the purchases of grain are chiefly made with real money, seldom by barter, and never on account or credit, they have to advance the sums requisite, with the understanding that the profits are to be divided between the owners and sailors in certain proportions; so many shares to each owner; so many to the captain; so many to the mate; and to the sailors individually so many, according to their respective merit. The sailors receive no pay nor wages; but they are allowed to take small investments on their own, to the amount of from 15 to 20 dollars' worth, with which they trade on their own account. Many of the ship owners and merchants are said to be quite illiterate, unable either to read or write'. Davy, *Notes and Observations*, 64.
75 Kardasis, *Ellines Omogeneis*, 122–23.
76 S. Gekas, 'The merchants of the Ionian Islands between East and West. Forming local and international networks' in M.S. Beerbuhl and J. Vogele (eds), *Spinning the Commercial Web. International Trade, Merchants, and Commercial Cities, c. 1640–1939*. Frankfurt: Peter Lang, 2004; Chircop, 'The British Imperial Network', 71.

77 D. Loromer, *Merchants and Reform in Livorno, 1814–1868*. Berkeley: University of California Press, 31–32.
78 Petition 162, CO 136/661, P.R.O.
79 Joyce, *The Rule of Freedom*.
80 D. Ladikos, 'Ta tachidromeia sti diarkeia tis Vretanikis Prostasias', *Praktika I enosi tis Eptanisou stin Ellada*, vol. I. Athens: Akadimia Athinon, 2005, 305–17.
81 *The Times*, 5 February 1831, p. 4, col. b.
82 *The Times*, 9 March 1835, p. 4, col. d.
83 G. Vlachos, 'Ta prota Ionika Atmoploia', *Kefalliniaka Chronika* 10 (Argostoli 2005): 491–500.
84 Nugent to Stanley, No. 33, CO 136/34, P.R.O.
85 Petition XXXX CO 136/122, 1844, The National Archives.
86 Petition No. 85, 3 April 1849, CO 136/776, P.R.O.
87 *Patris*, No. 29, 29 July/11 August 1849.
88 IIGG, 29 October/10 November 1838 and 12/24 April 1841.
89 The three merchants of Corfu who notified the rest of the business community to register also took the initiative to devise the rules of operation for the Exchange; ibid., 27 November 1843.
90 Petition No. 1083. 'Signor Inglessi. Differences between the Members of the Borsa', CO 136/801, P.R.O.
91 Emporodikeio 347 and 349; IIGG, 31 March 1856 and 2 September 1861.
92 The jurisdiction of the courts in settling commercial disputes was clearly specified in the commercial code.
93 The index of petitions recorded that the merchants were 'complaining against the administration of justice by the Commercial Courts in these Islands, for want of knowledge and experience on the part of the judges. And proposing that merchants should be elected as advisors in Commercial matters, as is done in all civilized countries. And beg his Excellency that a similar practice may be introduced in the Ionian States'. Petition No. 149, CO 136/1056.
94 Petition No. 400, 8 December 1857, CO 136/857.
95 C. Hadziiossif, *I Girea Selini. I Viomihania stin Elliniki Oikonomia, 1830–1940*. Athens: Themelio, 1993, 44.
96 Katsiardi-Hering, *I elliniki paroikia tis Tergestis*, 454–74.
97 D. Vlami, *To fiorini, to sitari kai i odos tou kipou. Ellines emporoi sto Livorno*. Athens: Themelio, 2000, 163; and Gekas and Grenet, 'Trade, Politics and City Space(s)'.
98 Katsiardi-Hering, 'Ta diktya emporikis diakinisis', in S. Asdrahas (ed), *Elliniki Oikonomiki Istoria IE'-IH'*. Athens: Katarti, 2003, 479.
99 V. Kardasis, *Syros. Stavrodromi tis Anatolikis Mesogeiou (1832–1857)*. Athens: MIET, 1987, 208.
100 Bakounakis, *Patra*, chapter 5.
101 Kardasis, *Ellines Omogeneis sti Notia Rosia*.
102 S. Gekas, 'A Sector "Most Beneficial to Commerce": Marine Insurance Companies in Nineteenth-Century Greek Port Cities', *Entrepreneurial History Discussion Papers* 1 (2008).

103 Ionian Senate Documents, Royal Greek Consulate, 26, Document 2842, I.A.K.
104 Kardasis, *Apo tou istiou eis ton atmon*, 32.
105 K. Papathanassopoulos, 'Naftilia, Kratos kai Politiki sto 19o aiona', in V. Kremmydas (ed.), *Eisagogi sti Neoelliniki Oikonomiki Istoria 18os–20os aionas*. Athens: Typothito, 1999, 122.
106 Paramithiotis came from Ioannina, on the mainland opposite Corfu, and migrated to the port in the early years of the protectorate. He was involved in several business activities, including insurance and banking. These activities were quite profitable, as his will shows; IAK, Notaries 605b, Aspreas Notary Documents, M. Paramithiotis will.

 Chapter 6

State Finances and the Cost of Protection

The finances of colonies and colonized states have not received the attention they deserve by historians of colonialism.[1] Research on colonial fiscal systems offers important insights into the history of the British Empire; however, the establishment of colonial institutions and public finance has often been ignored in histories of British imperialism.[2] This chapter shows the ways in which the finances of the Ionian State were crucial for Ionian attitudes to the protectorate, which did not have control over its own finances but was constrained by the semi-colonial relation with the British Empire. The revenues of the Ionian State from imports and exports duties determined the capability of Ionian governments to spend on public works and promote the modernization project that British commissioners and Ionian liberals shared.

The case of the Ionian Islands shows the fiscal impact and the limits of development in regions under colonial rule or, in the case of the Ionian State, in semi-colonies. The principle of self-sufficiency that guided imperial policy – at least in theory – mattered more for the Ionian State, given the policy of British governments of requiring colonies to pay for their expenses. Such technicalities could not account for the significant transfer of resources and revenues from the southern – and more productive – Ionian Islands to the capital Corfu, and from Corfu to London via the Ionian Bank. The needs of the Ionian State administration dictated the fiscal policy of transfers, but revenues stayed on the islands and were divided very unevenly. On the other hand Ionian State officials failed to collect sufficient revenue to pay for local administration and sustain a project of public works, despite the sophisticated bureaucracy they had installed and the pre-existing bureaucratic structures they found and improved. At the end the bureaucracy cost too much for the revenue they could collect, and the Ionian State took a downward spiral of debt and ever-increasing fiscal needs.

Histories of colonial budgets and administrations stress local variations and 'clusters of enclaves' rather than a uniform picture.[3] The Ionian Islands add to this complex picture since they were operating semi-independently of the British Treasury. As the cost of administration increased in the Ionian State, public spending decreased, especially since public investments such as schools, roads and other services needed maintenance. The inelastic cost of protection had long-term consequences not only for the welfare of Ionians but also for the legitimacy of the regime. While, however, the 'Second Empire' introduced a dichotomy after the 1850s between the increasingly autonomous colonies of white settlements and the dependent possessions, the idiosyncratic Ionian State predated the dichotomy. Classification schemes, some more comprehensive than others, solve the problem – but only partially.[4]

Sometimes it is preferable to listen to contemporaries' views; in 1860 the British House of Commons parliamentary committee discussion distinguished between Mediterranean colonies and colonies generally, especially on the issue of fortifications and other defence expenses. While naval supremacy was considered paramount and indeed non-negotiable if this supremacy was to continue for the colonies outside the Mediterranean, in 'the Middle Sea' the Ionian Islands stood out according to one Member of Parliament, compared to Malta and Gibraltar; the Ionian Islands, which the MP had visited 'not long ago', questioned 'very much the sense in which they could be said to be defensible, even at the present very heavy charge at which we hold the military occupation of them'. The debate that followed reveals the ambiguity and even awkwardness with which the Ionian Islands were considered:

> Do you consider them Colonies? – Not in any sense of the term, except that they are involved in our Colonial administration, and may, I presume, be considered to come within the scope of the inquiry of this Committee. Is there not a stipulation of treaty that the Ionian Islands shall contribute a certain sum only towards their own defence? – I believe there is. The amount, I think, is 25,000 L a year? – I think they did contribute 35,000 L, but it is now 25,000 L, the extra 10,000 L having been remitted by this country. That contribution of 25,000 L is a good deal complained of by the people of the Ionian Islands, or rather by their politicians, whom I should a good deal distinguish from the people, but I think without any reason whatever. It is a very limited sum, and does not exceed one-tenth part of our own charges, and I do not think it possible to conceive that in any political condition they would be subject to a lower charge than 25,000 L for their defences.[5]

Even after the mandatory payment for the cost of protection was reduced from 35,000 to 25,000 pounds, the Ionian Islands were paying more than many other colonies and dependencies, including some extremely strategic ones, such as Mauritius (5,000), Malta (6,200) and Ceylon (24,000). This amount was on top of the imperial expenditure that in 1860 amounted to 280,061 spent on the presence of 4,294 soldiers, the officers and their expenses. Concern with the Ionian budget was of high priority in both Corfu and London since, according to British principles, colonies and dependencies had to pay for their expenses, including those incurred by the British army. After 1797, every occupation army in the Ionian Islands extracted revenues for the funds necessary to sustain it. This was clear from the start of the period of British occupation. When Campbell, commander of British forces, occupied – or 'liberated' – Zante in 1809, he set as one of his priorities the increase of revenues to pay for the expenses of the British army and the needs of the local population. In 1813 he increased revenues from taxes from 54,000 to 80,000 dollars per year. Currants represented 48,000 dollars per year, which was between 50 and 80 per cent of all revenues from exports, a high percentage that remained at these levels during the Ionian State. In Kefalonia the total amount of revenues was 47,500 dollars per year, which came mostly from taxes on currants (20,000). In Lefkada revenue reached 35,302 per year, 9,750 of which came from tithe (a 10 per cent tax on annual agricultural production).[6] The administration received tenders for allocating the collection of taxes and customs to tax farmers for up to six years to fend off insecurity after successive changes in government.

In the 1810s, colonies such as the Cape, Mauritius and Ceylon were expected to pay a proportion of their military expenses in an attempt to balance budgets that were often in deficit, following periods of war;[7] the same principle applied to Corfu and the Ionian Islands. According to the constitutional charter, the Ionian government carried the financial obligation to cover protection costs. The sum was fixed at £25,000 per year, a sum that the Ionian Treasury did not pay during the Maitland administration but was large enough in the following decades to drive the budget into a permanent deficit. The annual income of the Ionian State amounted to no more than £160,000 in very good years. The cost of military protection for fortifications and other defence expenses at times reached a third of Ionian expenditure. For the first fifteen years of British rule (1818–34), when the value of Corfu as a naval and military post was much higher than later in the period, the government spent £190,850 on the Corfu fortifications, £77,206 on the construction of barracks and £46,370 on their renovation – an extraordinary total of £314,426.[8] The staggering amount in relation to the islands' revenues reflected the importance of Corfu for British colonial presence in the Mediterranean. By the 1860s when British forces left the island, they decided that if they could not keep the fortified port then no one should be able to, let alone the Greeks; British forces blew up the main fortifications to neutralize the island and deprive the Greek Kingdom of a secure base close to the Ottoman Empire, and reduce the temptation for another power to seize the island. In 1864 all the money that the Ionian state had spent during the fifty-year period went up – literally – in smoke.

The freeze on spending on military protection under Maitland's fiscal administration led to what appears to be a significant surplus, but this was also due to the way in which the amounts and items of the budget were calculated. In 1823, a few months before his death, Maitland announced to the assembly that the Ionian State finances were sound, with 707,875 Spanish dollars revenue and 590,518 expenditure, leaving a surplus of 117,357.[9] Olive crops failed in Corfu after a year of prosperity, however the 'price for currants [was] high beyond all precedent, owing to the destruction of the currant plantations of the Morea, in the contest in that peninsula'. On the islands of Cephalonia, Zante and Ithaca this meant increased revenues from Ionian exports. The war of independence that ravaged the Morea (the Peloponnese) benefited currant producers and boosted Ionian State revenues, which depended on tariffs collected at the customs office. These revenues paid salaries and provided funds for public works. Expenditure for salaries in relation to revenues grew over the period; consequently, expenditure for public works but also education was scaled back significantly, and had dwindled to small sums by the 1850s. The ability of the Ionian State to carry out public works and improve living conditions on the islands depended on the annual revenue and the available expenditure, but the Ionian government paid substantial sums for British protection that in the end undermined development projects of the Ionian State.

Between 1815 and 1848 the Ionian State spent £456,311 on artillery and defence; of these Britain paid only £148,684 and the Ionian State the remaining £307,627.[10] In 1827 there was a deficit for the first time due to the increased spending on public works that year. By the late 1830s, high salaries and the overall poor financial administration were taking their toll on public finances. This situation led to the gradual abandoning of the public works project that the first commissioners had embarked on, and started to undermine the strong state that Maitland had established.

The growth of government spending by Maitland in the Ionian State contrasts with his record in managing the finances of Ceylon. When Maitland took over, the colony of Ceylon was in the red; the efficient but costly system of colonial administration that North and Dundas had set up was in need of radical reform. Maitland succeeded in drastically reducing government expenditure but he did not unburden the colony of debt since finances remained in the red. In one year Maitland

Table 6.1 The finances of the Ionian State, 1821–34.

Source: Martin, *History of the British Possessions*, 399.

Year	Revenue	Revenue (according to Napier)	Expenditure		
			Civil	Military	Total
1821	125,884		87,178	18,202	105,380
1822	134,666		92,587	17,629	110,216
1823	129,565		100,304	19,844	120,114
1824	156,353	178,689	92,217	33,588	125,805
1827	124,945		143,631	20,983	164,614
1828	168,248	187,118	128,120	31,427	159,547
1829	139,405	171,646	115,311	32,502	147,813
1830	146,922	182,487	117,468	29,287	146,755
1831	131,052		108,386	28,920	136,676
1832	165,519	189,939	115,550	25,428	140,978
1833	144,073		129,145	27,077	156,222
1834	190,791	200,846	128,695	27,821	156,517

reduced the deficit to £60,000 but overall for the period 1807–18 the average deficit was around £100,000.[11] In Corfu finances improved under Maitland because very small sums were spent on fortifications, although the construction of the palace cannot be considered a productive investment; however, it did provide employment although mostly for the Maltese bricklayers and masons. While annual revenue under Maitland exceeded £100,000 his expenditure did not exceed £87,000. Unlike Maitland, Adam spent £154,000 on fortifications over seven years, or £22,000 annually.[12] Under Adam revenue went up to £140,000 per year, all of which was spent besides the £130,000 surplus that Maitland left. Most expenses related to public works but were also for the summer palace ('Mon Repos') that Adam built at a cost of £20,000, a project that, together with the Palace of St Michael and St George, was highly symbolic for British power, seen at the centre of the photograph in the book's cover. The works that provided Corfu with water and the increased number of schools built on the islands consumed most of the budget, with additional expenses for fortifications and other naval and military needs – an overall total of about £50,000 per year. Given that the average annual revenue was about £140,000, this was a large amount – more than a third of it – a sum that the next commissioner, Nugent, brought down to £35,000. Adam left no surplus to his successor but he did assist Ionians in times of need. Napier and the rich inhabitants of the island tackled the minor crisis caused by the grain deficit in Kefalonia in 1824, and provided relief to those who suffered from a devastating earthquake in Leukada in 1825.[13]

In the following years the money allocated for fortifications and other military expenses varied as different commissioners changed the sum that the Ionian State was required to pay; in 1833 only £15,000 was spent, in 1834 the contribution was fixed at £35,000 a year, and remained so until the end of 1843; so for the nine years between 1834 and 1843 military expenditure totalled £315,000. State finances improved under Nugent who, despite inheriting no surplus from Adam, left more than £126,000 in the public coffers.[14] On the contrary, Douglas, commissioner between 1835 and 1841, returned the Ionian fiscal balance to the red; the surplus left by Nugent was all spent and the government under Douglas ended with a large debt of more than £150,000 despite the highest revenues ever collected during the protectorate.[15] Under Seaton (1843–49) the debt increased even further, reaching £216,000 by the end of his term, despite his declared intention in his inaugural speech in the Ionian Assembly to reduce the debt he had inherited from Douglas and Mackenzie.

The cost of military protection was extraordinary for the fiscal capabilities of a small state, whose population depended overwhelmingly on agricultural production and was vulnerable to fluctuations of the olive and currants crops. British colonial officers expressed concerns about the cost and purpose of British military presence but no officer was more outspoken and pragmatic than Napier, Resident of Kefalonia in the 1820s and subsequently military commander of India. Napier believed that eight regiments, responsible for keeping the peace to a rather small population present in Corfu, was a large force. The operation of two custom houses, one in the port of Argostoli and a second in the larger port of Lixuri, health offices and law courts (both ports were important for the local economy and its exports) burdened the budget of Kefalonia but brought in much-needed revenue. Kefalonia was particularly difficult to govern; the Black Mountain, covered in thick forests, provided refuge to those breaking and escaping the law. The main problems, however, were at sea; the countless small beaches and coves made smuggling easy and enforcing quarantine very difficult, what Napier called 'those curses of the Mediterranean'. To cut spending, Napier proposed than Ithaca and Paxos lose their local governments since they were sufficiently close to large islands, Kefalonia and Corfu respectively, and so they did not need separate local governments.

Similar to the principle of self-financed, self-governed colonies, during the first few years of the protectorate's state formation commissioners faced the costs of running each island. Such a plan would most likely raise constitutional issues, given the structure of the Ionian State as the 'United States of the Ionian Islands'. Ionians would benefit from reduced spending by central and local government, but above all Napier's purpose was 'to govern the seven islands without expense to Britain'.[16] He estimated that if the average annual revenue of the state stood at £140,000 per year, this amounted to only fourteen shillings and a few pence to each person in a population estimated at £190,000. The British statesman wondered how he could increase this amount and while in India he always wrote about how much he missed his years in Kefalonia; increasing taxation would harm the economy of the islands. The main challenge in managing the budget efficiently was how to allocate funds for seven local governments (one on each main island) and one general government.

This, however, was a very noble cause. Napier had thirty-seven constables under his command in the 1820s, a small police force for a large population but still considerable given the fiscal capabilities of the island. Kefalonia was peculiar since out of more than sixty thousand people only four thousand lived in the port and capital Argostoli, and a few thousand in Lixuri. Kefalonia, unlike Zante and Corfu, was not only the most difficult but also the most expensive island to govern. Napier addressed these challenges in two ways: firstly, by extending the road network, building roads around the island and through its main mountain passages; and secondly, by extending the operations of the courts, the police, the customs house and the health office. He insisted that no more than a thousand soldiers would be enough, and perhaps more appropriate, for a garrison on the islands, an argument he based on his thirty-eight years of military service. For twelve of those years Napier was inspecting the Ionian militia that the British had created after the occupation of the southern Ionian Islands, the force that was instrumental later on in the Greek war of independence, and its first, very significant victories against the Ottoman army.

Napier's term as resident of Kefalonia is impressive even if it was not representative of the state as whole, not least because few other residents left such a detailed record. Napier's residency also left a positive financial balance; by contrast, the central government's finances derailed in the early 1830s. In Kefalonia between 1820 and 1827 the average revenue was £32,111, while expenses during the same period averaged at £13,385, leaving a balance of £18,726. Scandalously, Napier argued, these funds were paid to the general treasury at Corfu, as part of the contribution collected from all islands to the capital of the Ionian State: 'Corfu has been enriched at the expense of the islands of Zante, Cephalonia and Ithaca'.[17] If the issue was causing resentment to Napier, the resident of British authority on one of the islands, it is almost certain that it was causing resentment among Ionians too. Kefalonia alone sent

£150,000 pounds between 1822 and 1830; in return the central government completed the public works of a lazaretto, two market places, one in Argostoli and one in Lixuri, a prison and two lighthouses, all for a cost of £20,000 pounds (a rather small amount for all those works), leaving £130,000 that was sent to Corfu.

What was all this money sent to Corfu spent on? According to Napier it went to 'extravagantly paid idlers (English and Greek)', a reason why many Ionians in Corfu expressed distress when they heard of Adam's departure from Corfu and his next appointment as governor of Madras. The personal strategies, choices and agendas of British commissioners and residents on each island mattered in the administration of the islands. Napier accused Adam of failing to protect the people from 'the supreme council, the senate, the lawyers, and the feudal chiefs', so he was no liberal reformer, expressing his contempt for the institutions of the Ionian State as well as for the commissioner's policies. Internal divisions among the Ionian elite could lead to violent hostilities and a repetition of the events in the early years of the nineteenth century. Blaming 'Capo D'Istria' (Kapodistrias) for generating factionalism among the Corfu elite to serve Russian interests, Napier plays the foreign intervention card. Maitland's response to placate and lure Corfiots who supported Capo D'Istria was to found an order of knighthood that was called the Order of Saint Michael and Saint George. This was an honouring system that rewarded colonial officers overseas and one of the most prestigious orders, awarded to Thomas Maitland who in turn extended it to many members of his Ionian government, initiating a pattern that was to become common in other colonies with members of the colonial service granting to native elites membership to the order.[18] Napier is cynical and can hardly conceal his sneer at the Corfu elite who were blinded by the creation of this 'noble' and aristocratic order, followed by a 'uniform' that members of the order wore, ridiculing them even further. Corfu merchants and the political class were keen to support the new balance of power since it included a fair amount of new ceremonial pomp, as seen by Maitland's public presence in 1816 and the ball for five hundred people thrown at the 'palace'. Napier argued that Maitland lured many of the potential supporters of Kapodistria by public office and a salary 'by which he bribed a vast number of influential, though needy, families'.[19] Incidentally, this is what Gladstone also thought when he visited and stayed on the islands in 1861, admitting some of the failure of the protection. British rule in the Ionian Islands and the establishment of the Ionian State was a moment when Ionian aristocracy believed they could negotiate their relationship with the new rulers, who changed every few years. For these reasons Corfu elite families offered their support and service to British rule, especially since most of them did not object to Maitland's despotism; according to Napier, not much had changed since the end of Venetian rule.

The financial administration of Napier in the 1820s shows that individual colonial governors could make a difference and that they were crucial in the governance of the protectorate; Napier demonstrated such in his efficiency in managing the island's government. His achievements in infrastructure works and road construction, however, were short-lived; soon after his departure Commissioner Adam (apparently out of personal dislike towards Napier) abolished the system of forced labour for road construction and replaced it with a tax on cattle, a pointless measure given that very few cattle were ever imported to Kefalonia.[20] Nugent, the third high commissioner, attempted to establish a public fund of about £30,000 that was lying unused, for growers to borrow from it, essentially providing a state loan, but opposition to the scheme as we saw in the previous chapter was fierce. His term lasted only three years and his greatest achievement must be the neat financial administration that led to a surplus, also a result of reduced military expenditure.

In the mid-1830s Ionian State finances deteriorated. The failure of the currant crop in January 1833 reduced the government's income dramatically. That year Nugent abolished a duty on imported grain to relieve the poorest inhabitants but as a result revenue decreased by £15,000; the following year a reduction to the olive oil export duty saw revenue plummet from £62,901 in 1834 to a mere annual average of £18,000 in the following five years.[21] However, spending continued to go up; the assembly did not reduce civil list expenditure, the wages of the Ionian State administration and employees, while compensation for relief to olive growers and the purchase of a new government steamer led to serious deficits.[22]

Douglas was concerned about the current accounts deficit, which had grown substantially during his term. The most worrying item was the costs of the contribution to the military protection by the British forces, which had stood at £34,000 since 1834. Douglas in his speech to the Legislative Assembly in 1837 warned that the apparent surplus was false because it included the Pensions Fund and other savings. The 1834 Municipal Finance and Roads Act had taken control of finances away from the hands of central government and opened the way for corruption, even though Napier had claimed exactly the opposite ten years earlier. The good news was that the reduction of custom duties had reduced smuggling and brought more revenue to the treasury. Seaton's reforms in the 1840s are well known for their political implications, the opening up of a public sphere (through the press) but also the Pandora's box for the issue of union, by allowing opposition delegates to set the agenda inside as well as outside the assembly; Douglas was also a reformer, and his reforms during the period 1835–41 met the support of most Ionians in the British-Ionian state. Douglas focused on education, reform of the legal codes and the creation of a financial institution, based on Nugent's previous scheme, which evolved into the Ionian Bank. Development of the judicial system, reform of the Penal Laws, and public health legislation were all part of the commissioner's ambitious agenda. Nowhere was he influenced more, however, by his previous colonial experience in New Brunswick, Canada than in the creation of a bank, especially in the charter of the bank and the conditions for its operation, such as the number of notes to be issued, and especially on the issue of liability,[23] a very thorny and novel issue at the time. Douglas even used the charter of the New Brunswick Bank as a model to propose an Ionian government bank, that he called 'Bank of the United States of the Ionian Islands'.[24] The main and crucial difference between Canadian territories under British rule and the Ionian Islands was competition; the New Brunswick Bank had to compete with other similar banks, even if in different cities, whereas in Corfu, Argostoli and Zante, where the Ionian Bank opened, an exclusive monopoly was created and the Ionian State stifled any similar attempts to create competitive banks.

The Ionian Bank, 'to the benefit and satisfaction of the Ionian community'

In 1826 changes in the operation of banks and the financial sector in Britain allowed the establishment of joint-stock companies for the first time. Banking conditions in areas of British colonial influence such as the Ionian Islands lacked organized financial institutions, which made those areas very promising for British overseas banking ventures. The deteriorating fiscal condition of the Ionian State convinced Commissioner Douglas to invite British capital for the creation of a bank that would enable the Ionian State to borrow to satisfy its fiscal needs.[25] The Ionian Bank was one of the first colonial banks created through a network of London bankers with substantial support from the Ionian State, which used their accounts and expertise in return for banking monopolies in colonies.[26] These exclusive banking rights were essential for the bank's performance, operation and power, since they were granted this monopolistic advantage, a development that would not have happened if the islands had not been under British rule.

Plans for an Ionian State bank emerged when Nugent, commissioner in the early 1830s, created a state fund for lending to farmers to allow them to escape the vicious cycle of moneylending and debt that most people were caught in. The landownership and landholding relations were extremely complicated in the Ionian Islands, and contracts included borrowing on security of the crop in advance of harvest, also known as forward contracts; this was the main way producers secured cash to buy the necessary grain for the year. The plan of Commissioner Nugent in 1833 was to provide loans at low interest (6 per cent) and promote agricultural production to relieve growers from their unbearable debts that carried interest four or five times as much. When the plan to attract the necessary funds from merchants and others in Corfu failed and Nugent was replaced by Douglas the plan took a decisive turn. Soon after he arrived in Corfu and was informed about local conditions, Douglas sent a memo to the Colonial Office where he outlined his plans, ideas and goals for an Ionian State Bank. Douglas gave seven reasons why a bank should be created 'upon Joint Stock principles': (1) the need to provide loans to currant growers and relieve them from their indebtedness to moneylenders; (2) to provide credit secured on property to landowners who needed it; (3) the need to stamp out the practice of '*prostichio*', the forward contracts in the sale of olive oil and currants at very low prices; (4) the existence of the pawnshop-style '*Monte di Pieta*', run by the government and private individuals, whose transactions and capital could be carried out and administered by the bank; (5) the need to alleviate the practice of hoarding due to the lack of a safe place of deposit, resulting in low circulation; (6) the need to transport specie from one island to another, which could be substituted by bills; and (7) the increased need for credit by merchants who shipped agricultural commodities when paying clearances and export duties at the Custom House.[27]

In 1838, after the attempt to attract local capital failed and state deficit kept growing, Douglas approached bankers in London already involved in other colonial banking ventures,[28] with the idea to establish a British-funded bank in the Ionian Islands. Douglas asked Wood, agent of the Ionian Islands in London, to approach certain 'capitalists' for the establishment of the bank with British capital.[29] The agreement was signed on 1 February 1839 on the same terms as the law passed by the Senate in 1837; the bank was set up with capital of 100,000 pounds divided into four thousand shares of 25 pounds each. The origin of capital, overwhelmingly from London, since only eight hundred shares were reserved for Ionian investors, determined the relationship between the bank and the Colonial Office, as well as the dynamics of Ionian merchants and the Ionian State government.

The discounting at the bank of bills, its main operation and source of profit, had already reached 150,000 pounds by 1844. The reports of the directors' board meetings show the activities and performance of the bank and reveal the confidence regarding the continuing success of the bank's operations. The relationship between the Ionian Bank managers, in Corfu and on the other islands, played a crucial role for the finances of the Ionian State. The government depended on the bank through loans and the use of its safe for the state's money. Six months after the bank had started operations, Commissioner Douglas asked for and received a 10,000-pound loan for three years at 6 per cent, a very low annual rate.[30]

British power was grafted on Ionian coins too, revealing the symbolic as well as the actual dimension of its presence. On 28 October 1818, the Parliament of the Ionian State legislated on the new bronze coins. They resembled British coins, with the emblem of the Ionian State on one side with the cyclic inscription 'Ionian State 1819', and nymph Britannia on the other side with a simple but emphatic cyclic inscription 'Britannia'.

Despite the first volatile decade that produced insignificant, yet steady profits, the latter rose dramatically in a 'take-off' during the last years of the protectorate that continued throughout the nineteenth century. With the exception of the short period from 1852 to 1854, when bad harvests did not allow high levels of profit, the performance of the bank can be described as utterly successful; by the time the Ionian Islands were ceded to Greece, the bank's profits had reached £50,000. The London bankers claimed that the bank would bring prosperity to the people of the islands by relieving them of the burden of usury; British officers serving on the islands made celebratory claims that the evils of the society (namely hoarding, idle use of capital and usury) would be eliminated.

A handful of foreign merchants controlled 70–80 per cent of the total currants exports. Three companies, Toole, Barff & Co., and Lucatto controlled the trade, while Barff was involved in the trade of both Kefalonia and Zante, and exported from Patras as well. The bank financed the currant trade as seen in the discount of bills and lending throughout the period, and established a network with influential local people on the islands. The London board of directors chose people they knew (and could trust) as the branch managers, who, together with the superintendent, had the most important role as seen in the reports they sent to the London headquarters. The posts of accountants and cashiers were reserved for English employees, such as Lechner and Thomas, and local merchants such as Ernest and George

Toole. Merchants in Kefalonia and Zante took over the posts of local directors – Lucatto and Bassian in Kefalonia, Barff and Santorini in Zante – all involved in the currant trade. In Corfu, the centre of the bank's operations on the islands, the bank's managers decided they needed people of local political (not just commercial) influence, such as Elia Vassilachi and Dr N. Zambelli, both members of the Senate, and among the most important shareholders of the Ionian Bank. Therefore the bank was fully integrated with – if not controlled – the islands' commercial life, and had some leverage in the state's politics too.

Initially the bank was met with anything but enthusiasm by capital holders in Corfu, who attempted to prevent the founding of the bank with a last-minute counter project; this project lacked both banking knowledge (as the bank's representative in Corfu noted) and the necessary support from the British commissioner, who was determined to establish the Ionian Bank even if this meant circumventing the assembly. The participation of Ionians as shareholders was limited from the beginning of the bank's life, when only 888 shares out of 5,000 (or 15 per cent) were reserved for them.[31] In 1860 the number of shares reserved for Ionians had remained unchanged as the distribution of these shares among Ionians shows. Thirteen out of the twenty-six shareholders lived in Corfu (50 per cent); only three resided in Kefalonia, and five in Zante, while Fels & Co. and a few other merchants had extensive operations in more than one place – Zante, Corfu and Patras. Barff, Lucatos, Bassian and Fels were the only merchants of commercial houses involved in the currant trade. The rest of the shareholders as their titles show were members of the gentry; old aristocrats with substantial income, primarily from land. Among them were the Theotokis, Solari and Rivarola families in Corfu. There were also members of the professions, lawyers and some intellectuals. The example of the Zambeli relatives reveals some of the characteristics of a new emerging group of people with a multi-faceted role in the economy and the state.

Ioannis Zambelis (1788–1856) came from a noble family in Lefkada.[32] He was educated in law in Italy where he became related to the poet Ugo Foscolo and other intellectuals at Pisa University. The artistic circle led him into becoming a playwriter and a poet. On his return to the Ionian Islands he served in the judiciary at the highest level and became a member of the Supreme Court of Justice. He joined the Filiki Etaireia (the Friendly Society), the main association for the preparation for war against the Ottoman Empire. His son, Spyridon, or Spiridione for contemporaries (1810–78), was also educated in Italy, in Bologna and Pisa, and received a doctorate in law. On his return to Corfu, he married the adopted daughter of Woodhouse, general treasurer of the Ionian State, and embarked on the writing of several studies of Byzantine history, which earned him an international reputation to the extent that he is still considered among the founders of the field in Greece. He was elected to the Ionian Assembly, but his scholarly work is what he is best known for. Napoleon Zambelis (1816–[unknown]) also studied law in Italy and France. Better known as a political journalist, he founded the reformist newspaper *Patris* [Country] as soon as freedom of the press was granted to the islands. He was also elected to the Ionian Parliament, and his political career included appointments as secretary of the Ionian Assembly and senator; he was one of the main proponents of the need to reform the terms of British protection. Spyridon, with a hundred and four shares (or 12 per cent) was the principal shareholder of the Ionian Bank, while Napoleon with twenty-five shares (or 3 per cent) was appointed local director of the Corfu branch in 1842.

The Zambelis family were distinguished members of the Ionian bourgeoisie, highly educated, serving in important posts in the state administration, involved in politics and owning shares in a British banking institution; they were also very wealthy. Above all, they acquired a number of new roles as company directors and shareholders. Merchants were either indifferent or unable to obtain shares in the Ionian Bank, especially since the owners of shares were unlikely to sell shares that secured a dividend of 5 per cent per year. The fact that merchants did not choose to purchase shares does not mean that they did not conduct business with the bank, which was there to facilitate trade through credit and the discounting of bills of exchange, the necessary instrument of commerce. Before long though merchants founded their own local-capital companies, focusing on the insurance and banking sector, as well as getting involved in attempts to systematize agricultural production. None of these projects, however, challenged or even competed with the privileged position of the Ionian Bank in the Ionian economy and within the state.

From the 1840s onwards the government funded public works with increased borrowing from the Ionian Bank. The building of hospitals, piers, prisons, roads and drainage projects were all financed with loans from the bank.[33] From its early days the Ionian Bank lent increasingly to the Ionian government with rates of up to 6 per cent for short-term loans (three months) and 5 per cent for longer terms (seven months to two years).[34] The deterioration of public finances in the early 1850s, a period of crisis, is reflected in the levels of state borrowing; between March and September 1852 the Ionian government borrowed £31,000.[35] The board of directors of the British bank were never too keen on lending to the Ionian government but were equally reluctant to refuse, given that the bank operated mainly in the Ionian Islands and enjoyed a special relationship with London, where the bank's board of governors met. It is there that the board stated that the Ionian Bank, was going to operate 'to the benefit and satisfaction of the Ionian community',[36] but not always to the satisfaction of the Ionian State.

The Downward Spiral: State Finances, 1840–1860s

The shift from tax farming to tax collection of customs in the ports created the need for a bureaucracy, making customs employees by far the largest group within government. These changes had political as well as economic consequences, creating a large number of government employees, and of aspirants actively seeking employment. Excessive spending in the 1830s, however, had created another novelty in the Ionian State, the national debt. In the 1840s the Ionian budget was subject to the approval of the assembly. Ionian expenditure was mostly military, that is it was stuck in the eighteenth century or the Napoleonic Wars period at best. In this sense the Ionian State was much more a warfare state than a welfare state, even though the period from 1814 until the 1850s was one of the most peaceful in modern history (with the exception of the 1820s, which only indirectly affected the islands). The state did provide some administrative functions and services – education, health and salaries – while a large chunk of the budget was spent on the criminal justice system and policing.[37]

It would be unfair to say that Commissioner Seaton did not try to reduce expenditure, starting from the military contribution; in 1844 he decided that one-fifth of the annual revenue should be paid into the military budget, which brought the sum to an average of £25,633 a year, still a considerable amount.[38] Commissioner Ward (1849–55) accepted some of the constitutional changes that Seaton introduced, including the right of the assembly to review finances. The assembly proposed cutting the salaries of officials (the civil list) by half; Ward, fearing that such a drastic measure would alienate his supporters and further undermine his position, cut expenditure for public works instead.[39] In 1850, Ward fixed the contribution at £25,000 a year until 1863 (in total £350,000), bringing the overall cost of protection expressed in amounts spent on military expenses from 1825 until 1863 to an extraordinary £1,200,000 – or equivalent to the total revenue of the state for eight to nine years. Most of it was spent on fortifications and renting lodgings, until new barracks were constructed.[40]

By 1860 the Ionian government was facing chronic problems of tax collection; one report talks about difficulties in collecting the rents of property that belonged to the state: 'The charge made for the supply of water by the Aqueduct in Corfu can scarcely be collected except from the garrison and a few public institutions ... The people have never been accustomed to direct taxation – even for lighting the streets, maintenance of roads, or other purposes of public utility'.[41] In the last twenty years of the protectorate, revenue averaged about £172,000, well above the average of the whole period. Taxation was unfair, however, and burdened mostly agricultural producers, although Maitland and the first government had already targeted tax farming in 1818 with the Second Act of the First Parliament. Oil was taxed quite heavily, and the rate increased by three-quarters of a taller to two per barrel until 1825 when it was set at 18 per cent.[42]

The export duty on oil and currants averaged about £60,000 per year. The remaining revenue came from fees for the Health Office (£5,000), by the monopoly of salt and gunpowder, the post office establishment and port dues. By the end of the period, permanent deficits from year to year led to a total debt that exceeded £300,000; one-third of it was arrears of military contribution to Britain that did not incur any interest. Since agricultural production was volatile, revenue was subject to significant variations. In 1858 an extraordinary currant crop enabled the government to pay off £30,000 debt, but in 1860 the oil and currant crops were poor, while import duties from grain remained low at £23,218, and those from general merchandise at £30,993, a total of £54,211. Export duties brought in £27,578 from olive oil and £27,078 from currants, a total of £54,656. In 1860 revenue was only £140,855. Expenditure for the civil list, including interest on debt, cost £62,470, the judicial establishments, courts of justice, police and gaols £25,042, education £12,880 and public works £2,671. The annual charge for military expenditure was £25,000 and total expenditure was £151,187, showing a deficit of £10,000.[43] By the end of the period even increased revenues could not sustain mounting expenses, and a project for public works, education and other items of important public spending had passed into insignificance, especially since the period of British rule was coming to an end and British diplomacy had found a way out of the political impasse of the colonial experiment in the Ionian Islands.

In 1863 the debt of the Ionian State stood at £232,506; or at £220,070 according to a different estimate.[44] Vikelas, in 1868, estimated that the 'Ionian debt' stood at £430,000, without detailing how he reached the conclusion.[45] £90,000 was cancelled by Great Britain in a 'haircut' of Ionian debt when the islands united with the Greek Kingdom. The largest part of the debt included government orders (£75,085) and money borrowed from the Ionian Bank (£70,300) as well as money from pension funds. The very large (for the time) debt was about twice the annual revenue of the Ionian State. In 1863, Kirkwall quotes George Marcoran who suggested to him that the contributions of Ionians to the protectorate exceeded £1 million throughout the period, and were approximately £1,200,000. Andreadis has calculated this sum as being even higher, at £1,395,957,[46] but in any case the derailment of public finances is clear. Until 1849 and the devolution of control over finances to the assembly, the high commissioner in office was ultimately responsible for the monetary resources of the country, and therefore responsible for the large debt that accumulated over the period.

By the end of the protectorate the Ionian State had meagre financial resources and the debt was mounting; this state of finances eroded the state's ability to allocate money for public works and social assistance projects and maintain whatever legitimacy it had gained during the first half of the period of British rule. Revenue collection failed to improve during the period, not only because of volatile exports but also due to smuggling. In 1859 Commissioner Young admitted that the unguarded coasts and ports of several of the islands rendered any attempts to improve revenue hopeless, a situation fiscally unsound and politically 'demoralising'. The cost of some public establishments remained high in relation to the fiscal capabilities of the state, since more Ionians were moving to the cities and requiring assistance or some sort of safety net. Young noted that 'the Foundling Hospital at Zante costs a sum of £2,282 annually, being more than [a] third of the whole Municipal Revenue. It is not to be wondered at, that a Municipality complains of poverty when [a] third of its moderate revenue is devoted to rearing the illegitimate children of the population'.[47] The comments of the high commissioner on the Foundling Hospital of Zante focused on the corruption and maladministration of funds but sidestepped the reduction of funds to the Municipal Authority of Zante. If less than £7,000 was allocated for the needs of the whole island it is clear how far removed, financially at least, the central administration in Corfu was; as a result, the state of public establishments on all the islands deteriorated after years of underfunding.

State Finances and Civil Service

In the few years that Maitland ruled the Ionian Islands he oversaw the creation of a system of government, civil service, administration of justice and financial management that was based on his experience from Ceylon and Malta, but adjusted to local conditions, and aimed to improve a colony's government; this included the organization of public finances too. Unlike his term in Ceylon, however, Maitland was fortunate enough to find among Ionians a number of experienced state officials, who he was quick to employ, realizing that 'importing' more administrators from Britain would be costly and perhaps undesirable. Maitland also introduced a system of pensions for state officials in which up to a third of their salary was withheld for pension contribution, similar to the pensions assured to colonial service officials in Ceylon; while, however, the pensions system in Ceylon had concerned British nationals only, the Ionian State created a pension fund for all its employees, the overwhelming majority being Ionians. In 1830 the Ionian Parliament passed an act that established a fund for the supply of retirement pensions for life to be granted to 'civil functionaries'.[48] The appointment to civil service became one of the most effective tools of control British commissioners used to maintain support for the protectorate.

Commissioners controlled the finances of the Ionian State until the 1840s reforms of Seaton, and exercised this right with little restraint when it came to administering the salaries of Ionian employees to increase their influence among Ionians. Before the 1817 constitution there were 467 employees on the islands, mostly in Corfu, who received a salary of more than 100 tallers, while the total cost of the civil list was £22,687 pounds. In 1819, less than two years later, the number of civil servants had jumped to 570 (22 per cent increase) while the total cost for their salaries had more than doubled to almost £50,000 pounds.[49] Until 1817 the president of the senate, the Head of State, used to receive 1,515 'tallers' – dollars, and the senators 909 tallers; after 1817 their salaries roughly quadrupled, to 6,222 and 3,110 tallers respectively.[50] In 1835 the Ionian State paid £25,513 (or 45 per cent of total expenditure) on the salaries of judges, registrars, assistants and messengers. Money was not allocated equally of course; the president received £450 pounds, judges £320, registrars £120, deputies £78 and messengers £26 and £30 pounds. In Corfu 43 people were employed in the 'Judicial Establishment', in Kefalonia 51, in Zante 44 and in Lefkada 30, and on the smaller islands 43 – in total 211 people, excluding the *'avvocato generale'* or public prosecutor – attorney general, one on each island who received £425 pounds in Corfu, the *'avvocato fiscale'* or minister of finance £300 in Corfu, Kefalonia and Zante, £200 in Lefkada and £150 in Ithaki, Kythera and Paxos.[51]

The expansive policy of the Ionian State when it came to salaries was particularly influential in Corfu. In 1820 there had been 43 people from Corfu employed in the central (or 'general' as it was called) government, while in 1862 there were 156, a nearly fourfold increase that partly explains the bureaucracy that the Ionian government maintained. Other offices such as the Ionian Navy employed Ionians, but also foreigners from Malta, Sicily, Corsica and Naples. These were among the first naturalized Ionians since Ionian citizenship was required for employment in the government.[52]

By 1860 there were many more public employees, and salaries were more proportionally allocated; in 1820 nine government functionaries received 40 per cent of the total civil list amount, while in 1860 fourteen employees received 13 per cent; but in 1855 there were still 2,200 government employees out of a total population of about 240,000, a high number for such a small state.[53] In 1857, £66,251 was spent on salaries, which had increased to £71,000 by 1863. That year, the last of the protectorate, a different calculation brings the total number of state employees to 1,551 – perhaps on the low side, given the different estimates; only 26 of those were English but they earned far higher salaries than Ionians.[54] The 1864 the Treaty of London obliged Greek governments to continue paying pensions to British subjects who had served as Ionian State employees until the 1920s, probably when the last employee died;[55] the repercussions and the terms of the transfer of the Ionian Islands to the Greek Kingdom continued for decades after the merging of the two states, and show the obligations of the treaty for the Greek State. From a comparative perspective, in 1868 Greek State employees (3.5 times the population of the Ionian Islands) numbered 3,553, while the municipal functionaries numbered 5,119 in total.[56]

During the same period, the finances of the Greek Kingdom were for the most part in a deplorable state; this state of finances led some

Table 6.2 Public expenditure, 1847–48.

Source: CO 136/1220

Expenditure	1847	1848
Civil Establishment	53,782	54,405
Judicial Establishment	19,635	19,758
Education	11,281	10,916
Rents of Public Offices	1,569	1,679
Public Works	10,331	5,407
Contingencies and Collection of the Revenue, including the purchase of paper	1,592	470
Contingencies of the General and Local Governments	17,006	13,358
Military Protection	8,441	30,128
Total	123,637	136,121

economic historians locating in 1826 the first default of the Greek State, when the most it amounted to was a provisional revolutionary government.[57] The fiscal problems after independence dwarfed whatever challenges the Ionian government faced in an otherwise sound administration. The general neglect of cultivation in the last few decades before the 1821 revolution, the eight years of the revolutionary war, and the destruction of Morea in 1827 by the Egyptian army presented Kapodistrias, and later Otto, with great challenges. Kapodistrias was aware of how severe the situation was when he said that Greece was a country 'in which the scheme of social order is scarcely traced out, and in which anarchy finds a perpetual refuge in the recesses of the mountains'.[58] The lands owned by Muslims were used as collateral for borrowing from France and Britain during the war of independence. Many villagers, notables among them, had squatted on land left behind by Muslim landowners, and trespassed to such an extent that it was impossible to implement a land distribution system that would be fair, or even to ask those who had occupied land to abandon it. Instead, the state maintained its power through refusing to recognize land ownership unless titles could be verified. The absence of a strong landowning class delayed and definitely changed the course of the political system, which constrained the power of landowners and their involvement in politics, and led to their decline.[59]

The budget deficits were financed by the Ionian Bank, which lent to the Ionian State from the early 1840s onwards. In the Greek Kingdom only 5 per cent of the public revenue relied on the taxation of currants, whereas the Ionian government's revenues from currants were ten times as much. Fluctuations in the price of currants did not therefore affect significantly the Greek Kingdom finances, but they affected Ionian finances enormously. Another difference was the regular surpluses of the Greek Kingdom (every year except 1858), as opposed to the constant deficits in Ionian finances after the 1830s. The course of Ionian finances was related to the changing political circumstances in the Ionian State as well as the international political events of the 1820s, the 1840s, the 1850s and the 1860s, especially those on the Greek mainland. The capacity of the state to collect revenues rested on its administrative capabilities and mechanisms – in the case of the Ionian State, in the customs houses. This is why Napier insisted on the importance of the customs department, which in Kefalonia employed thirty-two staff in the large and smaller ports around the island in Argostoli, Lixury, Asso, Guiscardo, Prinos and Sami.[60] The Ionian State was a large trading economy, and for this reason relied heavily on taxing imports and exports to sustain the cost of administration. This was not elastic, despite adjustments to the amounts spent on protection and defence. The main advantage of the import and export taxes was they were easy to collect, which explains the importance of Customs Offices.

The Ionian State taxed only goods exported and imported, burdening mostly agricultural producers and the urban poor, and privileging British–imported goods to the benefit of its revenues and the merchants of the islands. The Greek Kingdom followed a trade policy that protected all local production, especially in industry, whereas British-Ionian governments followed a regime of high tariffs on all goods exported within the islands as well (given that they were in theory provincial states united under the protectorate). The presence of an indirect taxation oriented regime in the Ionian Islands led to lower revenues, diminishing spending on public works and the ability of the Ionian State to pursue the well-being of its subjects, one of the pledges of British protection.

The initial positive signs of fiscal administration under Maitland benefited from the additional revenues. In the Greek State the sums spent on public works were practically insignificant, and only in the 1880s reached half of the sum spent in other southern European states, and barely exceeded the 2.5 per cent of the revenues. Spending on education drew only 3 per cent of public spending without calculating, however, the amounts spent by municipalities.[61] There are significant differences compared with the Ionian State in the amounts spent on education, and especially on public works and road construction. Similarities emerge, however, on the level of spending on the expenses of the king, similar to the expenses on the high commissioner and his administration, where both states exceeded their capabilities to construct the symbolic and real sites of power, the seats of government, namely the palaces in Athens and Corfu. In the period 1833–42, three items (public debt, military spending and the king's expenses) took almost 80 per cent of annual spending.

These funding capabilities determined the mode of governance and tested the structures of the Ionian State. The resident controlled the Executive Police, the Health Office and the Post Office, and presided over the municipal council either in person or through his secretary. In Kefalonia between 1818 and 1845 police directors and inspectors hardly made a decision without reporting to the British resident, who through his contacts in the police force controlled public affairs and oversaw issues of public order and security, while his officers followed public and private meetings; he was also responsible for issues of public health that were important for the safety of the whole population. The regent worked closely with the resident, who read the correspondence with the Senate in Corfu besides his private correspondence with the commissioner. In this way the Kefalonia government were well informed about the security and public affair issues discussed and approved by the Senate, as well as about all legislation passed. The resident, always a British military officer, controlled the island's garrison and could declare a state of siege.[62] Until 1848–49 when the Electoral Law came into effect, liberalizing the electoral process and freeing it from the grip of commissioners, elections were under the direct control of the resident who exercised fraud at will. Despite the pledges of British officers and writers about the elimination of corruption, there was extensive corruption between the resident and the chief medical officer, especially during the period of the cholera outbreak in Kefalonia in 1850, when there was extensive abuse of power. These examples amount to a pervasive culture of corruption at a local level, and on the island of Kefalonia especially, both at the level of appointing state officials and consequently at the level of administration.

The municipal council appointed five committees that served the role of ministries: the first one was responsible for agriculture, public instruction and public industry; the second oversaw commerce and shipping, the third the market police; the fourth was responsible for public order (policing) and the benevolent establishments; and the fifth was responsible for religion, and 'moral and public economy'.[63] The duties of these committees overlapped, forming a particularly dense network of control, surveillance and rapid reaction, in case of disorder, insubordination or even worse, revolt. The first commission supervised a body of inspectors for damages to crops by flocks, called *'picchetti'*, who succeeded in constraining smaller pastoralists, not the well-connected ones, whose flocks continued grazing unsupervised. In education, Marinos Solomos doubted the ability of the committee to manage public instruction, following the recommendation of school principals. The General 'Archon' of Education, the principal government official, did not always communicate with the local (island) official. Solomos, who served as director of education in Kefalonia in 1845, was well aware of the issues that schools, students and teachers faced. He commented extensively on education, clearly an important field of public policy, arguing that the bad condition of schools induced students to go to Athens (or elsewhere), spending 25–30 tallers per month; and he hardly had any good things to say about the Ionian University. The Kefalonia treasury spent £12,000 on public instruction, but Solomos stated that 'there are schools without students, and teachers without schools', and he condemned false registers of students that meant the local government received more funding from Corfu.[64] By the end of the period, Ionians from all classes expressed grievances that evoked frustration rather than hostility towards British rule. The surplus of most years in the 1820s, 1830s and early 1840s gave way to the deficits and cutbacks from the late 1840s to the early 1860s. This course of public finances and change in the spending capabilities of the Ionian State explains Ionians' discontent, as people from various classes had additional reasons to challenge British rule and support union of the islands with Greece.

Notes

1. One exception can be found in J. van Zanden, 'Colonial State Formation and Patterns of Economic Development in Java', *Economic History of Developing Regions* 25(2) (2010).
2. L. Gardner, *Taxing Colonial Africa: The Political Economy of British Imperialism*. Oxford: Oxford University Press, 2012.
3. L. Benton, *A Search for Sovereignty: Law and Geography in European Empires, 1400–1900*. Cambridge: Cambridge University Press, 2010, 37.
4. Davis and Huttenback divide the empire into four categories: Britain itself, colonies with responsible government, all other colonial possessions regardless of the state of constitutional development, and India. L. Davis and R. Huttenback, *Mammon and the Pursuit of Empire: The Political Economic of British Imperialism, 1860–1912*. Cambridge: Cambridge University Press, 1986, 338.
5. Reports from Committees, Volume XIII, 1861, xvi–xvii
6. Stavrinou, 'Stoicheia tis dimosias zois sta notia Eptanisa'.
7. Manning, *British Colonial Government*, 468.
8. A. Dousmanis, *I en tis Ioniois Nisois apostolic tou Lordou Gladstone*. Corfu, 1875, 461.
9. Speech of Maitland to the Assembly, 5 April 1823.
10. Jervis, *History of the Island of Corfu*, 322.
11. Manning, *British Colonial Government*, 461–62.
12. Kirkwall, *Four Years in the Ionian Islands*, vol. I, 120, 124–25.
13. Chiotis, *Istoria tou Ioniou Kratous*, vol. II, 16–17.
14. Kirkwall, *Four Years in the Ionian Islands*, vol. I, 134.
15. Ibid., 152.
16. Napier, *The Colonies*, 31.
17. Ibid., 39.
18. D. Cannadine, *Ornamentalism: How the British Saw Their Empire*. Oxford: Oxford University Press, 2001, 86–88.
19. Napier, *The Colonies*, 50.
20. Kirkwall, *Four Years in the Ionian Islands*, vol. I, 121. In East Asia, systems of coerced labour were retained or rebuilt in both British and Dutch colonies; Bayly, *Imperial Meridian*, 10.

21 Cottrell, *The Ionian Bank*, 12.
22 *The Times*, 24 April 1841, p. 6, col. b.
23 B. Walker, *A History Banking in Canada*. Toronto, 1899, 23.
24 Cottrell, *The Ionian Bank*, 21.
25 S. Gekas, 'Banking Expansion, Success and Failure in the British Mediterranean; the Ionian Bank, 1840s–1930s' (with A. Apostolides) in John A Consiglio et al. (eds.), *Banking in the Mediterranean: A Historical Perspective*, Farnham: Ashgate, 2012, 175–196.
26 Cottrell, *The Ionian Bank*.
27 CO 136/76, Draft Act, No. 154, Douglas to Glenelg, Corfu, 22 August 1836. National Archives, London.
28 This was the Farrer-Wright group; Cottrell, *The Ionian Bank*.
29 BLPES Ionian Bank, 9/4, History of the Ionian Bank Ltd. Prepared by R.H. Fry.
30 Ionian Bank Archive, 3/1 Minute Books and Corporate Records, Letter of 25 November from the Manager of Zante, recorded 14 December 1840. British Library of Political and Economic Sciences, LSE.
31 Emporodikeio [Commercial Court] files, 699, I.A.K.
32 Chiotis, *Istorika Apomnimonvmata*, vol. 6, 418–23.
33 Cottrell, *The Ionian Bank*, 200.
34 Ionian Bank Archive, 3/1 Minute Books and Corporate Records.
35 Cottrell, *The Ionian Bank*, 268.
36 IIGG, No. 478, 10/22 February 1840.
37 It is interesting that in England it was only after 1829, and more so after 1856, that professional police forces and state prosecution officers appeared; until then most functions of the English criminal system had been administered by local governments and parishes; R. Harris, 'Government and the Economy, 1688–1850', in Roderick Floud and Paul Johnson (eds), *The Cambridge Economic History of Modern Britain. Vol. I. Industrialisation, 1700–1860*. Cambridge: Cambridge University Press, 2004, 204–37.
38 Paximadopoulou-Stavrinou, *Politiografika Ionion Nison*, 51.
39 Kirkwall, *Four Years in the Ionian Islands*, vol. I, 204.
40 Progoulakis, *Anamesa stin timi kai to chrima. I Kerkyra sta chronia tis agglikis kyriarchias 1814–1864*, 73.
41 Ansted, *The Ionian Islands in the Year 1863*.
42 Progoulakis, *Anamesa stin timi kai to chrima*, 64.
43 Ansted, *The Ionian Islands in the Year 1863*, 471.
44 Kirkwall, *Four Years in the Ionian Islands*, 335–36, Vol. I; for a different estimate, see G. Dertilis, *Atelesforoi I telesfori? Foroi kai exousia sto Neoelliniko Kratos*. Athens: Themelio, 1993, 128.
45 D. Vikelas, 'Statistics of the Kingdom of Greece', *Journal of the Statistical Society of London* 31(3) (Sept. 1868): 287.
46 A. Andreadis, *I Enosis tis Eptanisou kai I dioikisi tis Prostasias*, Athens, 1907, 16.
47 IIGG, No. 441, 28 November / 10 December 1859.
48 Moschonas, *Agnosta kai spania monofylla*, 23.

49 G. Papanikolas, 'The Ionian Islands: what they have lost and suffered under the thirty-five years' administration of the Lord High Commissioners sent to govern them : in reply to a pamphlet entitled "The Ionian Islands under British Protection"'. London, 1851, 54.
50 Andreadis, *I Enosi tis Eptanisou*, 12.
51 Resolution, Second Session of the Fourth Parliament, 5 June 1835.
52 Chiotis, *Istoria tou Ioniou Kratous*, vol. A, 261.
53 Progoulakis, *I timi kai to chrima*, 78.
54 Kirkwall, *Four Years in the Ionian Islands*, Vol. I, 306.
55 A. Antoniou, 'Dimosionomikes epiptoseis tis enosis tis Eptanisou', *Proceedings, I enosi tis Eptanisou me tin Ellada* ['Fiscal Consequences of the Union of the Ionian Islands with Greece', *Proceedings, The Union of Eptanisos with Greece*], vol. I. Athens: Academy of Athens, 2005, 551.
56 Vikelas, 'Statistics of the Kingdom of Greece', 272.
57 C. Reinhart and K. Rogoff, *This Time Is Different: Eight Centuries of Financial Folly*. Princeton, NJ: Princeton University Press, 2009, 12. The authors date the first default of Greece to 1826.
58 McGrew, *Land and Revolution in Modern Greece*, 95.
59 G. Dertilis, *Istoria tou Ellinikou Kratous* [History of the Greek State] *1830–1920*. Vol. 2. Athens, 2006, 697.
60 Napier, *The Colonies*, 499–500.
61 K. Kostis, 'Dimosia Oikonomika', in Kostas Kostis and Sokratis Petmezas (eds), *I anaptyksi tis ellinikis oikonomias to 19o aiona*. Athens: Alexandreia, 2006, 301–2.
62 Solomos, *Geniki Dimosionomiki tis Kefalonias*, 29.
63 Ibid., 39.
64 Ibid., 42–45.

Chapter 7

BUILDING A MODERN STATE
Public Works and Public Spaces

The Roads to Modernity

The design and execution of public works projects is at the heart of debates on colonialism and development across time and space.¹ Public works are also central in histories of the relationship between colonizers and colonized – the colonial encounter – and between any regime and its subjects as they can either generate legitimacy, discontent or both. Colonial architecture was never only about aesthetics or pragmatism, and the ordering of colonial cities, in India for example, started even before the formal imperial takeover.² The roads that British administrators built in Kefalonia figure prominently in arguments about the legacy of British rule in the Ionian Islands, and understandably so.³ Napier oversaw the construction of an impressive road network following the method pioneered by McAdam, a Scottish road trustee, who after experimenting concluded that roads should be constructed with broken stone and ditches dug for draining the road bed; in 1815 he was appointed surveyor general of the Bristol roads, and his method spread fast. The first roads constructed according to the McAdam method were in Kefalonia in 1822, in the United States of the Ionian Islands; in the other United States, of America, road construction according to the McAdam method began in 1823. Napier was so impressed by McAdam's innovation that he wrote a memoir, just like McAdam, and adjusted the method to suit the characteristics of the Kefalonia landscape and its workforce.⁴ The technique was so successful that by the late nineteenth century all roads in Europe were constructed according to this method.⁵

The public works project, an essential characteristic of the modern state, distinguished the Ionian State from the Greek Kingdom. The inability of Otto's regime in the Kingdom of Greece to transform the territory into a modern state is evident in the inability to build a communications and roads network that would allow the state to penetrate into areas and populations indifferent or even hostile to central authority.⁶ The two states, though, shared the conviction to modernize cities and societies, to elevate them to what was perceived as the appropriate European standard. State formation in the first two decades of the Ionian State was linked with colonial projects of architecture, engineering, road and infrastructure development that stamped the Ionian Islands with the British imperial seal. The construction of palaces (two in Corfu) and the public buildings on other islands had a considerable impact on public finances. Road construction, however, was the most extensive, visible and costly of a number of public infrastructure works that changed the colonial landscape of the islands. These projects involved the application of modern ideas, such as those about sanitation in the operation of markets, for example, and the need to incarcerate people in humane conditions, but they also defined the role of the state towards its citizens. Such interventions in the urban landscape carried highly symbolic and functional value; the palace, the Ionian Assembly, hospitals, prisons, markets, banks and roads still shape the urban and rural landscape of the islands, at least those that have survived the disastrous bombardments and earthquakes of the twentieth century. Although the passage of time has erased some of these symbols of modernity, the historical record is indisputable. Public works of infrastructure and communication integrated the islands' country population into urban markets, transferring even more power to the commercial, administrative and military hubs of Corfu, Zante and Argostoli; roads lowered town–country transportation costs and were supposed to improve the income of peasant families. The building of closed markets where trade would be more regulated, with standardized weights and measures and increased circulation of money, were all measures beneficial for the Ionian economy and aimed to produce a sense of order. Trade was also streamlined by removing the circulation of different currencies that had been hurting the peasants and poor consumers the most.

The first colonial officials of the Ionian Islands – Maitland and Adam in Corfu, Napier in Kefalonia and Fitzroy in Zante – started the transformation of the cities and islands under their command. Delivering on pledges of a colonial modernizing project required large amounts of public spending since roads, ports, sanitation and water systems were absent or at best rudimentary on all the islands, even in cities with a long urban history such as Corfu and Zante. In the first three decades of the Ionian State, spending on public works increased from 11 per cent of revenues and peaked at 28 per cent in 1844. The construction of the canal in Santa Maura was such a project. The taxation imposed on the inhabitants distinguished electors resident in the city (*corpo dei Sincliti abitanti nella Citta*) and merchants whose ships would benefit from the canal and would have to pay different tolls depending on their tonnage. This law, in effect from April 1820, came after the uprising of many residents against the new taxation, and confirmed the privileges of the urban commercial groups at the expense of the country's population who only in theory benefited from lower transportation costs.

There is no doubt that public works in the British protectorate improved the daily lives of Ionians, at least in the first few decades of British rule. Most villages of the islands were connected to each other, and especially the towns with paths, while wagons had been almost totally absent before the new roads were built. In 1806 when the Russian army and navy conducted the Second Archipelago (Aegean) cartographic expedition in the Mediterranean and the first survey of Corfu, the commanding officer suggested that there was little concern about an enemy invasion since all roads leading from the coasts to the interior were in such a bad state that it would be impossible to transport artillery and therefore a survey of the country was not really necessary.[7] Transportation of goods was conducted with mules, horses and donkeys. In 1824, when road construction began in the Ionian State, there were only twenty miles of roads on all islands; by 1842, the year when funding available for such works peaked, 366 miles had been completed, transforming the landscape of the islands, extending the reach of the state to the country, and increasing the ability of people to transport and communicate. Even today, most roads follow the same British plan of the nineteenth century.

Until the period of British rule, forced labour was imposed mostly on the rural population and on those who could not afford to buy their obligation off. For Marino Salomon, one of the Ionian intellectuals who shaped colonial governmentality in the Ionian State, although forced labour in road construction was imposed on the people they nevertheless realized the benefits of their toil, and the fair manner in which it was administered, and were therefore content.[8] It is unlikely that many Ionians shared similar feelings. Beyond contemporary perceptions by even some of the most acute Ionian commentators, forced labour in road construction enabled the colonial Ionian State to reorganize power relations in the country. The 'progress' of the Ionian protectorate, however, was a project that Ionian governments found it impossible to sustain; commissioners and Ionian government politicians sounded less and less convincing from the 1840s onwards, and many Ionians of all classes criticized the government for failing to keep its promises.

The construction of a dense and efficient road network improved the ability of the country's population to bring their crops to the ports, and improved communication between distant and previously inaccessible villages. It was the plague outbreak of 1815–16 that had highlighted this need for roads to Maitland and his staff. The federal system meant that responsibility for public works (and road construction) moved back and forth between local and central government, and suffered from dwindling Ionian State finances. The draining of Chalikiopoulos Lake, close to Corfu town, initiated by the French imperial army, aspired to rid the population of the malaria-infested waters. In Kefalonia, de Bosset was the first British officer to design and begin road construction, between 1810 and 1814. Until that time people from the country had rarely communicated with the port of Argostoli. The road network in Livatho, the plain in the south-western part of the island, improved the livelihoods of the villagers and the economy of the region, according to the notables of the villages, who offered a sword as a token of their gratitude to de Bosset.[9]

The project of road construction offered a first-class opportunity for the military staff of the Ionian colonial government to 'map' systematically the population of the country for the first time; it is telling that the registers used for road construction were the same as those compiled for the 1817 constitutional charter to form the Ionian militia. In 1822 the Senate resolved that road construction in the suburbs and country of Corfu would begin on 15 May every year. All residents were obliged to work, with the option for those who could afford it to buy their obligation off. The authorities divided the population into six 'classes' with the respective obligations depending on whether or not they possessed animals, and if so, how many. The Senate updated the resolution three years later, dividing the population to ten 'classes'; for those who could afford to could buy their obligation off the ratio of days of work to the amount in dollars was four to one (200 days of work 50 dollars, 160 days 40 dollars, all the way to the tenth 'class' of residents with 20 days obligation for 5 dollars). A day's work was estimated at 30 oboli, and the project included the registration of all men able to work by the Executive Police.[10]

Forced labour combined with modern means of registration and classification. The obligation to work was expressed in monetary terms and was supervised by the police; road construction associated forced labour and supplemented the meagre income of the country's population, especially during years of bad harvest. The government offered paid labour to the poorest willing to work on road construction at 14 oboli per day 'to every man worthy of working well', 11 oboli for those aged over 66, and 9 oboli for children 10 to 15 years old. The concept of child labour (at least if aged over 10) and other limits on who was able to work did not exist – only different pricing. A rare announcement followed this measure in unusually political language, probably the first such statement in a non-bureaucratic language that addressed the people of the country in the nineteenth century:

> Residents of the country! While the administration never neglects the smallest thing to improve your fortune and construct all the more roads in the country of the island, offering you the greatest benefit which at no previous age none of the previous administrations thought to execute. The incomparable benefit which you above all classes will feel, must motivate you to aid in such a valuable work by going many of you in the days you are called to work forced labour with your turn, work by which your greatest happiness derives.[11]

This was essentially a form of poor relief; in England, parishes employed the poor in road maintenance after the new poor law was introduced in 1834.[12] In conditions of poverty the first government of the Ionian State turned road construction from an infrastructure project into a policy of supplementing the income of the rural poor with paid labour. This policy offered employment (even for limited periods) combined with punitive surveillance measures that the police, the village notables and constables were responsible for: 'Every man that will notify the Executive Police that a registered obligated worker is missing will not work for six months as a reward'. This was an important incentive targeting those escaping forced labour as the government 'out-sourced' the disciplining of the country's population. From a practical point of view the order also ensured that the majority of the men were coerced to work. There were special privileges for those in charge of supervising; all officials of the militia, village notables, the constables and their fathers and children were exempted from the obligation to work on the roads. For those who did dodge their forced labour obligation the penalty was 25 oboli, unless they presented a certificate of illness, signed under oath by the notables, the priest and two militia captains.[13] These measures drew dividing lines among the country's population between those in charge of maintaining order – the notables, the constables and the militia captains – and the rest of the population. These new hierarchies emerged through the supervision of road construction, and the role of notables as assessors of harvests reinforced existing hierarchies of properties and landownership, establishing additional relations of dependence to landowners.

Road construction created new hierarchies but also brought unexpected consequences; 1824 was a year of bad harvest and thousands of villagers worked on Napier's extensive and ambitious project of constructing roads hoping to secure the much-needed additional income. Fields were left uncultivated, and in the winter some people, especially children, died of hunger. Napier intervened and helped residents of Argostoli, Lixuri and the surrounding rural areas by requesting grain from Corfu and organizing food distribution to those in need.[14] The developmental projects of the Ionian State could stumble upon the adversities of the Ionian agricultural economy. Still, Napier's record in Kefalonia is impressive; within a few years he completed 134 miles of roads in a rugged and mountainous terrain, most of them suitable for carriages, at a cost of £17,849. In 1885, William Bruce, a British traveller, marvelled at the work that Napier and Kennedy had achieved: '134 miles of road over a rugged mountain range more than 5,000 feet high, only 21 miles incomplete when control was taken from his [Napier's] hands; 113 miles fit for carriages, 96 miles having been cut or blasted through solid rock, as well as Bridges, Conduits, Mile-Stones and Guarding parapets. This vast work was executed by labour on the corvee system and at the marvellously low cost'.[15] Napier mobilized the population through the forced labour system that required everyone to work one day every three weeks. While people could chose not to work and pay instead, Napier used the system very strictly and justly, and set an example by assigning to the road-building project the resources and manpower of the resident, engineer, servants and soldiers.[16] The forced labour system was abolished in 1830 and road construction continued with money from a road fund created by the Road Act of 1828.

Subsequent governments, however, did not carry out infrastructure improvements or maintenance. Reports dating thirty years after the construction of roads in Kefalonia urged central authorities to take action. Kefalas, a local official in Kefalonia, stressed to the resident of the island that the roads around Lixuri had become impassable due to neglect; decay of the wooden bridges that linked Lixuri with the countryside and the villages was extensive. Growers submitted petitions highlighting that only traces of the original roads could be discerned. Villagers from the Lixuri area complained that the sums they paid in tax for road maintenance were wasted as they could neither reach their fields regularly for work nor use carts to bring back their produce.[17]

After the initial success of the 1820s the Ionian government gradually came to a compromise forced by the realities of fiscal pressures and the fear of extensive discontent in the country. More frequent access to the port cities meant more interaction between the people in the countryside and the urbanized Ionians; in some ways the gap narrowed but in other ways the differences were more visible; the wealth of some British and Ionians must have startled the poor peasants who entered Corfu for the market or for a religious holiday. Road construction and maintenance returned to the government's agenda in 1840 when Douglas and the Senate passed an act for the construction and repair of the roads in the country. The act called on all those living in the suburbs and the villages to work on the roads but no more than four miles' distance from their home.[18] By the 1840s the project of road construction was considered a partial success, but 'discontent and murmuring were the natural result'. The government ended statute labour and introduced a road fund with an additional tax on oil and currants, but the fund was hardly sufficient to complete roads according to schedule, much less to defray the expense of construction. Douglas returned to statute labour, given the dire state of Ionian finances, but restricted the obligation to branch-roads, seasonal labour and distance close to the villages of forced labourers especially during the sowing season. Flexibility and concessions worked: 'The result of this method is said to be very prosperous, and the extension of the roads by means of it rapid and great. In Corfu, where the most progress has been made, the use of carts has become common'.[19] Further correspondence confirms the dissatisfaction and frustration of locals, producers and landowners, who 'although they pay a large amount annually for road repair, their condition does not allow the transport of their products by carts'. Bridges were particularly damaged, and up to hundred villagers of several villages requested the building of a stone bridge instead of a wooden one. During the decade 1849–58 Ionian governments spent a mere £20,850, or just over £2,000 per year, £15,403 of which was spent in Corfu – £9,779 for pubic buildings and their maintenance expenses and £6,624 for road construction. Of the remaining £5,447, Zante received £3,866 and Kefalonia a mere £1,581. No sum was reserved for any public works on the other islands, which explains why when the Ionian Islands joined Greece there was not a single horse cart to be found.[20]

The road construction project of Ionian governments makes for an interesting comparison with the other new state in the region, post-revolutionary King Otto's Greece. In 1864, year of unification of the Ionian State and Greece, a mere 1,359 kilometres of road had been completed in the Greek Kingdom, two-thirds or about 800 km of which were in the Ionian Islands, constructed during the period of the Ionian State. In the years between 1828 and 1852 road construction in Greece under King Otto's governments had barely reached 128 kilometres, hindering domestic trade and the creation of a national market,[21] and limiting the ability of the Athens government to control distant and remote regions effectively. Instead a coastal trade developed around the ports of Piraeus, Patras and especially Hermoupoli, at the heart of the commercial economy of the new state. Otto's regime proved unable or indifferent towards constructing a basic communication network. The absence of such a network meant that the impact of the state was minimal and the influence of local warlords, chieftains and notables continued. The Ionian State, on the contrary, from its first years had generated a programme of constructing a road network and facilitated efficient and standardized communication within and between the islands with steamships. This had allowed the state to reach all islands and achieve an efficient administration.

Besides road construction that connected the villages with the islands' capitals, infrastructure works were an almost exclusively urban affair; the precedent of the canal in Sta Maura that failed when it sparked the uprising of 1819 was far from a promising start. The mole and aqueduct in Zante was the first such public project.[22] The two works served different purposes; firstly they served the export economy of the island, and secondly the well-being of the city inhabitants, who benefited when the 'sweet water' came from Mountain Scopo. The Parliament anticipated that the new port works would 'regenerate' commerce in Zante, while abundant water supply in the city would make life much more comfortable. The government introduced an additional tax of 2 per cent on the value of the currants exported from the island, effectively transferring the cost to the producers since merchants were able to negotiate lower prices when buying the crop and incorporate the additional export tax within the selling price.

Colonial Cityscapes: Designing and Ordering the Ionian City

When French general and military historian Frédéric Guillaume de Vaudoncourt visited Corfu in 1815, he discovered water could only be collected in cisterns or drawn from wells; as a result the city's population suffered from lack of adequate supplies of water.[23] Schemes that provided first Zante and then Corfu with water substituted the centuries-old cisterns and were essential in improving living conditions. In Zante, Resident Charles Fitzroy supplied the town with water in the early 1820s, an example followed by Commissioner Adam in Corfu a few years later. Fitzroy later (in 1850) defended his approach to the administration of the protectorate, contrasting his term in Zante and the rule of Napier and Nugent with the 'atrocities' under Commissioner Ward.[24] The task of supplying water in Corfu was much more formidable than in Zante since there were no springs close to town and water had to be brought from the village of Benitsa, around twelve kilometres distance. The project cost about £30,000,[25] indicating both the magnitude of the work and the fiscal ability of the Ionian State to carry out such public works, before the founding of the Ionian Bank and the potential for lending that the British financial institution brought. Some travellers were impressed already in the 1820s: 'The city of Corfu has gained through the British. It has become much cleaner and better lighted. Houses, colonades, and palaces have been built. Many English shops have opened, and for ready cash every luxury and comfort of life may be procured'.[26] These changes in Corfu and other Ionian cities did not go unnoticed by British and Ionians alike.

Improving water supply and living conditions addressed the urbanization of Corfu, and the government's intervention to regulate house building interfered with some property owners who formed an illegal syndicate to prevent urban expansion. In May 1825 the government, after being informed about written agreements between proprietors that prevented the building of houses, shops and other establishments, passed an act arguing that such obstacles were inappropriate in a city surrounded by walls and fortresses, and wholly inadequate to follow the increase in the population of the city and to stop unclean and unhealthy conditions. To this end the government ordered that all disputes and agreements on building extensions, more floors and alterations had to go through the civil courts through the 'method of *punti interlocutorie*', a questionnaire that both parties had to answer.[27] This is the first time the expert knowledge of civil engineers, a rare profession in the Ionian Islands, was introduced in a dispute-solving institutional mechanism, the civil court, and reflected the need to regulate construction of private buildings.

British travellers instantly saw and recognized Zante – as well as Corfu, even more perhaps – as a quintessentially Mediterranean port. Two things caught the eye of well-travelled British visitors: dress and architecture. Holland, when he arrived in Zante in 1814, noticed immediately

> an assemblage of people ... uniting the Venetian with the Greek in their external costume and manner; a body of soldiers of the Greek regiment, their dress at this time little altered from its national character; in other parts of the area the red-faced English soldier, curiously contrasted with the natives of the country, in the feature and expression of his countenance as well as his military dress; and in addition to these, Corsican and Calabrian soldiers, sailors from various parts of the Mediterranean and a few Greek merchants, habited in the fashion of continental Greece. This singular national mixture is found in many of the Mediterranean ports, as will be familiar to the memory of all who have traversed the streets of Gibraltar or Malta.[28]

The frequency of earthquakes had enforced a different architectural style from that of Corfu. Small, usually one- or two-storey houses were the norm. Not even government buildings or that of the resident governor and the collector of customs or those of *signori* and wealthy foreign merchants could be distinguished – at least from the outside. The centre of the town was the square of St Mark, named after the one in Venice. An arcade of jewellery shops was full of 'heavy and clumsy articles, which show the degree of taste possessed by the inhabitants'.[29] The principal coffee house, one the town's social hubs, was also located in the square. Here, the town's bourgeoisie, lawyers, physicians and merchants spent their time. Next to the square the principal guard of English soldiers was also located, demonstrating British authority ready to protect the seat of the representative of the British protection, the resident governor. Next to St Mark's Square the market of the town, or Piazza dell' Erbe, was located: 'a narrow, dirty lane, where the country people expose their vegetables, fruit, eggs, cheese, etc. for sale'. A symbol of the old social hierarchies and a manifestation of changing social customs, the Caffe de' Nobili was also located there. Murray noted that it was named after a time when only the noble citizens were admitted, but 'now they have become more liberal and people fond of market-cries, dirt and peculiar smells, may go wither without a pedigree. I could not forbear visiting the spot a few times'.[30] 'Recorded' conversations among those frequenting the coffee houses are supposed to have been about international politics: 'on the short-sighted policy of Russia; on the electors of Germany whose health is still drank by these kind gentlemen; on the good qualities of the King of Naples; on Napoleon's arrival in England e&'.[31]

Throughout the nineteenth century and especially during the period of British rule, British and other European writers left impressively detailed descriptions of their visits and travels to the Ionian Islands:

> The landing at Corfu is not unlike that at Gibraltar. The same low, narrow, dirty entrance, and total absence of decent accommodation. The same crowd of bipeds and quadrupeds, the same mixture of fish and oranges. The crowd, seen at the water gate of the city, does not diminish as we advance further into the great thoroughfares. We, at first, pass through a kind of market, a bazaar always so full of human beings, and stalls of fruit and vegetables, that it is really difficult to get on. And if, as is the case, picturesque effect is produced by an admixture of every conceivable style of all kinds of objects, natural and artificial, living and dead, very few places in the world are superior to Corfu. The narrow streets of this part of the town combine all that is most striking in Gibraltar, Genoa, Algiers, Bologna, Turin and Marseilles. Arcades, under whose shelter all classes meet; gloomy recesses, open, indeed, towards the street, but so black in their own darkness, that the Greek or Jew seated within is as

Figure 7.1 'View from the New Fortress'. View of the port, the closed market and the British ships and smaller boats. Kerkyra, 1856–60. Fotografikes Martyries. Mouseio Paleopololis – Mon Repos, Kerkyra. Eforia Archeotiton Kerkyras, Elliniko Ypoyrgeio Politismou kai Athlitismou.

invisible as the spider in its web; houses of rich Greeks, where the rooms are luxuriously furnished, but which can be visited only by entering dirty, shabby doors, and climbing dirtier, shabbier staircases.[32]

These scenes of exotic disorder in the public and private sphere, in the image as well as the soul of the city, is a trope in several accounts of Ionian urban landscape.[33] Corfu and the other Ionian islands became increasingly part of the 'Grand Tour', as British travellers increasingly spent time there. Usually a part of a larger trip to the 'Levant', the Ionian Islands soon captured the imagination of Victorians as one of the first 'exotic' stops en route to the East after leaving Trieste. Travelling increased, facilitated by the comfortable and fast steamers that Lloyd of Trieste provided.[34]

Arriving in Corfu by boat was clearly as exhilarating in the nineteenth century as it is today. The tall, narrow and colourful houses, the two impressive fortresses, the old and the new, on the two edges of the town, and the well-protected port survived the destruction of the city's fortifications by the British army in 1864; the scene is not far from what a nineteenth-century traveller would have seen from the Austrian Lloyd steamer, on its first stop en route to the Levant. This was the image that captured Mousson as the steamer approached the port of Corfu: 'Between these rocks lays the town, as if imprisoned, with the houses reaching the seaside, having only little space, as if to get some air'.[35] Mousson noted the importance of the port for Mediterranean trade, and described the dimly lit shops of small traders and the seedy taverns. This image, however, of the town as a maze of narrow alleys cutting through unusually tall buildings does not only appear in visitors' and foreigners' accounts. A local newspaper, on the occasion of a small fire, describes the town in very vivid colours, while arguing for improvements by the authorities, urging them to adopt safety measures to prevent a catastrophic fire: 'This town, which on the outside appears majestic, on the inside presents the most appalling condition. Houses are crammed one on top of the other, many of them reaching up to five or six floors. Streets are narrow and winding. Dirt flows everywhere. There are many districts in which no sunlight goes through whatsoever, and because of that, neuralgia and paleness are the benefits for those living there, especially for the women'.[36]

In 1836 the Zante municipal authorities passed statutes that demonstrate the intention of the town's authorities to organize urban society according to Western models. The Ionian State created commercial spaces that included the regulation of the market, the introduction of weights and measures, and granted licences to traders on designated stalls for the sale of goods, following regulations of the previous periods, especially of the Septinsular Republic. The building of markets in Corfu, Argostoli and Lixuri served aesthetic as well as functional purposes, and regulated prices to the town, its sites and its functions. Measures for the cleanliness of the streets and houses, from human waste to garbage, were introduced, as were measures for the restriction of prostitution, which was common in Corfu, the busiest port of the islands and the naval base, but with little effect. Measures for the opening hours of wine shops and for keeping order in the streets, especially during the carnival days, when disguise provided an excellent opportunity for ridiculing those untouchable to social criticism during the rest of the year, continued the long tradition of similar Venetian regulations. This restriction of economic and social life by the state and the intention to harmonize Ionian society according to Western notions was not limited to daily activities. Notorious for their late nights of fun and noise until early morning, Ionians were considered predisposed to bad behaviour; and this is why, for instance, tobacco shops closed at

Figure 7.2 Views of main street in Corfu. The signs of two hotels can be seen on the street in the top photograph. Kerkyra 1856–60. Fotografikes Martyries. Mouseio Paleopololis – Mon Repos, Kerkyra. Eforia Archeotiton Kerkyras, Elliniko Ypoyrgeio Politismou kai Athlitismou.

eleven, because apart from selling tobacco they also attracted persons of 'suspicious character', as it was specifically mentioned.

Ionian governmentality included the ordering of cities. A series of decrees of the Corfu municipal council during the 1840s and 1850s aimed to Westernize Ionian urban society and change the dominant British views on Greeks and Ionians as dirty, disorganized and uncivilized; it was instead the practical application of the ideology of British rule on the organization and control of society, and the assertion of power by those who embraced this ideology over those who failed even to comprehend it. The establishment of a state organized according to Western norms and ideas became more sophisticated with the construction of prisons, lunatic asylums, hospitals and other controlled places of modernity (such as the poorhouse and, of course, schools), but also through state mechanisms that provided the institutional and ideological context; the urban elite contributed and ran these institutions willingly. The Savings Bank, the Society for Improvement of Agriculture, the Reading Society, the Ionian Society, sanitary committees and philanthropic associations and initiatives offered sites for a coherent pursuit of interests and positive interaction with the British administration and the resident on the islands. The British-administered state performed the traditional role of surveillance and punishment, instituted by laws and decrees, and applied by the police. The Ionian State adopted the British model of social organization and the practices that derive from it (surveillance, rationalization, and 'progress'). Ionian liberals administered philanthropic associations and activities at a time when worsening the fiscal situation of the Ionian State did not allow it to act decisively and improve living conditions in the suburbs or many of the town's districts, or even in the poorest villages. The state encouraged philanthropy not only because it confirmed the role and presence of British colonial rule and concurred with its ideology but also because of the inability of the state to respond to the demands of Ionians for education, better living conditions, and especially a viable income from the agricultural produce and the commercial activity of the port.

There was more to Corfu than the bustling port and the narrow, dark alleys; this image of the town captured the imagination of contemporaries and dominates their accounts. Another image concerns the transformation that took place during the period of British rule that altered the urban landscape of Corfu, Argostoli, Lixuri Zante, Lefkada, Gaios (in Paxos) and Vathi (in Ithaca). In every Ionian port new modern buildings of aesthetic as well as public value and utility reflected the era of British influence. The palace of St Michael and St George on the Esplanade in Corfu, an impressive building built by Maitland that became the seat of the lord high commissioner and the government, signified the power of the new rulers and their intention to remain for some time. In Kefalonia, Napier modernized the towns of Argostoli and Lixuri, building moles, courthouses and markets.[37] Napier, in his own book of memoirs and discussion of the islands' administration, without concealing his contempt for Adam, the high commissioner at the time, maintains that Kefalonia provided an extraordinary opportunity for development, while Argostoli transformed during his time as resident, to everyone's satisfaction except Adam's.[38] Civic buildings, new streets, squares and mansions, as well as port facilities, impressed Napier's brother when he visited: 'Order, diligence and frugality in public offices and public expenditure, good roads, handsome buildings, schools, commodious quays for the landing of merchandise, a prison, two lighthouses, increased shipping and more widely extended commerce'.[39] Henry Napier of course was hardly an objective observer.

A new market was built in Lixuri in the same building as other 'public services' such as the court. Central and local governments regulated commerce and justice by concentrating them in the same space. Similarly, the buildings erected in Corfu during the 1830s and 1840s changed the town's urban landscape. A new prison (1835), a lunatic asylum, hospitals (both in Corfu and Kefalonia), branches of the Ionian Bank (on all three islands), the new Exchange (1843), and of course the Ionian Academy, the University of Corfu, right in the heart of Corfu town, indicate the construction boom in new buildings of functional and symbolic value. British architectural interventions reflected the image of a new order by constructing in essence a 'new town'.[40] This new order expressed a belief in structuring the town along rational lines, with new streets as an extension of the prominent Esplanade, and the older streets of the Saint, the Waters and the street of Merchants in Corfu. Sanitation and well-structured buildings and streets were in absolute contrast with the maze of dirty narrow alleys of the 'old town'. The public utility of the buildings and their function as instruments of a more effective central administration was expressed by the construction of the market in Corfu for the sale of foodstuffs, finished in 1834 but planned as early as 1820.

The British military command of Corfu gradually abandoned the traditional and principal function of the town's walls during the years of *Pax Britannica* in the history of the Ionian Islands. This enabled the transformation of fortifications and barracks into prisons, schools, hospitals and lunatic asylums – all buildings that served social needs. This shift started in the 1840s with the gradual degradation of Corfu as a naval/military station, and the increasing importance of Malta in

PUBLIC BUILDING AT LIXURI, CONTAINING THE MARKET SHOPS, COURT HOUSE, AND LANCASTRIAN SCHOOL; COST £4223.

Elevation of the North Front of a Building erecting in Argostoli to contain the Public School, The Assembly Rooms, The Exchange, a small Amateur Theatre, and the "Monte di Pietà." Estimated Expence £6000.

Figure 7.3 Napier's plans for a multipurpose civic building (top) and a market in Lixuri (bottom). Napier, *The Colonies*, plates 8 and 9.

serving this function. The transformation of urban space followed ideas that originated in Britain and gained popularity on the islands among intellectuals, liberals and British officials who catered for imperial needs. Contemporaries perceived buildings of public utility as serving specific roles, but also as architectural achievements and contributions to Ionian development and progress, elevating Ionian urban space to standards similar to British or European ones. In Douglas's rhetoric, for instance, cleanliness and order were synonyms for a 'civilized' society, and it was precisely what Ionian society was lacking. Douglas's views reflect the debate that was taking place during the same period in British towns, already with inhumane conditions for the working classes of the industrial revolution.

One British observer, Ansted, identified the 'ethnic' origin of the urban population based on prevalent Victorian ideas, infused by anti-Greek sentiments of content:

> Of the inhabitants of the town and suburbs, it may be said that they form three very distinct groups. One third consists of Jews, who resemble their brethren elsewhere, but are a superior class with fewer distinguishing marks. Another third is an admixture of Turks, Maltese, Italians, Albanians, Dalmatians and many other races; all indeed, of that mongrel class, for which the shores of the Mediterranean have been notorious from time immemorial; these are, as it where the followers of the British garrison. They live largely upon them, and are a pestiferous race that cannot be got rid of. They do not give credit to anybody. Only the remaining third can pretend to be Greeks: but even these are not Greeks of pure descent, being greatly mixed up with the remains of the old Venetians. On the whole, they form a tolerably respectable and not unimportant body. They are intensely national, often without or against apparent reason.[41]

In Corfu, the *Epirotes*, the merchants who originated from Epirus, established their own church, the *Panagia ton Xenon* or the 'Madonna of the Foreigners'. Just like the Christian Orthodox merchants of Livorno or Trieste, in Corfu where there was a predominantly Orthodox majority, merchants of a different origin established their distinct identity (and thus network), by building the church right at the heart of the marketplace. Among the trustees of the church was Spyridon Dimas, a member of the Kandonis and Seremetis partnership.[42] Despite the large number of Roman Catholic merchants, there were no obvious differences among Orthodox merchants; however, no identification of the merchants as a group can ignore the presence of Jewish merchants.

Corfu and its Jewish History

After the fall of Venice, the republican French took over the Ionian Islands in 1797 for a brief period of eighteen months and granted citizenship to all residents of Corfu, regardless of religion. The constitution of 1803 offered (limited) religious freedom to minorities such as the Roman Catholic rite and the Jewish religion, and declared the Eastern Greek Orthodox religion as the religion of the state.[43] In 1808, under French imperial rule, a special edict was issued forbidding the harassment of Jews and reiterating the commitment of the French authorities to protect the Jewish population. Shortly before Corfu became part of the British Empire in the form of the administrative and commercial capital of the Ionian Islands, in 1812–14, the Jewish merchants in Corfu amounted to 26 per cent (36 out of 139).[44] The constitutional charter of 1817, granted to the Ionian State, confirmed this tolerance of Jews and Roman Catholics.[45] The period of British rule, by contrast, is considered the continuation of a 'downward trend ... when Corfiote Jews, though in theory equal to Greek Christians, were subject to more ill-treatment than they had been at any time in their past as old imperial protection for Jews', while during the Ionian British protectorate 'the incidence of anti-Jewish outbursts rose dramatically; there are widespread accounts from the period detailing the desecration of cemeteries, the disruption of Jewish funerals by jeering onlookers, and the escalation of the Eastertime physical assaults that occurred annually on the island until World War II'.[46]

One of these accounts is in the *Jewish Chronicle* from 1858, hardly an unbiased observer: 'The position of the Ionian Jews is that of the man between the two stools ... The Jews only exist to give sport to their Greek task-masters'. Besides the significant but almost ceremonial stoning of the Jewish district every Easter, this assessment of British rule is gloomier than the actual experience of most Jews who lived in Corfu. There is no evidence that the outbursts 'rose dramatically' and no incidents were mentioned until 1861, when the vandalism of the Jewish cemetery was quickly condemned by the Orthodox Archbishop of Corfu, and was attributed to the publication of the first Jewish newspaper. In fact a careful reading of the *Jewish Chronicle* from 1845 reveals a very different picture, since the Jews are

> those of the higher class merchants, and trade chiefly in cloth and linen; the middle class consists of artisans and for the greater part tailors. The lower classes are the most numerous; they are dealers in old clothes, porters, and sailors. They have, in the midst of a very poor population, attained to a very comfortable circumstances and even riches. The Greeks hate them and seize every opportunity for injuring and ill-treating them; so that their situation would be very pitiable, if the English did not take them under their protection. Twenty years ago, no Jew dared show himself in the streets during the holy week; but things have changed since that time.[47]

Another contemporary observer offered a fairly positive account of the British protectorate:

> The town is almost exclusively occupied by foreigners and Jews. The principal merchants and shopkeepers are Englishmen, Russians and Sicilians; the petty traders are Maltese and Italians; and occupying every position, from highest to lowest, are the Jews. Yet, although despised and insulted for centuries, and even at the present day wearing a distinctive garb, the Jews are now aptly revenging themselves on their oppressors; for since British rule has caused life and property to be held sacred, the power of the money dealers is beginning to manifest itself and they are by degrees monopolising the whole of the retail trade between the Islands.[48]

The word 'monopolizing' may be too strong, but the description of the omnipresence of Corfu Jews in the city's commercial life is accurate, as seen by the percentage of their participation in the port's economy.

The main question, however, of whether or not Ionian Jews saw their rights curtailed during the period of the Ionian State, remains. It is not appropriate to compare an institutional setting such as the Ionian State with the previous period of French occupation, or with the even lower status of the islands and their people as a dominion during Venetian rule. Ionian Jews saw their political status improve after 1864, when every man over 21 years old had the right to vote, whether Jewish or Christian. The union of the Ionian Islands in 1864 meant that for the first time since the emergence of the Greek Kingdom significant Jewish minorities were living in Greek cities; understandably Jews as heterodox and heterolingual minorities were sceptical towards the policies of their new state. This was not, however, the first time that Ionian Jews had to renegotiate their status and protect their community in the transition from one political authority to another. It has been argued that this change almost by itself 'brought the Greek state against the dangerous combinations of the elements that comprise Greek anti-Semitism'.[49] At the same time the transition to the Greek State also brought Ionian Jews into the political process at a national level for the first time, and 'forced' the Greek State to consider its policy on minorities. A much more historical approach is to examine those first few years of participation in the political process, because they are extremely important for understanding the transition.

During the period of British rule, living conditions for Corfu and Zante Jews as well as for the rest of the urban population improved. The Jewish quarter in Corfu was considered very vulnerable due to the bad hygiene conditions, but also due to popular superstition;[50] but when running water came to Corfu and Zante in the 1820s it was accessible to all and therefore reduced the death rate of the population. For everyone who lived in Corfu, whether Christian or Jewish, harsh living conditions and the constant threat of disease were equally serious dangers as any superstition that could escalate into violence. Community organization was important during such crises; the Jewish population shielded itself against the cholera outbreak in 1855–56, when Jewish authorities set up their own assistance facilities against the disease, as the Sanitary Commission praised in their report after the disease had ebbed. As the commission itself admitted, the Jewish community formed a philanthropic committee and adapted a building to serve as a cholera hospital; their measures were remarkably effective, despite the fact that their district was one of the most populated and, thus, vulnerable areas of the town to contracting the disease;[51] no such organization had existed in previous centuries.

In the 1820s the law to regulate the legal profession dictated that only indigenous or naturalized Christian Ionians over 21 years old and registered as lawyers could exercise the profession, a term that obviously excluded and discriminated against Jewish law graduates. Assistant lawyers (*avvocato–interveniente*) had to fulfil the same qualifications, with the exception of their Christian faith, a clause that reflects the fact the many Jews already worked as court secretaries and could not be dismissed simply for belonging to the 'wrong' religion.[52] Assistant lawyers served also as scribers and secretaries of the courts and the prosecutor's office; they could only practise law, however, after several years of service and after passing the exams set by the Council of Justice of the Senate.

In the 1850s Jewish merchants were excluded from the commercial tribunal. On 8 March 1858 *Ta Kathimerina* newspaper argued that it did not intend to examine all aspects of the 'Israelites issue' to the benefit of Jews, because the author did not want to strengthen the spirit of wickedness against them. The issue was one of the exclusion of Jews from the right to get elected in the Exchange, but not from the right to vote.[53] While the lists of merchants were compiled, the minister of commerce took into serious consideration the laws of the state, which did not give political rights to Jews and considered the matter not according to his own beliefs but according to the law. In an attempt to redress this injustice, eight Jewish merchants petitioned the high commissioner to be admitted to appear before the commercial court as assessors.[54] The newspaper article challenged the appeal of the Jewish merchants to the decision of the Exchange. The Ionian Senate concluded that the minister of commerce 'had to interpret the Law according to the sense and the tolerance which that Law and our political institutions demonstrate'. The Exchange could not have gone against the laws of the state, and accepted the Jews as eligible for election. The author clarified that the intention of the Exchange Council was not to 'stroke the superstitions of the people, because those are absent among us, and if they existed, the Council would never sacrifice the right of one part of society to them'. These examples show that there was discrimination against Jews by various institutions, and limits to their employment opportunities, but there was also room for negotiation and in fact improvement of their status during the fifty-year period of British rule.

The most important development in some respects is the publishing of the bilingual (in Greek and Italian) newspaper *Cronaca Israelitica* by Iosif Nachamuli from 1861 until May 1864. It is interesting that the newspaper, which was also a platform for the campaign for full civil and political rights for Ionian Jews, provoked hostility as well as praise and support from Ionian liberals.[55] The publication of the newspaper sparked the extraordinary decision of the Corfu Christian commercial elite to exclude the Jewish traders from the Corfu Exchange, the beginnings of modern economic/political (as opposed to medieval/religious) anti-Semitism.[56]

Bureaucratic rationalization in the Ionian State allocated population into fixed categories, designed for the empire as a whole, without distinguishing between Romaniotes and Sephardim Jews. This technical amalgamation evolved into an actual classification of the Jewish population into one 'community', masking both the differences of origin and language of liturgy as well as the class distinctions associated with wealth and access to resources (mostly political). The electoral list of 1865 provides a first mapping of the occupational distribution in Corfu town among Christians and Jews, at the crucial turning point after the islands became part of Greece. Merchants constituted 40 per cent of the total number of the recorded electors. Jewish craftsmen, mostly tailors, were 22 per cent; retailers, pedlars and shopkeepers formed another 27.5 per cent. Jewish labourers, 47 per cent of the total (and 83 per cent in the second district) were mainly porters, contrary to contemporary accounts of nineteenth-century Corfu that associate Jews with usury, the local bourgeois elite and the owners of capital. A very high percentage of Jews contributed to the port economy; merchants, retailers (mainly pedlars) and dockworkers, that is 67 per cent of the Jews of the second district. The above data demonstrate the extent and diversity of Jewish participation in the port economy.[57] Despite this participation, Jews remained second-class citizens in terms of their political rights until the end of British rule and the moment of union with Greece.

The number of Jewish merchants can also be estimated according to the electoral list and the merchants' lists devised by the chamber of commerce and published in the *Gazette*. The percentage of the Jewish recorded merchants is presented here as part of the rest of the working population of the town. The Jews predominantly lived in the second district (according to the division of the town for the requirements of the list) in which the ghetto of the town was also situated. Only Jews who chose to become Greek citizens were recorded, while the rest were considered 'foreigners'. The decision to become a Greek citizen or not probably depended on the origin of the different and separate, until the end of the nineteenth century, Jewish communities; one Greek-speaking, the other Sephardim Italian-speaking and, in general, more wealthy.

The percentage of Jewish merchants (40) recorded in the 1865 source indicates the diversity of the merchant group in terms of religion. Jews were the second largest group after the Christian Orthodox urban population. The percentage of Jews involved in the retail trade (27.5) included many pedlars (60 out of 113), while the shopkeepers were basically wine and spirits sellers. A very high percentage of the Jewish craftsmen were tailors (127 out of 194), most of whom, however, did not usually maintain a 'workshop' for selling their handmade clothes; most of which were made at home, where the clothes were stored as well, increasing the danger of fire for the town and the transmission of viruses on the occasion of an outbreak – or that is what contemporary Christians thought at least.

The extremely low percentages of proprietors should not surprise us, since Jews were not allowed to own property, only in the Jewish quarter, and clearly not many of them considered themselves as proprietors. Similarly, the prohibition to practise law and medicine under British rule, which had just ended at the time the source was created, explains the equally low percentage of Jews belonging to the professions. The domination of the olive oil trade by Jews often led to accusations of monopoly, or more accurately monopsony, since they were in position to buy the produce in advance for past debts and then sell it on as profitable terms as possible. However, this was no different practice than the one followed by the currant merchants on the islands producing the precious fruit in Zante and Kefalonia. The percentage of the total population related to the port economy is only 37 per cent, if not less, since not all retailers were directly involved in the port economy.

City and Suburbs

The town walls reinforced a sense of community among the urban dwellers of the Ionian Islands; the Italian terms *cittadini* and *contadini* for the people of the town and the country respectively, used even after the islands had passed under British rule, substantiate this division etymologically. Being homogeneous (Greek-speaking and Orthodox), people in the countryside could probably identify with each other easier than with the townspeople, although differences between villages must have existed, but not with a considerable impact on any sense of community. The dichotomy and cleavage between town/country, and their importance for identities, is also evident in the recurrent eruptions of conflict with the landowners being attacked in their country villas and fleeing to town to save themselves from the villagers, who entered the towns and burned contracts and other proof of subordination and control, and perhaps threatened the lives of the people in the towns.[58]

Another traveller, the Swiss Albert Mousson, was more revealing in his description of the suburb of Manduki: the Parga refugees (eight hundred families) had settled in Manduki, where at the beginning they earned a living as beggars living in shanties. Mousson noted that they were fishermen, sailors and workers.[59] The enclosed town was not only spatially separated from the suburbs, but the separation was also economic and social. All commercial activity took place at the port and in the market street, 'the street of the merchants' as it was called, as well as in the fancy English shops along the esplanade for the more affluent consumers, who Mousson could not help but describe as beautiful.

A 'neutral' but by no means objective observer of the time, the French traveller Buchon, wrote in 1841, the year that is probably the end point of the period of affluence at least for some Ionian families, when he visited some country houses: 'Everywhere there is an air of affluence that is very pleasant ... In every house that I went I found the tables laid as if everyone expected their friends'.[60] Buchon was equally interested in the popular feelings, claiming that there were contradictions among them, especially on the issue of loyalty and Greek national consciousness. Similarly to other islands, the Zante infrastructure works convinced observers such as Buchon that British protection was benevolent and instrumental in raising the standard of living, especially of the urban population. On the other hand British authorities never really dealt systematically with Lefkada, especially after the insubordination of peasants in 1819, leaving it more or less to its own devices and those of the British residents. This explains the extremely strict term of rule of Resident Temple (1820–28), who punished particularly harshly the Lefkada supporters of the Greek Revolution, claiming the principle of neutrality. The revolt of 1819, however, was triggered by the extra taxes for the construction of the canal of Lefkada from the port to the fortress. The work was finally concluded in 1843, under Commissioner Seaton, long after the British had realized that a port exposed to the Ottoman mainland opposite would not be secure. In 1824 a general census of the Ionian Islands took place. This census shows a new group of recently arrived immigrants from Epirus and Dalmatia who run taverns, barber shops and other establishments. The earthquake of 19 January 1825 was devastating. In one of the first resolutions to manage the humanitarian crisis, the government acknowledged that living conditions for people in Lefkada were not great even before the disaster struck, and the commissioner approved 150,000 tallers to rebuild the city and the villages destroyed. The resolution ordered the appointment of a committee to conduct evaluations of properties, give compensation, and manage disputes among the owners of buildings destroyed. Compensation, however, came in the form of loans to rebuild homes and secured existing debts, obligations and other claims on properties destroyed. This was a complicated process, since all the churches but one had collapsed and new ones had to be built.[61] The government built homes for seventy-two families over the following two years. In 1827, the first building regulations were passed; the buildings erected after the 1825 earthquake were generally modest, with two-floors, and the ground floors were made of stone to resist future earthquakes. There were some public works on the road network but the second part of the British protectorate should be best remembered for the construction of schools, in the villages as well as in the towns, and for the organization of public education on the island.[62]

In the Greek Kingdom the need to construct public works placed extra pressures on the treasury; road building, telegraph installation, and gas lines absorbed ten to twelve million drachmas.[63] Large-scale public works projects, however, began in 1861: the laying of the Athens–Piraeus railway in 1861 and the drainage of Lake Kopaida in 1867, the Patras–Tripolis road and the bridging of the Corinthian isthmus were financed with large contributions from private capital but still created deficits during the 1860s. All surplus production was to be sold on the market and generate profits that would cover the expenses of running the prison. Prisoners could also be used to clean the streets, a menial and extremely unpleasant task that very few people undertook and so were offered by auction, going to those offering the best price for the contract. Street lightning, introduced by de Bosset in 1810, was also contracted, for six month periods, but irregularities and a lack of illumination point to an unreliable service, especially for the 1840s. In practice only one street was illuminated – the street of the police station and the resident's house.[64]

Plans for the development of the small colonial state by British authorities in London and the representatives of British power on the islands included the reordering of public space. The practices followed were firmly based on the dominant ideology of the time, a religious belief in progress, which would improve living conditions for the inhabitants in these states, and enable them to govern themselves without the British protection. The Ionian Islands, mostly their urban societies, went through a transformation still evident today. Throughout the fifty-year period a few broad trends can be identified: the administrative capabilities of the colonial state decreased, allowing the increase of power asserted by groups outside the immediate sphere the British-Ionian authorities; collection and exchange of information between 'colonizers' and 'colonized' increased and both adapted to changing conditions on the islands; Ionians repeatedly used existing state institutions and mechanisms (petitions, justice apparatus) to accommodate their own interests; and reorganization of public space was less successful than had been desired by the British authorities but still changed the outlook of the towns if not the habits of their people, as sociability between the British and Ionians remained limited, being mostly through philanthropic associations and balls at the palace, to which only the elite were invited.

Notes

1 M. Lange, J. Mahoney and M. von Hau, 'Colonialism and Development: A Comparative Analysis of Spanish and British Colonies', *American Journal of Sociology* 111(5) (March 2006): 1412–62.
2 P. Mitter, 'The Early British Port Cities of India: Their Planning and Architecture circa 1640–1757', *JSAH* XLV (June 1986): 96–114.
3 G. Moschopoulos, *Istoria tis Kefalonias*, vol. 2 (1797–1940). Athens: Kefalos, 1988, 76; Cosmetatos, *The Roads of Cefalonia*.
4 J. McAdam, *Remarks on the Present System of Road Making: With Observations, Deduced from Practice and Experience* (8th edn). London: Longman, Hurst, Rees, Orme and Brown (Paternoster Row), 1824. Retrieved 26 September 2011.
5 I. Berend, *An Economic History of Nineteenth-Century Europe: Diversity and Industrialization*. Cambridge: Cambridge University Press, 2013, 136.
6 Kostis, 'The formation of the state in Greece, 1830-1914', in F.Birtek and Th. Dragonas (eds), *Citizenship and the Nation – State in Greece and Turkey*, London & New York: Routledge, 2005, 21.

7   A. Postnikov, 'From Charting to Mapping: Russian Military Mapping of Corfu in the Early Nineteenth Century', *Imago Mundi: The International Journal for the History of Cartography* 53(1) (2001): 83–96.
8   Solomos, *Geniki Dimosionomia tis Kefallinias*, 63–64.
9   Cosmetatos, *The Roads of Cefalonia*, 23–26.
10 15/07/1822, E.A. 849, υποφ. 67, Γ.Α.Κ.
11 26/03/1823, E.A. 849, υποφ. 67, Γ.Α.Κ.
12 M. Daunton, *Progress and Poverty: An Economic and Social History of Britain, 1700–1850*. Oxford: Oxford University Press, 1995, 447–74.
13 24/10/1824, E.A. 849, υποφ. 84, Γ.Α.Κ.
14 Hiotis II, 17.
15 H. Cosmetatos, *Reports on the Roads of Cefalonia*. Argostoli: Corgialeneios Museum, 1990, 24.
16 N. Patricios, *Kefallinia and Ithaki: A Historical and Architectural Odyssey*. Danbury, CT: Rutledge Books, 2002, 142.
17 Arxeio 421, Doc 2, K.B, 11 and 12 November 1857.
18 1st Session, 7th Parliament, Act II, 28 March 1840, K.V.
19 Davy, *Notes and Observations*, 76–77.
20 Andreadis, *I Enosi tis Eptanisou*.
21 Nicos Mouzelis, *Modern Greece: Facets of Underdevelopment*. New York: Holmes & Meier, 1978, 15.
22 Third Session of the First Parliament of the United States of the Ionian Islands, No. XXV, 20 April 1820.
23 de Vaudoncourt, *Memoirs on the Ionian Islands*, 419.
24   Charles Fitzroy, *Ionian Islands. Letters by Lord Charles Fitzroy and documents from other sources on past and recent events in the Ionian Islands*. London: 1850.
25 Kirkwall, *Four Years in the Ionian Islands*, vol. I, 113–14.
26 Muller, *Journey through Greece*, 65.
27 Second Session of the Second Parliament, No. XXXII, Corfu, 10 May 1825.
28 H. Holland, *Travels in the Ionian Islands, Albania, Thessaly, Macedonia, etc. during the years 1812–1813*. London: Longman, 1815, 34.
29 J. Murray, *A Handbook for Travellers in the Ionian Islands, Greece, Turkey, Asia Minor, and Constantinople*. London, 1845, 18.
30 Ibid., 29.
31 Ibid., 29.
32 Ansted, *The Ionian Islands in the Year 1863*, 12.
33 Gallant discusses extensively the painting by William Dodwell; T.W. Gallant, *I empeiria tis apoikiakis kyriarchias. Politismos, taytotita kai eksousia sta Eptanisa 1817–1864*. Athens: Aleksandreia, 2014, chapter 3.
34 Mousson, *Ein Besuch auf Korfu*, 47–49.
35 Ibid., 54.
36 Ibid., 58–60. Newspaper *Astir*, No. 640, 1/1/1859.
37 Kirkwall, *Four Years in the Ionian Islands*, vol. I, 115.
38 Napier's account of his years as resident ends with excellent drawings of the buildings erected in Argostoli during his time.
39 H. Napier, *Journal of Captain Henry Napier*. Manuscript, Corgialenios Museum, Argostoli, 1829, 66–67.

40 G. Zucconi, 'Corfu brittanica: Architettura e strategie urbanistiche nella capitale dello Stato Ionio', in A. Nikiforou (ed.), *Corfu: Storia, Vita urbana e Architettura, 14o–19o secc.* Corfu: Archivi di Stato di Corfù, 1994, 95–103.
41 Ansted, *The Ionian Islands in the Year 1863*, 14.
42 Document 7516, Arheio Ioniou Gerousias [Ionian Senate Archive], 5th Parliament, 1/6/1836–20/2/1837, documents 7068-9863, I.A.K.
43 Konidaris, 'I thesi ton thriskeftikon koinotiton'.
44 Executive Police 1319, Town Population Register 1812–1814, I.A.K.
45 Chapter I Article 3 & Chapter V Section I Article 1–3, Constitutional Chart of the United States of the Ionian Islands, in R.M. Martin, *Statistics of the Colonies of the British Empire in the West Indies, South America, North America, Asia, Austral-Asia, Africa and Europe*. London: W.H. Allen & Co., 1839, 258–70.
46 K. Fleming, *Greece: A Jewish History*. Princeton, NJ: Princeton University Press, 2007, 37–39.
47 'The Jews of Corfu', *The Jewish Chronicle*, 1845, 177–78.
48 Jervis, *History of the Island of Corfu*, 261–62.
49 B. Pierron, *Evraioi kai christianoi sti neoteri Ellada: istoria ton diakoinotikon scheseon apo to 1821 os to 1945*. Athens: Polis Editions, 2004, 12.
50 Iakovos Typaldos Pretenteris, *Peri tis en Kerkira choleras kata to 1855*. Kerkyra: Typografeio tis Kyvernisis, 1856, 8.
51 Report of the Extraordinary Central Health Commission, 16 January 1856. IIGG, No. 225, 28 January 1856.
52 Act KA' (21) of the 8th Senate of the United States of the Ionian Islands, 1845, Atti di Parlamento, Korgialenios Library.
53 *Ta Kathimerina*, No. 154, 8 March 1858.
54 Petition No. 400, 8 December 1857, CO 136/857, National Archives, London.
55 D. Varvaritis, '"The Jews have got into trouble again...": Responses to the Publication of "*Cronaca Israelitica*" and the Question of Jewish Emancipation in the Ionian Islands (1861–1863)', in *Quest. Issues in Contemporary Jewish History. Journal of Fondazione CDEC* 7 (July 2014): 30–51.
56 Ibid., 41.
57 Gekas, 'The Port Jews of Corfu'.
58 The fears were not unjustified at all, since invasions in the towns, burnings and general insubordination occurred on several occasions on the islands between the seventeenth and nineteenth centuries: in Corfu in 1610, 1640, 1642, 1652, 1678, and sporadically in the eighteenth century, but not until 1865 on the issue of electors (the villagers were asking for greater representation than the town in the national elections; in Kefalonia 1640–44, 1648; in Kethyra 1780, 1794. The most significant period in recent times, however, was the years 1797–1802, when all the islands were practically ungovernable, following the advent of the French revolutionary spirit and rule. All rebellions were crushed. Omada enantia sti lithi. *Kyriarchia kai koinonikoi agones ston Elladiko choro*. Athens: Anarhiki Arheiothiki, 1996, 135–43.
59 Mousson, *Ein Besuch auf Korfu*, 86.
60 A. Buchon, 'Voyage dans l' Eubee, les Isles Ioniennes et les Cyclades en 1841', Paris 1911, in D. Zivas, *I Architektoniki tis Zakynthou apo ton 16o mechri tom 19o aiona*. Athens, 1970, 12.

61 Second Session of the Second Parliament, Act No. XXVII, Corfu, 22 April 1825.
62 M. Lambrinou, 'Oikodomikos kai poleodomikos programmatismos. Dimosia erga stin Agglokratoumeni Lefkada', in Panagiotis Moschonas (ed.), *To Ionio Kratos 1815–1864*. Athens: Kentro Meleton Ioniou, 1997, 229–37.
63 P. Petrakis, 'The Borrowing Requirements of the Greek Public Sector, 1844–1869', *Journal of the Hellenic Diaspora* 12 (1985): 45.
64 Solomos, *Geniki Dimosionomia tis Kefallinias*, 86–87.

 Chapter 8

'Progress'
State Policies for Ionian Development

In May 1819, Parliament increased taxes on imported tobacco in an attempt to encourage cultivation of the crop on the islands. Some Ionians did respond; in 1825 Attanasio Androni(s), who held land in Mandouki outside the Corfu city walls, planted tobacco. Andronis petitioned against his landowner, claiming that he unlawfully took a part of the land leased and segregated it from the remainder, making it harder to grow tobacco.[1] These were exactly the kinds of disputes that Ionian and especially British officials preferred to stay out of; there was no comment, reply or action noted in the petitions register, which was the usual response of Ionian bureaucrats to a petition. The Ionian State prioritized issues of public order and construction of public works, but also promoted the islands' economy through the necessary institutional framework, albeit with limited success. In the 1820s the government promoted agriculture, recognizing that increased exports would mean increased revenues. Parliament passed the first act promoting economic policy in April 1823.[2] This was the first of a series of measures adopted to promote agriculture but also 'arts' and 'commerce'. The resolution created a parliamentary committee, which pledged to enquire about the obstacles that hindered agricultural progress, consider what measures could be taken to alleviate these obstacles, and investigate where land could be cultivated or improved. Other duties included suggestions for the consolidation of landed property. The resolution also called for the publication of the committee's conclusions, both in Italian and Greek, thus introducing a new mode of governance – accountable, transparent and, in theory at least, open to deliberation. Projects such as the savings bank and the committees for the improvement of agriculture were part of the same concept seeking to improve Ionian economies and societies; this process included regularization and control of key professions and occupations in the cities, such as doctors, lawyers but also porters and other labourers such as fishermen. These groups and individuals promoted their interests in a negotiation with the state through petitions, an invaluable source for historians to understand how Ionians perceived their condition and their relationship with the state authorities.

The Agricultural Society formed in January 1836 for 'the development of agriculture',[3] and soon after the government approved a fund for the Societa Agraria, the Agrarian Society.[4] The Agricultural Society was part of the same liberal project that aimed to instil the principle of saving, a bourgeois value par excellence, to the 'poorer classes'. The project involved the publication of balance sheets of savings banks in Malta and Paris to demonstrate the performance of these establishments and propagate the inauguration of the Ionian savings banks. It is very unlikely that tenant farmers had any savings to deposit, not because they were not frugal enough but because they were locked in a cycle of over-indebtedness.[5]

Collection of data and generating knowledge was another policy instrument to improve agricultural productivity; there was a venerable tradition of Ionian bureaucracy as seen by the census and registers of 1830–32.[6] The committee sent three questionnaires to local committees to investigate how much land was cultivated, the existing irrigation system, the number of animals and many more questions regarding all aspects of agriculture and the processing of agricultural goods, including oil presses and the potential for producing silk and butter. The committee was also interested in the reasons why vegetables were not cultivated near the houses, and suggested ways to turn rural households into self-sufficient units instead of buying vegetables from the city. Questionnaires were distributed to and collected from all Ionian Islands with the aid of the Executive Police and the village primates (*primate*).[7]

In March 1837 another society 'of agriculture and industry' aimed to improve both areas, and 'introduce' to each island new techniques, crops ('herbs and roots'), and products: the manufacture of silk, the keeping of bees, the improvement of oil products, wine and brandy, and the expansion of soap manufacturing. The initiative took place under the auspices of the government. The regent of each island was responsible for compiling a list of subscribers and every person available to cooperate for the advancement of 'national agriculture and industry'. There was an annual fee as well of six shillings for the treasury of the society on each island. The sums would be distributed according to the traditional allocation of resources: 700 pounds for Corfu, Kefalonia, Zante and Santa Maura, 300 for Cerigo and Ithaca, and 316 remaining for Paxo. Every society had an executive of four members and a president; the president of the Municipal Magistrate of Agriculture would serve ex officio, for three years. In an organization that reminds of a public holding company, the subscribers met in meetings, legal when a majority of meetings convened, and approved the accounts. In the spirit of accountability, the accounts and reports of the society would be published every three months in the *Ionian Gazette*.⁸

Douglas remained convinced that transparency ought to be the mode of government. More developmental works followed; in June 1837 the act 'for promoting and carrying into effect the draining of marshes and valleys in the Ionian Islands, for preserving the cultivation of the land and for the benefit of Public Heatlh' passed.⁹ The resolution ordered the municipal councils to produce a detailed review of all the lands covered in stagnant waters, unproductive and flooded, and as such hazardous to public health. The law required the mobilization of other state services; the agrarian committees, the Executive Police, the civil engineers, the road inspector and the land surveyor, on the islands that had one. The act directed municipal councils to start from the lands closest to the city, making the plan more useful to Corfu and Argostoli in Kefalonia, but also the city of Lefkada where traditionally people's living conditions were hampered by marshland. There were concrete financial plans to promote agriculture. The government would advance loans at 4 per cent per year to help proprietors, tenants and landholders to execute the works. This was a stimulus indeed, showing the availability of funds in the government treasury, one of the last years with a budget surplus. The Agrarian Society would advance the money to those deemed creditworthy and with a plan to drain the marshland, making it effectively an agricultural fund. If some proprietors or tenants refused to cooperate they reserved the right to work with other villagers and even to create anonymous companies and procure capital through shares for the cultivation of these lands. The portion cultivated would remain in public ownership and would yield dividends of up to 6 per cent. This transformed the uncultivated and unhealthy land into an object of speculation, taking it out of the control of the landholders or even the landowners in order to create a land market. This project also stalled as another attempt to create a property market failed. McKenzie, the commissioner in 1842, visited Kefalonia and founded a cooperative for the 'encouragement of arts and professions' of Kefalonia; this was a shareholding company, under the auspices of the high commissioner, that is the government, that nevertheless failed and was abandoned.¹⁰ Other efforts concerned the processing of olive oil to produce soap. Caustic soda had to be imported and the act of April 1842 sought to 'animate the cultivation and petrification of riscolo' (saltwort), which was necessary for soap making.¹¹ The technique required using raw materials such as olive oil, boiled with soda ash and sea salt for several weeks. The law aimed to promote a sector of agriculture linked with manufacture and export, to 'augment national prosperity'; in fact all resolutions relating to agriculture express the progressive, developmental spirit in a discourse that leaves little doubt that government officials knew very well which sectors of the islands' economy could do better and required encouragement, so they legislated accordingly. Very little, if anything, happened in the saltwort sector. As was often the case with such regulations and the bureaucracy of the Ionian State, those interested in investing and cultivating saltwort would have to submit their tender to the municipal council, for five years.

Following the uprising of 1849 in Kefalonia, and its suppression which in the international press earned Commissioner Ward the reputation of a ruthless despot, Ward was eager to appear as a modernizer and a benevolent ruler. He nominated two committees in April 1853, the first was 'charged with an Enquiry into the state of Agriculture in Corfu, and the means of improving it by the introduction of new modes of cultivation, especially in olive oil production; the second will investigate all matters connected with the Tenure of Land, and with the relations that exist between Landowner and Colono'.[12] The letter Ward sent to the president of the Senate shows the ambitions of both committees, a statement of rationalization of governance following the example of practices followed in Britain. The document summarizes the philosophy guiding the British administration of the Ionian Islands with practices applied back home behind a facade of self-government with a seemingly just and benevolent administration that established committees manned by the local elite. The people Ward called the 'intelligent classes' formed the committee enquiring into the state of agriculture in Corfu and recommending remedies for its deplorable condition. This was another spasmodic response to the agricultural issue. Although Ward recommended the appointment of two committees, the Senate decided to merge them and appoint one committee to deal with all issues raised by the British ruler. Politicians, merchants and landowners formed the committee for agricultural reform. The people appointed were: 'Prestantissimo Cavaliere D. Allessandro Damaschino, President; Members: Noble Signor Spiridion Conte Bulgari q.m. Cristodulo; Noble Signor Elia Vasilachi; Prestantissimo Dr Pietro Braila Armeni; Noble Signor Alessandro Grollo; Noble Signor Dr Demetrio Curcumeli; Conte Alessandro Theotochi; Noble Signor Arseni Papadato; Noble Signor Andrea Chiriachi q.m. Eust; Noble Signor Teodoro Ventura; Noble Signor Antonio Candoni; Signor Ben. Aristide Pieri, Secretary'.

The members of the 'intelligent classes' assumed the task to conduct the inquiry with the mandate to settle the property rights maze on all the islands, but in Corfu in particular. Ward, just like others before him, had identified rightly that the settlement of the property relations was a necessary condition for the development of agriculture and the improvement of living standards among the 'poor classes' in the country; the propertied themselves were called in to assist the state in reforming agriculture. The committees on agricultural reform resulted in no improvement or reform whatsoever, and offered no solution to the problem of indebtedness and patronage that tied peasants to landlords and merchants. This enduring weakness of the Ionian State, its inability to define and enforce property rights, created stagnation and lack of incentives to improve agriculture. Ionian and British officials were very good at diagnosis but exceptionally idle in finding a cure.

The Ionian State was never short of ideas or incentives; in 1844 the Parliament passed another act for promoting the work of the Agricultural Society and for 'encouraging the classes of agriculturers and cultivators', deciding to give prizes to the most 'industrious and diligent agriculturer'. The prizes would not exceed fifty pounds, and would come out of the Agricultural Society.[13] No law was void of social and political rationale. In 1845 another law linked directly the progress of agriculture with the clandestine presence of criminals on the island of Santa Maura.[14] The law used the promotion of agriculture as a pretext for imposing order that apparently was slipping out of control in the rural areas. A special force was created on the island, called 'Corpo di Guardie Campestri', or Rural Guard, made up of locals only, under the authority of the few constables of the island, with powers to arrest anyone they suspected of any crime. The law confirmed previous and existing regulations for the control of the countryside with a militia, but apparently in need of reform. Any time an armed band appeared on the island the rural guard would have to hand them over to the Executive Police; the force would be armed, under the direction of the Executive Police, with no less than fifty-five men and six officers nominated by the director of the Executive Police, all to be no younger than 24, and no older than 40. The men of the guard had to be 'sane, strong and of known conduct and activity'; the police were able to check on almost every permanent resident of the islands and most foreigners, who were obliged to report upon arrival and have their travel documents stamped. The rural police force aimed to guard against trespassers of gardens, vineyards and orchards, which it was forbidden to enter without the approval of the proprietor, tenant, worker, gardener or other responsible person, or else was subject to a two tallers per day fine. The Rural Guard men would receive a stipend of nine tallers per month, a modest monthly wage of an unskilled worker. This rather secure income, however, was far better than the insecurity of the precarious status that the overwhelming majority of Ionians experienced.

Who would pay for the force? This was contentious because it became obvious that the people of Santa Maura would have to pay, with extra taxes: for every kilo of wheat imported into the island, they were charged an additional 2.5 dinars; for other grains, 1.5 dinars per kilo; for every barrel of oil exported abroad or to other islands, 6.5 dinars per kilo; and for every barrel of wine exported, 2 dinars. This was no mean tax hike, especially during periods of poor harvest. There would be a separate financial administration, reviewed by the regent and the resident of the island, and a special official would pay the militia individually. The issue was thorny on the island of Santa Maura because crossing from the mainland was exceptionally easy, with it being so close, and could apparently cause diplomatic headaches for the Ottoman authorities.

Honorary Secretary Captain Portlock, in his speech, laid out the philanthropic and developmental ambitions of the Agricultural Society. The speech, a fine documentation of contemporary perceptions of political economy, reveals the principles and mentality that the society's founders wanted to instil in proprietors who lacked the knowledge to develop their property and augment their wealth, and the tenant farmers of the islands who had neither.[15] Captain Portlock advised both groups to invest their savings, no matter how small, and urged them not to despair if they did not see their situation improve immediately, because once they started accumulating their capital they could buy an ox, and their means to social affluence would increase after they entered this brave new world of profitable and capital-intensive agriculture. Both the savings bank and the society pledged to 'save' the rural poor from their destitute condition. The speech shows how distant some British officials were from Ionian realities.

A series of other laws buttressed the state that Maitland introduced and rekindled the developmental project that had begun during the Septinsular Republic and the period of French occupation. In 1820 the law 'fixing the necessary conditions that will be able to build manufactures' – rather ambitiously – was passed, but not much was 'fixed'. Another, but more realistic, Act of Parliament legislated on the operation of public markets in Corfu (28 March 1820), to complement the series of regulations on food markets. Public order occupied the minds and legislative work of the first Parliament, with resolutions on the cleanliness of Corfu and the handling of human waste.[16] Public works included the construction of a canal and mole in Sta Maura and the reorganization of public space with the service of lighting at night and the cleanliness and construction of roads, in a single act (18 April 1820). The construction of a mole and aqueduct in Zante was approved, and the government also regulated the administration of saltworks with an institutional framework to a centuries-old resource in Corfu (and the smaller one in Sta Maura), but also intervened in labour markets, as the act for the establishment of the porters' as a professional group shows. A resolution of 1 February 1819 had regulated the tariffs porters could charge, but it effectively created the framework for the operation of the porters as a guild (Fraglia dei Facchini). The continuities with the previous organization of the guild system are difficult to establish; however, it is telling that the first guild the Senate chose to regulate was that of the porters, because of their vital role in the smooth operation of the harbour and commerce. Among the main obligations of the chief porter and his inferiors was the registration of all men working as porters, and the verification by the Civil Police.[17] The Municipal Police published also in the same resolution the tariff for all modes of transportation, distances and goods carried by the porters, with different lists for the profit margin of porters and a separate list with the profit reserved for the porters' fund. The extremely detailed resolution tells us more about the sophisticated public policy and regulation of the transportation services than it does about whether the rules actually worked in practice.

Reforms and Reactions: Letters to the State

One of the first tasks of the British-Ionian administration was to record and regulate a range of occupations that would lead to a more efficient control and regulation of labour markets, continuing a tradition from previous regimes. Ionian State authorities introduced reforms to regulate labour markets and the professions, trades and workers. Ionian cities already had an impressive division of labour since the early modern period, as reflected in the labour and professional organization in the fraternities or *'scuole'*, occupational guilds that regulated trades.[18] British and Ionian officials as well as the Ionian Academy recorded occupations and professions with the aim of rendering 'the government of the island more ordered and correct', a declaration revealing of the governmentality introduced under British rule. The task was given once again to the Executive Police, which in 1818 recorded 'arts and labour' and issued licences for the right to exercise the trade. Records of shopkeepers and artisans show the division of labour and specialization present in Ionian cities. Thirty occupations of 'artisans and labourers' were recorded in Italian and Greek in the sectors of jewellery, construction, fruit and vegetable sellers, bakers, tailors, barbers, barrel makers, confectioners, hat makers, innkeepers and cheese sellers, to mention but a few.[19]

In 1820 the government approved the *'corpo'* or association of porters, changing the previous labour framework that allowed porters to appoint their own colleagues as workers. The government's intervention to control and regulate the sensitive and important sector of port labour and services demanded that they form a body with three appointed 'leaders', one of them responsible for the treasury of the association.[20] This was not a grass-roots organization, although there is no evidence that many porters objected to it, but reminds more of a state-led initiative to establish a corporatist control of the labour market. The Senate approved the porters' association with a resolution in 1820 that aimed at the smooth operation of the port. The savings and self-help fund that was created for the porters in times of sickness or other need also included a sum for a small pension; this was an innovation at a time when no state structures for social insurance or other wealfare institutions existed, only these self-help associations. Through the association the government regulated porters' wages according to the services they offered; proceeds from association profits were distributed to sick porters, except 21 per cent of the fund in reserve. The assistance fund was the first institution of social welfare. Porters received money to buy medicine and visit doctors in cases of sickness or injury, while their families received a sum in cases of death. The leaders of the various groups of porters received a wage, effectively a trade union officer salary, and were obliged in return to control and report to the government (the police) the number of porters at any time, and also to help the army in case of fire.[21] The *corporazione,* or union of porters, was divided according to service of transport offered and according to religion and rite (Greek Orthodox, Catholic, Jewish). This form of association predated by fifty years the workers' fraternity of Corfu founded by Christian and Jewish workers, perhaps itself a continuation of this organization of porters in a workers' association and the traditional *'scuole'*, the fraternities. Registration of porters and the licence they received from the police was the same process as followed for merchants, brokers and shopkeepers; all were obliged to keep accounting books and be available for control by government officials. Manual labour such as the porters, the merchants and the brokers were the most important groups for commerce and the ports, and essential for the revenues of the Ionian State, and therefore under regulation by the government.

Doctors were a prestigious group in Ionian societies, for some British observers to an extraordinary extent: 'The swarm of D.C.L. and M.D. who now infest the several islands and who, for want to employment, lounge about the streets, in a perfect state of moral, industrial and professional idleness and vacancy, smoking their cigarettes, and discussing politics, of which they do not so much as understand the terms. This state of things becomes a matter of serious reflection, when the prospects of the succeeding generation are taken into consideration'. Out of the 663 electors in Corfu in 1849, 131 were doctors.[22]

The reaction of many Ionians was to petition the government collectively or individually to improve their condition or express a grievance to the central administration. This practice contradicts the argument of many British and a few Ionians about the alleged political immaturity of Ionians and their 'childlike' behaviour towards political institutions fit and reserved only for some nations and withheld from others. Some petitions reveal impressive knowledge about regulations; in 1825 Spiridione Avierino, Pietro Curcumelli and Giovanni Cipriotti, proprietors of fishing boats, were prohibited from fishing in the harbour and begged some exemption from the general regulations, founding their claim upon their citizenship as Ionians.[23] Soon after Ionian citizenship had been established, fishermen sought to gain from their Ionian status, showing that there was competition with those employed and working in Corfu.

More fishermen submitted four petitions in 1826 and 1827 'praying to be permitted to fish during the night'. That year requests also asked for exemption from the custom duty on fish.[24] These petitions reflect the ways in which groups and individuals perceived petitioning; Ionians who shared a common trade saw greater chances of success in collective action, even if, in the case of fishermen at least, in groups of no more than three, five or ten. In the 1820s petitioning was still an early practice, and collective agency through petitions did not necessarily take place at an organized level of representation of an occupational group or guild; instead, it was the expression of collective organization of a few individuals protecting established interests and asking for special but fair treatment from the state authorities so that they could earn a living.

Fishermen lived in the two districts outside the town walls, south and north of the town, in Anemomilos and Manduchi respectively.[25] Permission to fish at night continued to be the main issue of a petition signed by five fishermen from Anemomilos in 1837 and of several other petitions throughout the period. Fishermen described their living conditions, the impossibility of learning a different trade, since that was the only one they could earn their 'daily bread' with, which often left them depending on 'the charity of the Christians'.[26] The petitioners struggled for survival and occasionally supplemented their income with begging for charity in the town, an all too familiar image in the writings of contemporaries and travellers who visited Corfu. The prohibition of fishing at night was part of the quarantine laws to prevent the plague through contraband trade, but it affected considerably the 'unique means of subsistence' of the inhabitants of Anenomilos (Molino a Vento). They emphasized that night was the only time when they could 'apply their industry'; if they were not allowed to fish at night, it would be like 'taking away their daily bread'. Just like all petitioners, however, these six fishermen and fishmongers stated their belief in 'the equity characterising His Excellency'. The request clashed with the sanitary measures of the Ionian State, established from the period of Venetian rule and implemented strictly during the period of British rule. Petitions with the same subject from the 1825s to the early 1860s show how persistent fishermen were in trying to solve a recurring issue, namely the prohibitions put on fishing by an over-regulating government.

Fishermen opened with a long compliment to the high commissioner for his 'zeal and accomplished virtue'; they interestingly pointed to the absence of a firm law on the regulation of the fish market, which caused 'both the fishmongers and the society great damage', relating the request to the greater benefit of society. Fishmongers asked for a designated fish market because the rented one was too expensive compared to the profits of the retailers; in this case fishermen actually requested regulation since fishermen came 'from abroad and deprive locals from their bread'. The petitioners were cautious not to ask for a monopoly but for a strict regulation. The documents supporting the petition included correspondence with the municipal council that argued against the construction of a fish market since there were no funds for such a project in the public fund.[27] By the late 1850s, money for public projects similar to the ones of the 1820s–1840s period had run out.

Restrictions on the fishermen's trade was part of the regulation of all economic activity that Ionian-British government authorities designed and implemented during the period of the Ionian State. These regulations affected the activities and livelihoods of most Ionians who expressed their grievances through petitions. Butchers, bakers, coach proprietors, carpenters and masons, gardeners, blacksmiths, shopkeepers, coffee-house keepers, ship owners, and, most frequently, merchants petitioned the office of the high commissioner and addressed him personally. This practice reflects the earlier organization of society and occupations in guilds under Venetian rule, but only to an extent.[28] In the Ionian State every individual was entitled to a petition. Not all groups, however, filed the same number of petitions, nor were the requests of the same content. Butchers, for instance, filed several petitions over the years, of which the most impressive perhaps is a petition sent in April 1860. Butchers referred to the time of interim government under Colonel Robinson, between 1814 and 1816, when the islands were held under British occupation and claimed established rights showing an impressively enduring institutional memory as an occupational group:

> On the erection of the meat market in the time of Colonel Robinson, the Collector General of Customs, a decree was issued by the Senate to the effect that when the Government had reimbursed the money spent for the erection of the shed that they should be exempted from the payment of the rent they are bound to pay. They vow by His Excellency to recommend to the Senate that they may be exempted from paying the arrears due by them to the Government, but if that cannot be accorded that at least they may pay in instalments and that their debt be somewhat redeemed.[29]

Other petitions confirm strong local identities and a sense of injustice that emerged when imperial priorities or simply new practices sidestepped what petitioners considered local interests. In March 1852, during the worst economic crisis of the protectorate, thirty-five carpenters and blacksmiths requested that one of the two Ionian steamers, the aging *Ionia*, bought in 1827, remain in Corfu for repairs, instead of sending it to Malta.[30] The carpenters and blacksmiths who signed this petition contrast their previous repairs to the *Ionia* with unsatisfactory repairs done elsewhere. That is why they pray that the steamer may be repaired in Corfu, where facilities, tools and expertise could be found. The main argument related the general economic benefit the income from repairs would bring to carpenters and blacksmiths, but also to villagers selling the timber necessary for the repairs. Craftsmen and artisans worked together on issues specific to their occupations, demonstrating collective unity that resembled the guilds (fraternities) of the Venetian times but with the new conditions that emerged during the period of the Ionian State, and the right to petition the government to address their issues. In 1860 several porters of Zante, the 'only ones who enjoy the Custom House and Merchants' confidence', reminded the government of the time when a fire broke out in the Custom House store containing cottons, and they put it out. The eleven porters requested a regulation of their trade and protection from unfair competition from a clique of porters who received 17 pence per 1000 weight, well below the fee set by the government.[31]

Petitions very quickly became a space for negotiation and accommodation of groups' and individuals' interests between the state (regional and central) authorities and the rest of Ionians. In September 1825 the

Figure 8.1 Man in Corfu. Kerkyra 1856–60. Fotografikes Martyries. Mouseio Paleopololis – Mon Repos, Kerkyra, Eforia Archeotiton Kerkyras, Elliniko Ypoyrgeio Politismou kai Athlitismou.

'Albanians of Potamo', a village outside Corfu, prayed to be relieved from labour on the roads, the obligation of all country folk when road construction came to their area. The petition was rejected with a rationale that reveals the attitudes of British (or Ionian?) officials to a group clearly regarded as foreign and not very welcome: 'These people derive advantages form the roads at least equal to those which accrue to the natives of the same contado. Must work, if they don't like us they may leave us and we shall lose nothing by their going'.[32] There were clearly limits to the tolerance that British and Ionian authorities were prepared to show, especially when it came to minorities who were foreign to the Ionian Islands.

Most petitioners were looking to secure some regular income through employment or to receive some funds from the government as assistance or compensation for services offered. This was the case from very early on in the history of the protectorate and it shows the great expectations many Ionians held from their new masters. In the first year of petitions submitted to the government and logged in the index of petitions, 64 out of 280 petitions (or 23 per cent) were indexed with the word 'employment' in the subject category, by far the most popular request of petitioners.[33] Men but also women (mostly from the cities, especially Corfu) petitioned the government trying to avoid a tax or other obligations. For many Ionians the freedom to petition the authorities offered an opportunity for a negotiation with the state that many of them took up, sometimes in collective petitions, and sometimes in individual ones.

Ionians negotiated with the Ionian government and promoted their individual and collective interests. Anastasio Gangadi on 15 August 1825 prayed employment from the government and grounded his claim on former services as an inspector of roads, to which the government official replied that 'the petitioner did no more than his duty as inspector and was paid for it', dismissing claims for permanent employment. There was a limit to how many people the Ionian government could employ, even at times when Ionian finances presented a surplus. Many Ionians sought to test the limits of employment by the government, especially women. Dona Vaga Bonifation ('*Lavatrica*' – cleaner) worked as a public midwife and on 20 August 1825 requested that a salary be granted for her services, but the government's response stated that only services by professional doctors were reimbursed.[34] Women often asked for assistance from the government regarding employment but also money. Teodora Vrami prayed for an advance of $500, an extraordinary sum for an individual to ask for, from the government or from anyone else for that matter, prompting the following response: 'I have no doubt this is a case of great distress but it is utterly impossible to the Government to make any loan of money on such grounds, I shall be very glad under Mr Lovends benevolent directions personally to give such assistance as may be reasonable, or to subscribe to any fund he will suggest for the purpose of aiding this and similar cases of distress'.[35] While it is not clear in which distress Teodora found herself, it must have been extreme.

Ionians born on the islands or naturalized expected to be employed by the state on a more permanent basis; in fact this was the reason many of them became naturalized Ionians in the first place. Nicolo Costantino, a rope-maker working for the Ionian flotilla, begged employment on 21 October 1825; in many such cases the government, unable to hire whoever asked for work, chose to keep those craftsmen at bay and promised to employ them whenever work became available.[36] Others were luckier, depending on their conduct. Since its early days the Ionian State had built up a system of surveillance to prevent and identify crime but also for more day-to-day yet equally important purposes, such as when someone asked for employment. Antonio Pieri asked for employment at the port office and his petition was referred to the police official of Coast and Harbour. The report that came back was very positive: 'knows the petitioner very well and recommends him for employment'.[37] Beyond the obvious duties of police directors on each island, providing references for various individuals seeking employment or suspected of subversive political conduct were among their main tasks.

The crisis of the 1850s created unemployment and emigration, and Ionians turned to the government for assistance. In January 1855 Michele di Majo, a naturalized Ionian, supervisor of repair works, who served for years in the Ionian flotilla but was unemployed for several months, requested a free passage to Constantinople to support his family and claimed the philanthropy of the commissioner, but his request was denied.[38] Maria Reggini, a widow, was employed in the hospital at Manduchio during the cholera outbreak in the suburb and the building of the hospital, and begged for pension assistance after the dangerous work there. The destitute mother of a young girl pushed her to petition the commissioner for assistance, effectively a reward for her services during the months of the cholera outbreak. Reggini asked for a small monthly sum to support her and her family. Kogevinas, a doctor and director of the hospital in June 1856, confirmed that Maria Reggini had worked under the supervision of Iakovos Typaldos Pretenderis and was forced to resign afterwards since she could not perform her duties any longer.[39]

Other Ionians felt entitled to a pension or at least a small sum that would guarantee them a decent income. Cristodoulo Ruggieri petitioned for employment because his father, Georgio Ruggieri, had served in the health office and the market for twenty-eight years. When Georgio died he left his family destitute; his son Cristodoulo prayed for a post in the customs office and a monthly wage to help his aging mother and his own family. The report from the police was positive, even if laconic: 'Cristodulo Ruggiero bears a good character. His father served the Ionian Government for a long time' [Director General (Police). 8 February 1855]. It is not clear whether he was offered a post in the customs office, but in the 1850s very few new civil servants were appointed given the rising expenditure and accumulating deficits of the Ionian State. What is interesting is that Cristodoulo's claim to employment was his father's good service to the Ionian Government for almost three decades, not his own qualifications, which shows how crucial the trust of government officials was.[40]

Some Ionians were more qualified and presented a better case for employment. Ioannis Scordilis submitted a petition in 1860 that shows how Ionians used career opportunities and requested employment in the context of pilot school establishments like the agricultural station of Kastellanoi village in Corfu, which Commissioner Seaton had opened in the 1840s. After graduating from the Ionian University, Skordilis became a private teacher in the village of St Mateo but he soon found out that he could not earn a living there since the villagers were very poor and unable to pay the teacher's and school's expenses. He therefore asked to be appointed to a public Lancastrian school that the government would open in the village. Scordilis's request accompanied the petition of the villagers of St Mateo for a school that had been submitted the previous year; the government could only encourage him to open a private school, which he did but found very quickly that he could not secure an income. Scordilis's case, as always, was referred to the police for a report; all public employees needed to have a clean criminal record and the report made special reference to his morality and education.[41]

The surveillance capabilities of the Ionian State were impressive. Record keeping, correspondence and communication between departments, and especially the police, ensured the surveillance of the most dangerous citizens, given their criminal or political activity. When Apostolo Dima requested employment the police report noted: 'Albanian, born in Corfu. He is claiming that he is of good conduct, owns property of 2,000 $'. He belonged, however, to a violent family:

> The eldest, named Demetrio, was expelled in the year 1836, on account of his bad conduct together with 13 of his companions. The second, named Apostoli, was sent away in August 1854 for the same reason – a return of the imprisonments undergone by him is herewith annexed. This may look a past in the violent thefts committed at [...] and at Govino against [...]. The third Brother is the Petitioner who is a well-behaved man. The fourth, Giorgio, is at present in prison, condemned for life conviction of the attempted aggression – theft against Co Trivoli. General Police Office, 1 Febr. 1855.[42]

Police surveillance was impressive and efficient, and it defined relations between the Ionian government and its citizens.

Women, more vulnerable than men, often begged for assistance, financial aid, intervention and release of their husbands or sons from jail. In 1860, Fotini Desylla from Mandouki begged that her son, who was in jail, receive pardon for a minor offence (theft) because she was unable to feed her six other younger children and her aged husband. Fotini asked her parish protest Elisaios Kallonas to write and sign the petition for her. Women used the opportunities offered by the Ionian bureaucracy to mitigate economic misfortunes and improve their condition. Finding themselves in dire straits women (and many men) resorted to this form of bureaucratic begging and sought philanthropy from the government. The Ionian official processing the petition requested a report from the local director of police, a standard practice in the system of surveillance. The police and its director personally exercised great power, since reports in favour or against the 'conduct' of the petitioner determined the course of the petition and the outcome of the request.

The residents of Mandouki, most of them refugees from Parga, were particularly vocal in their request for assistance. In 1852, more than thirty years after their arrival from Parga, Ioannis Vassilas had been serving as the priest of two churches in Mandouki and the poorhouse for four years without pay. Being in distress and close to absolute poverty with his large family and orphan grandchildren, to the point that he was unable to pay his rent, he requested to move, together with other poor refugee families from Parga, into an old building that belonged to an Englishman. This is a rare case where the government satisfied the petitioner's request; the municipal council stated that the building mentioned was not vacant but offered instead the old 'anatomy room' for the distressed priest and his family.[43]

Petitioning created a space of negotiation with the central authorities, building on an established tradition and realizing that collective petitions, such as the one submitted by the villagers of Perivoli, could have an impact. Village notables often acted as health deputies, keeping an eye on the boats that arrived and left from the port near their village. When the government ordered that only its employees in fewer designated ports located much further from Perivoli could provide the clean bill of health to alleviate corruption and potentially the spread of disease, people from ten villages complained that they could not easily reach these ports to send their goods. Even forty years after the plague of 1815 had exposed the lack of roads in southern Corfu to connect villages and the city, the petitioners complained about how difficult it was to send goods overland during some months of the year to take them to the ports of Mesoggi or Potamos. Health regulations harmed internal trade as well as shipping, since villagers and ship captains risked going to other ports, and villagers requested a return to the previous regulation so that 'tranquil and sensitive citizens do not suffer'. The priests and notables, as well as other people from five villages, signed the petition, which was also submitted in Italian, showing the complexities of Ionian State bureaucracy even in the 1850s, more than ten years after the government had passed another act pronouncing Greek as the language of the state.[44]

In 1851 several caulkers of Corfu articulated their request to organize themselves into a body and elect representatives.[45] In 1851 the crisis of the Ionian economy was already taking its toll. The caulkers, having formed an unofficial collective to write the petition, began by stating the 'everyday disorder which has caused misery to all the sectors of the caulkers' trade and dragged many masters and their families to desperation, poverty and decline'. They first argued against any form of monopoly imposed arbitrarily by three people, quite ignorant of the trade as well, they said. They emphasized the support and protection their trade enjoyed 'by all governments', and pointed to the practices in England and the other 'civilized places'. Most importantly, they pointed to the other occupational groups of Corfu that had been allowed to organize themselves as a body, showing that they were aware of developments in labour organization in Western Europe, and their impact on the labour reality of the Ionian Islands. The petition ended by explaining that, because of the irresponsible behaviour of the three individuals, the caulkers' trade and consequently their families' livelihood was in danger, and they ask to be allowed to elect a 'chief artisan', who would represent their interests.

The state's response to the request, by the high commissioner himself, was very cautious towards the organization of labour groups:

> The work cannot be done without wages to the employed, and their organisation as a body, will not give them more to do. In England, which is a ... civilised place, there is [sic] no Trade organisations, under the .... The men may form societies among themselves ... and I can say, from long experience, that these societies, when they meddle with wages, generally do more harm than good. Corfu, 28 October 1853.

This was a clear denunciation of organized labour and trade unionism, and contrasted with the enthusiasm that the state showed, allowing merchants to form a chamber of commerce, the most advanced commercial mechanism of the time. A chamber provided advice to the Ionian government; by contrast, forms of organization that would demand better wages and improved working conditions could be troublesome, as Ward stated according to 'long experience'. The idea of self-organization, therefore, was popular not only with merchants but also with artisans and craftsmen as well as porters. In June 1861 several porters of Zante requested to be allowed to elect a representative and thus constitute an organized body.[46] The petition is very similar to the demand of caulkers eight years earlier. Porters highlighted the importance of their trade for the port and commerce of the island among other labour groups. As the port activity increased, so did the determination of porters as an organized body to play a decisive role in it. Porters wished to make their position in a competitive port economy less precarious, and to secure a better income. These petitions expressed specific requests of occupational groups and demonstrate the proliferation of ideas about labour organization, and reflect a strong sense of occupational and class identity among Corfu shopkeepers, coffee-house keepers and bakers.

The Ionian State sought to 'Westernize' Ionian economies and societies, and obliterate any traits of an 'uncivilized' or at least unrestrained society. In this spirit, opening hours for shops aimed at protecting popular feeling from any sacrilegious business practices, such as keeping shops open during the mass hours and during religious holidays. In October 1853, thirty-two shopkeepers, tobacconists and coffee-house owners requested permission to open their shops on Sundays and other religious holidays from 9 in the morning instead of 12 noon, when the mass was over.[47] The coffee-house keepers' and tobacconists' claim touched upon a strictly religious matter for Greek Orthodox Christians, as the signatures (only in Greek) and the petition demonstrate.[48] The shopkeepers argued that they did not intend to provoke a religious scandal by keeping their shops open during the mass, which had caused the rage and intervention of the archbishop to the municipal council to forbid the opening of the shops. The director of police claimed that shops should not open at 9 as shopkeepers requested, but after 10 when the mass was finished in most churches. Coffee-house keepers argued that they were struggling to earn a living because of the tariffs they had to pay, the rents and the wages, and that they were waiting for the religious holidays to make a profit. Who were their customers? 'Η κατωτάτη τάξις των πολιτών' (the lowest class of citizens) and the 'working class'; these were the people who went to wine shops and started drinking from the morning 'forgetting the exercise of sacred duties'. Here was a view of the everyday and holiday life of the people, their leisure and their lack of attention to religious duties; lower-class Ionians preferred to spend their holiday in the coffee houses and at tobacconists' forgetting their daily worries, anxieties and troubles as they struggled to earn a living. Shopkeepers noted their interaction with the 'lower classes' and the 'working class', and presented themselves as the group providing a service for the less privileged of the community, while claiming to be devout Christians and trying not to appear sacrilegious and provoke the reaction of the Church.

Many groups resisted restrictions to their trades, advocating greater freedom and claiming that they represented and expressed the needs of the rest of 'society'. Bakers were traditionally intermediaries between grain merchants and the rest of the population, and an essential trade group for the urban population since villagers produced their own bread after they had milled their grain. Bakers submitted petitions that reveal their class identity, how they perceived themselves and other social groups, and demonstrate how state regulations affected 'lower middle class' or 'petite bourgeoisie' Ionians. Petitions by bakers in Corfu go back to 1825; when Gamma Chiotto returned from his trip to Malta where he learned how to establish a 'fabrica of Paste fine', a pasta-making factory, he realized that the regulations for bakers had changed and he could no longer bake bread of the first quality – the only one he knew how to make – and he asked for an exemption from the general rule, which was not granted.[49] The government introduced in the 1820s regulations for the activities of every trade, occupation and profession, which, according to the story told by Gamma Chiotto, was harming investment. The regulation caused instant complaints; Giorgio Servopoulo prayed to be allowed to sell 'white bread', not being permitted by the actual municipal regulations, asking the government to consider the damage he had sustained the previous year when he was forced to sell his bread at six farthings instead of ten, the old price.[50]

These issues appeared in several petitions by bakers, who were one of the most vital but also well-organized trades in the cities. In 1837 Corfu bakers requested permission to keep their shops open for longer hours, so that they can prepare bread for the 'well-to-do classes of the town' (*classe piu agiata della citta*).[51] Selling 'white bread' brought significant income to bakers, on top of the bread they were required and obliged to prepare for the less well-off classes. Bakers wanted to be able to open their shops and produce white or 'luxury' bread and work longer hours against the order of the municipal council; to this end they asked the high commissioner to intervene for the 'liberty of their industry' (*liberta della loro industria*). The discourse of liberalism was becoming popular. Bakers defended the right to produce bread of different quality for a different market; they also responded to the municipal council, which accused them of neglecting the poor by producing bread for the rich, saying that this was the practice of just one baker and that they should not collectively be held responsible. The petition, written in Italian and signed by thirty-four bakers of Corfu, shows a striking similarity with the petition that the Zante bakers submitted, twenty-two years later.

In the 1860s bakers in Zante still claimed their right to prepare and sell bread without government intervention. Unlike Corfu bakers, they first asked for the government to regulate the bread-making process and prevent malpractice, and then requested the right to produce bread for the rich on order and according to 'the principle of free trade'.[52] Bakers argued that bread prices were set according to the price of wheat and the 'fixed' labour needed to produce the bread, which had been abandoned for several years since market regulators were setting the price, causing harm and injustice. The practice was particularly unfair because it ignored the bakers' own condition, who were neither rich nor 'capitalists' [κεφαλαιούχοι].

Bakers underlined their dependence on grain merchants who gave them three months' credit, leaving them vulnerable to fluctuations in international markets but also to prices set by the government's regulator. When bankruptcies followed, bakers ended up either in jail or in the hands of their creditors, and so they requested regulation of bread prices that would take grain prices and labour costs into account. The neglect of the government's regulators had led to a decrease in the quality of bread. When market inspectors found the bread unsuitable they distributed it to the poor; bakers protested that bread found unsuitable for consumption was distributed to the poor and questioned the practice, arguing that poor Ionians' health was as vulnerable as everyone else's. If market inspectors regulated in a fair manner, no bread would be wasted and the quality would remain suitable for consumption by all Ionians, not just those who could afford good-quality bread.

Bakers expressed how they perceived their class identity in providing bread for both ends of the social scale and requested permission to do so, just as bakers on other islands were. The resident of Zante reported that plans were under consideration to allow the unregulated sale of bread for the rich, called *pane di lusso*, provided the bakers continued to produce bread for the 'lower and middle classes'. The terminology used is revealing of the class differences on an issue of everyday consumption, such as bread, for which no risks could be taken and about which social tensions could mount. Authorities listened to the bakers' demand and left the 'luxury bread' market unregulated, responding to the bakers' request.

In the 'public sector' the state was the most important employer for Ionians and this is why so many asked for employment by the state. In 1841 the Ionian government and Douglas personally oversaw the processing of the requests for employment, promotion or transfer (in a few cases) in government services. The state, during that period, was rarely seen as employer; however, for many Ionians the state was precisely that, especially when there were no dilemmas concerning the functioning of the protectorate, at least for the lower classes seeking employment and for many middle class Ionians aspiring to pursue a career in the Ionian civil service.[53] Ionians sent 257 letters with such requests, mostly from Corfu, seeking employment, and it is among those petitions that the full state of many distressed Ionians transpires, as they described their destitution, often asking not for employment but simply begging for charity to alleviate their poverty.

Notes

1 Petition 505, 1825, CO 136/1034, National Archives, London (hereafter N.A.).
2 Risoluzione del II parlamento (12 April 1823).
3 Resoluzione del V PARLAMENTO (19 January 1836).
4 Senate Resolution, IIGG, No. 267, 25 January / 6 February 1836. Hiotis mentions that the plan for the 'Agronomical Society' was conceived and presented to the Senate by Adam. Chiotis, *Istorika Apopnimonevmata Eptanisou*, 264.
5 The state welcomed proposals for subsidizing cultivations with 700 pounds for Corfu, Zante and Kefalonia, and 300 pounds for the smaller islands. The society directed the expansion of wheat cultivations to cater for the islands' deficiency in cereals, but also the proliferation of silk, honey and wine production. It also purchased agricultural tools and machinery. See ibid., 266.
6 D. Anogiatis-Pelé and E. Prontzas, *I Kerkyra 1830–1832. Metaxi fedouarchias kai apoikiokratias*. Thessaloniki: University Studio Press, 2002.
7 M. Kamonachou, 'Thesmoi agrotikou eksynchronismou stin Kerkyra to 19o aiona'. Vol B. Ph.D. Ionio Panepistimio, 2008, 140.
8 Act No. 60, 5th Parliament, 31 March / 12 April 1837.
9 Act No. 82, 5th Parliament, 7/19 June 1837.
10 Solomos, *Geniki Dimosionomiki tis Kefallinias*, 46.
11 Act No. 29, 7th Parliament, 2/14 April 1842, 'per animare la coltura e pietrificazione della pianta di Riscolo'.
12 IIGG, 2/14 May 1853. *Coloni* was the term used for the tenant farmers.
13 Act No. 62, 7th Parliament, 30 May 1844.
14 Act No. 21, 8th Parliament, 30 March 1845; 'per garantire nell' Isla di Santa Maura e sue adiacenze il progresso dell' agricultura, ed impedire la clandestine introduzione di malfattori'.
15 'A few words on Capital, addressed to Proprietors and Peasants, by Capt. Portlock, Honorary Secretary of the Agricultural Society'. IIGG, No. 88, 24 August / 5 September 1846.
16 Resolution 25 June 1819, and Police Notification 8 May 1820, Anagnostiki Etairia Kerkyras.
17 No. 6, Gazzetta degli Stati Uniti delle Isole Jonie, 8/20 Februrary 1819.
18 L. Zoes, *Ai en Zakyntho Syntechniai*. Zakynthos, 1893.
19 E.A. 849, subfolder 17.

20 4/11/1818, E.A. 849, subfolder 22, Γ.Α.Κ.
21 3rd Session 1st Parliament, No. XXVIII, 14-05-1820, Korgialeneios Library.
22 Jervis, *History of the Island of Corfu*, 238.
23 Petition 520, Register of Petitions 1825–1827, CO 136/1034, P.R.O.
24 Register of Petitions 1825–1827, CO 136/1034, P.R.O.
25 S. Gekas, '"Thalassovioti" – Living off the Sea: The Corfu Suburb of Manduki in the Nineteenth Century', in Anthony Hirst and Patrick Sammon (eds), *The Ionian Islands: Aspects of their History and Culture*. Newcastle-upon-Tyne: Cambridge Scholars Publishing, 2014.
26 Corfu 14 March 1837, Petition No. 26, Fishermen and Fishmongers pray to be allowed to fish at night. CO 136/661, P.R.O.
27 September 1859, No. 739, CO 136/874.
28 Nikiforou, in her study on public ceremonies, mainly religious processions, talks about the participation of the *scuole* (guilds) in these processions. In eighteenth-century religious processions for example, the *scuole* of shoe-makers, cheesemongers/grocers, and tailors took part in the procession. See A. Nikiforou-Testone, *Dimosies Teletes stin Kerkyra kata tin periodo tis Venetikis Kyriarxias, 14os-18os ai*. Athens: Themelio, 1999, 47.
29 Petition No. 425, Register of Petitions 1860 (January–July), CO 136/1056, P.R.O.
30 Petition No. 58, CO 136/810. 'Carpenters and Blacksmiths of Corfu. Request that the *Ionia* may not be sent elsewhere for repairs'.
31 Zante, 31 March 1860, Petition 2, CO 136/887, P.R.O.
32 Petition 373, CO 136/1034, N.A.
33 Index of Petitions, 1825, CO 136/1034, N.A.
34 Petition 356, Register of Petitions 1825–1827, CO 136/1034, N.A.
35 Petition 551, 1825, CO 136/1034, N.A.
36 Petition No. 508, 1825, CO 136/1034, N.A.
37 Petition No. 509, 1825, CO 136/1035, N.A.
38 Petition No. 10, CO 136/841, N.A.
39 Petition No. 118, June 1856, 136/851, N.A.
40 Petition No. 26, CO 136/841, N.A.
41 Petition No. 94, February 1860, CO 136/887, N.A.
42 Petition No. 21, 1855, CO 136/841, N.A.
43 Petition No. 52, 1852, CO 136/810, N.A.
44 Petition No. 40, 1855, CO 136/841, N.A.
45 3/20 November 1851. 'Several caulkers. Ask to be allowed to organise into a body with an elected chief, against the monopoly of three persons', Petition No. 309, CO 136/821, P.R.O.
46 Petition No. 244, 'Several porters of Zante. Praying that a chief may be appointed at their head', Register of Petitions 1861, CO 136/1059, P.R.O.
47 Petition No. 308, 'Several Shopkeepers. Opening hours', CO 136/821, P.R.O.
48 This is not to imply of course that all shopkeepers were Orthodox. In the Jewish quarter the majority of wine-house keepers were Jews. Nevertheless, the Orthodox shopkeepers, being the majority, felt they had to take the initiative on the matter of opening hours on religious holidays; Corfu had (and has) a lot. For the patron saint, Saint Spyridon, alone there are four

processions per year, during which his relics are exposed; plus Christmas (2 days), New Year, Good Friday, Easter (2 days), Epiphany and 15 August.
49 Petition 518, 1826, CO 136/1034, N.A.
50 Petition 279, 1826, CO 136/1034, N.A.
51 Petition No. 164, Bakers. Pray to be allowed to open their shops, CO 136/661
52 Petition No.340, CO 136/873, P.R.O.
53 'Register of Candidates for employment. Promotion and transfer in government service', CO 136/1250.

 Chapter 9

Poverty, the State and the Middle Class

From the 1830s onwards, and especially during the 'long' 1850s – from the late 1840s to the early 1860s – Ionians became preoccupied with the intensity and extent of famine, disease and dislocation, as well as the hopelessness that people both in the Ionian State and the Greek Kingdom felt. This prolonged economic, social and health crisis led to a crisis of legitimacy in both states and had significant political consequences.[1] In the case of the Ionian State the government, faced with the 'problem' of poverty, introduced institutions of 'public utility' and provided some relief. At the time, many Ionians and British did not distinguish between public works and charity; colonial state officials in North India took a very similar approach to even more pressing issues during the period of the 1837–38 famine.[2] In the Ionian Islands, unlike in North India on that particular occasion, the colonial state had introduced employment and wage labour for the poor – in road construction – as a form of poor relief much earlier (in the 1810s–1820s) and without the urgency that a famine imposed on colonial authorities as well as the suffering population. Similarly it was the need to employ the suffering poor and offer them much-needed income that spurred road building in that part of colonial India but not before the 1830s, much later than in Corfu and Kefalonia. In both India and the Ionian Islands, whether under conditions of famine or as part of planning for regional development, road construction served as a form of poor relief and extended the power and reach of the state into areas previously difficult to control and for that reason often considered 'dangerous', unknown and prone to crime. This extension of state power was part of the centralization and modern state-building process, with state infrastructure being the clearest manifestation of the increasing power of a state, allowing it to 'extend material and symbolic communications throughout the territory'.[3]

The question of poverty in the Ionian Islands was linked to the state of living conditions for the majority of the population. Ionians thought that the increase in the number of the urban poor was evident in the increase in the number of beggars and vagabonds; their presence became for the first time a 'social problem'. This was as much the result of the worsening economic condition on the islands as it was the outcome of changing perceptions on poverty and philanthropy. Difficulties of securing a living by relying on agricultural production combined with a more systematic recording of poverty. The increased numbers of abandoned illegitimate children is but just one example, which indicates the extent of impoverishment without being the only sign.[4] Fluctuations in the international economy had a multiple impact on the population, with migration being a standard strategy especially from the 1840s onwards, when the currant crop was abundant in mainland Greece and competition was fierce; Ionians migrated to where grain could be found, and was used as a reward for the labour of thousands of them.[5] The volatility of agricultural production forced hundreds of Ionians to seek the means of survival in the towns, where they could beg, while others sought some income on the mainland opposite. These inherent problems of Ionian agricultural production were at the heart of the reform initiatives. The population rise may not have been dramatic but it certainly put pressures on the peasant economy and made seasonal migration a forced choice for many villagers.

There is evidence that poverty was already becoming a cause for concern by the 1820s. In 1825 the Senate introduced the law on the 'poverty certificates' (*forma pauperis*) that authorities had to issue to those in need. The preamble states that there was 'an excessive quantity of the Poverty documents, presented by those wishing to be declared as poor', more than the quantity the law had made provision for. These documents were issued in a non-uniform way that needed to be regulated to prevent abuse – hence the statement that priests, village notables and constables now had to sign, confirming that the holder of the 'certificate' was totally poor, meaning of no immobile goods or other goods, and not exercising any craft or profession; this would then secure their daily subsistence from either day labour or public charity. The law introduced penalties of up to 50 crowns or one to three months prison sentence for those signing false documents,[6] in the hope of stopping the abuse and the certification of too many 'undeserved' poor. The law was reformed in 1845, again to 'end all abuses with regard to the stamped paper used for persons who are authorized to plead in *forma pauperis*'.[7]

Increasing poverty on the islands became a concern in the period after the 1830s saw an upsurge of begging in Ionian towns, and it was considered, for the first time, to be a problem worth eliminating. Tackling poverty, or at least aiming to limit its visible impact in the towns, became more systematically organized by the central and municipal authorities, the political class and the British administration, and the urban elite, largely through the voluntary associations. An estimate of the number of poor and the rate of impoverishment based on the data we have is extremely hard; however the number of decrees, municipal regulations and acts of government passed from the mid-1830s onwards against beggars, vagrancy and 'vicious mendacity' indicate an increased visibility of the poor outside churches and in squares, and perhaps an increase of the poor themselves, as well as of begging. The local and central authorities passed decrees and regulations that gradually developed into more punitive rules that aimed to improve behaviour in the cities, but also in the countryside. The decrees of Zante were all issued in 1835;[8] similar decrees were passed for all Ionian cities. In the following years, however, the attitude of the state towards the poor and poverty developed towards a more coercive and authoritarian direction. Even the more punitive decrees and regulations of the 1850s did not alter the everyday practices of Ionians or their attitudes on cleanliness, social conduct and economic behaviour. Changes in Ionian society caused by impoverishment are seen in increased demands for poor relief, which in turn put pressure on the urban elite, as well as the state, to provide for the rising numbers of poor in the towns.

The following 'report' is telling about social perceptions and state policies by several British officials towards the poor, and especially vagrancy:

> The poor in distress are almost entirely dependent on casual charity and are under the necessity of becoming beggars. In churches, it is true, collections are made for their relief; but although it is said the service is often disturbed by the importunity of beggars, the amount contributed is so inconsiderable as not to be deserving of mention. From his address to the Parliament, the late lord high commissioner, Sir Howard Douglas, appears to have been fully alive to the necessity of some active measures being taken to afford relief to the poor, and seems to have had in contemplation the establishing of alms-houses and providing constant funds for their maintenance. Sir Charles Napier considers the revenue from the convent-lands as the appropriate means for supporting the poor. He says, these possessions, which are extensive, 'have been acquired in legacies made by the devout and the repentant, for the use of the poor. To this use (he adds) I applied them, and had I not been interfered with, there would have been, in a few years, no destitute person in Cephalonia ... Had it been continued six years, no labourer in Cephalonia would have been without a competence; by which I mean, that every industrious man might have a cottage of his own, a garden of his own, be able to buy a pound of bread for 1.5 d, a pound of meat for 2.5 d., and a bottle of wine for 1 d., in all 5 d. a day, and receive from 10 d. to 15 d. a day for his labour. When it is recollected that no firing and very little clothing are purchased in this hot climate, and that a Cephalonian has no rent to pay,

I think this as good a condition as any labouring man can expect, in addition to certain refuge in a convent, when disabled by bodily affliction'.⁹

This is what a daily wage could bring in to an Ionian according to one of the considerate British officials, Napier.

The Savings Bank and the 'Poor Agriculturalists'

One cannot blame British and Ionian liberals, state officials and delegates for not trying; they transplanted institutions and practices from Britain to Ionian society with interesting if not always successful results. In 1835 a savings bank was established in Corfu for the benefit of 'poor industrialists', 'artisans, labourers and agriculturalists'.¹⁰ This was a foreign (Scottish in particular) plan borrowed from 'other states' that aspired to turn the lower classes of Ionians into an industrious people by offering some insurance and interest in case of illness, based on earnings of deposits. The 'experiment' of a similar institution would be 'under the immediate protection of the government'. The establishment of the savings bank was the first time the word 'experiment' was used. The government was authorized to nominate trustees on the respective islands to receive deposits every week, but no less than one shilling during a year and no more than 25 pounds per individual.

The founders of the savings bank institutions were concerned with moral as well as economic considerations, and stated that they sought to target usury; the Ionian State newspaper wrote that 'the aim of the Bank is not only to help the working classes gain profit, but to help them improve morally as well ... [it] will infuse into those classes that are deprived of the rudiments of good education, the love for hard work, prudence and thrift'.¹¹ The bank announced it accepted deposits of money from the Ionian poor for times of sickness, for retirement or for a dowry for the depositors' daughters. The bank lent on flexible and attractive terms, since money deposited could be withdrawn on any day of the week and without any notice. The bank's deposits, the names of trustees and reports of the meetings were published in the official newspaper, in the same spirit of accountability that had permeated Ionian state affairs from the 1820s onwards. The government appointed the trustees who ran the bank and accepted deposits held in the public treasury at 4 per cent interest. During the first fifteen years of the bank's operation only a few members of the executive and legislative bodies of the Ionian State, British officers, and higher clergy administered the bank. The first trustees were ten British 'Esquires', five priests (four Roman Catholic and one Orthodox), Gerostathis, the well-established merchant, and Elias Vasilakis as auditor, the resident of Corfu at the time and in 1848 the local director of the Ionian Bank.[12] This was clearly the time when locals did not get involved or were not invited to participate, with the few exceptions mentioned. The trustees occasionally found themselves in an awkward position. In 1838 the third annual meeting of the savings bank trustees identified the problems inherent in the ambiguous status of the establishment as neither a bank nor a charity: when three benevolent citizens deposited money for the endowment of 'two or three destitute girls' without mentioning the names of the girls, the trustees warned against such practice in the future.[13] In 1846, the annual general meeting registered twelve new trustees, among them merchants Spyridon Dimas and Andreas Chiriachis. The administration committee included Antonios Candonis and Gerostathi, but also Andrea Mustoxidi, the historiographer and politician, and Demetrio Curcumelli.[14] Gradually merchants and politicians became involved and served as trustees in the administration of the savings bank, and according to the annual report were chosen according to their character, as 'honourable', 'distinguished' and 'well known to everyone for their love of public good'.[15] Then years later, in 1848, 308 depositors had entrusted the savings bank with their money, a small number for the whole Ionian population but high for Corfu, the only place that the bank achieved some popularity. For this reason, perhaps, the annual general meeting expressed its conviction that the bank was advancing 'at a secure and stable pace'.[16] However, by 1847 the bank seems to have been of no interest to peasants, who suffered from the volatility of agricultural production. Trustees felt inclined to ask the clergy to start a campaign for informing the peasant population of the advantages of saving their money in the state's establishment. British rule incited peasants to deposit their meagre savings, and a year later the trustees associated the work of the bank with the operation 'of other philanthropic establishments'.[17] Still, the bank had more deposits in 1848 than in 1846, with 3,227 pounds compared to 2,933 two years earlier.

The failure of the savings bank project is not surprising given the downturn of the Ionian economy in the 1840s and especially the 1850s. Peasants and the urban poor not only had very little to save but could barely make ends meet, and during the crisis of the 'long 1850s' got further into debt. At the level of the bank's administration, the Ionian bourgeoisie found fertile ground for forging an identity. In 1849 there were ninety trustees, including the high commissioner, politicians, doctors of medicine and law, merchants, priests, British officers, 'nobles' and persons entitled 'Cavaliers' by the British and belonging to the imperial order of St Michael and St George.[18] This was 'ornamentalism' Ionian style.[19] Many commissioners continued the practice, introducing a new order to the title-obsessed Ionians with hundreds of them adding the prefix 'count' to their name. In 1841 this situation forced the government to legislate on the issue, passing an act 'to regulate the Manner in which title of "Count", possessed by Ionians, can be legally retained and inherited', and asking those using the title to prove it with documents to the authorities.[20]

These 'Counts' participated in the savings bank and shared with other members of the Ionian bourgeoisie the British-imported view of ameliorating the condition of the poor by teaching them to save for a rainy day; they also aspired to the social status conferred by their participation in the administration of the savings bank. Trustees of these banks ought to have inspired confidence so as to attract the savings of those for whom they were founded – the less well off, labourers, and so on.[21] The integrity of such a heterogeneous but well-respected group was thought to be reassuring for prospective savers. The list of trustees from 1849 included merchants Candonis, Chiriachis, Dimas, Economo, Gerostati, Giamari, Lavrano, Micrulachi and Scarpa, who contributed to the administration of the bank for reasons of status as well as knowledge and experience. Spyridon Dimas was appointed as one of the two *revisore* or auditors. Lawyers formed one-third of all trustees; seven were recorded as 'Esquires', seven belonged to the clergy, while ten were recorded as 'Count' or 'Cavalier' or both. The political role of the nobility after the end of Venetian rule was synonymous with their traditional monopoly of positions of political influence and power;[22] the significant participation of the nobility to the administration of the bank shows the new roles these people and their 'political' families adopted in the new social and political order of Ionian and especially Corfu society. By 1855 there was one savings bank in Corfu, Zante, Lefkada and Kythera, and, apparently, there was one established in Kefalonia in 1857, although no other information has been found on any of the savings banks other than the Corfu one.[23]

The British-Ionian state and the Ionian and British elite introduced practices to regulate economic and social life. This tendency coincided with practices followed in Britain during the same period. The problems Britain faced of course during the peak of the industrial revolution, urbanization, and deterioration of living conditions, can hardly be compared with the Lilliputian Ionian societies. Still, it is impressive that the model of social organization as well as the practices adopted were the same, namely the ones followed by the British bourgeoisie and the liberal state.[24] The increasing use of police force in the towns to remove the pariahs of Ionian society pushed them further towards its fringes and shows the inability to remove the conditions of poverty through philanthropy, and explains the choice to introduce more stringent measures.

The urban elite viewed Ionian society as a microcosm of Britain, the protective power, not only on issues of free trade and protectionism but also on matters of social organization. If Britain was on a mission to civilize and modernize the colonies, then the Ionian Islands, even though a semi-colony, were equally or even more suited to a benevolent and caring society, and as poor-less as possible. If every society has to come to terms and deal with its own poor, then surely the period from the 1830s onwards was the period when the British-Ionian elite decided that they had to modernize the ways in which they were treating their poor. The Ionian bourgeoisie, some serving for periods as state officials, converged on their views about treating the poor and creating institutions to manage poverty, to the extent that was possible.

Care and Discipline for the Poor: State and Civil Society

The history of charitable institutions in Corfu is no different from others in Western Europe, especially Italy. Corfu during the period of Venetian rule developed 'highly sophisticated structures of assistance for the poor', first created in sixteenth-century Venice and known as the *Scuole Grandi*, guilds and confraternities; this was 'the most successful example of co-ordination between state and voluntary organisations'.[25] The first hospital was built in Corfu in the sixteenth century for the treatment of the poor and pilgrims on their way to, and from, the Holy Land (Pellegrini), and the Catholic monastery, which it adjoined, administered it.[26] In the eighteenth century, the first philanthropic initiative by a priest and a merchant led to the erection of a civic hospital for the treatment of poor Christians, Roman Catholics and Orthodox, but not Jews.[27] Zante's hospital was founded in 1666 and was rebuilt in 1817, while in Kefalonia and Lefkada hospitals were founded in the 1710s.[28] The Venetian administration ensured that some of the money deposited at the Corfu *Monte di Pieta* (pawnshop), which was re-established in 1768, went towards the building of a new hospital, which was postponed.[29] During the protectorate the administration of philanthropy and charitable institutions was sanctioned by an act in 1820, which passed the administration of all funds and income related to ecclesiastical goods, to a state committee. As a consequence, the hospital allowance passed to the government. This resulted in the erection of a new building outside the town walls, near the suburb of Mandouki. Accounts from the nineteenth century speak of three hospitals, one for the poor, one for orphans and one for the 'aphrodisiac diseases of prostitutes'.[30]

In March 1832, physicians of Zante decided to change the existing practice of visiting poor patients in their houses and treat patients in a building erected or bought (the sources are not clear), especially for the purpose of treating the poor free of charge.[31] Physicians intended to create a sanitized (to the extent possible) environment, a sign of progress and 'civilization' that the British resident applauded. The establishment of the hospital for the poor also meant that, from then on, registration at the hospital, the only place where the poor had any hope of receiving treatment, also meant better monitoring of the poor who got sick; this was the moment when the 'great confinement' in the Ionian Islands took place.[32]

A similar development took place in Corfu in the late 1830s. In the same spirit as with the physicians of Zante and, perhaps, following their example, 'the noble Corfiotes Dr Angelos Koyevinas, Dr Spyridon Arvanitakis, Dr Christoforos Lavranos, Dr Konstantinos Mavroioannis, and Dr Ioannis Vrailas offered to serve for free as doctors and surgeons in the public hospital for the poor of this Island, and the Senate accepted immediately their offer and ordered that they are being praised accordingly'.[33] The newspaper applauded the initiative of the Corfu physicians, but its author was also confident that this initiative would be imitated as an 'act of distributive justice'. Such contemporary perceptions of poverty and charity show the expectations of Ionian society from its prominent members, the physicians in this case, who emerged as another group of experts in tackling disease and sickness. The problem of impoverishment, however, could not be solved by the benevolence of the islands' physicians alone. The situation demanded the intervention of the state, which prohibited begging for the first time in 1833. Two acts of Parliament from 1837 and 1840 show the gradual transition from understanding the 'problem' of vagrancy to disciplining, to a policy of 'zero tolerance' towards 'vagabonds'. Even the titles of the respective acts, 'Act of Parliament for putting a stop to Mendacity' and 'Act of Parliament for the Prevention of Vagrancy and vicious Mendacity', demonstrate the growing suspicion against anyone trying to secure a living by begging, whether they were 'deserving' or undeserving poor. The regulations aimed to discern those vagrants and beggars who did not deserve aid and should be incarcerated instead. In the following decade, the response of the state to the increasingly visible poverty in the form of beggars and vagrants in the Ionian towns, essentially criminalized poverty.

These policies were part of a wider project of social engineering introduced by the Ionian elite and state officials. On 22 March 1833, Commissioner Nugent authorized the Ionian Senate to build a poorhouse on the Avramis hill at the site of an old Venetian tower. The new establishment would provide care to a few poor inmates and overall respond to growing impoverishment, destitution, misery and injustice, which was forcing increasingly more people into begging and 'vagrancy'. In 1833, the Ionian State decided the establishment of a poorhouse on each island. The administration and funding for the institutions burdened the local councils and the resident of each island. If the resolution of the Senate remained vague regarding funding sources for the operation of poorhouses, the aims and the philosophy of the initiative were explicitly stated: the opening of poorhouses was directly associated with prohibiting beggars from 'disturbing' their fellow citizens, and taking them off the streets and out of the churches, the public places where begged; no excuse would be allowed for begging in the streets or in the churches, and the resident of each island would publish a decree 'to constrain and if necessary to discipline the violators'.[34]

In 1837 the government introduced new legislation 'for putting a stop to Mendacity', since it was 'necessary not only to put an end to the nuisance of begging but also to prevent the exhibition of Objects of suffering humanity, that is constantly taking place during the celebration of Divine Service'.[35] The poor were becoming a nuisance, and Commissioner Douglas took another initiative since the first task of every bureaucratic government was to record and register within two months all the 'lame, blind and others who, from bodily defects or from old age, are unable to procure their daily bread by any other means but begging'. The committee formed to supervise the disabled and other poor consisted of two priests and two heads of families, chosen by the municipal council in each village, adding an extra layer of surveillance and control by the village authorities. The other important task of the committee was to obtain voluntary subscriptions, introducing a state-sponsored and public–private philanthropic sector. The funds were to be collected in churches, supervising the alms that were traditionally collected for the poor. Once these funds were available, the police prohibited begging on the streets, and in houses and churches, under the threat of arrest.

In the 1830s the poorhouse project combined traditional forms of collecting funds with a modern style of administration. The Senate adopted measures for collecting contributions and donations during

Mass in the churches, but made little provision for the financial administration of the institution. On 10 May 1837 the Senate complemented the previous resolution and introduced new measures with the encouragement and endorsement of Commissioner Douglas. The administration of the poorhouse combined the two types of response by the Ionian State and society to poverty, confinement and philanthropy. A committee to distribute funds collected for the poorhouse was formed, and in 1846 it required a systematic recording of poverty, with information on everyone from the town and the suburbs who, according to the criteria of those surveying these areas, should be sent to the poorhouse. In its announcement the committee 'lured' beggars into appearing before the committee who in return would provide 'money, food, clothes, medical help ... to those worthy of help ... according to their needs'.[36]

Much stricter regulation followed. Prohibition of begging was only part of a broader disciplinary framework when, in July 1838, the 'lunatic asylum' regulations were published. Modernizing the terms of confinement followed the creation of the places of internment. The site had to be 'spacious', and the 'lunatics' would be employed on crafts that would keep them occupied and productive while provisions were taken to keep the more serious cases away from the 'hypochondriacs', and men separate from women.[37] In June 1840 the Parliament passed another act for the 'prevention of vagrancy and vicious mendacity', stricter than the previous ones and evidence that they had not perhaps produced the intended results.[38] The act started by stressing the 'fatal consequences that derive from these practices', and expressed the commitment of the government to 'clear these states of vagrancy and vicious mendacity', including deportation of those foreign beggars who were able to work but 'followed no vocation, art, or trade and have no property'. Native 'vagrants' had to produce 'sureties for their conduct', otherwise they would be put to subsidiary labour for at least a year and not more than three, either on their own island or any other, so the measure included internal deportation as well. Whoever continued begging would be sentenced to imprisonment at the 'House of Correction' for eleven to thirty days, and on repetition they would be subject to heavier penalties.

The poorhouse committee soon devised the 'internal regulation of the Poorhouse', which demarcated the 'obligations of the poor and the guards'.[39] This essentially was a more liberal version of a prison, since inmates could only go out for a few hours a day with the guard's permission, were prohibited from going to wine shops (the place where the lower classes socialized), let alone drink and stay out beyond a certain hour. A number of other internal rules regulated the life of the poor in the institution, prohibited contact between men and women, and ordered a guard to read the obligations of inmates on a weekly basis. These conditions of confinement probably lured only the desperately poor to join the poorhouse, trading their freedom for survival and dependence. These new and modern institutions of confinement, the poorhouse and the 'lunatic asylum', could not operate without a set of rules that was not only decided by the administration but was also published in the state newspaper.

The results of the survey recording the poor were published; in the period from 1 March to 20 June 1846, the poorhouse provided for 189 poor, of whom 43 were resident in the poorhouse. The report of the committee, though, was far from festive. At the end, they talk of 'many persons being in utter poverty' and rendering the work of the committee incomplete. Poverty was increasingly seen as a problem in Corfu and on the other islands, as economic pressure was taking its toll in the urban and rural societies. The poor of the town and country had to resort to begging or even being incarcerated in the poorhouse once they moved to the city.

At the same time, Douglas and the Ionian government responded to emergencies with state support at short notice, showing another aspect of social policy. In January 1841, Douglas conveyed the sympathy of the colonial office minister and Queen Victoria to the earthquake victims in Zante, and the financial support of £5,000; a lot more was necessary. Davy, in one of his last years as chief medical inspector in the Mediterranean, estimated that the overall destruction of villages as well as city buildings stood at 'no less than £300,000', an amount that Douglas reported as well.[40] A committee of British officers, headed by Adam, formed to administer the funds for the earthquake victims. Similar to many initiatives that would follow, the newspaper published the names and amounts donated for the Zante poor and the earthquake fund; by February 1841 the committee had already collected 870 pounds from Britain and $945 from the islands, recorded in the different currencies of each place.[41]

Policies and measures that criminalized poverty increased in the 1850s; at the same time Ionian State officials realized that to tame poverty required more measures and more funding. Declarations and resolutions were published 'for the knowledge and benefit of the public', and those interested were notified that they could receive the money to which they were entitled after their case had been examined, provided that they were recorded by the committee and their condition (poverty, illness or both) enumerated. The result was a more bureaucratic process aspiring to a more efficient government policy on poverty; the committee promised 'to publish every three months the tables, showing the number of ill admitted to the Poorhouse, the number of poor receiving aid, and the income and expenditure of the establishment'.[42] This was an obligation similar to the Ionian Bank and the new business practices of the time that were novel for the region. The spirit of the times called for an administration that was accountable, similar to the management of different but ideologically consistent institutions such as joint-stock companies but also the organization of poor relief; both were parts of the same project to rationalize and change the outlook, structures and function of Ionian societies, and were part of the logic of the Ionian and the savings banks and the poorhouse, with the same people involved in the administration of all three organizations.

Philanthropy reflected the ideology and worldview of the Ionian bourgeoisie and served as an important safety valve for the pressures of the emerging industrializing societies of the nineteenth century. Examples during the period of British rule in the Ionian Islands point to similar pressures, despite the absence of an industrializing economy. The personal initiatives of Lady Seaton (spouse of Commissioner Seaton) and the Ionian elite in the 1840s focused on the poorhouse, and raised money through the subscription of annual and extraordinary funds. In the case of the poorhouse philanthropy and confinement went hand in hand. As the problem of vagabond beggars – what contemporaries called 'vicious mendacity' – deteriorated, the British-Ionian administration and affluent Ionians demonstrated their determination to transform Corfu – and other Ionian cities like Zante too – by criminalizing poverty and putting beggars in prison, not just in the poorhouse. What they achieved is debatable; probably not very much, under the pressures of the deteriorating economy of the 1850s. The discourse on poverty and the initiatives reveal the attitudes of state and bourgeois society that in most cases were very close.

The operation, principles and practices of voluntary associations and committees established by the state leave little doubt of the British influence on them. Voluntary associations were important for middle class formation all over Europe.[43] In Corfu, publication of subscriptions and the annual meetings were the new features of a society largely influenced by British ideas; they indicate that a part of this society aspired to the British model of societal organization. The publication of proceedings and most importantly the proceeds raised by the voluntary associations, the accounts and reports of the savings bank, the Ionian bank and the insurance companies, and the legal obligation of these organizations to publish their holdings, echoes the principle of accountability, the cornerstone of bourgeois, liberal society.

The official newspaper published the philanthropic initiatives and the subscriptions of benevolent Ionians and praised them as an example to follow. This showcasing of power and status in Ionian societies through philanthropy and subscription funds made claims to power very public. Subscription funds confirmed the wealth of the middle- and upper-class Ionians who blended in philanthropic initiatives, a most bourgeois space. Most subscribers in lists published in the official newspaper were already established members of the community, government employees, Ionian liberals and nobles, merchants and lawyers, not lacking the titles to prove it either. Among them, foreigners, officers of the British garrison, consuls and commercial agents, were prominent. Ladies/spouses of the leading philanthropists, Lady Seaton especially, formed the Benevolent Ladies Society, which opened the first subscription list in 1844. Merchants' ladies participated in the Ionian Exhibition committee, while others from aristocratic, merchant and military families took the initiative. Lady Seaton opened a space in Corfu urban society, which women of the 'honourable' families hastened to fill, grasping the opportunity, following the activities of their husbands.

The spouses of several merchants donated the standard amount (4s 4d) while a few contributed more. The merchants (or their spouses) and bankers Gysi, Candonis, Gerostathis (or Jerostathi), Lavranos, Courage, Micrulachi, Charlton, Taylor, Loughnan and Zambellis appeared in all subscription lists examined. Social networks in philanthropy brought members of the British administration, a few wholesale merchants and bankers, the land-owning nobility, the judiciary and some intellectuals and professors in the Ionian Academy (Joss, Orioli) closer. The benevolent ladies' society collected funds and managed the school for poor children. A balance sheet accompanied the tables of contributions published to ensure transparency and proper administration of funds. In 1848 the sum for the 'Infant School for the Poor under the Patronage of LADY SEATON' was £45 17s 8d, a sum large enough to pay for the expenses of the school, teachers' salaries, rent, books, needles, repairs, desks, etc.[44] Coincidentally or not, the published list of subscriptions followed the publication of tables of the exchange with lists of prices and a table with the quarterly balance sheet of the Ionian bank. All three pieces of information expressed different aspects of economic and social activity on the islands, and all aspired to the same organizing principle of accountability, transparency and the joint-stock company ethic of management, as well as the public display of economic and social activity.

Poverty threatened social stability in Zante and Kefalonia. In the early 1850s poverty in the country was devastating, with some villagers having only fruit and vegetables and no bread to eat during the spring and summer months. In winter, however, they were forced to go to the towns and beg; those who did not receive much charity passed out and others died of starvation.[45] Bread riots broke out in Zante, people looted bakeries, harassed merchants and retailers, and the police forced bakers to distribute free bread to the people.[46] Children were particularly vulnerable wandering in the squares: 'Young men in lust stripping homeless, starving girls for the price of three oboli of their virgin shame. The police arrested many of the girls and put them either in monasteries or in prison, where they could find bread'.[47]

While in Zante poverty disrupted the social fabric, damaged morals and corrupted young girls creating potentially a moral panic, in Corfu, too, similar descriptions appeared in a newspaper accompanied by a very interesting and British-inspired proposal to solve the problem of vagrancy and begging, increasingly visibly in the town:

> Children aged six to fourteen, wander in the town jobless, filthy, a shame for the town. ... A Workshop, administered by four able artisans, should recruit where those youngsters [are] wandering in the town without any occupation and left to their own devices. With only the threat of being enclosed and obliged to work, most, if not all, would disappear from the streets ... Society does not want anymore to include any wicked, corrupt and idle citizens such as these from their very young age.[48]

This leading article accused both the reformists and the radicals that 'while they wanted to reform the State, they did not say a word about reforming the vices of the vagabond youngsters', aged 6–14, who were going around the town 'dressed in rags or semi-naked, uttering the worse blasphemies and the most vulgar expressions'. This new model of society that commentators envisaged included the establishment of a workshop that would not only confine but also teach 'idle' and poor youngsters how to conform with the rules of a bourgeois society, where idleness, time wasting and 'moral degradation' due to poverty had to be eliminated. Those unwilling or unable to comply, were not considered an appropriate spectacle in a modern urban environment, and if necessary would be locked away.

The Birth of the Corfu Prison

These plans were put into practice in the following few years, as the crisis peaked. In 1853, the police ordered the registration of everyone 'unemployed, wandering in the town or countryside with suspicious intent'. In June the same year, a police report identified the problem and attempted to account for the increase of the poor in Corfu town:

> Sir,
> It is my duty to report that the number of mendacious vagrants in town has started to grow every day. This is due to the fact that the poor of the country who, after being deprived of any income and unable to feed their families, allow their children to enter the town and earn a living from begging. It is lamentable to watch children, dressed in rags and barefoot, male and female, to wander around, sleep under the arches and in other places in the towns, at the mercy of mendacious vagrants of older age. ... I submit to Your Excellency the list containing 22 males and 3 females, the age of which ranges from 5 to 13 years. It does not mean that these are all the vagrants, but they are mentioned because creatures of this frail age are at greater risk than older ones.[49]

The problem caused alarm; the 'shocking' images of young children wandering in the town, vulnerable and manipulated by their parents, appeared recurrently in the Corfu press. The authorities decided to move towards a more coercive direction with the municipal regulation of March 1855. The rationale behind the resolution was the prohibition of vagrancy and begging according to the criminal code, 'whereas vagrancy in these Islands is unfortunately advancing and causes social moral damage' and 'whereas begging is often conducted by underage children of both sexes jeopardising their moral condition'.[50] Everyone arrested for vagrancy and begging was sentenced to hard labour (stone cutting) and imprisoned 'until they promise in paper or provide alternative means of guarantee that they will cease vagrancy and mendacious begging'. What is astonishing is that the regulation was extremely hard on children, the most vulnerable, according to the police report mentioned earlier: 'All children above twelve will be arrested by the Executive Police and will be subject to hard labour, in stone cutting'.[51] Only the 'really' poor would be sent to the poorhouse, the regulations of which were already in place. The means to ascertain whether an Ionian was a 'deserving' poor was the testimony of an official who documented the 'poor' status and condition – usually the parish priest or a village primate.

Such regulations made the poor more dependent on the clergy, especially in villages and parishes where most of the poor came from, and where priests were one of the main authority figures. The incarceration of the vagrants was a daily event:

> 3 March: They put a notice on the Residency Building walls by the Executive Police and from the 4 this month was put in practice and they summoned all the poor, lame, blind, and they brought them to the Police

to examine them. And those able to work will work on road building. Some they will be sent to the countryside. And everyday they arrest more and more.[52]

The regulations effectively criminalized poverty; Ionian societies joined societies with a long tradition of prohibiting begging and conforming the poor to their duty to work, regardless of age or sex. Poor relief through subscription funds and the poorhouse aimed to restrict begging, and prevent potentially dangerous rises in the numbers of paupers who threatened social peace and stability – or at least they were perceived as such – by introducing the concept of unpaid work.[53]

Inside the Blue Books a category of social statistics was created since the 1820s, the number of 'paupers', part of the overall project of colonial statistics in the British Empire.[54] The category is used in inverted commas because historians have demonstrated that definition of the condition of a pauper is subject to changes in attitudes to the poor over time, thus rendering the condition of poverty a social construct as much as a real hardship.[55] The following table shows how many 'paupers' were found and recorded on the islands. The numbers recorded confirm the scepticism with which contemporary statistics should be treated, and their value lies mainly in the classification process that probably shaped colonial and local policy; in Corfu, for instance, the measurement is more meticulous than in Zante, while no economic development could explain the rapid drop in the number of 'paupers' in Zante from 2,000 in 1855–56 to 237 in 1857. Surely, there are factors to explain the difference (the extremely harsh conditions in the years 1855–56, and, perhaps, migration and amelioration of living conditions in the following years); in any case, the figures should be treated with caution whilst taking them into account.

The development of the penitentiary and other nineteenth-century sites of confinement were instruments of social control and often reflected class conflicts; a revisionist history of prisons related the practices and routines of prisons to society's dominant conceptions of power, justice, 'correction' and reform.[56] Despite obvious differences in scope and content, all three works argue that in the years between 1760 and 1840 a rising middle class managed to abolish public rituals of corporeal punishment because they were not appropriate for the modern liberal and industrial society that the middle classes were building. In the last few years the studies on Asia, Africa and Latin America have enriched and elaborated the debate on the 'birth of the prison', showing how colonialism, race and prisoners themselves shaped the histories of the prison and reform practices, and paid attention to the culture of

Table 9.1 Number of recorded 'paupers' in the Ionian Islands.
Source: Blue Books of Statistics, CO 136/1419–1427, T.N.A.

Year	Corfu	Kefalonia	Zante	Sta Maura	Ithaki
1855	250	1,600	2,000	150	1
1856	320	1,600	2,000	150	1
1857	187	1,000	237	62	2
1858	250	1,000	937	40	20
1859	155	1,000	900	40	20
1860	215	1,000	362	250	20
1861	340	1,000	710	350	20
1862	458	1,000	710	350	20

prisoners.[57] The case of the Corfu prison, a central component of the Ionian Islands criminal justice system and Ionian penology, adds to this emerging literature of global perspectives on the history of the prison; it is all the more interesting and potentially enlightening because it is situated on the borderline between Europe, non-European semi-colonized land and the Mediterranean informal colonial condition space.

One of the first British officials to identify the need for prison reform was Napier in Kefalonia. In his chapter on the prisons of the island, he noted with his special style that in both Argostoli and Lixouri 'the prisoners generally quitted at night, leaving a civil message for the jailor that they would be back in the morning, and kept their word, except in urgent cases, when they sometimes broke faith'.[58] Security, obviously, was a major issue in the Argostoli prison where guards had to kill two prisoners on one occasion to prevent everyone from escaping.

The psychiatric hospital, the poorhouse and the prison in Corfu (and the other Ionian cities to a lesser extent) represent the moment of 'discipline and punish' but also affirm the role of the state. Commensurate with the legal codes that predated these sites of modernity but came into effect in exactly the same period, signify for Corfu the birth of the (modern) prison. Focusing on lesser but more widespread crimes, such as theft and crimes against property or the failure to pay debts, the prison was populated with 'new-' as well as 'old-crimes' inmates. The prison became a model for the psychiatric hospital, its infrastructure and its constitution, and for the poorhouse, which was also built in the 1840s. While a 'revolution in social practice' took place in the United States in the 1820s, the emergence of a very similar disciplinary matrix in the 'other' United States, of the Ionian Islands, came soon after. In the United States the scale necessitated radically new practices, and the increasing militancy of the working classes in England also required new and sophisticated penitentiaries; it was the colonial framework that produced such modernizing reforms and the emergence of a set of disciplinary institutions in Corfu. The status of protectorate allowed colonial officials such as Douglas to employ the expertise of Ionians trained in Italy before they returned and developed the Ionian version of governmentality. Corporeal punishment did not go away as an option, or indeed as a practice, when Commissioner Ward treated with remarkable cruelty and excess those convicted for the uprising in Kefalonia in 1849, sending several Ionian members of the assembly to exile, in some cases for several years. The state, however, personified by the British commissioners (Douglas especially) and Ionian officials and reformers, was the source of disciplinary power but not of course on behalf of the industrial bourgeoisie, because it did not exist in Corfu; then on behalf of whom? Then there is the question of correspondence between the prison system and the actual everyday reality of prison life; did prison conditions really change that much after the revolution in disciplinary and especially penal practices? The work by Cozziris, the prison director in Corfu, provides an ideal account of an insider evaluating the penal system almost two decades after its inception. His work demonstrates the available discourses on prison reform, from Benthamite well-meaning suggestions to more social scientific approaches to prison management, introduced in French, Italian and German prisons. If the old adage, that 'a society's prisons reflect its humanity' holds, the Corfu prison is a marker of contemporary ideas about society's less docile members.

The prison was constructed in the early 1840s according to Jeremy Bentham's 'Panopticon' design, as a cellular, radial prison. Until the nineteenth century the fortress, built in the sixteenth century but upgraded by British forces, had been used as a military as well as a civilian prison. The fortress is now a tourist attraction but the prison built in the 1840s has been so successful that it is still used today as a penal facility, making it probably one of the oldest jails in Europe. In April 1840, Howard Douglas laid the foundation of the Corfu prison; until then prisoners had been kept in awful conditions in Venetian-medieval dungeons in the Old Fortress. Theotokis, in his memoir in 1826, described the prison as old, airless and infectious, and many times fatal for the prisoners.[59] The hill of San Salvatore, near the city walls, was selected as the best location for what was in its time a model work. The prison warden could watch everyone from the central room with the ten windows. Prisoners were employed in agriculture in the fields nearby as well as in workshops inside the prison; shoe-makers and carpenters were given the raw materials to create goods that would bring some revenue to the prison. In 1857 there were around 210 prisoners, 109 from Corfu and the rest from the other islands: Kefalonia (21), Zante (44), Lefkada (21), Kythera (7), Ithaki (7), Paxoi (7). Between 1857 and 1860, the Corfu prison housed 507 inmates in total. Most had been imprisoned for crimes against the person (70 per cent) or against property. The average age of inmates was 26, and most of them were illiterate, came from the countryside and were workers or peasants.

The reorganization of the prison system by Giovanni Cozziris, from Corfu, is one of the finest examples of Ionian governmentality. Published in 1861, the report is an impressive as well as long and detailed account of the state of prisons on all the islands, with a focus on Corfu prison, the seat of Cozziris's office. His book, *Statistica del Penitenziario di Corfu per gli anni 1857, 1858, 1859* [Statistics of the Penitentiary of Corfu for the years 1857–59] is the first work on penology in Greece, published in the Ionian Islands under British rule, in Italian. The book exemplifies all the characteristics of Ionian colonial liberalism in state building, as Cozziris was a 'product' of the education, professional culture and practice of almost five decades of colonial governmentality. The book complemented an earlier treatise by Spridione Androni, a liberal politician, lawyer and reformer.[60]

The regulation that Cozziris designed for the prison followed the principles of a mixed penal system that combined the isolation of prisoners at night and collective labour under strict silence during the day. This was a 'benevolent' yet autocratic system with a strong bureaucratic administrative content; the prison warden was the ultimate authority over the prisoners' lives. The prison, of course, was more than just a site of state oppression, so we need to go beyond the legislation and constitution of prisons as instruments, to avoid impoverishing the question of power.[61] The building of a new prison and the construction and operation of the first psychiatric hospital in Corfu, also in the 1840s (and also still in operation today) constitute a disciplinary panel of modernity. The psychiatric hospital received its own evaluation, in 1878, but published in Greek and much shorter than Cozziris's lengthy and meticulous account of the Corfu prison. The institution, as Tsirigotis acknowledged in his 1878 report, was a major departure from the previous horrible condition: 'lunatics' were held in prisons, mixed with the criminals and constantly abused by them; the psychiatric hospital should have been purpose-built, not as a conversion on the site of the old Venetian barracks of San Rocco suburb. It was in 1848 that two new large rooms were added, 'resembling in everything the rooms of the penitentiary'.[62] The model prison became the model for the psychiatric hospital, not only in the physical characteristics but in the constitution and regulations as well. By the time Tsirigotis completed his report the hospital was 'inadequate' because patients from all over Greece had overcrowded it; between 1852 and 1876 eighty-four men and twenty-one women had been hospitalized.

The Ionian Islands 'in the times of cholera'

The power that Ionian liberals exercised within or in combination with the state and in the public sphere is evident in regulations, discourses and practices of social control. The coercive means took the form of criminalizing begging, confinement and hard labour for anyone over twelve years old. This was the joint project of the state and the Ionian liberal bourgeoisie to achieve social control through philanthropy but also through force. Philanthropy emerged as a voluntary institution of bourgeois activism. In Corfu and on the other Ionian islands, the agenda of philanthropy was far wider than simply distributing aid to the poor, and was founded on the principle and practice of voluntary organization by merchants, lawyers, state officials and military officers. These groups played a pivotal role at a moment of crisis and social upheaval caused by the outbreak of cholera in the suburbs of Corfu in 1855; unlike the plague outbreak of 1816 forty years earlier, which had been the first test of British authority on the island, now social peace and urban tranquillity prevailed not only thanks to British officers, however experienced, but also thanks to Ionian doctors and affluent merchants aware of their social role and responsibility.

British and Ionian officials had been concerned with cleanliness, order and the prevention of disease since the early days of the protectorate for practical – military and sanitary – as well as ideological reasons. Compared to sanitary conditions in the 1810s, the image of Corfu that many British writers presented in the 1840s onwards was one of progress:

> When the British first occupied Corfu, the streets were nearly impassable from the offal of butchers' stalls, and the litter of the venders of vegetables, who have been allowed to establish themselves promiscuously throughout the town: but, by a series of sanitary regulations, the streets are, at present, remarkably clean, considering the character of the population. The case is, however, different with respect to the interior of the houses; for, with very few exceptions, they possess no convenience of any description; and a house which does, though of the commonest kind, is termed 'English fashion', and brings a higher rent. As the town is situated many feet above water level, it is astonishing that some better

system of drainage should not have been introduced; and if the inhabitants were ever attacked by any epidemical disease, the consequences would be frightful.[63]

Less than four years later, Jervis's grim prediction became reality. From late September 1855 until early January 1856 there were 884 people diagnosed with cholera, of whom 489 died.[64] The disease tested social cohesion and stability, and the historians' work is to identify 'the relationships, the institutions, the means of social control by which such stability were maintained'.[65] The Ionian State and bourgeoisie provided the institutions and means of social control to prevent conflict between people living inside the town and the people in the suburbs, especially in Mandouki where the disease broke out. Chiotis, the historian of the Ionian State, and Iakovos Typaldos-Pretenteris, appointed by the Extraordinary Sanitary Committee as director of hospitals during the outbreak, offer a gripping narrative; surprisingly, the story has not attracted historians' attention despite the obvious importance of the cholera outbreak for public health but also for the history of social relations. Typaldos-Pretenteris studied in Paris in the 1830s when cholera terrorized the French capital, and he gained invaluable experience that he used for the first time in 1850 during the cholera outbreak in Kefalonia, when bread riots broke out following the harsh winter; these were adequate qualifications for the extremely difficult task of administering the hospitalization and treatment of the disease-stricken and informed Pretenteris of the social implications of a widespread outbreak. His work is a detailed account of the outbreak and an important medical document on the symptoms of the disease and the recommended therapies; but it also resembles the work of a contemporary anthropologist. Pretenteris was not interested in simply providing the 'facts' about the disease but also in explaining and accounting for the reasons that led to its outbreak in the Mandouki orphanage. Hiotis, also a witness, stated (much earlier than comparative historians of our time studying cholera epidemics did), that 'no age or class of people escaped the disease', mentioning members of 'noble' families who had contracted the disease.[66] Hiotis writes in his account of the Zante outbreak in September 1856 about the paralysis of the whole town, but also about the altruism of doctors, priests, chemists and everyone else who was in a position to help the cholera-stricken, regardless of class or occupation.[67] Some Zantiotes denied that the cause of so many deaths in late September 1856 was cholera; but the event does not compare with the cholera outbreak in Mandouki and the ways in which doctors and other members of the elite handled the outbreak of the disease outside and inside their town. Whereas in Zante the urban folk (and especially its elite) had united to fight the menace, according to Pretenteris people in Mandouki refused to accept the solutions imposed on them for the city to protect itself, as if that was even possible.

Even a month after the disease had been diagnosed and confirmed, on 4 October 1855, Mandouki residents were not showing any trust whatsoever in the advice and therapeutic guidelines the town doctors were giving them. 'Unpleasant scenes, lack of trust, fear and terror' prevailed in the streets of Mandouki.[68] Pretenteris gave his own interpretation of the people's discontent, which led to the acute reactions against the doctors, and shows the cleavage between people in the suburb and those in the town at this moment of crisis:

> The people of Manduki attributed these cases to poverty and not cholera. The people thought doctors were poisoning them and did not believe anything about the disease; on the contrary, most of the people in the town were terrified, and thinking that the disease was contagious, were arguing and struggling to ensure the suburb and all cholera-stricken areas were in sanitary isolation.[69]

If the people of Mandouki were in denial, the people of the town were in panic. The lower-class suburb and its residents rejected doctors and turned down their offer to help them. This was not because they were superstitious but because they realized that trying to put the whole suburb in quarantine would mean the deaths of, perhaps, more than 101 people out of the 189 cases in Mandouki.[70] It is remarkable that this idea found supporters not only among the panicked crowd, but also among the sanitary committee, something that did not impress the people of Mandouki: 'This had the worse impact on the people of the suburb. As most of them were earning a living by working in town, they saw the isolation measure as the ruin of their living, and as a result they threatened with revolutionary movements in case the measure was put to practice'.[71]

The 'revolutionary movements', as Pretenteris called them, deterred the urban elite, doctors, state officials and merchants, and discouraged the sanitary commission from going ahead with the quarantine plan. Doctors were targeted because they were the only people from the town who were allowed access to the disease-stricken streets of Mandouki. The people were worried about securing their daily bread as well as dying from the disease, and if the suburb were to be put under quarantine they would have no means of subsistence. Given that most of them were boatmen and fishermen, living off the sea, as mentioned by several contemporary observers including Pretenteris, then

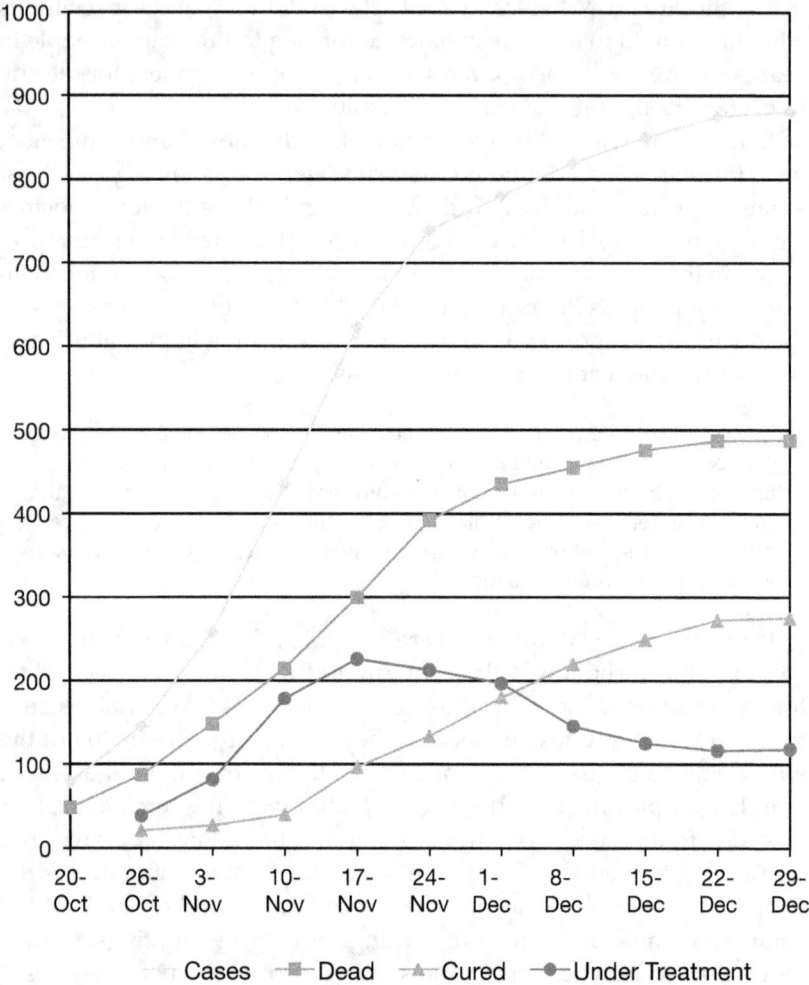

Figure 9.1 The peak of the cholera outbreak, Corfu 1855.

Source: *Ionian Islands Government Gazette*, issues October–December 1855.

during times of cholera, when the port would be closed, they would be facing strains anyway. Being isolated would deprive many of them of their only means of supporting themselves: begging. This case demonstrates the acute differences underlying the relationship between town and suburb, and the dependence of the suburb on the town for the survival of its people, in a literal sense. The case also confirms what contemporaries in Paris had recognized immediately – that 'cholera exacerbated class hatred'.[72]

Merchants offered a different solution. Soon after the outbreak of cholera and its diagnosis in September 1855, merchants formed a subscription fund for the necessary provisions to help the disease-stricken. They published a letter to the people of Corfu and the other islands in the *Ionian Gazette* where they portray their motives and aims, as they considered themselves responsible members of Corfu society with an obligation to stand up to the challenge posed to them:

> The cholera having, unfortunately, fallen upon the suburb of Manduki, in the lunatic asylum and the orphanage, and knowing that in the aforesaid suburb there are some inhabitants who are poor and in a destitute condition, Mssrs Antonios Kandonis, Frangiskos Scarpas, Konstantinos Baldas and Spyridon Topalis, hurried spontaneously to form a committee under the direction of the Archbishop of Corfu, Mr Athanasios Politis, which appeals to the philanthropists Christians, to contribute according to their means for the suffering ill and destitute immediately, now that there is still time. The Government, as a general paternal figure, will afford to complete the means and the rest. To this aim, a few days ago contributions begun and the programme of the said committee is published and the sum of money each signed to contribute to the relief of the suffering. The committee will also publish in the future the names of those who will subscribe. The programme and the subscriptions follow.
>
> Brothers,
> During the year 1850, cholera fell upon the sister Island of Kefalonia. During 1853, there was a great earthquake in Theva, in the Greek Kingdom, and the brothers here in Corfu were brave and contributed each according to their means. Already in the suburb of our Island, Mandukio, there have been cases of cholera, shaking our whole society. Whereas in one part of the suburb, the inhabitants belong to the worse class and condition, are deprived of even the daily bread, and without any means to endure the evil, for this reason, brothers, it is the duty of all the prosperous and the ones that have the means, to contribute according to their ability, to save the suffering, showing that we fulfil our Christian, brotherly and patriotic duty.
>
> Corfu, 12 October 1855[73]

The responsible and 'prosperous' citizens of Corfu reminded everyone of their charity record. In previous cases though, the threat was never as serious as 'in the times of cholera' that Corfu experienced in 1855. The disease, as millions of people came to realize when the bacillus left the Indian subcontinent for the first time, did not discriminate between wealthy and destitute, between the prosperous and those of the lowest class. The merchants of Corfu formed the subscription fund aiming to contain the disease on the outskirts of town simply because they were concerned not only with disruption of trade, but also with saving their own lives and the lives of their families. Of course, as usually happens, containment failed, and the disease entered the town. As the sanitary committee reported after the disease had killed its last victim, the subscriptions to the benevolent fund were instrumental in stopping the deadly virus. Merchants and companies donated various sums; among those individuals the leadership that Kandonis, Scarpas, Topalis and Baldas demonstrated earned them a special place in the urban hierarchy of Corfu town in the field of philanthropy. In the following weeks more than £250 was collected and donated by the merchants' committee to the central authorities for containing the disease and to cover the expenses of the health committee. In response, the committee gratefully thanked those who 'did their patriotic and Christian duty' in their report in January 1856, as soon as the disease had subsided.[74] The Corfu Jews were not part of the relief effort and did not receive any of the funds collected because their community organized its own committee. The Jewish quarter was considered very vulnerable due to the bad hygiene conditions, but also due to popular superstition.[75] As the committee itself admitted, the Jewish community's response was fast when they formed a philanthropic committee and adapted a building to serve as a cholera hospital; their measures were remarkably effective, despite being one of the most populated and thus vulnerable areas, as well as being one of the few areas in the town that contracted the disease.[76] The fact that the disease did not spare the town demonstrates that the plan to quarantine the suburb of Mandouki was futile and potentially destabilizing, even leading to conflict. The idea of containment, however, was far from a new one.[77] Given that the disease did not peak until the end of December, the fund was absolutely necessary for preventing the disease from ravaging the town. When the merchants formed the subscription fund in early October, the worst was still to come. The 'scientific' and close following of the disease allowed the better distribution and allocation of blankets, food and medicine to those in need.

The attitude of the 'lower classes' of Mandouki (as they were described by contemporaries) in attributing the symptoms of the disease not to cholera but to poverty and their harsh economic condition, indicates the cleavage between the inhabitants of the town and the suburbs. Their refusal to accept medical advice, and the real threat of open revolt in case of isolation, demonstrates the different expectations and choices of the people who lacked the power and means to face the disease. Historians of the cholera outbreak in 1832 in Britain have reached similar conclusions, stressing that the population divided into two groups: 'Those with power were expected to take action against cholera. Those without power were the likely victims. Each had a choice of action, quarantine, cleansing, medical provision, prayer or just doing nothing on the one hand, and flight, anger, alarm, obedience to regulations, or just doing nothing on the other'.[78]

The merchants of Corfu chose not to isolate Mandouki, a decision that would increase social unrest. Merchants and the urban elite provided the financial means, while the state and the physicians of the island facilitated the effort to turn the tide and stop the disease flooding the town. Philanthropy often served as a catalyst for maintaining social stability,[79] and merchants intended to restore trade and the town's economic and social peace. The fear of death that everyone felt regardless of social class also explains the reaction of all groups at a moment of social crisis.

The city's officials and notable residents were experienced with outbreaks of disease transmitted from areas east and west of Corfu. When news of cholera outbreaks on the mainland opposite or in areas of the Italian peninsula reached Corfu, the Ionian State authorities raised the alarm. Extreme measures were taken both in 1850, when cholera broke out in Kefalonia, and again in 1855 in Corfu. Ionian State medical officials had gained experience after the plague outbreak in southern Corfu in 1816, the first test of the British administration, and again after the first serious outbreak in Britain and continental Europe in 1832. In that year the *Ionian Gazette* published several theories on the causes of the disease and suggested therapeutic measures, and the Ionian State introduced surveillance practices to anticipate the transmission of the disease to Corfu. Dr Therianos, 'Public Physician' of the Ionian State, travelled to Ioannina, on the mainland opposite, as soon as news of an outbreak reached Corfu, and published a work with his ideas on the causes of the disease, which contained the views of the British Medical Council.[80] Quarantine and other sanitary measures, such as the establishment of a sanitary committee, were introduced in 1836, when news of the epidemic ravaging areas of the Austro-Hungarian Empire and Italy reached Corfu.[81]

It was only in 1850 after the Kefalonia cholera outbreak that the town and the suburbs were divided into districts, following practices that officials of the Septinsular Republic had introduced. The government appointed sanitary committees responsible for supervising hygiene and taking measures to prevent and if necessary stop the outbreak. Corfu and the suburbs were divided into eight districts, each with a sanitary committee appointed to supervise public health.[82] In early October 1855, when doctors had confirmed the nature of the disease to be a cholera outbreak, the division of the town into districts and sanitary commissions was reinstituted, with the aim to supervise sanitary conditions and prevent the spread of the disease from the suburbs to the town. The Greek term *'dimogerontes'*[83] is used to describe the members of the commissions, and the municipal resolution is a repetition of the 1850 one. As in the 1850 sanitary commissions, the participation of merchants is extended since they are the second 'group' after the physicians. Merchants, such as Candonis, Rallis, Topalis, Kollas, Baldas and Coraggios were among the commission members for the town of Corfu, while it is not possible to know how many, if any, of the Mandouki commission were merchants. Not surprisingly, among these merchants were the ones who had formed the subscription fund in October. Their initiative indicates a possible distrust of, or even disbelief in, the measures taken by the administration and their ability to prevent the disease from entering the town walls. It has to be remembered that the disease broke out not in the town but in one of the suburbs, in the lunatic asylum and the foundling house.[84]

By 1850 the people of Mandouki were also aware of the threat of cholera to their residential area. When High Commissioner Ward visited, perhaps the first and the last time a commissioner visited the suburb, the notables of Mandouki expressed their concerns. Ward, in an equally rare mention in a speech to the Ionian Assembly, pledged £2,000 to be 'distributed to the population' for improvement of the sanitary conditions and sewage facilities in the suburb. Sanitary conditions, Ward noted, were 'as dangerous to the public health, as it is offensive to public decency'.[85] The situation in parts of the town was equally alarming. The cholera epidemic of 1855 broke out in the orphanage in Mandouki, highlighting the failure of the Ionian government to provide decent sanitary conditions to some of its most vulnerable citizens, orphan children. The government and the commissioner personally had failed to respond to the people in Mandouki, who in 1851, years before the cholera outbreak, had complained about sanitary conditions in their suburb and had requested improvements following the visit of Ward to their district. After his promises to improve their health and living conditions were completely forgotten, residents of Mandouki wrote a petition, reminding him of the urgency of the situation and the risk they ran every time the disease reached Epirus on the opposite coast, to where many of them often travelled. The petition, written in April 1851, was signed by eleven residents of Mandouki who described the deplorable state of the suburb, requesting from the Senate – the executive of the state – the immediate adoption of measures to prevent an outbreak of cholera similar to that in Kefalonia a few months before. The people who lived in Mandouki petitioned the state authorities using this standard form of written negotiation between Ionians and their government to alert officials to the dangers of ill public health. Therefore the people of Mandouki were not unaware of or, at that stage, ungrateful for the plan by city doctors and state officials to quarantine the suburb.[86]

The residents of Mandouki continued to complain about the lack of latrines in the suburb and 'the great inconvenience they are put to on record of this great deficiency'.[87] The official in charge did respond with a memo, sending it to the Senate; by the late 1850s it was becoming clear to many in the Ionian government as well as in Ionian society that good sanitary conditions were absolutely essential for winning the hearts and minds of Ionians, especially in areas like Mandouki, struck by disease. Residents and 'the community' of Mandouki did not give up in their efforts to improve their living conditions. In August 1859, ninety-two residents of Mandouki, led by five priests who signed the petition first, stated their complaint that their suburb had been neglected by the government and that they had not had a good school for years, thus exposing the neglect of central government, in a district close to the capital, over the educational matters of many of its less affluent and influential citizens. Comparisons and implied competition is not absent from the petition either: 'the very important for the population, shipping and commerce community of Mandouki is altogether neglected by the government and is in a worse state than even the most inferior villages of the island'. There was not even a Lancastrian school in Mandouki, while Paxos, with a smaller population, enjoyed the privilege of a senator, a resident, a bishop, deputies and municipal councillors and, of course, schools, since given the federal structure of the Ionian State the island was, typically at least, a state. The only existing school in Mandouki operated with just one teacher who received four dollars per month, a meagre salary in 1859. The petitioners, in an impressive for its collective character petition, did not just ask for better pay for their teacher and a more organized school; they suggested that their children return to school instead of remaining idle, and offered suggestions for the curriculum: Greek, Italian, English, religion, geography, history, and practical naval education.[88] It was not only the urban elite that expressed their ideas and policy suggestions on their children's education. The Ionian state bureaucracy took the petition seriously, translated it (from Greek) and reported at great length; but the comment on the back of the petition was not hopeful. The petition was submitted to the Senate for their consideration, who acknowledged the fair entitlement of the people of Mandouki to a school, however concluded that 'more facilities for education cannot be afforded to the population in the suburb of Manducchio'. The interest of this suburb's residents for the educational needs of their children was not uncommon; in 1861 the villagers of Vasilikata in Kefalonia wrote to the resident requesting a change of teacher because after eight years their children had learned neither Italian nor Greek, and were unable to write even their own name.

The merchants of the town were involved in a number of other philanthropic funds, raising money for calamities in the Greek Kingdom, and also in the British Empire. Samartzis, a merchant who left a detailed chronicle, mentions in 1857 the formation of a committee by merchants Kefalas and Baldas, 'and other big merchants in order to help the destitute widows and orphans of the war in Indies, and in other places. They go around the town and each contributes according to their means'.[89] The fund was raised for the Indian Mutiny of 1857; news about the mutiny reached Ionians through newspapers, as was the case for other parts of the empire. Merchants demonstrated an awareness and sense of responsibility to help those in need in the protective power, indicating an attitude of collaboration and compliance with British rule. The initiative might have simply been a public relations attempt by merchants, although its importance for projecting their solidarity to the imperial power is obvious.

Philanthropy in Greek towns, as elsewhere in nineteenth-century Europe, assumed new forms when urban elites realized that poverty and other social problems had to be addressed in more organized ways, as increased urbanization and the spread of disease rendered city populations extremely vulnerable. This was most evident in relation to the series of cholera outbreaks in the 1850s in Corfu, Piraeus (and Athens) and Ermoupoli. The outbreaks decimated the population and proved that the state authorities, whether in Greece as a whole or in Athens in particular, were unable to cope with such emergencies.[90] Disease continued to afflict Greek cities throughout the nineteenth century, such as when smallpox exacted a heavy toll in the 1880s not only in Piraeus and Athens but also in Corfu and Kefalonia. Under these conditions it is not surprising that merchants played a critical role in responding to such crises.

In Corfu, philanthropic activity went hand in hand with an intensification of punitive measures by state authorities. The municipal and state authorities became gradually less tolerant of beggars, vagrants and 'idlers', especially in the case of males in general and young people. The creation of a poorhouse, and its funding and management by the Ladies' Benevolent Society, is a good example of the coexistence of punitive and philanthropic measures in the same initiative. At the same time, the state failed to provide for some groups who were particularly vulnerable, like people living on the margins of the town such as the Parga refugees in the Mandouki district. The petitions of the Mandouki inhabitants from the 1830s asking for improvements in their living conditions and for preventive measures to protect them from outbreaks of disease continued to be ignored, despite a visit by Commissioner Ward in 1852, which also failed to produce any results.

In Athens and Piraeus a few years later, new ideas about the treatment of the poor developed with increasing support from the more active and wealthy citizens. A variety of motives – individual and collective, public and private – determined the specific nature of these responses, which were also products of the need to maintain or gain social status and political power, particularly after 1864 with the introduction of universal male suffrage and votes for the poor. In Athens the founding of the Ελεήμων Εταιρεία [Merciful Society] aimed at helping the poor, but it was equally concerned to 'discover' those who fraudulently pretended to be poor and in need.[91] In Corfu, state control of poverty began in the 1830s in a more centralized and efficient manner. The Ionian government introduced the institution of the poorhouse and was responsible from the start for the registration of the local poor, although from the 1840s funds were raised through individual subscriptions to the Ladies' Benevolent Society. In Corfu the police and the prison system had been responsible for implementing a tougher policy towards the poor, through acts against 'vicious mendacity' since the 1830s. The British-influenced Ionian State was therefore more advanced in penalizing the poor and in adopting punitive treatment.

The growing concern of the urban elite in Corfu and Piraeus with real as well as perceived social problems was also the result of economic crises in the 1850s and the 1880s. There was however an important difference; in Corfu, merchants were more directly involved in responding to social issues and played an important role in the founding and administration of charitable institutions, cooperating actively with the forces of law and order, in line with the ideology and practice of the authorities. In Piraeus, by contrast, although factory owners were initially active in generating resources for the creation of an orphanage where young boys could learn a trade and thus form a new, well-trained and industrious working class, they later became indifferent and ceased to play a supportive role.[92] The spirit of educating the poor and transforming them from beggars to workers was most evident in the code of conduct of the orphanages in Piraeus and Ermoupoli in the second half of the nineteenth century, but these operated under the auspices of the local municipal councils and philanthropic societies.[93] The case of Piraeus corresponded most closely to the typology of European port cities in which leading members of the bourgeoisie, merchants and industrialists preferred individual philanthropic activities rather than policies designed to address contemporary social problems through education and school-based technical training.[94] The Athens bourgeoisie aimed to confine the poor to the poorhouse, while the Piraeus factory owners preferred to leave the treatment of the poor to the police, which in many cases meant the expulsion of foreign immigrants from the city. In Corfu, merchants and other members of the town's bourgeoisie chose to work with state authorities to confine the registered poor to the poorhouse, where they could receive training, while attempting to penalize those who refused to comply. Philanthropic institutions developed in Corfu earlier than in Greek cities, based on the centuries-old tradition of social control through various individual and collective, public and private mechanisms. Merchants formed new urban hierarchies through the introduction and operation of new institutions along British or West European lines, ranging from the savings bank to philanthropic initiatives in Corfu during the outbreaks of cholera in the 1850s. Merchants, together with Ionian professionals, lawyers, doctors and members of the state administration, enhanced their social standing through the administration of charitable and other urban institutions.

Towards the end of the period merchants, journalists and politicians affirmed their social hegemony through philanthropy and sermonizing. Their target was the urban poor and the residents of suburbs. Their sermons aimed at what they saw as 'social excess' by outcasts, such as prostitutes, beggars and those who refused to conform to the image required by the urban elite.

The connotations and the metaphors with the cholera outbreak a few years earlier are obvious. Images from the cholera outbreak were used to direct attention to the dangers of another disease, in this instance moral. Unlike cholera, degeneration did not kill instantly but slowly, creeping into the social body – or so the readers were told. Moral decline, however, constituted an 'enemy of society' all the same. The sight of prostitutes in public did not appeal to respectable citizens; children had to be protected from moral corruption and prostitutes had to realize their decadence and redeem themselves or remain isolated. Corfu philanthropists produced the moralizing discourse that appeared in Athens towards the end of the nineteenth century, ending the period of social exclusion and coercion that followed the post-revolutionary years.[95] Members of the commercial bourgeoisie with wide interests and aspirations, such as Marvoioannis, who would develop and realize political ambitions as a member of the municipal council in post-unification years, formulated an ideology aiming to implement stricter repressive measures to avoid social conflict and moral decadence. The project, which started in the 1830s with an attempt to sanitize the towns, continued until the late 1850s, showing remarkable continuities. If, however, the project was initiated by the British image of progress through an seemingly ordered urban space and society, it was undertaken and continued by those members of the commercial bourgeoisie who were prepared to sacrifice some of their time to commercial affairs to 'serve' their fellow citizens as urban leaders in voluntary associations. They also offered, of course, some of their money in times of crisis through philanthropic activities, the bourgeois activity par excellence.

One year after the union of the islands with Greece, an event that did little to eliminate poverty in Ionian towns, an article praising the ideological maturity of the voluntary association movement in Corfu appeared in the press. The article, a report on the 'performance' of the philanthropic society 'St Spyridon', praised its members and benefactors, and declared its belief in the intervention of providence for ameliorating the condition of the poor, together, of course, with the contributions of the rich. The short article ends with the hope that 'we will, at last, comprehend that only through private initiative and association such benevolent and philanthropic institutions are established, maintained and flourish. Without them societies fall ill and stagnate, or, even worse, decline. These are the principles that inspire us, and following them, we will benefit our society'.[96]

In Corfu the transition from the penal phase of punishment and incarceration to the phase of social inclusion through training, work and 'correction' was not only faster but took place within the space of a few years, under the influence of the discourse of progress. The merchant journalist Mavroioannis, editor of the self-proclaimed 'commercial and radical newspaper', argued for the segregation of prostitutes in one street and in houses to the benefit of the society as a whole. The article ended arguing for the cleansing of the town, implying a cleansing both literal and metaphorical;[97] no British high commissioner could have phrased it any better. By the time the British left the islands, the seeds of a bourgeois society were growing fast.

Notes

1 S. Gekas, The Crisis of the Long 1850s and Regime Change in the Ionian State and the Kingdom of Greece'. *The Historical Review/La Revue Historique* [S.l.], 10, (2013): 57–84.

2   S. Sharma, *Famine, Philanthropy and the Colonial State: North India in the Early Nineteenth Century*. New Delhi: Oxford University Press, 2001, 136.
3   M. Mann, *The Sources of Social Power*, vol. II. New York: Cambridge University Press, 2012, 380.
4   Gallant, *Experiencing Dominion*, 84. Gallant identifies three options/potential responses of the peasants to the problem of a rising population in harsh economic conditions: 'migrate – either seasonally or permanently – try to obtain new leaseholds, or selectively control numbers'. Ionian peasants did the first, in thousands, and Gallant argues that child abandonment was aimed at relieving the peasant household. Buying leaseholds was totally out of the question, given the inability of the large majority of peasants to pay even existing debts, let alone acquire new property, especially at times of bad harvests, such as the extremely volatile decades of the 1840s and 1850s.
5   The annual population movement was such that it really compromised the validity of the census, as high commissioners noted repeatedly: 'The apparent decrease [of the population], I conclude, might be attributed to the calculation having been made at a time when many of the labouring classes were absent in the Morea and other parts of Greece, whither they are accustomed to resort in search of work at certain seasons'. Parliamentary Papers, Accounts and Papers, 1847 xivi (1005), Reports Exhibiting the Past and Present State of Her Majesty's Colonial Possessions, 181–86. The same 'problem' in calculating the population change accurately was raised in the accounts of the years 1845 and 1846.
6   Act No. LXII, Third Session of the Second Parliament, Corfu, 20 March 1827.
7   Act No. I, First Session of the Eighth Parliament, Corfu, 20 March 1845.
8   Gallant considers these regulations, however, to have been more symbolic than substantive, instituted by the urban British-following and admiring elite, a token of their enthusiasm to demonstrate their readiness to incorporate the British worldview while it was merely a pretext for obtaining power for themselves; Gallant, *Experiencing Dominion*, 74.
9   Davy, *Notes and Observations*, 120–21.
10 Act XLV, Second Session, Fourth Parliament, 5 June 1835; and IIGG, No. 264, 4/16 January 1836.
11 IIGG, No 251, 1835, cited in Progoulakis, 'Anamesa stin Timi kai to Chrima', 191.
12 IIGG, No. 264, 4/16 January 1836.
13 IIGG, No. 369, 8/20 January 1838.
14 IIGG, No. 55, 5/17 January 1846. Curcumelli was initially in the 'opposition' party following Mustoxidi, only to declare his loyalty subsequently to the British administration. He was rewarded with the post of General Attorney of the Ionian State, and complied with Young's proposal in 1857 to colonize Corfu. To this end, he wrote a memorandum to the colonial office; this led to a public outcry in the press when the colonization plan leaked and Curcumelli was forced to resign. Biographical information in Chiotis, *Istorika Apomnimonevmata Eptanisou*, 54.

15 IIGG, No. 55, 5/17 January 1846.
16 General Meeting of the Savings Bank Trustees, IIGG, No. 107, 4 January 1847.
17 IIGG, No. 162, 24 January / 5 February 1848.
18 IIGG, No. 3, 8 January 1849.
19 Cannadine, *Ornamentialism*.
20 IIGG, No. 539, 18 April 1841.
21 A. Haldane, *One Hundred and Fifty Years of Trustees' Savings Banks*, Trustee Savings Banks Association, 1960, 17–18.
22 Karapidakis, 'Apo ton koinotismo stin politiki', 36.
23 Blue Books of Statistics, CO 136/1419–1427, T.N.A.
24 P. Joyce, *The State of Freedom: A Social History of the British State since 1800*. New York: Cambridge University Press, 2013.
25 S. Woolf, *The Poor in Western Europe in the Eighteenth and Nineteenth Centuries*. London and New York: Methuen, 1986, 23.
26 G. Kefalonitis, 'Istoria tou Astikou Nosokomeiou Kerkyras', *Kerkyraika Chronika* 13 (1967): 55–75.
27 The date is ambiguous. While Kefalonitis notes 1726 as the date when the merchant Delotis erected the first building, Vlassopoulos says that the hospital for the poor was founded in 1739. This is probably because the institution changed location several times during the eighteenth and nineteenth centuries. Chiotis, on his part, mentions two hospitals, one built in 1698 and the other built by the British. Chiotis, op. cit., 267.
28 Ibid.
29 Vlassopoulos, *Statistikai – Istorikai peri Kerkyras Eidiseis*, 114–15.
30 Kefalonitis, 'Istoria tou Astikou Nosokomeiou Kerkyras', 61. The Zante Medical Society was established in 1829 and its members paid a small subscription and created a forum for the discussion of medical issues and therapies, and the publication of medical texts. Chiotis, op. cit., 264.
31 The initiative was realized through a number of generous funds donated and money collected from theatrical plays, another distinctive form of sociability of the urban elite. IIGG, No. 66, 19/31 March 1832, and Chiotis, op. cit., 265.
32 Foucault has asserted that the question was 'to neutralise the houses of confinement as potential causes of new evil'. M. Foucault, *Madness and Civilisation: A History of Insanity in the Age of Reason*. London: Routledge, 2001, 206. Ironically, the outbreak in 1855 of cholera in the orphanage in the suburb of Manduchi, and cholera cases in the lunatic asylum, both 'isolated' places, demonstrated spectacularly the failure of the Ionian State to fulfil its basic goals regarding the health of some of its most vulnerable citizens.
33 IIGG, No. 379, 19/31 March 1838.
34 IIGG, No. 129, 3/15 June 1833.
35 IIGG, No. 336, 22 May / 3 June 1837.
36 IIGG, No. 61, 9/21 March 1846.
37 IIGG, No. 394, 2/14 July, 1838.
38 IIGG, No. 494, 1/13 June 1840.

39 IIGG, No. 65, 16 March 1846. This was part of a wider process of introducing internal regulations for the lunatic asylum and the prison.
40 J. Davy, *Notes and Observations*, Vol. II, 187.
41 IIGG, No. 531, 14 February 1841.
42 IIGG, No. 61, 9/21 March 1846.
43 R. J. Morris, *Class, Sect and Party. The making of the British middle class: Leeds, 1820–50*. Manchester: Manchester University Press, 1990.
44 IIGG, No. 168, 6/18 March 1848
45 Chiotis, *Istoria tou Ioniou Kratous*, 350.
46 These riots, rare as they may have been, are certainly worth investigating, a task still awaiting the social historians of the Ionian Islands.
47 Chiotis, *Istoria tou Ioniou Kratous*, 351. Obolos was the smallest monetary unit used in the Ionian States, for everyday transactions.
48 Newspaper *H Foni tou Laou* [The Voice of the People], No. 24, 4 November 1850, Arheio Dafni, I.A.K.
49 Corfu, 17 June 1853. Executive Police 1749, I.A.K.
50 IIGG, No. 175, 5/17 March 1855.
51 Ibid., Art. 2.
52 G. Karter and P. Samartzis (eds), *Kathimerousiai Eideiseis*. Athens: ELIA, 2000, 57.
53 C. Lis and H. Soly, *Poverty and Capitalism in Pre-Industrial Europe*. Bristol: The Harvester Press, 1979, 88.
54 R. Martin, *Statistics of the Colonies*, 599–602.
55 Woolf, *The Poor in Western Europe*, 39. In early modern Europe, for instance, the poor themselves hardly ever defined poverty. See R. Jutte, *Poverty and Deviance in Early Modern Europe*. Cambridge: Cambridge University Press, 1994, chapter 2.
56 D. Rothman, *The Discovery of the Asylum: Social Order and Disorder in the New Republic*. Boston and Toronto: Little, Brown and Company, 1971; M. Foucault, *Discipline and Punish*; M. Ignatieff, *A Just Measure of Pain: The Penitentiary in the Industrial Revolution, 1750–1850*. Chicago: Chicago University Press, 1981.
57 M. Gibson, 'Global Perspectives on the Birth of the Prison', *The American Historical Review* 116(4) (2011): 1040–63.
58 Napier, *The Colonies*, 326.
59 Theotoky, *Details sur Corfou*, 109.
60 S. Androni, *Alcune idee sopra le diverse istituzioni completive del sistema penitenziario*. Corfu, 1848.
61 D. Arnold, 'The Colonial Prison: Power, Knowledge and Penology in Nineteenth-Century India'. Subaltern Studies VIII: Essays in Honour of Ranajit Guha. New Delhi, 1994, 148–84.
62 C. Tsirigotou, *Statistiki tou en Kerkyra Frenokomeiou tou etous 1877. Ypovlitheisa eis to Ypourgeion Esoterikon*. Athens, 1878, 4.
63 Jervis, *History of the Island of Corfu*, 264.
64 Typaldos Pretenteris, *Peri tis en Kerkyra Holeras kata to 1855*, 4–5.
65 R. Morris, *Cholera 1832*. London: Croom Helm, 1976, 17.
66 Hiotis, *History of the Ionian State*, 365.

67 Ibid., 352.
68 One of the morbid traits of cholera is the speed with which it spreads. People can be healthy in the morning, pale, vomiting and with diarrhoea in the afternoon, and dead in the evening. These scenes must have caused panic among people who did not trust the doctors. Physicians could hardly do anything at this point anyway, before the disease peaked.
69 Typaldos Pretenteris, *Peri tis en Kerkyra Holeras kata to 1855*, 4–5.
70 Ibid.
71 Ibid., 6–7.
72 A. Briggs, 'Cholera and Society in the Nineteenth Century', *Past and Present* 19 (1961): 76–96.
73 IIGG, No. 209, 8 October 1855.
74 Report of the Extraordinary Central Health Commission, 16 January 1856. IIGG, No. 225, 28 January 1856.
75 Typaldos Pretenteris, *Peri tis en Kerkira choleras*, 8.
76 Report of the Health Commission.
77 In late medieval and early modern times, the practice of containment had been followed on the islands of Rhodes (1498–99) and Naxos (1676), where the inhabitants of the town abandoned it altogether, and undoubtedly in other places too. As Kostis notes though, the practice of isolation was difficult to follow in places with large and dense populations; Corfu was definitely one of them. See K. Kostis, *Ston Kairo tis Panolis*. Irakleio: Panepistimiakes Ekdoseis Kritis, 1995, 279.
78 R. J. Morris, *Cholera 1832*, London: Croom Helm, 1976, 18.
79 A. Maclaren, 'Bourgeois Ideology and Victorian Philanthropy: The Contradictions of Cholera', in A.A. Maclaren (ed.), *Social Class in Scotland: Past and Present*. Edinburgh: Donald, 1976, 36–54.
80 IIGG, No. 58, 23 January / 4 February 1832; and No. 85, 30 July / 11 August 1832.
81 IIGG, No. 297, 22 August / 3 September 1836.
82 IIGG, No. 89, 2/14 September 1850.
83 Gallant in the same chapter uses the term 'city fathers', which is an accurate translation.
84 Extraordinary Central Sanitary Commission – Report on Cholera, IIGG, No. 225, 28 January 1856. The irony is that these were the buildings that the British project of civilizing the islands had so much praised, but where they had utterly neglected to maintain basic conditions of hygiene. The fact that the disease also started from the orphanage shows the failure of the Ionian State to carry out the pledges of several high commissioners to these establishments of public utility.
85 IIGG, No. 101, 25 November / 7 December 1850.
86 Petition 1076, 22 April 1851, CO 136/1045, T.N.A.
87 Petition 71, Register of Petitions 1859, CO 136/1053, N.A.
88 Petition 423, 3 August 1859, CO 136/873, National Archives
89 Karter and Samartzis, *Kathimerousiai Eideiseis*, 103.
90 M. Korasidou, *Oi athlioi ton Athinon kai oi therapeftes tous. Ftochia kai filanthropia stin elliniki protevousa ton 19o aiona*. Athens: EIE, 1995; for Ermoupoli,

see C. Loukos, 'Epidimia kai koinonia. I cholera stin Ermoupoli tis Syrou (1854)', *Mnemon* XIV (1992): 49–69.
91. Y. Yannitsiotis, 'Social History in Greece: New Perspectives', *East Central Europe* 34–35 (2007–8): 278–79.
92. Ibid., 288.
93. V. Theodorou, Theodorou, V. 'Peitharchika systimata kai ergasia sta orfanotrofeia to B miso tou 19ou aiona', *Mnemon* XXI (1999): 55–84; Y. Kokkinakis, 'Filanthropia, techniki ekpaidefsi kai ergatika atichimata ston Peiraia to telefteo trito tou 19ou aiona'. *Mnemon* XXI (1999): 85–108.
94. R. Lee, 'Socio-economic and Demographic Characteristics of Port Cities: A Typology for Comparative Analysis?'. *Urban History* 25 (1998): 147–72; and Giannitsiotis, *Social History*, 294.
95. Korasidou, *I athlioi ton Athinon*.
96. Newspaper *Astir*, No. 20, 26 June 1865.
97. *I Eptalofos*, 5 / 14 May 1859. I.A.K., Archeio Dafni 183(3).

 Chapter 10

The *Literati* and the *Liberali*
The Making of the Ionian Bourgeoisie

The Powerful Class

Previous chapters have demonstrated the roles of some Ionians in commerce, state administration, and urban affairs, tackling issues of commercial policy and urban poverty. This chapter looks at the crucial role of education and journalism in fostering the new hegemonic class among Ionians. This class, despite its differences in terms of island of origin, sources of income, political affiliation and attitude towards union, had one underlying common identity: they were all liberals in the broadest sense, and some even adopted the term *liberali*, as their contemporaries called them. This chapter, on political liberalism towards the end of colonial rule, explores how liberal and modernizing middle-class Ionians, especially after the liberal reforms of Commissioner Seaton in the 1840s, became more vocal in the public sphere through newspapers that challenged both the old aristocracy and British rule, and transformed Ionian politics. Ionian liberals focused on reforming the Ionian constitution of 1817, but their demands extended to a range of social issues, the national (Greek) question and social inequality. From the 1830s onwards, liberal ideas in the sphere of politics and commerce produced a new configuration of power relations among Ionians, challenging submissive supporters of British protection and arguing for more liberalization in politics and freedom of trade as well as of expression. Education qualifications (in law and medicine) and wealth acquired through commerce and shipping, and more traditional forms of rent extraction or profits from agricultural surplus, translated into political activity that included creating a number of political and voluntary associations.

Greek historians have either underestimated or ignored the role of the bourgeoisie in their own making;[1] instead historians opted for other factors following mostly an old-fashioned dependency theory approach and tools drawn from political science and anthropology: comprador capitalism, foreign influence, clientelism and political patronage.[2] A previous generation of historians and social scientists were looking for a 'national' bourgeoisie and, not surprisingly, they failed to find it; the Greek world was so fragmented, especially in the nineteenth century, that a Greek national bourgeoisie sounds implausible and unconvincing, just like elsewhere in Europe, where bourgeoisies were distinguished by their local identities and civic pride. Once, however, historians started looking for local, urban identities that were central in the formation of bourgeois identity, whether in Hermoupoli, Piraeus or Patras, similarities as well as differences with European cities quickly emerged.[3]

Historians of the Ionian Islands, such as Moschopoulos and Paximadopoulou-Stavrinou, focus on class to explain the rebellions of 1848–49,[4] agreeing that it was the 'middle bourgeoisie' that was the most responsive, compared to other social classes, to the social and political ideas of the time. This was an Ionian version of the *Bildungsbürgertum* of fairly affluent Ionians educated abroad before becoming the bearers of liberalism and nationalism. Zervos Iakovatos distinguished the strata he considered as supportive to the issue of union (the lower and middle bourgeoisie) from the ones hostile to union, due to its long association with Venetian and subsequently British rule, the 'upper strata' as Iakovatos called them.[5] Iakovatos and historians of Kefalonia were concerned less with how Ionian society and state changed during the period of British rule and more with identifying the attitude of different strata to the issue of union. This issue and the rise of nationalism not only dominated the political life of the islands from the late 1840s onwards, but it has equally dominated historians' concerns ever since. The reason for that – and the case of Greece is not atypical in this respect – is the far easier to digest narrative of national integration and assimilation of new territories such as the Ionian Islands, to an expanding Greek State, told usually in a manner of national pride, expectation and anticipated fulfilment.[6] The focus on the issue of union serves extremely well the division into the three-tier social system. In the narrative of the nation unification project the landowning nobility is usually the evil collaborator, while the bourgeoisie is usually presented as split into two groups. One is the progressive one, a bourgeoisie that was aware of its national consciousness, from the ranks of which the group of the radical unionists emerged. The other group is the reformists, seeking to reform the Ionian State and not overthrow British rule. All the works that have addressed the issue of union focus on this 'three-party system', which contemporaries also expressed their views on. In the main works on the Ionian Islands, the Ionian assembly constitutes the only field of struggle for union with Greece, a struggle that is ultimately a constitutional one, since it takes place inside existing institutions by using them and not attempting to overthrow them by revolutionary movements.[7] In both the Ionian State and the Kingdom of Greece, modernization was a political project. In the Ionian Islands the project of reforming the state gave way to the demand for union with Greece and the idea that a stronger Greek Kingdom could result from union with the Ionian State.

This is not to say that local differences did not matter. The sources of social differentiation in Kefalonia (and to some extent in Ionian society in general) were the chronic problems of subdivision of property and the joint but unequal ownership of land between landowner and tenant farmer. For contemporaries, however, differences were clear between the aristocrats, who were the first class, the principal landowners and some big merchants unlike the 'nobles' of the previous Venetian century. They were the *signori*, the people English sources called 'the eminent and powerful gentlemen', 'the respectable citizens' ... 'People of this class maintained all power in their hands, just like during the period of Venetian rule ... they rotated to positions of public administration and government catering for their private interests. In exchange for their privileges they offered their total backing to the Protection and supported with their actions the Anglo-Ionian State'.[8]

Ionians of all classes talked about class distinctions in Ionian society. When the bakers of Corfu petitioned the high commissioner to allow them to sell bread to all classes, they wrote in Italian: 'Of the fourteen bakers that are accustomed to prepare the white necessary to the wealthiest class of the *Citta* [city], ten are inactive'.[9] For bakers there were two main classes, the wealthy and the poor; a simple but stark differentiation, and they were keen to be allowed to bake the white bread for the wealthy, upper classes, and the black for the lower, poorer classes. This chapter, however, focuses not on discourse and class language as previous chapters did, but on the role of education in the formation of the Ionian bourgeois class. This approach is consistent with many recent histories of industrialization and economic prosperity that attribute the great surge forward not to capital, resources, institutions and property systems but to education and the Enlightenment.[10] This chapter looks at the role of Ionians and some British officials, who designed the school system in one of the finest examples of colonial governmentality. Ionians were, from the beginning, poised to oversee the educational transformation that took place during the period of British rule but had its origins in the early nineteenth century.

Education Reform: Sowing the Seeds of Discontent

Another title for the chapter could have been 'educating the colonized' but this would be drawing too sharp a line between the colonizers and colonized. Instead it is crucial to see how the British took a hands-off approach to the educational system, in fact creating new educational institutions, including a university. Most importantly, many liberal and radical Ionians that challenged British rule in the 1850s had been educated in the Ionian State public school system. This aspect of the British colonialism in the Ionian Islands has not been discussed before as historians have studied changes in education as part of British reforms in the islands but missed the impact of education for the constitution of a civil society.

Between 1797 and 1815, the succession of foreign rule (French, Russian, French and British) brought in state and administrative institutions. The Septinsular Republic organized state education according to the 1803 constitution, which placed education under state supervision. In 1804 the Senate decided to open elementary schools, two on each of the larger islands and one on each of the smaller ones, and forty schools of basic education. As a young minister of the Septinsular Republic, Kapodistrias devised the education law of 1804; the Corfu politician worked again with ideas on how to organize education and the school system when he became governor of Greece in 1828. Private education, that is private schools with tutors, small classes and usually one teacher, remained widespread among affluent Ionians throughout the period of British rule; but the public school system expanded significantly as well, especially during the first decades of the protectorate when the state's finances allowed spending on education. The seeds of public education, however, were sown during the period of the Septinsular Republic. The resolution for the school that opened in 1805 in Corfu in a rare expression of purpose explicitly pledged to offer 'education for the young officials of the Illustrious Senate, the local government, services, the military and the clergy of the island of Corfu';[11] in other words for the technocrats of the state. Wealthy students – or rather their parents – paid three Venetian tallers per year, while poor ones, at least in theory, received free education. The government supervised both public and private schools, and four secondary schools opened on each of the major islands and taught Greek, Latin, Italian and French languages, grammar, geography, history, arithmetic, geometry, philosophy, religious catechism, natural history and, most interestingly, the constitution of the republic.[12] The revenue of monasteries was directed to pay for the education expenses and student fees, while private endowments were deposited to the establishments of the Monte di Pieta, wherever they existed. In addition, the state spent an amount, budgeted each year, granting pensions to retired teachers and founding a public library in each secondary school, which many private donations filled. The imperial French offered places for thirty Ionians to study arts and crafts in France and return to teach in their islands.[13] Once the British occupied the southern islands they appointed Platon Petrides, the chief interpreter for the British officials, as director of education, and also appointed a committee for each island. Textbooks were printed and a newspaper became the official publication of the state, published in plain Greek once a month. The British oversaw the first transition from a cultural milieu dominated by the use of the Italian language to the increasing use of Greek, which then remained for decades the lesser language in administration and among educated Ionians. Following the British takeover of the Ionian Islands, the constitutional charter of 1817, article 23, pledged that:

> the public instruction of youth being one of the most important points connected with the prosperity and happiness of any State and it being of the utmost importance, both to the morals and religion of the country, that it's pastors in particular should receive a liberal and adequate education, it is hereby declared to be a primary duty immediately after the meeting of Parliament, subsequent to the ratification of this Constitutional Chart by His Majesty, the Protecting Sovereign, that measures should be adopted by the Parliament for the institution in the first place of primary schools, and subsequently for the establishment of a college for the different branches of science, of literature and of the fine arts.[14]

The administration of education remained in the hands of Platon Petrides, the translator of British officials, appointed by Campbell in Zante. The Lancastrian method was used for the first time in Corfu in 1819 with 17 students – 5 from Zante, 4 from Corfu, 2 from Ithaca, 4 from Kefalonia and 2 from Paxos – all between 12 and 14 years old, a rather accurate reflection of the federal system introduced in education. Ionians who had trained in European universities were familiar with the Lancastrian method; out of the five teachers of Greek, Latin, Italian, fine arts and English, only one, the English teacher, was not Ionian. Two such schools opened, one in Corfu and the other in Leukada, which explains why no students from that island travelled to Corfu for their education. In 1826–27, the survey that the Ionian State conducted with the help of the police for administrative purposes included a questionnaire given to the notables of each village, asking them to provide information on the number and gender of pupils, the teaching material,

Table 10.1 Schools and pupils in the Ionian Islands, 1828.

Source: *American Journal of Education for the Year 1828*, Volume III, Boston, 1828, 624.

Island	Number of inhabitants	Number of schools	Number of 'scholars'
Kefalonia	49,857	2	157
Corfu	48,737	3	239
Paxos	3,970	1	40
Zante	40,063	13	363
Ithaca	8,200	1	87
Sante Maura	17,425	1	75
Cerigo	8,140	8	772
Total	176,392	29	1,733

the salary of teachers, and the type of education provided; all facets of a well-designed educational policy that the government promoted. According to the returns there were 121 Lancastrian schools in Corfu, with 2,342 students, boys as well as girls.[15] A year later a different report published in the prestigious *American Journal of Education* gave slightly different but more comprehensive numbers for all islands about the schools of 'mutual instruction':

The prospects were particularly dire, however, for the girls of Zante since 'the town does not afford the least means of instruction to females; and a doubt has been expressed to me, whether the girls would be allowed to attend the school, if one were established but as the Zantiotes are very jealous of their own dignity, they will blush when they find schools established in the other islands, while the women of Zante are permitted to remain in the most profound ignorance'; in the name of competition and progress even long-held conservative views about women could be left behind. The report would be proven wrong quite quickly. The journal's correspondents, Vamvas, Kalvos and Mrs Kennedy, most likely the wife of a British officer, made special mention of Kythera (Cerigo), where the British resident had built seven schools, an unusual number for such a small island, which schooled 772 children; even more impressive, however, than the number of students was the attitude to education: 'The order observed in these schools is scarcely exceeded in England; the progress is almost incredible: above all the female school of one hundred and thirteen pupils is admirably well managed. A great portion of the scholars, of both sexes, is a refugee from all parts of Greece; so that the benefits of the system will extend to the whole of the Levant'.[16] Contemporaries were very optimistic about the impact of education, from the Ionians Islands to the mainland, especially after the war of independence was over.

In 1828, Ionian officials, the British commissioner and his closest aides introduced the first major reforms in education. The Ionian Academy had started its long period of decline after the death of its founder, Lord Guilford in 1826. Several of the academy's professors were demoted to secondary school principals and appointed to other islands in the archipelago; some even refused to take up their new appointments and resigned in protest.[17] The law of 1828 subjected the academy to the control of the high commissioner and deprived it of its academic and political freedom, reduced its importance by closing the medical school and extended the powers of intervention of the central government. In 1830, Adam announced the opening of eighty-three new Lancastrian schools on the islands and offered an account of the school system to that date. The university operated in the old fortress with sixty-three students, very well paid professors (Karouzos, Professor of Law; Typaldos, Theology Professor; Vamvos, Moral Philosophy; Asopios, Greek; and Grasseti, Italian and Latin) and others all received 156 pounds, being among the highest paid in the Ionian State. The secondary school was also housed inside the old fortress with eighty-two male students, where Asopios, Grasseti and Vamvas taught without extra pay. The Lancastrian school was housed in the same building, where ninety-six students attended, and its principal and teachers were also among the very well paid, with annual salaries of 78 pounds and 26 pounds respectively. More Lancastrian schools in Corfu operated with funds provided by parents: three schools in town with fifty, forty-four and forty-two students; and two schools in Mandouki, one with seventy-two and another with sixty-nine students. Seventeen schools operated in the rural areas of the island, with between twenty-four and sixty students; one school with forty-five girls operated in Garitsa, while the report omitted another Lancastrian school in the suburb of Anemomilos with eighty students.[18]

The Ionian State created a special commission for public instruction, which Commissioner Nugent revised and improved; this was similar to other enlightened projects such as the public fund for lending to currant growers. In December 1832 the educational map of Corfu was changing fast, with 1,127 students in twenty-seven schools, while in Argostoli 799 children were in twenty-one schools, in Lixuri 150 students in three schools, in Zante 1,010 students in thirty-seven schools, in Lefkada 369 students in twelve schools, in Ithaki 435 students in seven schools, in Paxos 199 students in five schools, and in Kythera 194 students in five schools.[19] There were thirty-two public schools and 206 very small private 'schools', where locals and foreigners taught the children of most affluent Ionians, an impressive number that shows the 'market' for private tutoring and the number of people prepared to pay significant amounts for their children's education. The local aristocracy, the foreign families who lived on the islands and whoever could afford it sent their children to the several private schools that English female teachers operated in Corfu, Argostoli and Zakynthos. It is telling that the Ionian government, in the same year, spent less on the education of the whole population of the seven islands (6,171 pounds) than it did on the salaries of the priests. This meagre sum subsidized 7,315 students across all the islands, 4,583 boys and 826 girls.[20]

The level of education increased significantly during the first two decades of the Ionian State, even if it merely involved basic schooling, especially compared to the level of education in the years before the British protectorate. Education for girls catered for specific 'needs' and reflected society's expectations of gender roles. The Lancastrian method served as a training ground for bringing more teachers into education; in 1831, after twenty months of schooling, two girls were considered able to teach.[21] Protestant missionaries moved to the island and enjoyed logistical support from their base in Malta as well as in Corfu, as the government allowed the operation of girls' schools – the Kennedy School in Kefalonia and a Lancastrian girls' schools in Kythera. The initiative of Commissioner Adam's wife, the Corfu lady Palatianou, and other ladies of British officers, to establish schools for poor girls reflected the diffusion of education according to a British model, funded with money raised in Scotland and England; in 1829–31, five schools for girls opened according to this model: one in Corfu with a hundred and fifty students, one in Potamos with forty, another one in Garitsa with fifty-five, one in the suburb of Mandouki with eighty, and a fifth one in the village of Kinopiastes with twenty. This was the first cohort of educated girls in the Ionian Islands and the British environment, even if many of them left school during the period of olive harvesting.[22] Plans were drawn up to establish similar schools in Zante and Kythera, and funds were raised for this purpose.

Part of the enthusiasm that the appointment of Nugent as high commissioner of the Ionian Islands generated concerned his reforms in education. In 1833 the prominent liberal Ionian, Andreas Moustoxidis, was elected senator and was appointed president of the committee for public education.[23] In his first report, Mustoxidis attributed the low numbers of Ionian students in Kefalonia primary schools, for example, to the general ignorance of people towards education but especially to the 28 oboli per month for tuition fees. In 1834 there were 1,700 students in Kefalonia in a population of about 64,000; there were 85 schools, of which 12 were public and the rest private. In the same year (1831) in the new state of Greece under Governor Capodistrias, there were 125 schools with 9,246 students.[24] This was the result of the efforts that Capodistrias – an Ionian – had made for the education of the fledgling state.

The two sectors of private and public education that served Ionian children and their families are accurately depicted in the following table, which shows the results of the educational policy during the first two decades of the protectorate and the impressive spread of education in the Ionian Islands. Even small islands such as Kythera enjoyed high numbers of schools and of students. Girls were privately schooled on almost all islands, except Kefalonia where girls benefited form the public school system. More than half of the education budget went to Corfu, a sum that also covered the Ionian University expenses.

One of the interesting data in the table above is the number of private 'schools' and the number of female students that were taught in private schools by tutors and in their family homes. This is totally in accordance with the norms of the time, which did not allow girls to be educated even if their families could afford it. It is hard to explain why the fifty-nine families in Kefalonia and the forty-nine in Paxos thought differently, but this is what the government report recorded at the time. Another account, that of the Ionian committee for education and its general inspector, gave similar but lower figures but included also the amounts spent on the salaries of teachers, the principal expense in the education budget.

Ionian State officials introduced a plan for education and attempted to measure systematically schools and students in the same way that they recorded, for example, criminal activity to improve the organization of the police and the management of the population. They also designed a process for the selection of teachers in schools and the university through examination, although the Senate reserved the right to appoint the best candidate. This was part of the same Ionian governmentality project that put accountability centre stage, but also adopted a culture of numbers in public administration that would not leave such a crucial area for the control of the population unattended. The new provision for education of 1834 shows that teaching and 'schools' were housed in churches, especially in the villages and the suburbs, but also shows the ability of some areas of the country to communicate with each other, as schools operated in clusters, with students from smaller villages registered to the schools of the more populated ones. The planning shows the road and communication network in the country in 1834, when the roads system of the next twenty years was not yet in place. One of the most impressive elements in the report is the opening of the school in the village of Marathias, less than twenty years

Table 10.2 Schools and pupils, 1834.

Source: Martin, *History of the British Possessions*, 368.

Island	Public or free school	No of scholars in the public schools			Supported by government	No. of private schools	No. of scholars in the private schools		Total public and private scholars
		Males	Females	Total			Males	Females	
Corfu	4	294		294	3,261	67	1,955	353	2,602
Cephalonia	12	445	59	504	867	73	1,207		1,711
Zante	2	150		150	622	38	666	325	1,141
S. Maura	2	126		126	537	17	426	71	623
Ithaca	2	258		258	331	9	312	22	592
Cerigo	9	394	9	403	294	2	17	55	475
Paxo	5	122	49	171	257				171
Total	36	1,789	117	1,906	6,169	206	4,583	826	7,315

after the village had been devastated and all its houses burned when the plague ravaged southern Corfu.[25] Towards the end of Nugent's term, Mustoxidi was appointed as 'Archon' or minister of education, and he led the drafting of regulations for the operation of Lancastrian schools, self-funded and government-funded, public and private, in town and in the countryside. Mustoxidi resigned, however, in 1835 due to his conflict with the president of the Senate, Emmanuel Theotokis, and other pressures from those close to the commissioner. The main reason, however, was his profound disagreement with the Senate's plans for reform in education. The latter included the unacceptable – for Mustoxidi – decision of the general committee for education in February 1835 to introduce Italian as the language of correspondence and reports among the committee's members.[26] Politics and personal beliefs forced Mustoxidi to resign.

The Ionian government innovated in creating a 'college' in Corfu, a secondary school for preparing students for the university, similar to the ways Lancastrian primary schools prepared students for secondary schools. The college had a boarding establishment for students from other islands, and in 1840 it was flourishing, according to Davy, always a valuable source:

> The success of the college is most gratifying. It contains eighty scholars and the applications for admittance from parents and guardians are more numerous than can be favourably attended to. The expense incurred by students is exceedingly moderate, amounting only to eight, ten and twelve dollars a month, for the first, second and third years ... The expense to government, in the first instance, was, as anticipated, heavy; but the institution now pays its own expenses and with the increase in the number of scholars there will be surplus.

The report emphasized the 'moral and political good' of the establishment and the expectation that the college would bring to Corfu the youth of the several islands:

> Mingling together at an early age, pursuing the same studies, imbibing the same ideas, at a moment when the mind is most accessible to impressions, island and provincial jealousies and prejudices will be softened, and gradually destroyed; there will be no rivalry but to excel ... the most proficient will be provided for in the public service ... a national feeling will be centralized in and towards this capital (Corfu), as the place of their education; and this feeling is already fostering by the universal popularity of the measure.[27]

Davy, as was often the case, was extremely perceptive; education fostered a common Ionian identity from a very young age for the very first time and in unique ways. Within a few years many educated Ionians felt confident enough to pose a challenge to the British-Ionian government that had educated them, and even to undermine the state and try to end the protectorate.

Douglas, among his other plans to transform the protectorate into a colony, continued his predecessor's work and extended the reach and size of the state through education. By 1837, 102 public Lancastrian schools taught 4,348 students, while only ten of them educated 615 girls. Education offered the means to a younger generation of Ionians to rise to positions of power in administration, politics and commerce. A table with the names of students of the Ionian college at Corfu, written by Orioli, the headmaster, includes the names of Spiridion Cefala, Michele Dima, Andrea Scarpa, Spiridion Topali, Giacomo Tool and Marco Bassian (from Kefalonia) – all sons of established merchants.[28] This experience certainly advanced the qualifications and status of the sons of well-established merchants by providing a prestigious education.

Mustoxidi, in his famous memorial to the colonial secretary, summarized the state of Ionian education: 'One of the first duties of Parliament, dictated by the Constitution, after the Royal ratification, was the establishment of a college for the different branches of science, belles-lettres, and the fine arts. Has this been done? Certainly not. Acts of Parliament, resolutions, reports and regulations, are published in succession, for the purpose of re-organizing public instruction, but each one of the enactments destroys the other'. Mustoxidi accused the government of 'squandering' eleven thousand pounds: 'the Ionian youth flock to foreign universities to pursue their studies and the elementary schools are deserted'. Mustoxidi was genuinely upset that a Methodist had been appointed as inspector of the elementary and inferior schools, 'a man ignorant of our character, our customs, our religious rites, and our language, is appointed to superintend the education of the rising generation, the only hope of their families and of their country'. Mustoxidi's liberal views, however, transpire beyond his critique of the Ionian government: 'It was decreed that from that time forward, elementary school-books should first be approved by a conference of all the bishops of the state; and thus, in this enlightened age, a censorship is established, which extends beyond the just and necessary limits the influence of the clergy over public education'.[29]

In the 1840s there were still several private schools, the most common schooling before the affluent young Ionians left for Italian or other universities abroad. These schools advertised their services in the official newspaper, publishing information about tuition fees, courses, regulations and teachers for those Ionians who could afford to send their children to a private school, preparing them for membership of their island's elite, possibly a government position. Among the first to encourage and sponsor education was Commissioner Douglas; in 1836 under his patronage the 'Classical and Commercial School for young Gentlemen' was established.[30] Mrs Dickson opened her school in 1841, teaching at 'lower' and 'higher levels of Academic Study', with a fee of $1.[31] Schools were separated according to gender and the 'appropriate' courses taught.[32] Schools from abroad advertised their services on the islands too; an 'English Collegiate School' at St Julian's, Malta, combined 'religious and moral instruction' with the learning of very useful tools for prospective merchants, 'Arithmetic, Book-keeping, the elements of Mathematics', as well as several foreign languages. Those interested could visit James Taylor for a prospectus.[33] Merchants and landowners provided for their children's education with the desire that it not merely 'reproduce' elite positions and relations of power through education mechanisms, but educated the next generation of Ionians, schooled in their islands, often the same people who as young adults challenged the continuation of the protectorate; by educating Ionians the British-Ionian State to an extent sowed the seeds of its own demise. In 1843 a detailed report of all schools on the islands was produced. The report, submitted in May 1843, was signed by A. L. Dusmani, 'Secretary of the General Commission of Public Instruction' and Ettore Ricchi, 'General Inspector of Primary and Secondary Instruction of the State'.[34] This was one of the most impressive manifestations of the emergence of a systematic bureaucratic organization for the formation of education policy.

The amount that the Ionian State spent on education as long as state finances allowed determined the level of education; career opportunities for Ionians depended on the island on which they were born, and especially on their family's background. Ioannis N. Stamatelos (1822–81) was born in Lefkada to an affluent family, and received his basic education on the island.[35] In 1829, during his primary school years, the famous Athanasios Psallidas was the headmaster of the secondary school, and reported to his superiors in Corfu that the Lancastrian school lay deserted but not closed, since the teacher was there but students were missing, making the function of the secondary school problematic.[36] According to Psallidas's report there was no school building, as the Lancastrian school, when open, operated in a church, at least until the construction of a new school started in 1824; the building is still there but its function as a school did not last long. In 1835 the building housed the courts – for a remarkably long period, from 1835 to 1989. The relegation of education from the purpose-built school shows the lack of interest in primary education, even in the capital of the island of Lefkada.

The most remarkable failing in education, however, was the islands' university, the Ionian Academy.[37] Founded in 1823 and opened in 1824 in Corfu with spectacular fanfare that simulated antiquity to the point of re-enactment, after the death of its founder and director, Lord Guilford in 1827, the university fell into a prolonged decline. State funding was cut and the medical school closed for fifteen years; the number of students reduced from 240 in 1826–27 to less than 100 in the following years. Many physicians in the Ionian Islands had studied in Italy and the level of education that the university offered was very high.[38] The opening of the Athens university struck another blow and the competition with the much more acclaimed and centuries-old established universities of Pisa and Padova contributed to the decline; the university finally closed after the union of the islands with Greece in 1864. The evidence from the Athens university presents a mixed picture; while in the period 1837–52 there were 168 students who had come from the Ionian Islands, in the shorter period 1853–63 only 118 were registered.[39] This is because many Ionians continued to study in Pisa: for the period 1837–62 about 200 Ionians graduated from Pisa and 54 from other universities; in the period 1806–61 most students in Pisa came from Kefalonia (203) as opposed to 93 from Zante, 88 from Corfu, 28 from Ithaki, 26 from Lefkada and 18 from Kythera. Most Ionians studied law, and several of them (especially those from Kefalonia) medicine, and their presence in Pisa peaked in the 1830s and 1840s, declining sharply from the late 1840s onwards, and never recovering.[40] The few hundred Ionians who were trained in law returned to their island to work in the legal system, in the administration, or simply to manage their family estate in the litigation-obsessed Ionian society. A law degree, just as was the case sometimes with land, was much more a question of prestige than it was a matter of profit, let alone productive investment and employment.

A Special Profession

Training in law, a university degree and the experience in administration proved crucial for the fortunes of the Ionian State, but also for the challenges that Ionians posed to the British protectorate. At the beginning of the nineteenth century, lawyers in Corfu (those who practised law) only numbered twelve; there were tens of others who did not work as lawyers but looked after their own property and the properties of their relatives and friends, which was one of the main aims of training in law, together with the status and especially the right to political participation that the degree conferred upon its holder in Ionian society. In Corfu there were many more law practitioners, other than certified lawyers; twenty assistant lawyers (*intervenienti*) and many more notaries – thirty-two for the country, two for each suburb in Garitsa, Mandouki and Potamo, and sixteen for the city – fifty-six in total, according to a regulation dating back to Venetian Governor Andrea Dona in 1756. Before the British period the profession of lawyer (*avocato*) was open to everyone with a law degree. At least in the city, if not in the country as well, the regulation had been in place since 1810.[41]

In the 1820s the law to regulate the profession dictated that only indigenous or naturalized Christian Ionians over twenty-one years old and registered as lawyers could exercise the profession, a term that obviously excluded and discriminated against Jewish law graduates who had already practised law. Certified lawyers were required to have a very good knowledge of Greek but also English, besides the Italian that was compulsory in practice if not on paper. The law asked for a practice of one year in a law office, and introduced the Lawyers' Association on each island, placing with them the responsibility for examining candidate lawyers. Assistant lawyers had to fulfil the same qualifications except their Christian faith, a clause that reflects the fact the many Jews already worked as court secretaries and could not be dismissed simply for belonging to the 'wrong' religion. The law mentions the professions in English as advocate and attorney, and in Italian as *avvocato* and *interveniente*.[42] Only law degree holders could exercise the profession, and they also held the right to vote and progress to the office of prosecutor, appointed by the Senate. Assistant lawyers served also as scribers and secretaries of the courts and the prosecutor's office; they could practise law, however only after several years of service and after passing the exams by the Council of Justice of the Senate. By the end of the British period, state officials had registered ninety-five lawyers (excluding the other law practitioners).[43] In the electoral list of 1865, one year after the unification of the islands with the Greek Kingdom, there were fifty-five lawyers and fifty-one attorneys.

Lawyers were by far the most distinguished occupational, social and status group in Ionian society. A degree in law was an almost compulsory qualification for everyone who wanted to be somebody, but was also useful in providing an income and essential in managing the family estate. A law degree qualified for political participation; in 1849, out of 663 electors in Corfu, 131 were doctors of law. This troubled some British writers who believed that idleness bred discontent: 'for want of employment, [they] lounge about the streets, in a perfect state of moral, industrial, and professional idleness and vacancy, smoking their cigarettes, and discussing politics, of which they do not so much as understand the terms'.[44] There were clearly 'too many' lawyers in the Ionian States as opposed to civil engineers, a profession practically unknown. The situation worried Nugent who stated in a speech to the legislative assembly before leaving Corfu:

> I strenuously recommend that every young man in the States should be sent by his parents to learn an active profession. That of the law is doubtless honourable and a useful profession, in a State which is governed according to known laws, to which men may appeal through their advocates for justice. But the profession of the law in these States is too much crowded. The business becomes of a pretty sort; trifling litigation is encouraged, instead of being repressed, among the people; and the profession of the law becomes a less elevated, if not a less honourable, pursuit.

Ionian lawyers also instigated most of the resistance to British rule, and were among the most ardent reformers, politicians and even activists during the 1840s and 1850s when Ionian nationalism took shape.

Lawyers were one of the central groups in the process of class formation. The main forces of social differentiation in Kefalonian society, and for that matter in Ionian society in general, were the chronic problem of landed property (constant subdivision and joint but largely unequal ownership of land between landowner and tenant farmer), the system of British administration, which perpetuated the land problem by proselytizing the landowners, and the rapid development of shipowning commerce from the period of the Septinsular Republic (1800–1807) onwards. The social classes that could be discerned by the end of the protectorate were the principal landowners and the wholesale merchants. They are the ones who, until the middle of the twentieth century, people still called the 'masters' (*archontes*), the nobles of the previous centuries, the *signori*, those called in the English sources 'the eminent and powerful gentlemen', the 'gentry' and 'the respectable citizens'. People of this class maintained all power in their hands; just like during the period of Venetian rule, they rotated to positions of public administration and government, controlling them and, thus, catering to their private interests. In exchange for their privileges they offered their total backing to the protection, and supported with their actions the Anglo-Ionian State.[45] The best example is probably Demetrios Carouzos, who from the 'humble' beginnings of an assistant lawyer rose to become the very powerful regent of Kefalonia, thanks to his very good connections and trust of the British. Conflicts and synergies among liberal Ionians, however, were not about union with Greece necessarily, but about reforming the Ionian State. One of the main fields of bourgeois activism was the politics of liberal associations, political as well as literary and scientific, that became very popular during the 1830s and in the following decades.

Voluntary Associations and the Ionian Bourgeoisie

In 1836, the same year that the Agricultural Society was founded, 'young men, on their return from Europe', established the Reading Society, or *Anagnostiki Eteria*, of Corfu.[46] New ideas were expressed though the formation of voluntary educational–literary associations, a field of public activity for the European bourgeoisie. The society is still in the same building today and houses an important collection of documents and rare books.[47] When the society opened, the 'best selection of political newspapers and periodicals of England, France, Germany and Italy' was available in its reading room.[48] Merchants were among the founding members of these societies and interacted with politicians, lawyers, physicians and members of the Ionian administration. The society's founding members were all intellectuals, physicians, lawyers and politicians, plus some merchants and a few members of the nobility. One of the founding members and first president of the society was Petros Vrailas-Armenis, an emblematic figure of the Corfu liberal bourgeoisie. Son of a merchant from the Ottoman mainland, philosopher, and supporter of union with Greece from the ranks of the reformist party, Vrailas-Armenis became an important member of the Greek Parliament after union with Greece, as well as a member of the Academy of Athens. Martin Fels and Ernest Toole were the two merchants among the 'founders' of the society, evidence that there was interaction between some (foreign mainly) merchants with local literary circles and intellectuals. Theodoros Lavranos, another merchant, was also involved from the early years of the society; his father, Filippos Lavranos, had been a well-established merchant in Corfu since the early nineteenth century, and so Theodoros confirms a long and successful presence of the family in urban affairs. Business partners Dimas and Seremetis, wholesale grain importers, shareholders and landowners involved in most aspects of economic life in Corfu, joined the Reading Society in 1850. The process of 'embourgeoisement' of the Corfu urban elite continued and intensified towards the end of the nineteenth century and during the early twentieth century, when the offspring of nobles lost out in local politics, associations, and positions of urban authority, with the exception of the famous Theotoki family that produced a prime minister in the late nineteenth and early twentieth century, one of the most important and underestimated prime ministers in that period.[49]

Ionian liberals established institutions such as the Reading Society, which followed the trajectory of the *literati* of the academies that formed the first phase of Ionian governmentality since the eighteenth century and bear all the hallmarks of bourgeois society. The 'Ionian Association', on the other hand, encapsulated the scope of Ionian liberalism in tandem with the Ionian government; the association was founded in 1851 'for the development of intellect and the encouragement of agriculture, industry and the arts in all the Ionian Islands'.[50] In January 1860, Andreas Mustoxidis, president of the Ionian Society, historian and politician, and minister of education, announced in the *Ionian Gazette* the call for those interested in joining the 'Ionian Association for the encouragement of useful knowledge', and to meet in the theatre of the Ionian Academy.[51] The committee included cavaliers and counts, priests and doctors, musicians and intellectuals, highly representative of British-Ionian administration (Drummond Woolf, secretary to the high commissioner), the intelligentsia of Corfu (Mustoxidis, Vrailas-Armenis, Mantzaros), the medical establishment (including Dr Semo, the Jewish physician), the Church hierarchy (one for each Christian denomination, Roman Catholic and Orthodox), as well as senators (Grollo, Foresti, Mercati) and the bankers Loughnan and Zambelli also serving as treasurers of the society, applying their accounting skills to the society's service.

The annual report of the Ionian Society for the year 1861 included the balance sheet, signed by Zambelios, which shows that revenue came from subscriptions and offers by members. The donations had brought £71 5s to the society's coffers, adding to the existing £126 4s 10d, amounting altogether to £197 9s 10d, a considerable amount for a modest organization, excluding state support for the society's projects. In the balance sheet Zambelios notes that there is also the sum of £100 deposited in the Ionian Bank at an annual interest of 4 per cent. The expenses of the society amounted to £165 8s 2d of which £125 had been spent on organizing the Ionian Exhibition. This was the largest event organized by the Ionian State, aiming to bring international recognition of the protectorate, even if it was on its course to joining Greece. The competition organized by the Ionian Society awarded prizes for Ionian agricultural and manufactured products.[52]

The society was divided into two 'departments': one called 'Moral Sciences', one 'Natural and Mathematical Sciences'. In turn, these were divided into two 'classes', the first one that included physicians, local and British, and a second 'class' responsible for 'Agriculture, Commerce and Shipping'. Merchants, bankers and the senators or municipal councillors who had served as officers for commerce all joined, including Elia Vasilaki, regent of Corfu. Among them were the merchants Kyriakis, Seremetis, Kefalas, Baldas, Merkatis, Loughnan, Koraggios, Zervos, Scaramangas, Dimas and Scarpas. The other two 'departments' were 'Grammatology and Archaeology', while there was one for the 'Fine Arts'. The names of the people assigned to each department reveal the broadest participation of the urban elite possible; the participation of people with different professions, occupations and talents, brought together under the auspices of the Ionian Society to cultivate those 'sciences' in the respective 'departments'.

The first two aims of the society were the organization of the Ionian Exhibition and the completion and publication of *Kerkyraika*, the history of Corfu, postponed by the sudden death of the president of the society, Andrea Mustoxidi. Ionian urban society was not unfamiliar with the international exhibitions of the time. In 1850, a notice was placed in the *Gazette* about accommodation arrangements for those wishing to attend the Great Exhibition of 1851 in London.[53] The French ambassador in London made provisions for producers from the islands who wished to exhibit their products at the Paris Exhibition of May 1855.[54] In 1861, showcasing Ionian products at international exhibitions had become a matter of priority for High Commissioner Storks, as he was personally involved, calling upon the merchants of the islands to encourage the participation of producers in the local exhibition in February 1862 and to select Ionian products that would represent the Ionian State. Storks revealed his ambition and plans:

> In these states, little can be effected without the active and zealous efforts of individuals ... The local Commissions should consist of influential persons, who take an interest in the development of the Industry and productive resources of the Islands. It should be their endeavour not only collectively, but individually, to urge those producers with whom they may be in communication, to exercise their best skill in producing something worthy of remark, and to point out to tradesmen and manufacturers how great an advantage they would derive if their productions were to attract notice at the Exhibition in London and, thus, open a market in which their goods are not at present known.[55]

This was by far the most organized participation of Ionian products on the international scene. Everyone contributed their part: agent and merchant of the firm Fels & Co., and representatives of the Steam Ship Company, John Bibby, Sons & Co. of Liverpool, arranged for the company's ships to carry freight free of charge from Corfu to Liverpool: objects shipped by the Ionian Association for the exhibition of 1862, not exceeding the aggregate 15 tons measurement, and one passenger.[56] The preliminary exhibition in Corfu in February 1862 became a significant event for the islands, and for Corfu in particular. The Lloyd ships offered discounted prices for goods and tickets (40 per cent) for those wishing to travel to Corfu for the exhibition or to send their produce, and who were obliged to carry these goods from the other islands to Corfu.[57]

Merchants were appointed to the committee for the awards, and for certifying the quality of the products that would represent the Ionian Islands in the Great Exhibition. This was a very gendered process; merchants and company agents were appointed as judges to the committee and their wives as judges of the more 'feminine' products, such as embroidery, silks, laces, clothes, needlework and jewellery. The jury on currants comprised the merchants Martin Fels, A. Sargint and Woodley; on olive oil, the merchants Barr, Baldas and Gysis; on wine, Boyd, Dusmani and Major Peel; while on embroidery, ladies 'Signora' Valaoriti, Mrs Drummond Wolf, 'Contessa' Bulgari Aucler, Mrs Inglis, and 'Signora' Angela Scarpa. Equally, the jury on silks comprised Lady Buller, Lady Braila, Contessa Giovanni Dusmani; and on cloth and needlework, Lady Damascino, Mrs Barr, Contessa Annino, Signora Diamantina Scarpa and Signora Candoni. Paintings were judged by Conte Spiro Dusmani, Signor Machiedo, Signor Nicolo Vassilachi, Captain Hamilton Simpson and Major Darling; jewellery by Signora Lavrano, Contessa Flamburiari, Contessa Conemi, Lady Sargent and Mrs Wynn; and on cereal and commestibile, Federico Fels, Cavalier Cefala and Xenofonte Vasila. Other goods included leather, which Messrs. Seremetti, Sp. Marchetti and Taylor adjudicated; and tobacco which Messrs Colquhoun, Rodostamo, T. Zambelli, Vitalis and Strahan promoted.[58]

The members of the juries were selected according to specialization of the merchandise in which they were trading (e.g. Fels traded in currants, Baldas in olive oil, Vasilas in cereals, and Taylor in leather), and with the expectation that jury members would judge the quality of the various products such as wine, tobacco and jewellery as 'connoisseurs'. The committee, appointed by the municipal council of Corfu, summoned some of the members of the Ionian Society and their wives as the 'experts' in the jurisdiction of the products worthy to represent the states, reaffirming their authority. This is the moment that the gendered dimension of the bourgeoisie was manifested in this very public demonstration of status and authority for the international exhibition of 1862.

The Reading Society and the Ionian Association were genuine expressions of bourgeois liberalism, demonstrating aspirations to cultivate the arts and the sciences together with the economic development of the islands, and shows the convergence of Ionian and British officials, merchants and politicians. This was also an opportunity for those participating to reaffirm their status, but also actively promote business interests for the public and private good, through the promotion of Ionian exports at the Great Exhibition and in international markets. These were spaces of sociability as well as education, essential in the formation of class identities. The Reading Society and the Ionian Society were faithful to the 'civilizing mission' of the British middle class, aiming to impose their values and ideology, and transform working-class behaviour and ideals, through voluntary efforts;[59] only that they were created and run by Ionians. The Ionian Exhibition and the Reading Society offered prestige to their members and probably small economic gain to the Ionian State, but they projected the images of an affluent, extrovert and advancing society.[60] When the islands joined the Greek Kingdom and were set on a different historical trajectory, all these initiatives stalled. By then Ionian liberalism had become the hegemonic intellectual and political project in the British protectorate, and it was most clearly expressed in the field where ultimately all class differences are resolved: politics.

The *liberali*: Liberalism and the End of Colonial Rule

Ionian liberalism emerged through interaction with Western cultural registers, mainly through the education of Ionians in Italy but especially through their experience of British colonialism during the period of the protectorate. The constitutional tradition of the early nineteenth century formed the foundation for the liberal constitutional demands of the next generation of Ionian politicians in the 1830s and 1840s. Merchants and businessmen championed the liberal cause on the issue of free trade, adopting the spirit of colonial capitalism and helping to promote the imperialism of free trade. State policies on the regulation of a broad range of issues – such as health, markets, labour and order – fell precisely into this category of colonial liberalism, which found fertile ground in this part of the Mediterranean. Petitions as forms of interaction with state authorities, from all islands, reveal how widespread liberal views on education, commerce and even religion were among Ionians. The political and intellectual hegemony of Ionian liberalism took the form of a state project (besides its punitive-executive function) and as a civil society political movement. This movement predated the cause of union with Greece that matured only during the 1850s among some liberals – the more radical or opportunistic ones.

The discourse, practice and politics of liberalism in the Ionian Islands followed a different trajectory to the liberalism developed by intellectuals in the Greek Kingdom.[61] The post-revolution state truncated the aspirations of the most fervent liberals to the Greek Kingdom and the absolute power of its monarch. Ionian liberalism is also distinct from the liberalism that emerged in the eastern Mediterranean, as the impact of Western education, colonialism and the rise of Arab nationalism.[62] The ideas and political activism of liberals and radicals in the Ionian State matter precisely for their intermediate and bridging position in the spread of liberal ideas, even if the diffusion of ideas was hardly an even process; still, unless we consider Ionian liberals and their agency we miss a crucial link in the narrative of the history of Mediterranean liberalism. The debate has concerned Latin American historians for a long time and continues to enjoy popularity, often as a case of 'imported' liberalism among other approaches.[63]

The high levels of literacy among the members of the bourgeoisie, and long-established connections with France and Italy and the liberal reforms introduced in Ionian society by the French revolutionaries (1797–99), made it, at least in the eyes of their British rulers, highly probable that the Ionians might ask for further liberal reforms, greater participation in the decision-making process, or even independence and *Enosis* (Union) with Greece.[64] The education of Ionians in Italy equipped them with a sophisticated view of liberalism, a sense of historicism that for some Greek historians represents a 'historical school' and is evident in the fact that the Ionian State appointed Mustoxidi as the official historian of the state, following the earlier decision of the Septinsular Republic in 1806, another continuity between the two states; here was a state, so conscious of its historical role and presence that it appointed one of its most distinguished citizens as the official historian. From the early years of British protection, Ionian liberals sought to establish their status as worthy of European and therefore British liberalism. Some Ionians organized what was effectively one of the first instances of anti-colonialism, against what Ionians called *ksenokratia* (xenocracy).[65] Other Ionians, such as the grain merchants, were fervent supporters of liberal ideas and laissez-faire liberalism. Ionians structured their ideas and arguments for reform and, later, abolition of British rule based on political principles that were prominent in Britain, Italy, France and other centres of European liberalism.

Most Ionian liberals studied law in some of the finest Italian or French universities before returning to their native islands to enter politics or state administration as members of the government, usually in the judiciary or education. Some of the radical Ionians started their intellectual journey as liberals with demands first put forward to the representatives of British rule in the 1830s. One of them was Iosif Momferratos from Kefalonia, the centre of Ionian radicalism. In December 1843 he returned to his native Argostoli after his studies in Italy. Although he had trained in law he did not practise it but spent his time, together with his friends Elias Zervos Iakovatos and Gerasimos Livadas, debating the political and social condition of Kefalonia and the other islands. The three men became the main representatives of the radical 'movement' in Kefalonia, aiming for 'national reconstitution and radical progress', through the association that would be named Demotikon Katastima (Municipal Establishment), according to Momferratos.[66] The reforms of Commissioner Seaton allowed the opening of political clubs in Corfu, Argostoli and Zante; the one in Argostoli was named Koraes, after the famous Greek Enlightenment intellectual. In 1848 Koraes became explicitly political, and the radicals renamed it Demotikon Katastima. From that moment onwards this became the 'headquarters' of radicalism in Kefalonia, if not for the whole of the Ionian Islands. Momferratos wrote 'anti-protection' articles that were published in Athens because of the absence of a free press in the Ionian Islands. Momferratos, Zervos and a few other radicals insisted on the 'sovereign and unalienable right' of Ionians to demand union with independent Greece, declaring their uncompromising and non-negotiable position against the protectorate. The resistance of the radicals in the assembly took tangible forms; they refused to take the oath that they believed was unacceptable and humiliating.

Ionians evoked rights granted under the previous regime of Venetian rule, during the 1803 constitution and the constitutional charter of 1817, but within the established European Enlightenment register of rights. Beyond the origins of Ionian liberal thought, Ionian Greeks were certainly part of the 'liberal international' and shared much of the anti-imperial discourse that spread like wildfire on the Italian peninsula.[67] The *Ionian Islands Government Gazette* frequently included stories about conflicts between liberal Europeans and absolutist governments, but also about the major event of the Greek war of independence and its success in creating a post-revolutionary state in the south of the Greek peninsula and the Cycladic islands. Ionian radicalism grew through political clubs and societies that took after the Italian secret societies and connected to the 'political committees' in the Greek Kingdom, such as the 'Sacred Struggle' that demonized British protection, and were held responsible for destabilizing affairs in south-eastern Europe.[68]

Ionian challenges to the protectorate and a reform project date back to Kapodistrias's concerns about the constitutional sanctions of

Maitland's rule in 1819 that the Corfiote statesman took up to the highest level with Bathurst, during his visit to London. In the two decades that followed, commissioners Adam (1824–32), Nugent (1832–36) and Douglas (1836–41) fluctuated between a policy faithful to Maitland's original intentions under Adam and a liberal shift under Nugent. The latter allowed and even encouraged Ionians to challenge previous and especially future forms of rule in the protectorate, making them more confident to counter the policies of Douglas to promote social and economic development under an authoritarian and paternalistic rule. In many ways Nugent and Douglas created the conditions for the liberal surge of the 1830s and 1840s that was transformed by some Ionians into the dominant movement of union as more and more Ionians became disillusioned or outraged with the response of the government to the Kefalonia uprising of 1849 and the worsening economic conditions of the 1850s.

Nugent brought a new style but also substance to Ionian government. Declaring his admiration for Ionian history and virtues, Nugent promoted and supported the passing of no less than forty-two laws on improving prospects for Ionians in education, fiscal administration, commerce and agriculture. Nugent was also aware of Ionian sensitivities a few years after the war of independence; he cancelled the confiscation of property that belonged to Ionians who had taken part in the war. Loyal to the original declarations of the Ionian constitution, he established Greek as the official language in the courts even if Italian remained as the language of the state.[69] Douglas promoted a similar reform project. He used public funds to build and support schools, primary as well as secondary ones, extending Ionians' access to further education, and preparing many for university.

Three issues dominated the debate and concerned Douglas during his term: the freedom of the press, control over state finances and the accountability of the assembly, which was under the exclusive control of the commissioner. During Nugent's term, the Fourth and Fifth Parliament (1833 and 1844) passed two acts, 'recognizing the right of the Assembly to regulate and sanction the finance of these states'; effectively this was a constitutional amendment in everything but name, since the constitution gave to the commissioner absolute control over finances. Douglas, however, repealed Nugent's law that gave the assembly power over ordinary expenses, which covered the salaries of the commissioner, state officials and employees, the civil list. This is a sign that Douglas was prepared to accept a reduction in spending for military expenses, public education, and other items, but not the budget that gave him power and could earn Ionians' support for the government. Douglas also stated that he agreed with Maitland that control of the state's finances was the most important article of the constitution, although it contradicted the Treaty of Paris that had founded the right of Ionians to manage the state finances. According to article VIII of the constitution, the Senate appointed three ministerial officers to be responsible for three departments, the 'General', the 'Political' and 'Finance'.[70]

Arguments about the immaturity of Ionians to govern themselves persisted in the discourse of high commissioners; at least, by the time of Douglas, Ionians were 'advanced in education and refinement' although still unfit for self-government.[71] The 'constitutional issue' never faded away, it only subsided and then recurred on several occasions, often with the initiative of commissioners themselves. Douglas, for example, attributed the turmoil that was fermenting in 1839 to the elections of March, which had seen liberal Ionians elected in the Sixth Parliament; fifteen out of the forty members of the assembly formed a formidable opposition that focused on constitutional reform. The intransigence of Douglas when it came to the circulation of foreign newspapers, especially from Greece, that offered Ionians the opportunity to challenge the protectorate, not only upset Ionians but raised eyebrows in London, where his policies were considered unconstitutional, as noted by colonial office consul Stephens, whose opinions Colonial Secretary Normandy valued.[72]

The reform effort of the 1830s against Douglas's procrastination and uncompromising spirit culminated in the visit of Andreas Mustoxidis, one of the most distinguished Ionian liberals, to London, where he took Ionian grievances directly to the colonial secretary. Mustoxidis presented Normandy with a memorial criticizing Douglas and his policy on the islands, and outlined his project for constitutional reform. The memorial and the visit represent the pinnacle of the reform effort, and in both that document and in the response of Douglas that the colonial office elicited, liberalism was at the heart of the debate. The document shows the range of liberal demands that Ionians put forward. For Mustoxidi, Ionian political independence was enshrined in the 1803 constitution but went back to the period of Venetian rule and therefore could not be scaled back to the nineteenth century; Mustoxidi argued that the 1803 constitution introduced 'more liberal and equitable principles' than the British-designed constitution of 1817. Interestingly, though, Mustoxidi focused on Douglas more than on Maitland, castigating his despotic rule that had depressed the Ionian Islands like never before. More than a critique, however, the memorial proposed four demands for reform: freedom of the press, free elections, voting by ballot, and control of state finances.[73] Mustoxidis argued that the electoral system should be based on representation entirely free from nomination of the primary council, that the interval of two years between the successive sessions of the legislative assembly should be shortened, that the extraordinary as well as the ordinary expenses of the state should be voted on by the assembly annually, and that the freedom of the press should be established. In his response to Mustoxidis's memorial, Colonial Minister Russell acknowledged that the constitutional charter that Maitland had devised had an expiry date, 'to inquire whether the period thus contemplated by Sir Thomas Maitland has arrived; whether the people of the Ionian States have made such advances in the knowledge and habits indispensable to the right conduct of free institutions as would qualify them for any material enlargement of their existing franchises'.[74] Russell requested a full report from Douglas, precluding the outcome, and stating that at least some extension of liberties should be granted to the issue of free press and political representation. Moreover, for Russell the matter was one of imperial honour: 'It would not be to the honour of this country to have occupied the Ionian States for so many years, without having advanced the inhabitants towards some qualification for institutions more liberal than those which were granted to them, avowedly as a mere preparation for such change'.

Mustoxidis's memorial was scathing of Maitland's provisions and the powers he had invested the high commissioner with. The police, Mustoxidis argued,

> rules and directs with an absolute influence the inhabitants of the country's districts and at the time of the elections exercises a pernicious preponderance. And if it is added that not even a justice of the peace has been granted to these country districts, so that the peasants for the least offence are dragged from the most distant parts of the country to the town before the tribunal of justice, to become the laughing-stock of lawyers and at the expense of loss of time, of injury to their agriculture, the corruption of the manners and exorbitant costs, no one can but feel compassion for them.[75]

Mustoxidis condemned the arbitrary selection of memorials, private petitions and communications form the magistrates, and private petitions which were in the power of the president of the Senate, with the result that they could lie 'unnoticed from year to year and not infrequently are for ever abandoned to oblivion', as he could keep from them what he pleased and communicate to them what he chose. There were problems with how the police force worked: 'By what law does he [the high commissioner] appoint the inspectors of police and the officers of this branch, and even the constables, who are for the most part

Albanians, as if to restrain by foreign mercenaries the natural courage of the natives?' On the administration of state finances the question of power was at the heart of Mustoxidis's criticisms:

> The Assembly has the right of regulating the ordinary expenses of the state. The Senate persists in calling ordinary expenses only those belonging to the civil list, and all others that are caused by unforeseen events, by accident, or suddenly, are termed extraordinary in order to avoid presenting to the Assembly the budget, and in order not to ask for its previous approbation. The great privilege was that of inspecting the numerical correctness of the accounts. But it is in vain that the Assembly deliberates even upon the civil list, because it has already been modified; for when the Senate does not attempt to increase, it diminishes the sums fixed by the Assembly.[76]

The language issue, the continuous use of Italian in courts and the administration bothered Mustoxidi, who echoed Nugent in his frustration about most Ionians being tried in a language they could not understand.[77]

Douglas, in his response, contrasted the 'backward' Ionian institutions, economy and society with the advanced commercial world of the settler colonies, and therefore advised that the best policy for the Ionian Islands was to maintain strict control of the population. Russell, although liberal and open-minded enough to consider Mustoxidi's proposals, in the end accepted Douglas's objections and maintained the status quo, although Douglas had completed his term by the time the response was debated in the British Parliament.[78]

Journalism and the Making of an Ionian Public

The uprisings of September 1848 and August 1849 in Kefalonia convinced British colonial policymakers that liberalization of the Ionian protectorate regime was necessary to avoid an escalating crisis that could harm British interests. The crushing of the rebellions and the severe punishment and retribution inflicted by Commissioner Ward set back the reforms that the colonial office had approved, namely to grant freedom of the press and extend the right to vote. Once the law came into force, printing houses opened in Corfu, Kefalonia and Zakynthos that published newspapers, expressing the various political views towards a range of issues that gradually crystallized into the first political parties of the time and of Greek politics, other than the personality-centred and foreign powers-determined political formations that existed in Athens. Liberal and more radical ideas had been fermenting since the 1830s, if not earlier, when two parties emerged: the Reformists and the Radicals. Reformists advocated the reform of British protection and particularly of the Ionian State, and considered the prospect of unification with the Greek Kingdom unrealistic; Radicals demanded the abolition of the protectorate and unification with Greece. These political formations were formally represented in the Ionian Assembly in the elections of 1850, the first that were held following the extension of the franchise; twenty-one Reformists, eleven Radicals and ten government supporters were elected to that Parliament.

The circulation of newspapers in Ionian cities came after decades of slow but steady emergence of a civil society and opened a space of political communication, confrontation and negotiation without which the crystallization of groups of liberal Ionians into 'parties' and factions would be unthinkable. The political and national developments on the islands, in neighbouring Italy and the Greek Kingdom, and all over Europe in the 'spring of nations' in 1848 shaped the debates and the spirit that drove some Ionians to become journalists, political commentators or even radical nationalists who demanded union with Greece. Ionians who had studied in Italian and especially French universities were infused with liberal ideas, and drove a wedge into the much desired but always elusive 'tranquility' that the British so often sought.[79] The Ionian press followed the intellectual and political developments of the first half of the nineteenth century, but it was the new generation of Ionians who came of age in the 1840s who were ready to challenge the British and aristocratic Ionian social and political order by using the new medium of the newspaper and, to a lesser extent, the pamphlet. The number, content and impact of these newspapers is impressive; their publishers exposed and criticized the contradictions of British protection on the islands and encapsulated the struggle against 'xenocracy', as radical Ionians called it. The first phase in the history of the Ionian press highlighted the social and political inequalities in Ionian societies and struggled for reform or union, depending on the ideological principles that Ionians held, whether of liberalism or early socialism. Social demands, whether though reform or abolition of the regime of protection, figured prominently but gradually converged into the unequivocal and unconditional demand of union with Greece. The period from 1848 to 1862 saw a range of political and economic events: the economic crisis of the 1850s, and the height of the anti-colonial struggle – or rather more accurately the struggle against xenocracy – that challenged the legitimacy of both Ionian and Greek regimes and ended with the revolution against King Otto and his replacement by a different monarch. After 1864 the assimilation of institutions and practices in Ionian societies and economies dominated the local press. In every assimilation process something is lost in the name of integration; the political culture of Ionians with their local demands for social justice and equality succumbed to the nationalism of the day and the realization of the *Megali Idea*, the dream of expanding Greek territorial control to include all Greeks under one national state.

As soon as one of the main liberal demands of Ionians, freedom of the press, was addressed with the Seaton reforms of 1848, Ionians developed different media strategies depending on their loyalties and tried to influence the educated as well as the general public by shaping a public opinion for the first time. Government supporters published their own newspapers, attacking the opposition of liberals and especially radical unionists. Similar to the Italian states of the late eighteenth century, the development of public opinion through the new medium of the newspaper and the development of the public sphere did not oppose established authority but was even protected by the state.[80] It took Seaton, a liberal commissioner who thought that the time was ripe for Ionians to enjoy freedom of press, to unleash untapped forces and create a public opinion. We should not, however, assume that the separation between a public-bourgeois sphere and a plebeian-private sphere was all too rigid. The most radical Ionians, those liberals who wished to reform British protection but especially the fervent nationalists who sought to abolish it, opened up 'their' sphere to reach towards other groups, whether through a wide circulation of their newspapers or their mobilization in events that directly challenged or at least provoked British rule to respond. While there was a public sphere of those who subscribed to and read the newspapers and then voted for the liberals and the radicals to give them a combined majority in the Ionian Assembly, there was also a counter or parallel public of those who did not have the right to vote but whose support was necessary for realizing the radical dream of union with Greece.[81] The boundaries were not clear; many bourgeois Ionians hated the idea of including everyone in their liberal, even radical agenda, which was more middle-class oriented. Ionians would have to wait for the constitution of 1864, the first one of the unified kingdom, to vote, regardless of income or other qualifications.

The activism of unionists and reformists varied from island to island, from Zante and Corfu to the more 'radical' Kefalonia, which became the centre of radicalism in the 1850s. The newspaper *Mellon* published by Antonios Gaetas belonged to the Reformists of Zante until March 1851 following the intense debates and conflicts between Radicals and Reformists, while the newspaper *Rigas* was published by the Radicals in 28 April 1851. By the late 1840s the Seaton reforms had provided the stage for the conflict that simmered for about ten years within the liberal camp and divided liberals into Radicals (*Rizospastes*) and Reformers. Within this broad division there were fractions; Reformists, from 1852 onwards, were in turn divided into those supporting reforms within the British protection of the Ionian State and those in the opposition who sided with the Radicals and demanded union with Greece. This division did not prevent them from switching camps and collaborating on various laws with the government. Radicals, on the other hand, split in 1855 into two groups that formed distinct political programmes and clashed without any intention of working together to fulfil the aim of union with Greece. The two groups were classified as 'old' and 'new' Radicals and the division reflected differences between islands; the 'old' Radicals operated in Kefalonia with the main figures of Elias Zervos Iakovatos and I. Momferratos, while the 'new' Radicals clustered around politicians K. Lomvardos and G. Verykios from Zante. The debate became heated, with accusations from the 'true' Radicals writing against the 'unionists' of Zante who privileged union with Greece at the expense of every other social and economic issue that had plagued the islands for decades and exacerbated living conditions during the 'long' 1850s. This should not mask the politics of most Ionians, who subscribed to the unionist cause but also sought to correct the social and economic injustices of Ionian society.

Liberal Reformists dominated Ionian parliamentary politics following the extension of franchise in the 1849 reforms; they promoted the programme of state and social reforms and broadened the agenda of demands in the Ionian State. In those politically fluent times it was common to vote for some laws and protest against others but always within parliamentary practice and procedures, which distinguishes the politics of reform from the politics of unionists who sought to galvanize the population against British colonial rule and the continuation of the protectorate regime. Above all, the political clubs that opened became hubs of resistance against the Ionian State. Reformists promoted a broad agenda for the modernization of the state in the areas of education, prison reform, and more direct control of the state finances. The production and circulation of newspapers, articles and pamphlets as well as the speeches and parliamentary debates form a corpus of sources for the study of the liberal agenda and politics, which was far from the political immaturity caricature that the British portrayed about Ionians. Ionian radicals and their ideas were very much influenced by the revolutions of 1848 onwards and the Italian national question, and were certainly influential in the Ionian Assembly, as is evident in the declaration of union of 1850, but they were not necessarily 'the main political force in the Ionian Islands'.[82] Reformists in all their shades were much more influential from a history of the Ionian State point of view, and they were ambitious as well as pragmatic, seeking to reform the Ionian State as well as shaping Ionian civil society, essentially being part of both.

The Rise of Reformists as a Hegemonic Political Power

In 1848 and 1849, two rebellions against local and central state authority shook the island and Ionian societies. The suppression of the two rebellions, the second much more violently than the first, offered the opportunity for Ionians seasoned in legal discourse to raise issues of rights and liberties that had been violated. The issue was inherently political. Commissioner Seaton, who handled the rebellion of 1848, granted amnesty to most of those held responsible for the uprising, radicals Zervos Iakovatos, G. Livadas, Ioannis Typaldos Dottoratos, Ieronymos Typaldso Pretenteris and many more. All those sent to trial in normal – not military – courts were finally but reluctantly granted amnesty in the summer of 1849 by the next commissioner, Ward, as the trial would have revealed the role of the local police and British authorities in instigating the armed rebellion. When, in March 1849, the celebrations for the 25 March anniversary of the Greek Revolution were forbidden, the deployment of the High Police stirred Ionian Reformists who condemned the violation of rights in the arrests and detainment of people in Kefalonia. The police were always quick to hold the Radicals responsible for every public order and safety violation. What followed – the exile of three radicals, Zervos Iakovatos, Livadas and Typaldos Charitatos to Paxos – became the rallying cry for both Radicals and Reformists against the escalating suppression of the British commissioner and his regime. The ambiguity of the law on the measure of forced dislocation, allowing authorities to sent people to exile without clarifying whether this was a preventive or oppressive measure, stirred political antagonisms between the commissioner and the authorities and Ionians in all parties of the opposition.[83]

The suppression of the rebellions and the following stance of the authorities radicalized Ionians and accelerated developments towards the call for union of the islands with Greece. Reformists condemned the exile of Radicals, already elected to Parliament, to the islets of Othonoi and Antikythera, extremely isolated even today, let alone in the 1840s. The suppression deprived Radicals of maintaining a coherent group in Parliament, and essentially left Reformists as the only political force in the state to demand reform on a number of issues from civil liberties to better and more efficient administration under British protection.

Constitutional reforms in 1848 included the right to free press, the Senate and the Parliament. The extension of franchise, the right to control expenditure (especially extraordinary expenses), and the fact that the Parliament would consist, from then onwards, exclusively of people elected and not appointed by the commissioner, shows the progressive direction of British colonial policy in the Ionian protectorate. This, though, came at a price: the commissioner could no longer control the 'Senate' – the executive – as firmly; in the light of the freedom of the press, that would have stirred discontent and unleashed critical forces towards the government and British protection. Moreover, the continuing right of the executive to legislate when the Parliament was not sitting potentially stalled any reform effort of the Parliament. In a sense the British and the commissioner allowed discontent to be voiced in the press and in Parliament, but limited its impact by reserving the right to close down newspapers – presumably because they could destabilize public order – and by proroguing Parliament, if necessary, or simply seeing its term expire.

The second round of reforms in 1852 reveals the extent of the reform project that aspired to be a comprehensive improvement of the distinction between the three powers: the legislative, the executive and the judiciary. Reforms included the more frequent and longer sitting of Parliament, the withdrawal of the commissioner and the president of the Senate from the Supreme Council of Justice and the abolition of the High Police, all constitutionally sanctioned. Commissioner Ward submitted to the Tenth Parliament in 1852 a very different reform plan, in which he accepted with slight modifications almost all of the recommendations and proposals for reform, except, predictably, the abolition of the High Police. Ward also carefully maintained the centralized and controlling privileges of the residents on each island, the long arm of the central government.[84] Ward's recommendations barely touched on the thorny issue of the malfunction of the two bodies, the Senate and Parliament, a deficiency in the Ionian political system that suited Ward and his extraordinary measures to deal with Ionian insubordination of all kinds. The negotiations with the commissioner split the Reformists, opening a rift between Zambelios, not a parliamentarian any more, and Vrailas, representative of the Reformist group. The proposal that Ward submitted alienated and failed to gain the support of both the Reformists in opposition as well as the Radicals, who opposed any reform that did not lead to a declaration of union with Greece – not an option, of course, since the crisis of 1850 when the first such statement had been voiced in the assembly. This does not limit its significance in being the first coherent proposal to that date for state reform towards a more accountable and potentially democratic political society.

The reform effort accelerated in the 1840s when Zervos Iakovatos proposed universal suffrage in the Ionian State, and all Reformists voted in favour, including those supporting limited franchise for short-term political reasons and to protect their reputation; it was a very difficult issue to say no to. Those Reformists believing in limited franchise, however, prevailed over the long term. Anything else would have gone against both their ideological origins as well as their class position. Vrailas Armenis, for example, ever the philosopher, maintained that production depended on the securing of private property, without which there was no exchange of services or mutual rights, but confusion, expropriation and conflict.[85] Given that property was the main precondition for political rights, any negation of the 'sacred' right of property, watered down by arguments in favour of universal suffrage, would contradict the principles of the leader of the Liberal–Reformist party. The reforms of 1849 granted the right to vote to people who could prove their property, expressed in a different amount for each island, and according to profession: merchants, artisans who kept a store, shipowners and captains, brokers, civil servants (including retirees), university graduates, doctors, pharmacists, lawyers, assistant lawyers and notaries, professors, teachers at secondary schools and the college. Fewer people had the right to get elected: those owning property above the specified amount, merchants, retired civil servants and of course working ones, university graduates and lawyers.[86] The importance of those with a law degree (including those registered as lawyers or similar professions) is clear, and reflects the widespread belief about the importance of training in law for society, and in this case for office and the right to vote. In many ways, however, the definition of political capital is broad, expressed in property, knowledge, business acumen and – most importantly – state employment. This turned civil servants into a pool among the electorate for the selection of candidates potentially favourable to the government, but it is debatable whether the regime of the commissioner sought to gain votes by promising state employment (at any level). The law privileged some islands over others, and widened the gap between town and country more emphatically; Ithaki, given its large number of captains and shipowners, had many people voting in the 1861 elections, the ones with the most reliable registers. The amount of $3,000 for the city of Zante and $1,800 for the rural areas was forbidding for most people, and this is why the island occupied bottom place in the number of electors.[87]

When William Gladstone was appointed 'Extraordinary High Commissioner' and was sent to the Ionian Islands in 1858, he quickly dismissed calls for the unification of the islands with the Kingdom of Greece – the ultimate 'reform' – by stating that the Queen would not abandon the obligations of the 1815 treaty. It was as good an excuse as it was the official diplomatic line; he did concede though to a number of important constitutional reforms that could potentially and decisively change the structure of power in the Ionian State. *The Times* reported in January 1859 that 'the first assembly [session] of the Ionian Parliament is expected to be stormy, as independently of the all-engrossing patriotic question of union with Greece, which occupies the most prominent post in this session's programme, the deputies have many personal and local matters to discuss, one of which will, I hear, be brought forward this very day by M. Dandolo, the veteran leader of the ultra-Liberal Greek party, which motion amounts simply to the expulsion of four of the Cephaloniote members'. The reforms that Gladstone presented to that session included 'the form of government to be introduced to be a responsible government – a Lower and an Upper House; the former by popular election – to sit simultaneously for three months every year'. While Gladstone was dealing with one of the many international crises of his career on the ground, the commissioner, 'Sir John Young, and his lady embark[ed] to-day for Naples. They propose spending the carnival at Rome'.[88] The Ionian Assembly (Eleventh) Parliament was not content with the reforms proposed but also reconfigured the political coordinates in the camps of both Reformists and Radicals. The association of the constitutional reforms with the 'national' issue split both camps, as Radicals had split by 1859, and the 'old' Radicals refused to associate the two issues; the reforms passed with the votes of Reformists, who wished to avoid strengthening the position of 'new' Radicals in Parliament and society.

This chapter started with the opinions of fervent Radical Zervos Iakovatos and his analysis of Kefalonia and Ionian society. His views on the Reformists were no less compromising; he believed that Reformists suffered from a great disadvantage, the lack of political principles and theories that could become popular with Ionians; instead they were guided by their own interests and their wish to secure a position in government.[89] The reform effort of the 1840s that culminated in the electoral and more broadly constitutional reforms of 1849, 1852 and 1859 show that this was a very significant part of the Reformist agenda. Education, prison reform, law and the political system, as well as the economy, control over finances and civil rights were some of the main fields of modernizing reforms that Ionians, with the more or less supportive politics of different commissioners, achieved in promoting, and to some extent introduced. This form of politics distinguished the *liberali*, the liberal Reformists, more than any other social/political group in Ionian society, inside as well as beyond the Ionian Assembly. The inconsistency and contradictions of British protection, however, created an impasse that only the constitutional and legitimacy crisis in Greece as well as in the Ionian Islands could solve by the 'radical' reform of cession of the Ionian Islands to Greece, and the end of British colonialism in its protectorate version.

Notes

1. Koliopoulos and Veremis, *Greece, the Modern Sequel*; G. Dertilis, *Istoria tou Ellinikou Kratous*.
2. N. Diamantouros, *Oi aparches tis sygkrotisis synchronou kratous stin Ellada 1821–1828*. Athens: MIET, 2002.
3. There is only one work that has stressed this aspect of the Greek bourgeoisie: Y. Yannitsiotis, *I Koinoniki Istoria tou Peiraia 1860–1910*.
4. M. Paximadopoulou-Stavrinou, *Oi eksegerseis tis Kefallinias kata ta eti 1848 kai 1849*. Athens: Etaireia Kefalliniakon Istorikon Erevnon, 1980.
5. Ibid., 94.
6. Calligas uncovers the different agendas of the Radical Unionists of Kefalonia, who 'favoured major internal socio-political changes on the basis of the right of national self-determination', and the Radicals of Zante who 'redefined radicalism on purely unionist lines'. Calligas, 'The Rizospastai'.
7. D. Moschopoulos, 'Krisi nomimotitas sto Ionio Kratos'. Proceedings of International Conference, Corfu 22–25 May 1996. Corfu: Politistikos Syllogos Corcyra, 1998, 191–211.
8. Moschopoulos, *Istoria tis Kefalonias*, 88.
9. Petition No. 164, CO 136/661, PRO.
10. J. Mokyr, *The Enlightened Economy: An Economic History of Britain, 1700–1850*. Princeton, NJ: Princeton University Press, 2010.
11. Sp. Theotokis, 'I ekpaidefsi en Eptaniso' (1453–1864)', *Kerkyraika Chronia* 5 (1956). P. Rontoyannis, *I ekpaidefsi sti Lefkada, 1613–1950*. Athens, 1994, 60–61; N. Kourkoumelis, *I ekpaidefsi stin Kerkyra kata ti diarkeia tis Vretanikis Prostasias (1816–1864)*. Athens: Syllogos pros diadosin ton Ellinikon Grammaton, 2002, 61.
12. Chiotis, *Istorika Apomnimonevmata*, vol. 6, 224.
13. Ibid., 226.
14. The Constitutional Charter of the United States of the Ionian Islands, CO 136/7.
15. Kourkoumelis, *I ekpaidefsi stin Kerkyra*, 238–43.
16. *American Journal of Education*, 625.
17. Kourkoumelis, *I ekpaidefsi stin Kerkyra*, 261–62.
18. Ibid., 270–72.
19. Ibid., 272.

20 Martin, *History of the British Possessions*, 349.
21 N. Kourkoumelis, 'I ekpaidefsi tis Kerkyraias sto Ionio Kratos', *ΙΣΤ Diethnes Panionio Synedrio Praktika*, vol. 3. Athens, 2002, 137–57.
22 Kourkoumelis, *I ekpaidefsi stin Kerkyra*, 274.
23 P. Moschona, 'Ekpaidefsi stin Kefalonia to proto miso tou 19ou ai', *Kefalliniaka Chronika* 8. Argostoli: Etaireia Kefalliniakon Istorikon Erevnon, 1999, 305–19.
24 Belia Eleni, *I ekpedevsis is tin Lakonian kai Messinian sti kata tin Kapodistriakin periodon* [Education in Lakonia and Messinia during the Kapodistrias Period, 1828–32]. Athens, 1970, 27.
25 Kourkoumelis, *I ekpaidefsi stin Kerkyra*, 291.
26 Ibid., 296.
27 Davy, *Notes and Observations*, 103–4.
28 For the tables with the college students, see S. Asdrahas, *Eliiniki Oikonomia kai Koinonia, IZ kai IH aionas*. Athens: Ermis, 1988, 303–4.
29 British Parliament Accounts and Papers, Session 16 January – 11 August 1840, Vol. XLVIII, 12–13.
30 IIGG, No. 286, 6/18 June 1836.
31 'Mrs Dickson begs leave to inform her friends, and the public, that the second quarter of her School will be opened on Monday the 2nd August 1841. The course of education will embrace the English and modern Greek languages, Spelling, Reading, Penmanship, Geography, Arithmetic, Grammar, Composition, vocal Music, also plain, and ornamental Needle work. The Elements of higher branches of Academical study, such as Ancient and Modern History, Natural Philosophy, Botany, Mathematics, Astronomy, Rhetoric, Mental, and Moral Philosophy, together with the ancient Greek, will be taught to such pupils as are sufficiently advanced to prosecute them with advantage; and for these studies there will be some extra charge of tuition, Corfu, 27 July 1841'. IIGG, No. 553, 19/31 July 1841.
32 'Mrs Rosa Royst Piloto continues the girls school so long established in this capital, on the plan she has always followed, and which has given so much satisfaction. The children are taught all kinds of needle work and embroidery, modern Greek, Italian, the elements of the English Language (Mrs Piloto speaks English), Writing and Arithmetic. Mrs Piloto is particularly careful of the moral instruction of her scholars, and studiously attentive to their manners and dispositions, a part of education so important to them in after-life, and by a union of mildness, firmness and good temper, has been peculiarly successful with her pupils. Dancing, for those whose parents may wish it, considered as healthy exercise as well as an accomplishment. Terms usually moderate. The school is situated in the Calle de Santo, Casa Theotochi, No. 1267'. IIGG, No. 559, 30 August / 11 September 1841. In 1843, a 'Corfu Government School for young Ladies' opened, providing similar education, at a fee of £26 per annum.
33 IIGG, No. 63, 2/14 March 1846.
34 CO 136/1256.
35 Sklavenitis, 'Ioannis N. Stamatelos (1822–1881)'.
36 Rontoyannis, *I Ekpaidefsi sti Lefkada*, 123–24.

37 G. Henderson, *The Ionian Academy*. Edinburgh, 1988.
38 G. Pentogalos, 'The Medical School of Ionian Academy (1824–1828 and 1844–1865)'. Ph.D. Thesis, University of Thessaloniki, 1980.
39 K. Lappas, *Panepistimio kai foitites stin Ellada kata ton 19o aiona*. Athens: IEAN 39, 2004, 313.
40 Sideri, *Ellines foitites sto Panepistimio tis Pizas (1806–1861)*, Vols. A–B. Athens: IEAN, 1989–94, 440–67, 475–81, 518.
41 Vlassopoulos, *Statistikai*, 75.
42 Act KA of the 8th Senate of the United States of the Ionian Islands, 1845, Atti di Parlamento, K.B.
43 G. Progoulakis, *Anamesa stin timi kai to chrima. I Kerkyra sta chronia tis agglikis kyriarchias 1814–1864*. Athens: Istoriko Archeio-Emporiki Trapeza, 2003, 361.
44 Jervis, *History of the Island of Corfu*, 238.
45 Moschopoulos, *Istoria tis Kefalonias*, 88.
46 Chiotis, *Istorika Apomnimonevmata*, 260–61.
47 When researching in the society's library, the then president informed me proudly that the Reading Society was the bastion of the Corfu bourgeoisie in the nineteenth century.
48 Hiotis, *Istorika Apomnimonevmata*, 261.
49 X. Vlachos-Politis, 'To Telos ton Evgenon', *Deltio Anagnostikis Eterias Kerkyras* 24 (2001): 174.
50 Chiotis, *Istorika Apomnimonevmata*, 261.
51 IIGG, No. 450, 16/28 January 1860.
52 Praktika Ioniou Eterias 1860–61, Vol. A.
53 IIGG, No. 99, 11/23 November 1850.
54 IIGG, No. 79, 20 June / 2 July 1853.
55 IIGG, No. 505, 14/26 January 1861.
56 IIGG, No. 509, 11/23 February 1861.
57 IIGG, No. 553, 25 November / 7 December 1861.
58 IIGG, No. 559, 30 December 1861 / 11 January 1862.
59 R. Morris, *Class and Class Consciousness in the Industrial Revolution, 1750–1850*. London: Macmillan, 1979, 60.
60 Chiotis, *Istorika Apomnimonevmata*, 284.
61 Michail Sotiropoulos, 'European Jurisprudence and the Intellectual Origins of the Greek State: The Greek Jurists and Liberal Reforms (ca. 1830–1880)'. Ph.D. thesis, Queen Mary, University of London, 2014.
62 C. Schumann, *Liberal Thought in the Eastern Mediterranean: Late 19th Century until the 1960s*. Leiden and Boston: Brill, 2008; Ilham Khuri-Makdisi, *Eastern Mediterranean and the Making of Global Radicalism*. Berkeley: University of California Press, 2010; and the most relevant account of nineteenth-century liberalism in the Mediterranean, focused on Italian history: M. Isabella, *Risorgimento in Exile: Italian Emigres and the Liberal International in the post-Napoleonic Era*. Oxford: Oxford University Press, 2009. For a most interesting contribution from a Mediterranean perspective, see also, M. Isabella and K. Zanou, *Mediterranean Diasporas: Politics and Ideas in the Long 19th Century*. London: Bloomsbury, 2016.

63 V. Roldan and M. Caruso, *Imported Modernity in Post-Colonial State Formation*. Frankfurt: Peter Lang, 2007.
64 A. Liakos, *Italia è Grecia nel decenio dell' Unificazione Italiana*. Rome, 1983, 28–43.
65 In India, for example, it is difficult to find anti-colonial positions among Indian intellectuals before the 1870s; Bayly, *Recovering Liberties*, 14.
66 G. Alisandratos, *Keimena gia ton Eptanisiako Rizospastimo*. Athens: Benaki Museum, 2008, 27.
67 Isabella, *Risorgimento in Exile*.
68 R. Holland and D. Markides, *The British and the Hellenes: Struggles for Mastery in the Eastern Mediterranean 1850–1960*. Oxford: Oxford University Press, 2006, 47.
69 Paschalidi, 'Constructing Ionian Identities', 151.
70 Constitutional Charter of the United States of the Ionian Islands
71 Douglas to Glenelg, 21 June 1838, CO 136/88.
72 Paschalidi, 'Constructing Ionian Identities', 177.
73 British Parliamentary Papers, XLVIII (401): 'Memorial of Cavaliere Mustoxidi', 1840.
74 Copy of a Despatch from the Right Hon. Lord John Russell to Lieutenant-General Sir Howard Douglas, Her Majesty's Lord High Commissioner to the Ionian States, 21 December 1839, British Parliament Accounts and Papers, Session 16 January – 11 August 1840, Vol. XLVIII, 4.
75 Ibid., 10.
76 Ibid., 12.
77 P. Mackridge, 'Venise après Venise: Official Languages in the Ionian Islands, 1797–1864', *Byzantine and Modern Greek Studies* Vol. 38 (1) (2014): 76.
78 Paschalidi, 'Constructing Ionian Identities', 185.
79 Holland and Markides, *The British and the Hellenes*, 47.
80 M. Isabella, 'Italy, 1760–1815', in Hannah Barker and Simon Burrows (eds), *Press, Politics and the Public Sphere in Europe and North America, 1760–1820*. Cambridge: Cambridge University Press, 2002, 201–23.
81 For the notion of counter public and historical examples, see C. Calhoun, *The Roots of Radicalism: Tradition, the Public Sphere and Early Nineteenth-Century Social Movements*. Chicago and London: University of Chicago Press, 2012.
82 A. Liakos, 'To kinima tou Garibaldi kai ta Eptanisa (1860–1862)'. *Kerkyraika Chronika*, vol. XXIII, D Panionio Synedrio, vol. A. Corfu, 1980, 207–15.
83 Newspaper *Patris*, No. 34, 1849, 159–60.
84 See letter of Ward to P. Vrailas, 5 September 1852, in A. Kontoni, 'Fileleftheroi stochasmoi kai deksiosi tous ston Eptanisiako choro. Ideologia kai politiki ton metarrythmiston (1848–1864)'. Ph.D. dissertation, Athens, 1989, 182.
85 P. Vrailas-Armenis, *Scheseis tis viomixanias pros tin ithikin kai noitikin anaptyksin*. Corfu, 1853.
86 IIGG, No. 54, 31 December 1849; and IIGG, No. 117, 17/29 March 1851.
87 Kontoni, 'Fileleftheroi stochasmoi', 256–57.
88 *The Times*, 1 February 1859 (page 7, col. f).
89 Alisandratos, *Keimena gia ton Eptanisiako Rizospastismo*, 267.

 **Conclusion**

1864: The End of Colonial Rule?

On the 2nd of June the curtain fell upon the last act of the British protectorate in the Ionian Islands. A correspondent of the *Times* gave the following account of the closing scene: "a small fleet of troopships and transports clustered around the majestic Marlborough; near them lay a clumsy-looking paddle-wheel steamer, with 800 Greek troops forming the future garrison of Corfu, on board. The harbour was dotted with yachts and pleasure boats, the shores lined with a dense mass of people of all classes. At eleven o'clock the last remaining regiment in the citadel, the 4th King's Own, marched out, and their guard at the main gate was relieved by a Greek guard of gendarmerie. Meanwhile the approaches to the Palace of St. Michael and St. George were choked by crowds of townspeople and villagers from many a mile around, and there was hardly standing room in the reception hall, so eager were people to pay their parting respects to the Lords High Commissioners. When Sir Henry Storks, in a few grateful words in Italian, and in a voice which betrayed his emotion, bade them farewell, at least three-fourths of his audience were in tears ... crowded round his Excellency, shaking him by the hand, embracing him and conferring upon him not unfrequently those salutations which Englishmen generally reserve for the other sex ... At noon the Commander of the Forces, accompanied by his staff, mounted to the flagstaff at the citadel, and as the British red ensign was unfurled at the Marlborough's main our colours at Cape Sidero, Fort Neuf and Vido were simultaneously lowered, and the blue and white flag of Greece was hoisted in their place ... Until the last ship has become dim in the distance, crowds still gather upon the shore. 'Sono bono genti' [They are good people], said an old man, as with tears in his eyes he waved his hat towards the departing Britons. 'Adesso siamo liberi!' [Now we are free!], said a young man, as he lit a cigarette by way of inaugurating the new order of things.[1]

This emotive and vivid description of the 'last act' of the British protectorate through the pen of the British correspondent reflects many of the issues this book has tried to address. In many ways the report tells much more about the upper-class, Corfu city response and ambivalence towards the end of British rule than it says about Ionian societies more generally. The book has revisited the history of how the Ionian State formation under British colonialism, and explored the relationship and entanglement of state and class in Ionian societies. This history of the Ionian protectorate shows how this odd political arrangement of British colonialism, halfway between what was called 'responsible' government and colonial rule, fits mainstream histories of the British Empire. The book has highlighted the contradictions of British colonialism in the archipelago of the Ionian Islands in the Mediterranean. These islands were occupied first as a result of the islands' conquest during the Napoleonic wars and formally became part of the British Empire as a protectorate under the Treaty of Paris in 1815. From the 1840s onwards a liberal class became hegemonic in politics, commerce and the public sphere of Ionian cities; some of the more radical Ionians demanded union of the islands with Greece and contributed to the decolonization of this British 'possession', achieved in 1864 with increasing popular support. The ambivalent status of the islands in a form of protected colonialism laid the foundations of the constitutional conflict between British and Ionians. The modernizing attempts of British and Ionian officials created state institutions that failed because of deficits in public finances, conflicting interests among Ionians, and the oscillations of British colonial officials between autocratic and liberal forms of rule. This was a case of decolonization that set a precedent in British imperial politics in the Mediterranean, especially in the case of Cyprus in the twentieth century. The conception, planning and functioning of the Ionian State under British rule, and the regime of protection, is part of the history of modern Greece because besides the fifty years of British rule of those islands, the end of the protectorate meant the beginnings of more than a century of British political and economic influence, which often became outright domination over the country's fortunes.

State formation and British colonialism accelerated the formation of classes, defined by their role in the relations of production and distribution of agricultural goods, but also in the social hierarchies in towns and the country. By 1864 Ionians had become more clearly divided according to social and economic status, involvement in politics, and educational background, but also urban culture and consumption patterns. As the nineteenth century progressed 'aristocratic' background mattered less and less for public office as well as in the public sphere, although the powerful families capitalized on their past glory and status. Change was clearly visible, however. Around 1800 Kefalonia was essentially a premodern political field defined by conflict between the major families that required special envoys from the Septinsular Republic Senate to calm things down, and Zante had practically seceded from the federal state that was being formed, refusing to submit to Corfu's authority; but by the 1850s both islands had become a hotbed of radicalism in defence of the great cause of nationalism. The transition took place as members of some of the same families served in the Ionian State and became divided over very different issues from those of the previous century. Of the eighty-two parliamentarians elected from Kefalonia during the period of the protectorate, thirty-one held important offices in the state administration, whether as Senators, members of the municipal council, or members of the judiciary.

Class divisions dominated social relations in the Ionian Islands but the construction of a relatively efficient communication network and the overall extension of infrastructural power aimed at legitimizing British colonial presence and the control of the islands by British and local armed forces. The Ionian juridical and police apparatus provided the terrain for the ruling power bloc: the alliance of state officials, wealthy merchants, active intellectuals and career politicians. The liberal-bourgeois hegemony was established before, above and beyond the issue of union with Greece. The Ionian State, under the direction and authority of first commissioner, Maitland, established the monopoly of legitimate violence over the particular territory that constituted the British protectorate.

The political status of the Ionian Islands, neither a colony nor an independent state, was anomalous, and the Ionian State under British protection failed on several accounts for the following four reasons. First, by the time of union with Greece in 1864 the Ionian State was bankrupt, with debts exceeding £200,000 or approximately 150 per cent of the state's average annual revenues. Second, during the fifty years of British rule the Ionian State failed to tackle constant indebtedness of the peasants, the most pressing issue of the Ionian economy, consistent with the imperial 'policy' of non-intervention to areas that risked upsetting the local elites and thereby jeopardizing their much-needed support. Third, the progressively deteriorating fiscal condition of the Ionian State compromised any public works projects that had moved ahead in the early years of the protectorate but had to be abandoned later. Fourth, the arrival on the political scene and in the Ionian public sphere of a new generation of liberal Ionians in the fields of commerce and politics replaced the old political class by means of the new media of newspapers, commercial mechanisms and voluntary associations.

In the nineteenth century, new European states were being formed in conditions of dependence. The example of 'independent' Greece in 1828 after a prolonged war is well known as the first successful nationalist revolution. Less known is the emergence of the Ionian State, first in the form of the 'Septinsular Republic', under Russian and Ottoman protection and control, and subject to tribute to the Ottoman Sultan;

then, under British control, formally a 'protection', the 'United States of the Ionians Islands' raised a number of issues on state formation under colonial rule in the region that this book has addressed. The new practices of organized control of the population (legislation, police forces, bureaucratic organization) did not create a state that was all powerful, omnipresent and rigid; the semi-colonial condition of the Ionian State allowed more space for experimentation, negotiation and accommodation of the occasionally conflicting but sometimes converging views of the British and Ionians, depending on their class interests. The purpose of the liberal colonial state was to have enough mechanisms and regulation in place for the practice of government to exist independently of the officials responsible for its implementation. An Ionian bureaucracy was put in place that inherited the Venetian period's culture of state administration, and continued a tradition of state formation that started in the early 1800s following the French republican interlude, or break, and the Septinsular Republic. Projects of collecting and organizing information and generating colonial knowledge were introduced by British as well as by Ionian state officials. These were the political technologies of the colonial state and the tenets of British imperial rule. Historians of this period have studied the content of the colonial archive, and extracted the evidence found in the Blue Books, but not analysed the form or the underlying assumptions that are revealed once the historian zooms out from the Ionian state register. By the end of the period, Ionians were skilled enough in the modern practices of administration to devise their own schemes for education, agriculture and prison reform, to mention only some of their contributions to public policy. These projects of colonial governmentality were conceived and produced by both British and Ionian officials.

The project to organize the state under autocratic rule behind a facade of a representative assembly exposed the contradictions of the Treaty of Paris in 1815 and most importantly laid the foundations for the failure of the British protectorate. The pledge of high commissioners to improve living conditions and moral standards that would legitimize British colonial rule remained an empty promise, especially after 1840; the Ionian economy adjusted to British requirements but the Ionian State fell into deficit under the heavy costs of protection, extravagant spending on salaries, and financial mismanagement. Despite the various versions of rule tried by different commissioners and their Ionian counterparts, ranging from autocratic to liberal, depending on the ideas and disposition of each commissioner, local pressures became insurmountable. This was a gradually failing protection that in the end was not desirable in the eyes of the majority of Ionians of different classes and occupations, even in Corfu, which got the most out of the protectorate. The British had failed to win the tolerance – if not the support – of Ionians, and the prospect of a new king and dynasty in Greece in 1863 impelled the British to cede the islands and instead to secure their influence over Greece, as a united territory. Despite these failures of the Ionian State, forms of indirect rule such as the protectorate, or colonial rule in all but name, were applied later in the nineteenth century in Cyprus (1878) and Egypt (1882).

Timothy Mitchell has shown how in colonial Egypt the state created markets 'formatting' and not just regulating them.[2] It will be difficult to find other examples, in the British Mediterranean or beyond, where such a dense matrix of regulations and rules ordered, or at least attempted to regulate, urban (primarily) societies such as were introduced in the Ionian State. The British-directed colonial Ionian State introduced a series of liberal reforms in the islands' markets and created a space for the emergence of civil society, as well as a new form of state knowledge and bureaucracy that was much more compatible with West European states, and certainly compatible with colonial office perceptions and categories. This was part of the liberal modernity, as it was 'defined by new bureaucracies, forms of statecraft, the growth of trade and consumption, and the emergence of civil society'.[3] During the fifty years of British rule the Ionian State failed to change the basic institutions of the rural economy and tackle the constant indebtedness of peasants; such was, after all, the typical colonial approach of non-intervention, avoiding jeopardizing the much-needed support of local elites. The deteriorating fiscal condition of the Ionian State stalled any public works projects; only a few were completed in the early years of the protectorate, but were abandoned later. The history of the Ionian State offers another perspective to the history of liberal modernity, characterized by bureaucratic practices, statecraft, commerce, consumption patterns and the rise of civil society.

This civil society was the work of Ionian state officials, merchants, intellectuals and some British colonial officers who redefined power relations based on liberal values as well as their colonial background. The Ionian colonial state pledged liberal principles, although the first years of the protectorate were autocratic. Ionians created a public sphere of parties, political groups, philanthropic and literary societies, clubs and social events, but also developmental projects.

One of the commonalities was the liberal discourse of progress and 'enlightened' rule, and the policies to create infrastructure and other public works that in theory would render British rule benevolent and even acceptable to Ionians.

The transportation system of steamships that connected the islands' ports with Trieste, Livorno and other cities in Greece and the Ottoman Empire ensured the steady flow of people, products, ideas and fashions. Beliefs, values, modes of political discourse and agency, but also lifestyle, distinguished the Ionian State middle classes from other classes and from Ionian elite groups of previous decades, but also distinguished them from the Greek bourgeoisie in the Greek Kingdom and the Ottoman Greeks in major Ottoman cities.[4] Once the Ionian Islands became part of Greece in 1864, many Ionians settled in Athens and germinated Athenian society with their ideas, and they excelled in politics, the university and public administration.[5] Educational and social capital as well as economic enabled Ionians to produce but also consume a colonial modernity much earlier than other parts of the empire.[6]

The decision of Britain to cede the islands to Greece is often seen as an international relations act of politics, on the occasion of the new dynasty installed in the country under the auspices and the blessing of the most influential of the 'protecting powers', or as a failure of British imperial administration.[7] 'English diplomacy' played a part in the revolution of 1862 that split some of the radicals into monarchists and anti-royalists. The contradictions and asymmetries of the Ionian State protectorate reached an impasse in the 1850s; a crisis of legitimacy forced decolonization and the cession of the islands to Greece on the occasion of the expulsion of King Otto in 1862 and the change of dynasty soon after.[8] Decolonization of the islands in 1864 owed much to the ten-year or more constitutional struggle of the radicals and to a lesser extent the rather timid mobilization of the Ionian people against British rule; nevertheless, the decision to cede the Ionian Islands to Greece was a decision made by the British in their own time and on their own terms, notwithstanding the political developments in Greece and the overthrow of King Otto in 1862.

This book has also focused on the formation of the Ionian State and the initiatives of a group of merchants and intellectuals who, together with British officials, shaped and benefited the most from the policies of this state. The diverse responses to British rule, and the different experiences of Ionians depending on class, wealth, status, gender, religion and educational capital, are there for the historian to elicit from an array of sources from the period. The responses and attitudes of 'peasants' – agricultural growers, people who lived in the Ionian countryside, and the 'disturbances', as the British called them – explain Ionian 'resistance' to colonial rule, but only to an extent. The monolingual and generally homogeneous Ionian country (Greek and Christian

Orthodox) was very different from the town of Corfu, for example, where Greek Orthodox, Roman Catholics and Jews lived within the confines of the town walls. Neither the rural areas nor the towns, however, could have been ruled without the assistance of Ionians themselves. From the first months of rule on the islands, British officials imposed strict order and developed a sophisticated system of policing, hierarchies, surveillance and control that was to last with few changes until the end of the period. British authorities ensured an overall peaceful rule of the islands, despite the often-portrayed image of Ionians as 'insubordinate', unruly and too troublesome for the British to be worth the trouble of ruling them.

Ionians, whether traditionalists or modernists, were all exposed to modern ideas of social and economic organization, and shaped their politics accordingly. Far from being united, middle-class Ionian liberals were unreservedly modern in at least one sense: they embraced the project to 'improve' social practices, institutions and their societies, distinguishing themselves from the previous generations and their Venetian-ridden traditions, and to reform the state and the political system of the protectorate. Ionian liberals strove for their own project of modernity, not the British patronizing, civilizing and therefore colonial modernity. This was not another case of passive reaction to the colonial authority that imposed modernity on an indigenous society and compelled it to define its modernity in juxtaposition. Whereas an earlier generation of conservative Ionians invited, supported and worked with British officials, the 'generation' of the 1830s and the 1840s challenged, criticized, sought reform, and even rejected British rule for a future joined with the fortunes of the Greek Kingdom. British commissioners and their appointed and controlled (until 1850) governments realized how much they needed educated, trained and experienced Ionians for their colonial modernizing project. Some Ionians cooperated and joined associations, committees and state institutions but others stayed well away as they challenged the British-protected Ionian State.

There were differences among Ionians of course, not least because of British colonial perceptions and projects designed and realized by the various commissioners and their aides for the Ionian Islands. These differences depended on each island and its local tradition and culture, but also on the reach of the state. Ionians with bourgeois values – liberal, modernizing and cosmopolitan with novel business culture and university-level education – also challenged an earlier generation of landowning aristocrats, who first heard the death woes of the Venetian social and political order and who swiftly adjusted to the various occupying powers; this was the legacy of the Septinsular Republic to the subsequent 'United States of the Ionian Islands'. The Ionian bourgeoisie of merchants, state employees and professionals differed also from their predecessors as the hegemonic social group in their inclusiveness of other groups, whether through the project of reform or the demand for unification; whereas the previous generation spoke of the 'people' hypocritically and vaguely, many middle-class Ionians actually came from 'the people' and were certainly more justified to speak (and especially write) on behalf of them.

The meaning of 'middle class' varied and still varies significantly. So what did it entail to be middle class in Ionian cities? This book has shown that the sociological indicators of income, occupation and (in some cases) housing do not suffice for a meaningful understanding of the middle-class condition of many Ionians. Where do we draw the lines between upper, middle and lower classes? Middle-class politics was born and grew in tandem with the emergence of an Ionian public sphere. The middle class was a project of Ionians, British and other foreigners on the islands who worked for the state or worked as, for example, merchants, teachers, or representatives of foreign powers.

Modernity was ushered in in the late eighteenth century when the Republic French arrived. Modernity in the Ionian State was an aspiration as well as a condition, expressed by Ionians and British who embarked on state building for a period of fifty years. The rise of the middle class in politics and society on the various Ionian islands reflected the economic condition but was not an even process. The rise of the middle classes was determined by the previous history of each island as well as by their collective fortunes during the long period of Venetian domination and the brief but seismic times of the French republicanism, the Ionian Republic and the British and French occupation of 1797–1814.

Middle-class Ionians, educated, and informed about European – mostly Italian but also French and British – ideas of economic and social organization, were eager to adopt the colonial project to suit their own circumstances, realities and agendas. Against the backdrop of British-inspired discourses of a corrupt Venetian-Ionian past, liberal Ionians willingly adopted this image to suit their own ambitious rise in politics and the Ionian public sphere. The Ionian middle class that emerged at the end was precisely that – Ionian, and not British colonial or Greek national, since the Greek Kingdom integration project, which many of them joined with ambivalence in the 1840s and with enthusiasm in the 1850s, had barely formed. Above all, the result of the fifty years of the Ionian State (1815–64) was a contradictory and fragmented middle class, navigating its way through various forms of state control, its Venetian past, its British present and its Greek future. Middle-class Ionians sought and achieved to empower themselves against both the (initially) superior Ionians of the previous generation, many of whom collaborated with the British until the end, and against the lower classes who set their own agenda. The age of reform that began at the end of Venetian rule ended with the integration of the islands with the Greek Kingdom, marking the beginning of a new trajectory for those island – but far from insular – urban societies.

The Ionian bourgeoisie therefore were more than just 'a middle class'. They drew on their island and family traditions, appropriated a way of life that was modern, with goods and consumption patterns imported from European cities but adjusted to the history, culture and Ionian mentality. The formation of the Ionian Islands bourgeoisie can compare with the emergence of class relations and colonial modernity in other parts of the world. Class was an identity inextricably linked with the religious, national and local identities that Ionians fashioned in their newly created public sphere. Ionian State officials legitimized British authority and colonial presence through the extension of infrastructural power.

The importance of Ionian social and intellectual life for the development of the Greek State after unification was celebrated accordingly in a first demonstration of national pride. Ionian societies and their distinct formation similar to those of Western Europe are supposed to have brought 'clear and exact social formations to the then vague and unformed conditions of Greek society'.[9] The first Ionian delegates, eighty-four new ones that joined the Greek Parliament, expressed their enthusiasm, pride and ambition that the 'liberation of the Eptanisos will be the beginning of the regeneration of the whole Orient', and Greek state officials, dignitaries and delegates acknowledged the crucial role Ionians played in 'preserving Greek language, culture, history and religious traditions'.[10] Ionians contributed to the political culture of Athens in novel and indeed radical ways, originating in the organized and structured form that gave rise to the first parties in Greek (and Ionian specifically) politics.[11] It was at this moment of the first encounter between Ionian and Greek delegates that some Ionians declared their ideological roots in political liberalism, the principles of the French Revolution, the Enlightenment and the radical liberal movements in Italy and elsewhere in Europe in 1848.[12]

The political realities of Ionian and Greek governmentality are absent from debates on democratization and liberalization in Greece. Whatever debate there is has been dominated by discussions regarding the country's history in the last forty years, from the end of the dictatorship until the recent crisis. The beginnings of liberal democracy in Greece and of the modern state are to be found not only in the post-revolution, post-Ottoman Bavarian-ruled Greece, but especially in the Ionian protectorate, despite the conditions of protection and British colonialism or perhaps because of it. Liberal democracy was based on the division of powers, the rule of law, self-government and self-determination. Contemporaries were aware of the significant role Ionians played in the formation of nineteenth-century Greek political culture. The story of Ionian politicians, liberal officers and government employees, university professors, artists and intellectuals following unification remains to be written; some of the key liberal ideas and themes in the history in Ionian society and later in Greek society – modernity, progress, reform, constitutional rule – were to be found in the main tenets of Ionian liberalism. Despite the regime of protection and colonialism, Ionian liberals and proponents of liberal democracy, within the limits that caused splits among the Reformists and Radicals, were unable to use their experience once they had transferred their seat of power from Corfu to Athens; the great opportunity for Greece to become a liberal democracy and not a constitutional monarchy, based exclusively on parliamentary politics and not on the powers of the monarch, lost significant ground and it was subsequently abandoned. This is why Ionians did not really contest the role of the monarch as the head of state, and accepted the constitutional state of Greece, with the exception of Momferratos, the exemplary figure of Ionian liberalism and Greek republicanism. The contribution Ionians could offer to the Greek political order and culture transpired from the very first session, when they participated with important interventions on the content of the new constitution and on legislation on education issues, the freedom of press, and the rights of Greek citizens. Ionians were assimilated into the Greek Kingdom, since their previous state entity, the Ionian Republic, had dissolved and therefore there was no option to retain their previous citizenship or accept the new one, as was the case in previous treaties between Greece, the Ottoman Empire and the Powers, Britain, France and Russia.[13] Ionian delegates proposed an amendment to the constitution declaring that the people appoint the legislative power (instead of the king), but it was rejected. Despite the fact that Ionian delegates comprised nearly a fifth of all Greek Parliament members, they were disproportionately dynamic, creating the opportunity to challenge the establishment and the institution of monarchy, but they ultimately failed to prevail and engrave their democratic and indeed republican ideas in the constitution of 1864.

The Ionian State regime of protection was founded on the contradiction between British pledges about self-government and the illiberal practices followed at times, the cases of prorogued Parliament and the declaration of martial law. Still, the legal and overall institutional framework that developed during the fifty-year period was far more liberal than anything comparable in Greece at the time, especially during the period of Otto's interregnum, the period of absolute monarchy (1833–43). In the end the British protectorate failed because of these inherent contradictions that grew more acute by the decade, culminating in the liberal project of state reform and the nationalist demand for union with Greece. The British protectorate as a state project that was neither a colony nor an independent state could not fulfil the dominant vision of the times, the economic and national integration of Greeks into a single state. Despite the main target of the *Megali Idea*, the expansion of Greece to the north and east of its borders, the integration of the Ionian Islands was nevertheless a very important step. The reason this chapter of Greek history has not received the recognition and analysis that it deserves is because there was no revolution, such as the glamorous and glorified 1821 landmark that dominates national historical consciousness, or the Balkan wars of 1912–13 that saw the sacrifice of thousands of Greeks in the name of territorial expansion and the fulfilment of the *Megali Idea*.

The legacy of British rule in the Ionian Islands and Greece resonates in the present through tourism and popular culture (Corfu is the only place in Greece where they play cricket and drink ginger beer) that foster the islands' post-colonial condition. This unusual case of British colonialism, assuming that there was anything 'usual' in the range of British imperial experience, demonstrates the inherent colonial contradictions in the fields of government, in the piecemeal transformation of the Ionian economy, and in the absence of long-term development despite the introduction of modernizing reforms. These contradictions at the end became insurmountable. The rise of a liberal and nationalist bourgeoisie included people who initially challenged and later rejected British rule and determined to some extent the course of the islands' history and their cession to Greece. This particular case of British colonial 'protected' rule predated the subsequent history of British colonialism elsewhere in the Mediterranean, in Cyprus and Egypt, with equally contradictory results. In Greece the Ionian Islands served as the catalyst for the extension of British influence from Corfu to Athens and created the colonial conditions that shaped the post-colonial British–Greek relations until the 1940s. The history of the Ionian State reveals the origins of the often self-imposed identity of Greece as a 'colony', an argument that today is once again dominating discussions about the country's present and its future. This book has argued that the colonization of

Greece begun with the Ionian Islands two hundred years ago and it could be argued that it continues today with Greece as a 'debt colony'. In any case it is crucial to understand who the colonizers were and what the role of the 'colonized' was in the formation of the Ionian state. There can be no colonialism without the locally stationed agents who will implement the practices, policies and projects of the colonizer often making them their own. There can be therefore no real 'de-colonization' without radical social change.

Notes

1. *The Public Ledger*, 26 July 1864.
2. T. Mitchell, *The Rule of Experts: Egypt, Techno-Politics, Modernity*. Berkeley: University of California Press, 2002, Chapter 2.
3. Gunn and Vernon, *Peculiarities of Liberal Modernity*, 12.
4. Exertzoglou, 'Cultural Uses of Consumption'.
5. Gardikas-Katsiadakis, 'Ioannis A. Valaoritis'.
6. Joshi, *The Middle Class in Colonial India*.
7. B. Knox, 'British Policy and the Ionian Islands, 1847–1864: Nationalism and Imperial Administration', *English Historical Review* (1984): 99, 392, 503–29.
8. S. Gekas, 'The Crisis of the Long 1850s and Regime Change in the Ionian State and the Kingdom of Greece', *The Historical Review/La Revue Historique* 10 (2013): 57–84.
9. N. Svoronos, *Episkopisi tis Neoellinikis Istorias*. Athens: Themelio, 1985, 91.
10. G. Moschopoulos, 'Oi protoi Eptanisioi sto Elliniko Koinovoulio (1864). Ypodochi, ideologika minimata, "metakenosi", politiki anadiarthrosi tou Koinovouliou', in A. Argyriou, K. Dimadis and A. Lazaridou (eds), *O ellinikos kosmos anamesa stin Anatoli kai ti Dysi 1453–1981*, vol. B. Athens: Ellinika Gramma, 1999, 71.
11. A. Liakos, *To Risorgimento kai I Megali Idea. Ellinoitalikes politikes kai ideologikes scheseis 1859–1862*. Thessaloniki.
12. K. Dimaras, *Istoria tis Neoellinikis Logotechnias*, 5th edition. Athens, 1972, 314–26.
13. D. Christopoulos, *Poios einai Ellinas Politis? To kathestos ithageneias apo tin idrysio tou ellinikou kratous os tis arches tou 21ou aiona*. Athens: Vivliorama, 2012, 63–64.

Bibliography

UNPUBLISHED SOURCES

British Library of Political and Economic Sciences, London School of Economics

Ionian Bank Archives, 3/1, 9/4.

Corfu General State Archives (G.A.K.)

Ektelestiki Astynomia 849, subfolder 22 4/11/1818.
E.A. 849, subfolder 67, 15/07/1822, Γ.Α.Κ.
E.A. 849, subfolder 67, 26/03/1823.
E.A. 849, subfolder 17.
E.A.1749, Corfu, 17 June 1853.
E.A. 1719, 1/91.
E.A. 22, subfolder 44, Catalogo degli Parghi abitanti a Manduchio, 25/02/1821.
E.A. 849, subfolder 27, Notification, 30/06/1819.
E.A. 1319, Town Population Register, 1812–1814.
Ionio Kratos 232a, Register of Corfu Merchants, Corfu, 1818.
Eptanisos Politeia, F. 473, subfolder 3, and Passports, F.2.
Notaries 605b, Aspreas Notary Documents, M. Paramithiotis will.
Ionian Senate Documents, Royal Greek Consulate, 26, Document 2842.
Emporodikeio 347, 349, 699.

Arheio Dafni

Newspaper *I Foni tou Laou*, No. 24, 4 November 1850.
Newspaper *Astir*, No. 20, 26 June 1865.
Newspaper *Astir*, No. 640, 1/1/1859.
Newspaper *H Foni tou Laou*, No. 24, 4 November 1850.
Newspaper *I Eptalofos*, 5/14 May 1859.

British Parliament Accounts and Papers

Session 16, January – 11 August 1840, Vol. XLVIII, 4, 10, 12–13.
British Parliamentary Papers, XLVIII (401): 'Memorial of Cavaliere Mustoxidi', 1840.
Constitutional Charter of the United States of the Ionian Islands.
Parliamentary Papers, Accounts and Papers, 1847 xivi (1005), Reports Exhibiting the Past and Present State of Her Majesty's Colonial Possessions, 181–86.

Korgialeneios Library, Argostoli, Kefalonia

1st Parliament, Verbali dell' Assemblea Legislativa, 22 April 1819.
No. XIV, 2nd Session, 1st Parliament, 22 May 1819.
No. XXVIII, 3rd Session, 1st Parliament, 14 May 1820.
No. XVIII, *Atto che fissa la graduale riforma delle Leggi, Atti emanati dal secondo Parlamento degli Stati Uniti delle Isole Jonie sotto la Costituzione del 1817 durante la sua seconda sessione tenuta nell' anno 1825*. Corfu, 1825.
2nd Session of the 2nd Parliament, No. XXXII, Corfu, 10 May 1825.
No. XLV, 2nd Session, 4th Parliament, 5 June 1835.
No. XXI, 8th Parliament of the United States of the Ionian Islands, 18/30 March 1845.
1st Session, 7th Parliament, Act II, 28 March 1840.
No. XXIX, 7th Parliament, 2/14 April 1842.
No. XL, 5th Parliament, 12 April 1837.
No. LXXXII, 5th Parliament, 7/19 June 1837.
No. LXII, DEL VII PARLAMENTO (18/30 May 1844).
No. VI, 1st Session, 2nd Parliament, 22 March 1823.
No. XII, 1st Session, 2nd Parliament, 20 May 1823.
No. XXV, 3rd Session, 1st Parliament, 20 April 1820.
No. LXII, 3rd Session, 2nd Parliament, 20 March 1827.
V Parlamento, b. 139, Verbali del Senato, 6 June 1835.
Newspapers: *O Fileleftheros, Filalithis, Nea Epohi, Alitheia, Foni tou Ioniou, I Diaolapothiki, To Mellon, Patris, Enosis, O Horikos*
Arxeio 421, Doc 2, 11 and 12 November 1857.

British Library

BL Manuscripts, Add. 43217, ff. 238b–239.
Praktika Ioniou Eterias 1860–61, Vol. A, Ekdothenta ypo Napoleontos Zambeliou, Tamiou kai Iakovou Polyla, Grammateos, Kerkyra 1861 [Minutes of the Ionian Society, 1860–61. Published by Napoleon Zambelios, Treasurer and Iakovos Polylas, Secretary, Corfu 1861].

National Archives, London

Foreign Office 348/1, Commercial Letters.
CO 136/5, Maitland to Bathurst, 27 February 1816.
CO 136/7, Maitland to Bathurst, 1 March 1817.
CO 136/34, No. 33, Nugent to Stanley.
CO 136/76, Draft Act, No. 154, Douglas to Glenelg, Corfu, 22 August 1836.
CO 136/88, Douglas to Glenelg, 21 June 1838.
CO 136/122, Petition No. 40.
CO 136/122, Despatches, No. 59, 1844,
CO 136/186, Maitland to Bathurst, 6 May 1817.
CO 136/187, Earl Bathurst to Sir Thomas Maitland (L.H.C.), 29 August 1816.
CO 136/206.
CO 412/207.
CO 136/661, Petition Nos. 26, 31, 95, 162, 164, 185.
CO 136/695, Petition No. 367.
CO 136/787.
CO 136/776, Petition No. 85.
CO 136/801, Petition Nos. 118, No. 1083.
CO 136/810, Petition Nos. 52, 58.
CO 136/821, Petition No. 308.
CO 136/832, Petition No. 105.
CO 136/841, Petition Nos. 10, 21, 26, 40, 56, 97.
CO 136/857, Petition No. 400.
CO 136/873, Petition Nos. 340, 423.
CO 136/874, Petition No. 739.
CO 136/887, Petition No. 94, February 1860.
CO 136/887, Petition No. 2, 31 March 1860.
CO 136/1107, Maitland to William A' Court, 23 November 1818.
CO 136/1034, Index of Petitions 1825–1827, Petition Nos. 279, 356, 373, 505, 518, 520, 551.
CO 136/1034, Register of Petitions 1825–1827, Petition Nos. 505, 508.
CO 136/1035, Petition No. 509.
CO 136/1041, Register of Petitions 1837–1841.
CO 136/1045, Petition No. 1076, 22 April 1851.
CO 136/1053, Petition No. 71, Register of Petitions 1859.
CO 136/1056, Petition No. 425, Register of Petitions 1860 (January–July).
CO 136/1056, Petition No. 149.
CO 136/1059, Register of Petitions 1861, Petition No. 244.
CO 136/1085.
CO 136/1241.
CO 136/1256.
CO 136/1419–1427.
CO 136/1392–1426, Ionian Islands Blue Books of Statistics.

Corfu Reading Society (Anagnostiki Etaireia)

Register of pharmacists, shopkeepers and manufacturers, subject to taxation for the daily cleaning of streets (according to the Senate resolution 3 September 1818), Reading Society, Monofylla, 28/10/1818, V-8.
Reports from Committees, Volume XIII, 1861, xvi–xvii.
Resolution 25 June 1819, and Police Notification 8 May 1820.
Resolution, 2nd Session, 4th Parliament, 5 June 1835.
Resolution, 5th Parliament, 7/19 January 1836.
Resolution, 2nd Parliament, 12 April 1823.
Senate Resolution, 11 November 1818, Anagnostiki Etairia Library, Corfu.
Senate Resolution, No. 267, 25 January / 6 February 1836.

Ionian Islands Government Gazette

IIGG, No. 58, 2 November 1815.
IIGG, No. 4, May 1817.
IIGG, No. 6, Gazzetta degli Stati Uniti delle Isole Jonie, 8/20 Februrary 1819.
IIGG, No. 58, 23 January / 4 February 1832.
IIGG, No. 66, 19/31 March 1832.
IIGG No. 85, 30 July / 11 August 1832.
IIGG, No. 129, 3/15 June 1833.
IIGG, No. 264, 4/16 January 1836.
IIGG, No. 286, 6/18 June 1836.
IIGG, No. 297, 22 August / 3 September 1836.
IIGG, No. 336, 22 May / 3 June 1837.
IIGG, No. 369, 8/20 January 1838.
IIGG, No. 379, 19/31 March 1838.
IIGG, No. 394, 2/14 July, 1838.
IIGG, No. 411, 29 October / 10 November 1838.
IIGG, No. 469, 9/21 December 1839.
IIGG, No. 478, 10/22 February 1840.
IIGG, No. 494. 1/13 June, 1840.
IIGG, No. 531, 14 February 1841.
IIGG, No. 539, 18 April 1841.
IIGG, No. 553, 19/31 July 1841.
IIGG, No. 559, 30 August / 11 September 1841.
IIGG, No. 598, 30 May 1842.
IIGG, No. 676, 27 November 1843.
IIGG, No. 46, 3 November 1845.
IIGG, No. 55, 5/17 January 1846.
IIGG, No. 63, 2/14 March 1846.
IIGG, No. 61, 9/21 March 1846.
IIGG, No. 65, 16 March 1846.

IIGG, No. 79, 22 June / 4 July 1846.
IIGG, No. 88, 24 August / 5 September 1846.
IIGG, No.107, 4 January 1847.
IIGG, No. 162, 24 January / 5 February 1848.
IIGG, No. 168, 6/18 March 1848.
IIGG, No. 3, 8 January 1849.
IIGG, No. 54, 31 December 1849.
IIGG, No. 101, 25 November / 7 December 1850.
IIGG, No. 89, 2/14 September 1850.
IIGG, No. 117, 17/29 March 1851.
IIGG, 2/14 May, 1853.
IIGG, No. 93, 26 September / 8 October 1853.
IIGG, No. 79, 20 June / 2 July 1853.
IIGG, No. 116, 6 March 1854.
IIGG, No. 175, 5/17 March 1855.
IIGG, No. 209, 8 October 1855.
IIGG, No. 225, 28 January 1856.
IIGG No. 739, September 1859.
IIGG, No. 441, 28 November / 10 December 1859.
IIGG, No. 450, 16/28 January 1860.
IIGG, No. 505, 14/26 January 1861.
IIGG, No. 509, 11/23 February 1861.
IIGG. No. 553, 25 November / 7 December 1861.
IIGG, No. 559, 30 December 1861 / 11 January 1862.
IIGG, No. 628, 23 March / 4 April 1863.

The Times Newspaper

1 December 1815.
22 May 1816.
5 February 1831, p. 4, col. b.
1 July 1833.
22 July 1825, p. 2, col. e.
30 August 1833, p. 3, col. b.
1 February 1859, p. 7, col. f.
1 May 1816.
10 November 1827.
20 November 1819.
20 October 1800, p. 2, col. c.
24 April 1841, p. 6, col. b.
30 August 1833, p. 3, col. b.
6 February 1816.
8 December 1819.
8 March 1864.
9 March 1835, p. 4, col. d.
30 August 1833.

PUBLISHED SOURCES

Acemoglu, D., S. Johnson and J.A. Robinson. 'The Colonial Origins of Comparative Development: An Empirical Investigation', *American Economic Review* 91 (2001): 1369–401.

——. 'Institutions as the Fundamental Cause of Long-Run Growth', in P. Aghion and S. Durlauf (eds), *Handbook of Economic Growth*. Amsterdam: Elsevier EB, 2005, 385–472.

Agriantoni, Christina. *Oi Aparhes tis Ekviomixanisis stin Ellada ton 19o aiona* [The beginnings of industrialization in Greece in the 19th century]. Athens, 1986.

Alisandratos, Giorgos G. *Keimena gia ton Eptanisiako Rizospastimo*. Athens: Benaki Museum, 2008.

Anastassiadis, Tassos and Nathalie Clayer (eds.). *Society, Politics and State Formation in Southeastern Europe during the 19th Century*. Athens: Alpha Bank Historical Archives, 2011.

Andreadis, Andreas M. *I Enosis tis Eptanisou kai I dioikisis tis Prostasias*. Athens, 1907.

——. *Peri tis oikonomikis dioikiseos tis Eptanisou epi Venetokratias* [On economic administration of the Ionian Islands during Venetian rule], Vols I and II. Athens: Karavias, 1914.

——. *I Eptanisiaki Dimosia Oikonomia kata tin periodon 1797–1814*, Athens: Karavias 1936.

Androni, Spiridione. *Alcune idee sopra le diverse istituzioni completive del sistema penitenziario*. Corfu, 1848.

Anogiatis-Pelé, Dimitris. 'Ta Ionia Nisia: apo tin politiografia sti statistiki tou plithismou' [The Ionian Islands: From politiografia to population statistics], Z' Panionio Synedrio [7th Panionian Synedrio]. Lefkada, 2002, 389–97.

Anogiatis-Pelé, Dimitris, and Evangelos Prontzas. *I Kerkyra 1830–1832. Metaxi fedouarchias kai apoikiokratias*. Thessaloniki: University Studio Press, 2002.

Ansted, David T. *The Ionian Islands in the Year 1863*. London, 1863.

Antoniadi, Sofia. 'Katasticho tou 1645 peri tis oikonomikis katastaseos tis Zakinthou' [Cadastral of 1645 on the economic administration of Zante], *3o Panionio Synedrio Proceedings*. Athens, 1967, 6–15.

Antoniou, A. 'Dimosionomikes epiptoseis tis enosis tis Eptanisou', *Proceedings, I enosi tis Eptanisou me tin Ellada* ['Fiscal consequences of the union of the Ionian Islands with Greece', *Proceedings, The union of Eptanisos with Greece*], vol. I. Athens: Academy of Athens, 2005.

Arnold, David. *Police Power and Colonial Rule. Madras 1859–1947*. New Delhi: Oxford University Press, 1986.

——. 'The Colonial Prison: Power, Knowledge and Penology in Nineteenth-Century India'. *Subaltern Studies VIII: Essays in Honour of Ranajit Guha*. New Delhi, 1994, 148–84.

Arvanitakis, Dimitris. *To rebelio ton popolaron (1628). Koinonikes antitheseis stin poli tis Zakynthou*. Athens: ELIA, 2001.

———. 'Oi taraches tou 1640 stin Kerkyra', 6th Panionio Synedrio, Zakynthos 1997, in N.E. Karapidakis, 'Politikos politismos sta Eptanisa kata tin period tis enetokratias', 7th Panionio Synedrio. Athens, 2002, 35–47.

———. 'I autoviografia tis Martinengou: i rogmes tis siopis kai I pollaples diastaseis tou kosmou' [The autobiography of Martinengou: The ruptures of silence and the multiple dimensions of the world], *Ta Istorika* 22(43) (2005): 397–420.

Arvanitakis, S. 'I Zakynthos kata to proto miso tou 16ou aiona' [Zante during the first half of the sixteenth century], *Ta Istorika* 20(39) (2000): 358.

Asdrachas, Spyros I. *Eliiniki Oikonomia kai Koinonia, IZ kai IH aionas*. Athens: Ermis, 1982.

———. 'Feoudaliki prosodos kai gaioprosodos stin Kerkyra tin epochi tis Venetikis kyriarchias', in S. Asdrachas, *Oikonomia kai Nootropies*. Athens: Ermis, 1988, 57–76.

——— (ed.). *Greek Economic History, 15th–19th Centuries*, Vol. I. Piraeus Group Bank Cultural Foundation, Athens, 2007.

———. 'Eisagogi', in S. Asdrachas (ed.), *Greek Economic History, 15th–19th Centuries*, Vol. I. Piraeus Group Bank Cultural Foundation, Athens, 2007.

Asdrachas, Spyros, and N. Karapidakis. 'To anthopino dichty', in S. Asdrachas (ed.), *Elliniki Oikonomiki Istoria 15th–18th Centuries*. Athens: PIOP, 2003, 71–149.

———. 'Oi megaloi tomeis', in S. Asdrachas (ed.), *Elliniki Oikonomiki Istoria 15th–18th Centuries*, Vol. I. Athens: PIOP, 2003, 151–218.

Assante, F. *Il mercato delle assicurazione marittime a Napoli nel Settecento*. Giannini, Naples, 1979.

Baghdiantz, Ina Mccabe, Gelina Harlaftis and Ioanna Pepelasis Minoglou (eds). *Diaspora Entrepreneurial Networks: Four Centuries of History*. New York, 2005.

Bakounakis, Nikos. *Patra. Mia elliniki protevousa ton 19o aiona*. Athens: Kastaniotis, 1995.

Ballantyne, Tony. 'Colonial Knowledge', in Sarah Stockwell (ed.), *The British Empire: Themes and Perspectives*. London: Blackwell, 2008.

Baster, A.S.J. *The International Banks*. London: P.S. King & Son Ltd., 1929.

Bayly C.A. *Imperial Meridian: The British Empire and the World, 1780–1830*. London and New York: Longman, 1989.

———. *Recovering Liberties: Indian Thought in the Age of Liberalism and Empire*. Cambridge: Cambridge University Press, 2012.

Belia, Eleni. *I ekpedevsis is tin Lakonian kai Messinian sti kata tin Kapodistriakin periodon*. Athens, Grafikai Tecnai Papoulia, 1970.

Benton, Lauren. 'Colonial Law and Cultural Difference: Jurisdictional Politics and the Formation of the Colonial State', *Comparative Studies in Society and History* 41(3) (2000): 563–88.

———. *Law and Colonial Cultures.Legal Regimes in World History, 1400–1800*. Cambridge: Cambridge University Press, 2001.

———. *A Search for Sovereignty: Law and Geography in European Empires, 1400–1900*. Cambridge: Cambridge University Press, 2010.

Berend, Ivan. *An Economic History of Nineteenth-Century Europe: Diversity and Industrialization*. Cambridge: Cambridge University Press, 2013.

Bjelovucic, Harriet. *The Ragusan Republic: Victim of Napoleon and its own Conservatism*. Leiden: Brill, 1970.

Block, Brian P., and John Hostettler. *Hanging in the Balance: A History of the Abolition of Capital Punishment in Britain*. Sherfiel Gables: Waterside Press, 1997.

Bokos, Giorgos D. *Ta monofylla tou kerkyraikou tyografeiou kata tin periodo tis gallikis kyriarchias sta Eptanisa (1797–1799, 1807–1814)*. Corfu: Ionio Panepistimio, 1998.

Bosset, Charles de. *Parga and the Ionian Islands; a refutation of the mis-statement of the quarterly review and of Lieut.-Gen. Sir Thomas Maitland on the subject; with a report of the trial between that officer and the author*. London, 1821.

Botta, Carlo Giuseppe Gulielmo. *Storia Naturale e medica deli Isola di Corfu*. Milan, 1798.

'Bowen, George Ferguson. 'Ionian Administration', *Quarterly Review*, xci (Sept. 1852).

Braudel, Fernand. *The Mediterranean and the Mediterranean World in the Age of Philip II*, Vol. 1. New York, San Francisco and London: Harper & Row, 1972.

———. *Civilisation and Capitalism, 15th–18th Century: The Perspective of the World*, Vol. 3. London: Harper Collins, 1985.

Briggs, A. 'Cholera and Society in the Nineteenth Century', *Past and Present* 19 (1961): 76–96.

Buchon, A. 'Voyage dans l' Eubee, les Isles Ioniennes et les Cyclades en 1841', Paris 1911, in Dionisis Zivas, *I Architektoniki tis Zakinthou apo ton 16o mechri tom 19o aiona* [The architecture of Zante from the 16th to the 19th century]. Athens: Techniko Epimelitirio Ellados, 1970.

Burroughs, Peter. 'Imperial Institutions and the Government of the Empire', in Andrew Porter and Roger Louis (eds), *The Oxford History of the British Empire. Vol. III, The Nineteenth Century*. Oxford: Oxford University Press 1999, 171–221.

Butlin, S.J. *Australia and New Zealand Bank: The Bank of Australasia and the United Bank of Australia Limited 1828–1951*. London: Longmans, 1961.

Caglioti, Daniela Luigia. 'Voluntary Societies and Urban Elites in Nineteenth-Century Naples', in Graeme Morton, Boudien de Vries and R.J. Morris (eds), *Civil Society, Associaitons and Urban Places: Class, Nation and Culture in Nineteenth-Century Europe*. Aldershot: Ashgate, 2006, 39–53.

Cain, P.J. 'Character and Imperialism: The British Financial Administration of Egypt, 1878–1914', *Journal of Imperial and Commonwealth History* 34 (2006): 177–200.

Cain, P.J., and Anthony G. Hopkins. *British Imperialism, 1688–2000*, 2nd edn. London: Longman, 2000.

Calhoun, Craig. *The Roots of Radicalism: Tradition, the Public Sphere and Early Nineteenth-Century Social Movements*. Chicago and London: University of Chicago Press, 2012.

Calligas Eleni. 'The "Rizospastai" (Radical-Unionists): Politics and Nationalism in the British Protectorate of the Ionian Islands, 1815–1864'. Ph.D. dissertation, London School of Ecoomics, 1994.

Cannadine, David. *Ornamentalism: How the British Saw Their Empire*. Oxford: Oxford University Press, 2001.
Chatziioannou, Maria Christina. *Oikogeneiaki Stratigiki kai Emporikos Antagwnismos. O Oikos Gerousi ton 19o aiona*. Athens: MIET, 2003.
Chanock, Martin. 'Making Customary Law: Men, Women and Courts in Colonial Northern Rhodesia', in M. Wright and M. Hay (eds), *African Women and the Law*. Boston: African Studies Centre, Boston University, 1982.
Chapman, Stanley. *Merchant Enterprise in Britain: From the Industrial Revolution to World War I*. Cambridge: Cambridge University Press, 1992.
Chatterjee, Partha. *The Nation and its Fragments*. Princeton: Princeton University Press, 1993.
Chiotis, P. *Istoria tou Ioniou Kratous apo tis systaseos autou mechri enoseos (1815–1864)*, Vol. B. Corfu, 1878, 19.
———. *Istorika Apomnimonvmata Eptanisou*. Vol. 6. Zakynhtos, 1887.
Chircop, J. 'The British Imperial Network in the Mediterranean 1800–1870: A Study of Regional Fragmentation and Imperial Integration'. Unpublished Ph.D. thesis, University of Essex, 1997.
———. 'Old Age Coping Strategies of the Ionian and Maltese Poor, 1800–1865', *Hygiea Internationalis, Journal of the History of Public Health*, vol. 5, no.1, Linkoping, 2006, 51–73.
Chouliarakis, Michales. *Geographiki, Dioikitiki kai Plythismiaki Ekseliksis tis Ellados, 1821–1971*. Athens: EKKE 1973–74.
Christmas, Henry. *George Augustus Frederick Fitzclarence, The Literary Gazette: A Weekly Journal of Literature, Science, and the Fine Arts*, Volume 5. London: H. Colburn, 1821.
Christopoulos, Dimitris. *Poios einai Ellinas Politis? To kathestos ithageneias apo tin idrysio tou ellinikou kratous os tis arches tou 21ou aiona*. Athens: Vivliorama, 2012.
Ciriacono, S. 'Venetian Economy and Commerce in Modern Times: The Case of Olive Oil Production in Corfu', and M. Constantini, 'The Trade Policy of Venice towards its Possessions in the Eastern Mediterranean', in A. Nikiforou (ed.), *Kerkira, mia Mesogiaki synthesi: nisiotismos, diktiam anthropina perivallonta 16os–19os aionas*. International Conference Proceedings, Corfu, 22–25 May 1996, 1998.
Clancy-Smith, Julia. *Mediterraneans: North Africa and Europe in an Age of Migration, c. 1800–1900*. Berkeley: University of California Press, 2011.
Clogg, Richard. *A Concise History of Modern Greece*. Cambridge: Cambridge University Press, 2nd edn, 2002.
Cochran, Peter. *Byron's Romantic Politics: the Problem of Metahistory*. Cambridge: Cambridge Scholars Publishing, 2011.
Cohn, B.S. *Colonialism and its Forms of Knowledge: The British in India*. Princeton, NJ: Princeton University Press, 1996.
Cooper, David, 'Public Executions in Victorian England: A Reform Adrift', in William Thesing, *Executions and the British Experience from the Seventeenth to the Twentieth Century: A Collection of Essays*. London: McFarland, 1990.
Cooper, F., and A.L. Stoler. *Tensions of Empire: Colonial Cultures in a Bourgeois World*. Berkeley: University of California Press, 1997.

———. 'Between Metropole and Colony: Rethinking a Research Agenda', in Frederick Cooper and Ann Laura Stoler (eds), *Tensions of Empire: Colonial Cultures in a Bourgeois World*. Berkeley: University of California Press, 1997, 1–56.

Cosmetatos, Helen. *Reports on the Roads of Cefalonia*. Argostoli: Corgialeneios Museum, 1990.

———. *The Roads of Cefalonia*. Argostoli: Corgialenios Library, 1995.

Cottrell, P.L. *The Ionian Bank: An Imperial Institution, 1839–1864*. Athens: Alpha Bank Historical Archives, 2007.

Darwin, J. *The Empire Project: The Rise and Fall of the British World-System, 1830–1970*. Cambridge: Cambridge University Press, 2009.

———. *Unfinished Empire: The Global Expansion of Britain*. London: Bloomsbury Press, 2012.

Daunton, Martin. *Progress and Poverty: An Economic and Social History of Britain, 1700–1850*. Oxford: Oxford University Press, 1995.

David, Scott. 'Colonial Governmentality', *Social Text* 43 (1995): 191–220.

Davis, L., and R. Huttenback. *Mammon and the Pursuit of Empire: The Political Economic of British Imperialism, 1860–1912*. Cambridge: Cambridge University Press, 1986.

Davis, Norman. Vanished Kingdoms: The Rise and Fall of States and Nations. London: Penguin, 2011.

Davy, J. *Notes and Observations on the Ionian Islands and Malta*, Vol. II. London, 1842.

Debonos, Angelo-Dionysis. 'Stoicheia stafidikis politikis stin Kefalonia tou 19ou aiona'. *Kefalliniaka Chronika*. Argostoli, 2005, 271–96.

De Bosset, Charles Philippe. 'Proceedings in Parga, and the Ionian Islands', *The Quarterly Review*, 1820.

Dellis, G. Ioannis. 'Ta anthropina dikaiomata sto Syntagma (Katastasin) tis "Eptanisou Politeias" tou 1803. Epidraseis ton ideon tou evropaikou diafotismou sti thespisi tous', in *Eptanisos Politeia (1800–1807): to proto aneksartito elliniko kratos*. Corfu: G.A.K. – Archeia Nomou Kerkyras, 2001, 57–77.

Demponos, Angelo-Dionysis. *I Peitharchiki Prostasia. Apo tous Agones tou laou tis Kefalonias*. Argostoli: Dimos Argostoliou, 1985.

Dendias, Michael A. 'Symvoli eis tin meletin tou Ionikou Syntagmatos tou 1803. O thesmos ton eforon', *3 Panionio Synedrio*. Athens, 1967, 58–64.

Dertilis, G. 'Oikonomia kai diamorfosi Kratous stin Ellada tou 19ou aiona', in C. Agriantoni, *Oi Aparhes tis Ekviomihanisis stin Ellada*. Athens: Emporiki Trapeza tis Ellados, 1986.

———. *Atelesforoi I telesforoi? Foroi kai exousia sto Neoelliniko Kratos*. Athens: Themelio, 1993.

———. *Istoria tou Ellinikou Kratous* [History of the Greek State] *1830–1920*. Vol. 2. Athens: Estia, 2006.

Desmond, Gregory. *Malta, Britain, and the European Powers, 1793–1815*. London: Associated University Press, 1996.

Desyllas, Christos Th. *I Trapeza ton ftohon. To Monte di Pieta tis Kerkaras (1630–1864)*. Athens: PIOP, 2006.

Diamantouros, Nikiforos. *Oi aparches tis sygkrotisis synchronou kratous stin Ellada 1821–1828*. Athens: MIET, 2002.

Dimakopoulos, Iordanis. 'To Anaktoro ton Agion Michail kai Georgiou', in Ennio Concina and Aliki Nikiforou-Testone (eds), *Kerkyra: Istoria, Astiki Zoi kai Architektoniki 14os–19os ai.* Corfu: Politistikos Syllogos 'Coryra', 1994, 105–11.
Dimaras, K.Θ. *Istoria tis Neoellinikis Logotechnias*, 5th edition. Athens, 1972.
Dixon, Willis. *The Colonial Administrations of Sir Thomas Maitland.* London: Longmans, 1939.
Dousmanis, A. *I en tis Ioniois Nisois apostoli tou Lordou Gladstone.* Corfu, 1875.
DuPont, Jerry. The Common Law Abroad: Constitutional and Legal Legacy of the British Empire. Littleton, CO: Rothman Publications, 2001.
Epstein, S.R. Freedom and Growth: The Rise of States and Markets in Europe, 1300–1750. London and New York: Routledge, 2000.
—— (ed.). *Town and Country in Europe, 1300–1800.* Cambridge: Cambridge University Press, 2001.
Exertzoglou, Haris. 'The Cultural Uses of Consumption: Negotiating Class, Gender and Nation in Ottoman Urban Centers during the 19th Century', *International Journal of Middle East Studies* 35(1) (2003): 77–101.
Fairlie, S. 'The Corn Laws and British Wheat Production, 1829–76', *Economic History Review* XXII (April 1969): 88–116.
Faruk, Tabak. *The Waning of the Mediterranean, 1550–1870: A Geohistorical Approach.* Baltimore, MD: Johns Hopkins University Press, 2008.
Filaretou, Georgiou N. *Ksenokratia kai Vasileia en Elladi (1821–1897).* Athens, 1897.
Fiore, Jordan D. 'Carlo Botta: An Italian Historian of the American Revolution', *Italica* 28(3) (1951): 155–71.
Fitzpatrick, Peter. 'Custom as Imperialism', in J.M. Abun-Nasr and U. Spellenbert (eds), *Law and Identity in Africa.* Beitrage auf Afrikaforschung, 1 (1990): 15–30.
Fitzory, Charles Lord. *Ionian Islands. Letters by Lord Charles Fitzroy and documents from other sources on past and recent events in the Ionian Islands.* London: 1850.
Fleming, K.E. *The Muslim Bonaparte: Diplomacy and Orientalism in Ali Pasha's Greece.* Princeton, NJ: Princeton University Press, 1999.
——. *Greece: A Jewish History.* Princeton, NJ: Princeton University Press, 2007.
Follet, Richard. *Evangelicalism, Penal Theory, and the Politics of Penal Law Reform in England, 1808–1830.* Basingstoke: Palgrave, 2001.
Foucault, M. *Discipline and Punish: The Birth of the Prison.* New York: Pantheon, 1977.
——. *Madness and Civilisation: A History of Insanity in the Age of Reason.* London: Routledge, 2001.
Fragkiadis A. 'Agrotiki oikonomia kai ekswteriko emporio', in K. Kostis and S. Petmezas (eds), *I anaptyksi tis ellinikis oikonomias kata ton 19o aiona (1830–1914).* Athens: Alexandreia, 2006, 153–74.
Frangiaskos, Emm. N. 'O Korais kai I Ioniki Akadimia (1808–1814)', *O Eranistis* 3 (1965): 177–98.
Franks, M. 'Cadastral Kerkyra: The World System in Eighteenth-Century Venetian Commodity Production', *Journal of the Hellenic Diaspora* 24 (1998): 41–67.

Frary, Lucien J. *Russia and the making of modern Greek identity, 1821–1844*, Oxford: Oxford University Press 2015.

Fusaro, Maria. *Uva Passa. Una guerra commerciale tra Venezia e l'Inghilterra (1540–1640)* [The ripe grapes. A commercial war between Venice and England]. il Cardo, Venice, 1996.

Gallagher, John, and Ronald Robinson. 'The Imperialism of Free Trade', *Economic History Review*, 2nd series, 6 (1953): 1–15.

Gallant, Thomas W. 'Honor, Masculinity, and Ritual Knife-Fighting in Nineteenth Century Greece', *American Historical Review* 105(2) (2000): 359–82.

———. *Modern Greece*. London and New York: Arnold, 2001.

———. Experiencing Dominion: Culture, Identity and Power in the British Mediterranean. Notre Dame: University of Notre Dame Press, 2002.

———. 'Tales from the Dark Side: Transnational Migration, the Underworld and the "other" Greeks of the Diaspora', in Dimitris Tziovas (ed.), *Greek Diaspora and Migration since 1700: Society, Politics and Culture*. Aldershot: Ashgate, 2009, 17–30.

———. 'When "Men of Honour" Met "Men of Law": Violence, the Unwritten Law and Modern Justice', in Efi Avdela, Shani d'Cruze and Judith Rowbotham (eds), *Crime, Violence and the Modern State, 1780–2000*. London: Edwin Mellen, 2010, 69–92.

———. 'Women, Crime and the Courts in the Ionian Islands during the Nineteenth Century', *Historein* 11 (2011): 138–56.

———. *I empeiria tis apoikiakis kyriarchias. Politismos, taytotita kai eksousia sta Eptanisa 1817–1864*. Athens: Aleksandreia, 2014.

———. *The Edinburgh History of the Greeks, 1768 to 1913: The Long Nineteenth Century*. Edinburgh: Edinburgh University Press, 2015.

Gardikas-Katsiadakis, Helen. 'Ioannis A. Valaoritis: The Life of a Typical Greek Nineteenth-Century Bourgeois?', in P. Carabott (ed.), *Greek Society in the Making, 1863–1913: Realities, Symbols and Visions*. Aldershot: Ashgate, 1997, 55–69.

Gardner, Leigh A. *Taxing Colonial Africa: The Political Economy of British Imperialism*. Oxford: Oxford University Press, 2012.

Gatrell, V.A.C. *The Hanging Tree: Execution and the English People, 1770–1868*. Oxford: Oxford University Press, 1994.

Gekas, Athanasios (Sakis). 'The Commercial Bourgeoisie of the Ionian Islands under British Rule, 1815–1864: Class Formation in a Semi-colonial Society'. Ph.D., University of Essex, 2004.

———. 'The merchants of the Ionian Islands between East and West. Forming local and international networks' in M.S. Beerbuhl and J. Vogele (eds), *Spinning the Commercial Web. International Trade, Merchants, and Commercial Cities, c. 1640–1939*. Frankfurt: Peter Lang, 2004, 43–63.

———. 'The Port Jews of Corfu and the "Blood Libel" of 1891: A Tale of Many Centuries and of One Event', *Jewish Culture and History* 7(1–2) (2004): 171–96.

———. 'Thesmoi kai eksousia stin poli tis Kerkyras sta mesa tou dekatou enatou aiona'. *Istor* XV (2007): 107–44.

———. (with Panos Krokidas). 'Public Health in Crete under the Rule of Mehmed Ali in the 1830s', *Egypt / Monde Arab* 4(3) (2007): 35–54.

———. 'A Sector "Most Beneficial to Commerce": Marine Insurance Companies in Nineteenth-Century Greek Port Cities', *Entrepreneurial History Discussion Papers* 1 (2008). http://www.ehdp.net./ p001/p001.pdf.

———. 'Credit, Bankruptcy and Power in the Ionian Islands under British Rule, 1815', in Karl Gratzer and Dieter Stiefel (eds), *History of Insolvency and Bankruptcy from an International Perspective*. Södertörn academic studies 38, Huddinge, 2008, 83–118.

———. (with Mathieu Grenet). 'Trade, Politics and City Space(s) in Mediterranean Ports', in Carola Hein (ed.), *Port Cities: Dynamic Landscapes and Global Networks*. London: Routledge, 2011, 89–103.

———. 'Banking Expansion, Success and Failure in the British Mediterranean; the Ionian Bank, 1840s–1930s' (with A. Apostolides) in John A Consiglio et al. (eds.), *Banking in the Mediterranean: A Historical Perspective*, Farnham: Ashgate 2012, 175–196.

——— (with Manuel Borutta), 'A Colonial Sea: the Mediterranean, 1798-1856. Introduction', in *European Review of History: Revue Européenne d' Histoire*, 19 (1) (2012):1-13

———. 'Colonial Migrants and the Making of a British Mediterranean', *European Review of History – Revue Europeenne d' histoire* 19(1) (2012): 75–92.

———.'The Crisis of the Long 1850s and Regime Change in the Ionian State and the Kingdom of Greece'. *The Historical Review/La Revue Historique*, [S.l.], 10, (2013): 57–84.

———. '"Thalassovioti" – Living off the Sea: The Corfu Suburb of Manduki in the Nineteenth Century', in Anthony Hirst and Patrick Sammon (eds), *The Ionian Islands: Aspects of their History and Culture*. Newcastle-upon-Tyne: Cambridge Scholars Publishing, 2014.Gibson, Mary. 'Global Perspectives on the Birth of the Prison', *The American Historical Review* 116(4) (2011): 1040–63.

Goodison, William. *Historical and Topographical Essay upon the Islands of Corfu, Leucadia, Cephalonia, Ithaca, and Zante*. London, 1822.

Gott, Richard. *Britain's Empire: Resistance, Repression and Revolt*. London and New York: Verso, 2011.

Gourgouris, Stathis. *Dream Nation: Enlightenment, Colonization, and the Institution of Modern Greece*. Stanford, CA: Stanford University Press, 1996.

Greene, Molly. *Catholic Pirates and Greek Merchants: A Maritime History of the Early Modern Mediterranean*. Princeton, NJ: Princeton University Press, 2010.

Griffiths, P. *To Guard my People: The History of the Indian Police*. London: Ernest Benn, 1971.

Gunn, Simon. 'From Hegemony to Governmentality: Changing Conceptions of Power in Social History', *Journal of Social History* 39(3) (2006): 705–20.

Gunn, Simon, and James Vernon (eds). *The Peculiarities of Liberal Modernity in Imperial Britain*. Berkeley: University of California, 2011.

Gupta, A. *Crime and police in India (Up to 1861)*. Agra: Sahitya Bhavan, 1974.

———. *The Police in British India, 1861–1947*. New Delhi: Concept, 1979.

Gupta, Subhash. *Capital Punishment in India*. New Delhi: Deep & Deep Publications, 1986.

Habermas, Jurgen. *The Structural Transformation of the Public Sphere*. Cambridge, MA: MIT Press, 1989.
Hadziiossif, Christos. *I Girea Selini. I Viomihania stin Elliniki Oikonomia, 1830–1940*. Athens: Themelio, 1993.
———. 'Class Structure and Class Antagonism in Late Nineteenth-Century Greece', in Philip Cabaret (ed.), *Greek Society in the Making, 1863–1913*. Aldershot: Ashgate–Variorum, 1997, 3–18.
Haldane, A.R.D. *One Hundred and Fifty Years of Trustees' Savings Banks*. Trustee Savings Banks Association, 1960.
Hall, Catherine (ed.). *Cultures of Empire: Colonizers in Britain and the Empire in the Nineteenth and Twentieth Centuries*. Manchester: Manchester University Press, 2000.
Hanioğlu, M. Şükrü. *A Brief History of the Late Ottoman Empire*. Princeton, NJ: Princeton University Press, 2008.
Hannell, D. 'A Case of Bad Publicity: Britain and the Ionian Islands', *European History Quarterly* 17 (1987): 131–43.
———. 'The Ionian Islands under the British Protectorate: Social and Economic Problems', *Journal of Modern Greek Studies* 7(1) (1989): 105–32.
Harlaftis, Gelina. 'To emporonaftiliako dikyto ton Ellinon tis Diasporas kai I anaptyksi tis ellinikis naftilias ton 19o aiona: 1830-1860', *Mnemon* (15), 1993: 69–127.
———. *A History of Greek-Owned Shipping: The Making of an International Tramp Fleet, 1830 to the Present Day*. London: Routledge, 1996.
———. 'Mapping the Greek Maritime Diaspora from the Early Eighteenth to the Late Twentieth Centuries', in Ina Baghiatz McCabe, Gelina Harlaftis and Ioanna Pepelasis Minoglou (eds), *Diaspora Entrepreneurial Networks: Four Centuries of History*. Oxford: Berg, 2005, 147–71.
———. 'From Diaspora Traders to Shipping Tycoons: The Vagliano Bros', *Business History Review* 81(2) (2007): 237–68.
Harris, Ron. 'Government and the Economy, 1688–1850', in Roderick Floud and Paul Johnson (eds), *The Cambridge Economic History of Modern Britain. Vol. I. Industrialisation, 1700–1860*. Cambridge: Cambridge University Press, 2004, 204–37.
Henderson, G.P., *The Ionian Academy*. Edinburgh, 1988.
Herzfeld, Michael. 'The Absent Presence: Discourses of Crypto-Colonialism', *South Atlantic Quarterly* 101(4) (2002): 899–926.
Hionidou, V. 'The Demographic System of a Mediterranean Island: Mykonos, Greece, 1859–1959', *International Journal of Population Geography* 1 (1995): 125–46.
———. 'Nineteenth-Century Urban Greek Households: The Case of Hermoupolis, 1861–1879', *Continuity and Change* 14(3) (1999): 403–27.
———. 'Dimographia' [Demography], in K. Kostis and S. Petmezas (eds), in *I anaptyxi tis ellinikis oikonomias kata ton 19o aiona (1830–1914)* [The development of the Greek economy during the nineteenth-century]. Athens: Alexandreia, 2006.
———. 'From Modernity to Tradition: Households on Kythera in the Early Nineteenth Century', in Silvia Sovic, Pat Thane and Pier Paolo Viazzo (eds),

The History of Families and Households: Comparative European Dimensions. Leiden and Boston: Brill, 2016, 47–68.

Holland, Henry. *Travels in the Ionian Islands, Albania, Thessaly, Macedonia, etc. during the years 1812–1813.* London: Longman, 1815.

Holland, Robert. *Blue-Water Empire: The British in the Mediterranean since 1800.* London: Allen Lane, 2012.

Holland, Robert, and D. Markides. *The British and the Hellenes: Struggles for Mastery in the Eastern Mediterranean 1850–1960.* Oxford: Oxford University Press, 2006.

Hook, Gail. 'Mr. Fenech's Colony: Maltese Immigration in British Cyprus, 1878 to 1950', *Journal of Cyprus Studies* 13 (2007): 27–51. `Hyam, R. 'The Primacy of Geopolitics: The Dynamics of British Imperial Policy, 1793–1863', *Journal of Imperial and Commonwealth History* 27(2) (1999): 27–52.

Ignatieff, Michael. *A Just Measure of Pain: The Penitentiary in the Industrial Revolution, 1750–1850.* Chicago: Chicago University Press, 1981.

Isabella, Maurizio. 'Italy, 1760–1815', in Hannah Barker and Simon Burrows (eds), *Press, Politics and the Public Sphere in Europe and North America, 1760–1820.* Cambridge: Cambridge University Press, 2002, 201–23.

———. *Risorgimento in Exile: Italian Emigres and the Liberal International in the post-Napoleonic Era.* Oxford: Oxford University Press, 2009.

Isabella, Maurizio, and Konstantina Zanou (eds). *Mediterranean Diasporas: Politics and Ideas in the Long 19th Century.* London: Bloomsbury, 2016.

Ithakisios, D.D. 'I ekseliksi ton vasikon dimografikon charaktiristikon tou plithismou tis Eptanisou kata tin period tis Agglikis Prostasias kai ti methenotiki period 1815–1864–1900', *Epistimoniko Synedrio Praktika*, vol. A. Athens: Vouli ton Ellinon – Akadimia Athinon, 2005, 475–530.

Jayawardena, Kumari. *Nobodies to Somebodies: The Rise of the Colonial Bourgeoisie in Sri Lanka.* London and New York: Zed Books, 2000.

Jervis, Henry Jervis-White. *History of the Island of Corfu and of the Republic of the Ionian Islands.* London: Colburn, 1852.

Joshi, Sanjay. *The Middle Class in Colonial India.* New Delhi and New York: Oxford University Press, 2010.

Joyce, Patrick. The Rule of Freedom: Liberalism and the Modern City. London: Verso, 2003.

———. *The State of Freedom: A Social History of the British State since 1800.* New York: Cambridge University Press, 2013.

Jutte, R. *Poverty and Deviance in Early Modern Europe.* Cambridge: Cambridge University Press, 1994.

Kalafatis, Thanasis. 'Paragogi kai emporia stafidas sta Ionia Nisia (16os–19os ai.)', *Praktika Z Panioniou Synedriou*, vol. B. Athens, 2004, 567–77.

Kaldis, William P. *John Capodistrias and the Modern Greek State.* Madison: University of Wisconsin, 1963.

Kalliga, Eleni. 'To Syntagma tou Maitland gia ta Eptanisa (1817). Ionies katavoles kai vretanikoi stochoi', *Istor* 3 (1991): 93–120.

Kalpagam, U., 'Colonial Governmentality and the Public Sphere in India', *Journal of Historical Sociology* 15(1) (2002): 35–58.

Kamonachou, M. 'Thesmoi agrotikou eksynchronismou stin Kerkyra to 19o aiona'. Ph.D. Ionio Panepistimio, 2008.

Kapetanakis, Panayotis. 'I pontoporos emporiki naftilia ton Eptanison tin epochi tis Vretanikis katochis kai prostasias kai I Kefalliniaki yperochi (1809/1815–1864)'. Ph.D., Ionian University, 2009.

——. 'The Ionian State in the "British" Nineteenth Century, 1814–1864: From Adriatic Isolation to Atlantic Integration', *International Journal of Maritime History* XXII(1) (2010): 163–84.

——. 'Shipping and Trade in a British semicolony: the Case of the United States of the Ionian Islands (1815-1864)', *Cahiers de la Méditerranée* 85, 2012, 269–283, URL: http://cdlm.revues.org/6770.

Karapidakis, N. 'I Kerkyraiki eugeneia ton archon tou IZ aiona', *Istorika* 3 (1985): 95–123.

——. 'Apo ton koinotismo stin politiki: koinoniologia ton dianoumenon kai ton anthropon tis politikis drasis ston eptanisiako choro (teli tou 18ou aiona arches tou 19ou)', in A. Nikiforou (ed.), *Eptanisos Politeia (1800–1807): ta meizona istorika zitimata*. Corfu: G.A.K – Archeia Nomou Kerkyras, 2001, 33–41.

——. 'Oikonomia kai emporio (eisagogi)', in Chrysa Maltezou (ed.), *Venetokratoumeni Ellada, Proseggizontas tin Istoria tis*. Athens and Venice: Elliniko Institouto Byzantinon kai Metavyzantinon Spoudon, No. 10, 2010, 227–52.

——. 'Departement de Corfu, 1798: Les troubles', in Tassos Anastassiadis and Nathalie Claire (eds), *Society, Politics and State Formation in Southeastern Europe during the 19th Century*. Athens: Alpha Bank Historical Archives, 2011, 235–54.

Kardamitsi-Adami, Maro. 'Astiki Architektoniki', in Chrysa Maltezou (ed.), *Venetokratoumeni Ellada, Proseggizontas tin Istoria tis*. Athens and Venice: Elliniko Institouto Byzantinon kai Metavyzantinon Spoudon, No. 10, 2010, 407–32.

Kardasis, Vasilis A. *Syros. Stavrodromi tis Anatolikis Mesogeiou (1832–1857)*. Athens: MIET, 1987.

——. *Apo tou istiou eis ton atmon, Elliniki Emporiki Naftilia 1858–1914*. Athens: MIET, 1993.

——. *Ellines Omogeneis sti Notia Rossia 1775–1861*. Athens: Alexandreia, 1998.

Karlafti-Mouratidi, Fotini. *I techni tou psomiou sti venetokratoumeni Kerkyra: to sitari, oi choroi, oi anthropoid*. Athens: Poreia, 2009.

Karouzou, Evi. 'Thesmiko plaisio kai agrotiki oikonomia', in Kostas Kostis and Sokratis Petmezas (eds), *I anaptyksi tis ellinikis oikonomias to 19o aiona*. Athens: Alexandreia, 2006.

Karter, G., and P. Samartzis (eds). *Kathimerousiai Eideiseis*. Athens: ELIA, 2000.

Katsiardi-Hering, O. *I elliniki paroikia tis Tergestis* (1750–1830). 2 vols. Athens, 1986.

——. 'Ta diktya tis ellinikis emporikis diakinisis', in S. Asdrahas (ed.), *Elliniki Oikonomiki Istoria IE'-IH'*. Athens: Katarti, 2003, 461–81.

Kefalonitis G., 'Istoria tou Astikou Nosokomeiou Kerkyras' [History of the Civil Hospital of Corfu], *Kerkyraika Chronika* 13 (1967): 55–75.

Kendrick, Tertius. *The Ionian Islands*. London, 1822.

Khaled, Fahmy. *All the Pashas's Men: Mehmed Ali, his Army, and the Making of Modern Egypt*. New York: Cambridge University Press, 1997.
Khuri-Makdisi, Ilham. *Eastern Mediterranean and the Making of Global Radicalism*. Berkeley: University of California Press, 2010.
Kirkwall, V. *Four Years in the Ionian Islands. Their Political and Social Condition*. 2 vols. London, 1864.
Kitromilides, P.M. 'An Enlightenment Perspective on Balkan Cultural Pluralism: The Republican Vision of Rhigas Velestinlis', *History of Political Thought* 24 (2003): 465–79.
Knox, Bruce. 'British Policy and the Ionian Islands, 1847–1864: Nationalism and Imperial Administration', *English Historical Review* (1984): 99, 392, 503–29.
Kokkinakis, Y. 'Filanthropia, techniki ekpaidefsi kai ergatika atichimata ston Peiraia to telefteo trito tou 19ou aiona'. *Mnemon* XXI (1999): 85–108.
Koliopoulos, John S., and Thanos M. Veremis. *Modern Greece: A History since 1821*. London: Wiley-Blackwell, 2010.
———. *Greece. The Modern Sequel. From 1821 to the Present*. London: Hurst & Company, 2004.
Kolsky, Elizabeth. 'Codification and the Rule of Colonial Difference: Criminal Procedure in British India', *Law and History Review* 23(3) (2005): 631–83.
Konidaris, Ioannis. 'I thesi ton thriskeftikon koinotiton sta syntagmata tis Eptanisou Politeias (1800–1807)', *Eptanisos Politeia (1800–1807)*, Praktika Synedriou, Argostoli: Etaireia Kefalliniakon Istorikon Erevnon, 2003, 47–56.
Konstantinidou, Katerina. *'To kako odevei erpontas...'. Oi limoi tis panolis sta Ionia Nisia (17os-18os ai.)*. Venice: Hellenic Institute of Byzantine and Post Byzantine Studies, 2007.
———. 'Thesmoi koinonikis pronoias', in Chrysa Maltezou (ed.), *Venetokratoumeni Ellada, Proseggizontas tin Istoria tis*. Athens and Venice: Elliniko Instituto Byzantinon kai Metavyzantinon Spoudon, No. 10, 2010, 187–210.
Kontoni, Anna. 'Fileleftheroi stochasmoi kai deksiosi tous ston Eptanisiako choro. Ideologia kai politiki ton metarrythmiston (1848–1864)'. Ph.D. dissertation, Athens, 1989.
Korasidou, Maria, *Oi athlioi ton Athinon kai oi therapeftes tous. Ftochia kai filanthropia stin elliniki protevousa ton 19o aiona*. Athens: EIE, 1995.
Koskinas, Nikos. 'Emporoi kai emporiko diktyo ton Ionion Nison (1815–1864)', Praktika Θ' Panioniou Synedriou, Paxoi 26–30 May 2010, vols Α'-Β', Aliki Nikiforou (ed.), Παξοί, Εταιρεία Παξινών Μελετών, 2014, 411–440.
Kosmatou, Eftychia. 'La population des Iles Ioniennes XVIIIème-XIXème siècle', Ph.D.
Dissertation, Université de Paris I, Paris 2000.
Kostis, Kostas. *Ston Kairo tis Panolis* [In the times of plague]. Irakleio: Panepistimiakes Ekdoseis Kritis, 1995.
———. 'The formation of the state in Greece, 1830–1914', in F. Birtek and Th. Dragonas (eds), *Citizenship and the Nation – State in Greece and Turkey*, London & New York: Routledge, 2005, 18–36.
———. 'Dimosia Oikonomika', in Kostas Kostis and Sokratis Petmezas (eds), *I anaptyksi tis ellinikis oikonomias to 19o aiona*. Athens: Alexandreia, 2006, 293–335.

———. Ta kakomathimena paidia tis istorias. I diamorfosi tou neoellinikou kratous 18os–21os aionas. Athens: Polis, 2013.
Kostis, Kostas, and Sokratis Petmezas (eds), *I anaptyksi tis ellinikis oikonomias to 19o aiona*. Athens: Alexandreia, 2006.
Koukou. Eleni. *Istoria ton Eptanison apo to 1791 mechri tin Anglokratia* [The history of the Ionian Islands from 1797 until English rule]. Athens, 1999, 3rd edition.
Kourkoumelis, N.K. *I ekpaidefsi stin Kerkyra kata ti diarkeia tis Vretanikis Prostasias (1816–1864)*. Athens: Syllogos pros diadosin ton Ellinikon Grammaton, 2002.
———. 'I ekpaidefsi tis Kerkyraias sto Ionio Kratos', IΣT *Diethnes Panionio Synedrio Praktika*, vol. 3. Athens, 2002, 137–57.
Krater, G., (ed), *P. Samartzis. Kathimerousiai Eideiseis*. Athens: ELIA, 2000.
Kremmydas, Vasilis. 'Gia dyo endiaferouses viomichanies sti Zakyntho', *Praktika E Panioniou Synedriou*, vol. 1. Argostoli: Etaireia Kefaliniakon Istorikon Erevnon, 1989.
Ladikos, Dionisis. 'Ta tachidromeia sti diarkeia tis Vretanikis Prostasias', *Praktika I enosi tis Eptanisou stin Ellada*, vol. I. Athens: Akadimia Athinon, 2005, 305–17.
Laidlow, Zoe. *Colonial Connections 1815–1845: Patronage, the Information Revolution and Colonial Government*. Manchester: Manchester University Press, 2005.
Lambert, D., and A. Lester (eds). *Colonial Lives across the British Empire: Imperial Careering in the Long Nineteenth Century*. Cambridge: Cambridge University Press, 2006.
Lambrinou, Maria. 'Oikodomikos kai poloedomikos programmatismos. Dimosia erga stin Agglokratoumeni Lefkada', in Panagiotis Moschonas (ed.), *To Ionio Kratos 1815–1864*. Athens: Kentro Meleton Ioniou, 1997, 229–37.
Lane, F.C. *Venice, A Maritime Republic*. Baltimore, MD: Johns Hopkins University Press, 1973.
Lange, Matthew, James Mahoney and Matthias vom Hau, 'Colonialism and Development: A Comparative Analysis of Spanish and British Colonies', *American Journal of Sociology* 111(5) (March 2006): 1412–62.
Lappas, Kostas. *Panepistimio kai foitites stin Ellada kata ton 19o aiona*. Athens: IEAN 39, 2004.
Lee, Robert. 'The Socio-economic and Demographic Characteristics of Port Cities: A Typology for Comparative Analysis?'. *Urban History* 25 (1998): 147–72.
Leontsinis, G.N. *The Island of Kythera: A Social History (1700–1863)*. Athens: National Capodistrian University of Athens, S. Saripolos Library 55, 1987.
Le tre costituzioni (1800, 1803, 1817) delle sette isole Jonie ed i relativi documenti con l' aggiunta dei due progetti di costituzione del 1802 e 1806 e delle modificazioni e riforme alla costituzione del 1817. Corfu, 1849, 153.
Liakos, Antonis. 'To kinima tou Garibaldi kai ta Eptanisa (1860–1862)'. *Kerkyraika Chronika*, vol. XXIII, D Panionio Synedrio, vol. A. Corfu, 1980, 207–15.
———. *Italia è Grecia nel decenio dell' Unificazione Italiana*. Rome, 1983.

———. *I Italiki Enopoiisi kai I Megali Idea. Ellinoitalikes politikes kai ideologikes scheseis 1859–1862*. Thessaloniki: Themelio, 1985.

Liata, Eftychia. 'The Anti-Semitic Disturbances on Corfu and Zakynthos in 1891 and their Socio-political Consequences', *The Historical Review / La Revue Historique*, Institute for Neohellenic Research, Volume IV (2007): 157–69.

Lis, C., and H. Soly. *Poverty and Capitalism in Pre-Industrial Europe*. Bristol: The Harvester Press, 1979.

Lithgow, William. *Travels and Voyages through Europe, Asia and Africa, for Nineteen Years*. Edinburgh: A. Murray and J. Cochran, 1770.

López, A. Ricardo, and Barbara Weinstein (eds), *The Making of the Middle Class: Toward a Transnational History*. Durham, NC: Duke University Press, 2012.

Loromer D. *Merchants and Reform in Livorno, 1814–1868*. Berkeley: University of California Press, 1987.

Loukatos, Spyros. *I Eptanisiaki politiki scholi ton Rizospaston*. Argostoli, 2009.

Loukos, Chistos. 'Epidimia kai koinonia. I cholera stin Ermoupoli tis Syrou (1854)'. *Mnemon* XIV (1992): 49–69.

`Lountzis, Ermannos. *Peri tis politikis katastaseos tis Eptanisou epi Eneton*. En Athinais: X. Nikolaou Filadelfeos, 1856.

Lynn, M. 'British Policy, Trade, and Informal Empire in the Mid-Nineteenth Century', in A. Porter, *The Oxford History of the British Empire*. Vol. 3, The Nineteenth Century. Oxford: Oxford University Press, 1999, 101–21.

Lyrintzis, Christos. *To telos ton tzakion. Koinonia kai politiki stin Achaia to 19o aiona*. Athens: Themelio, 1991.

MacGachen, Frederic Stewart. *The Ionian Islands: A Sketch of their Past History, with Reference to their Position under our Protectorate*. London, 1859.

Mackridge, Peter. *Language and National Identity in Greece, 1776–1976*. Oxford: Oxford University Press, 2009.

———. 'Venise après Venise: official languages in the Ionian Islands, 1797–1864'. *Byzantine and Modern Greek Studies* Vol. 38 (1) (2014): 68–90.

Maclaren, A.A. 'Bourgeois Ideology and Victorian Philanthropy: The Contradictions of Cholera', in A.A. Maclaren (ed.), *Social Class in Scotland: Past and Present*. Edinburgh: Donald, 1976, 36–54.

Madden, Frederick, and David Fieldhouse (eds). *Imperial Reconstruction, 1763–1840: The Evolution of Alternative Systems of Colonial Government*. New York and London: Greenwood, 1987.

———. *The Dependent Empire and Ireland, 1840–1900: Advance and Retreat in Representative Self-Government: Select Documents on the Constitutional History of the British Empire and Commonwealth*, Vol. V. New York: Greenwood Press, 1991.

Maltezou, Chrysa. 'Eptanisa', in *Istoria tou Ellinikou Ethnous*, Vol. 10. Athens: Ekdotiki Athinon, 1975, 215–29.

———. 'Nisia tou Ioniou. I Teleutaia periodos tis Venetikis Kyriarxias (1699–1797)', in *Istoria tou Ellinikou Ethnous*, Vol. 11. Athens: Ekdotiki Athinon, 1975, 212–18.

Mann, Michael. *The Sources of Social Power*, Vol. II. New York: Cambridge University Press, 2012.

Manning, Helen Taft. *British Colonial Government after the American Revolution, 1782–1820*. New Haven, CT: Yale University Press, 1933.

Martin, Robert Montgomery. *History of the British Possessions in the Mediterranean*. London: W. Nicol, 1837.

——. *Statistics of the Colonies of the British Empire in the West Indies, South America, North America, Asia, Austral-Asia, Africa and Europe*. London: W.H. Allen & Co., 1839.

Mavrogiannis, Gerasimos. *Istoria ton Ionion Nison*. Vols. A and B. Athens, 1889.

Mavrogordato, John. *Modern Greece: A Chronicle and a Survey 1800–1931*. London: Macmillan & Co, 1931.

Mazarakis, Anthimos. *Viografiai ton endokson andron tis nisou Kefallinias*. Venice, 1843 (Athens: N. Karavias, 1999).

Mazzacane, Aldo. 'Law and Jurists in the Formation of the Modern State in Italy', *The Journal of Modern History* 67 (1995): S62–S73.

McAdam, John Loudon. *Remarks on the Present System of Road Making: With Observations, Deduced from Practice and Experience* (8th edn). London: Longman, Hurst, Rees, Orme and Brown (Paternoster Row), 1824. Retrieved 26 September 2011.

McGrew, William W. *Land and Revolution in Modern Greece, 1800–1881: The Transition in the Tenure and Exploitation of Land from Ottoman Rule to Independence*. Kent, OH: Kent State University Press, 1985.

McKnight, James Lawrence. 'Admiral Ushakov and the Ionian Republic: The Genesis of Russia's First Balkan Satellite'. Thesis dissertation, University of Wisconsin-Madison, 1965.

Mercati, P. *Saggio Storico Statistico della Citta et Isola di Zante*, Zante 1811, published in J. Davy, *Notes and Observations*, Vol. II, Chap. 2, London, 1842.

Merry, Sally Engle. 'Law and Colonialism. Review Essay', *Law & Society Review* 25(4) (1991): 889–922.

Metcalf, Thomas R. *Ideologies of the Raj*. Cambridge: Cambridge University Press, 1995.

Misra, Maria. 'Colonial Officers and Gentlemen: The British Empire and the Globalization of Tradition', *Journal of Global History* 3 (2008): 135–61.

Mitchell, A. 'Bourgeois Liberalism and Public Health: A Franco-German Comparison', in J. Kocka and A. Mitchell (eds), *Bourgeois Society in Nineteenth-Century Europe*. Oxford: Berg, 1993.

Mitchell, Timothy. *The Rule of Experts: Egypt, Techno-Politics, Modernity*. Berkeley: University of California Press, 2002.

Mitter, Partha. 'The Early British Port Cities of India: Their Planning and Architecture circa 1640–1757', *JSAH* XLV (June 1986): 96–114.

Mokyr, Joel. *The Enlightened Economy: An Economic History of Britain, 1700–1850*. Princeton, NJ: Princeton University Press, 2010.

Morris, H.F. 'A History of the Adoption of Codes of Criminal Law and Procedure in the British Colonial Africa, 1876–1935', *Journal of African Law* 18(1) (1974): 6–23.

Morris, R.J. *Cholera 1832*. London: Croom Helm, 1976.
——. *Class and Class Consciousness in the Industrial Revolution, 1750–1850*. London: Macmillan, 1979.
——. *Class, Sect and Party. The making of the British middle class: Leeds, 1820–50*. Manchester: Manchester University Press, 1990.
Moschonas, Emm. I. *Agnosta kai spania Monofylla Syllogis N. Karavia 1797–1863*. Athens: Vivliopoleio Karavia, 1967.
Moschonas, N.G. 'Forologikes metarrythmiseis stin Kefallinia kata ta teli tou IZ aionos', *Trito Panionio Synedrio, Praktika*. Athens, 1967, 228–39.
Moschona, Panagiota. 'Ekpaidefsi stin Kefalonia to proto miso tou 19ou ai.', *Kefalliniaka Chronika* 8. Argostoli: Etaireia Kefalliniakon Istorikon Erevnon, 1999, 305–19.
——. 'Ta Ionian Nisia kata tin periodo 1797–1821', in *Istoria tou Ellinikou Ethnous*, vol. 11. Athens: Ekdotiki Athinon, 1978, 382–402.
Moschopoulos, D. 'Krisi nomimotitas sto Ionio Kratos'. Proceedings of International Conference, Corfu 22–25 May 1996. Corfu: Politistikos Syllogos Corcyra, 1998, 191–211.
Moschopoulos, G.N. *Istoria tis Kefalonias*, vol. 2 (1797–1940). Athens: Kefalos, 1988.
——. *O Thesmos tis Astynomias sta Eptanisa. Ta kefalliniaka archeia tis Ektelestikis Astynomias (1815–1864)*. Argostoli: G.A.K. Archeion Nomou Kefalonias, 1997.
——. 'Oi protoi Eptanisioi sto Elliniko Koinovoulio (1864). Ypodochi, ideologika minimata, "metakenosi", politiki anadiarthrosi tou Koinovouliou', in A. Argyriou, K. Dimadis and A. Lazaridou (eds), *O ellinikos kosmos anamesa stin Anatoli kai ti Dysi 1453–1981*, vol. B. Athens: Ellinika Gramma, 1999, 65–74.
Mousson A. *Ein Besuch auf Korfu und Cefalonien im September 1858*. Zurich, 1859 (Greek translation). Athens: Istoritis, 1995.
Mouzelis, Nicos P. *Modern Greece: Facets of Underdevelopment*. New York: Holmes & Meier, 1978.
Mponi, K. 'I symvoli tis Ithakis kai tou Kalamou eis to yper aneksartisias agona tou ethnous', *Praktika Tritou Panioniou Synedriou, 23–29 Spetemvriou 1965*, Vol. I, Athens, 1967, 240–45.
Muller, Christian. *Journey through Greece and the Ionian Islands, in June, July and August*. London, 1821.
Murray, J. A handbook for travellers in the Ionian Islands, Greece, Turkey, Asia Minor, and Constantinople. London, 1845.
Napier, Charles-James. *Memoir on the roads of Cefalonia*. London: Ridgway, 1825.
Napier, Charles James. *The Colonies, Treating of their Value Generally – of the Ionian Islands in Particular: The Importance of the Latter in War and Commerce*. London: T. & W. Boone, 1833.
Napier, Henry. *Journal of Captain Henry Napier*. Manuscript, Corgialenios Museum, Argostoli, 1829.
Nikiforou-Testone, A. *Dimosies Teletes stin Kerkyra kata tin periodo tis Venetikis Kyriarxias, 14os-18os ai*. Athens: Themelio, 1999.

Nikiforou, Aliki. *Ta diavatiria tou 19ou ai. ton archeion tis Kerkyras (1800–1870)*. Corfu: G.A.K. Archeia Nomou Kerkyras, 2003.

——. (ed). *Syntagmatika Keimena ton Ionion Nison*. Athens: Idryma tis Voulis ton Ellinon, 2008.

Nikolaou, Chrysa. 'I oikonomiki sygkyria stis gamilies symperifores. Oi katholikoi stin Kerkyra (1815–1864)', in Aliki Nikiforou (ed.), *Θ' Panionio Synedrio, Praktika vol. A*. Paxoi: Eaireia Paxinon Meleton, 2014, 333–57.

Norman, Bertram. 'An Anatomy of Income Distribution', *American Economic Review* 2(1) (1972): 30–37.

O'Brien, Patrick Karl. 'European Economic Development: The Contribution of the Periphery', *Economic History Review*, 2nd Series, 35(1) (1982): 1–18.

——. 'The Costs and Benefits of British Imperialism 1846–1914', *Past and Present* 120 (1988): 163–200.

——. 'Colonies in a Globalizing Economy, 1815–1948', GEHN Working Paper No. 08/04, London School of Economics. http://www.lse.ac.uk/collections/economicHistory/GEHN/GEHNPDF/WorkingPaper08POB.pdf

Omada enantia sti lithi. *Kyriarchia kai koinonikoi agones ston Elladiko choro*. Athens: Anarhiki Arheiothiki, 1996.

Osborn, M. *Global Lives: Britain and the World, 1550–1800*. Cambridge: Cambridge University Press, 2008.

Osterhammel, Jurgen. 'Semi-Colonialism and Informal Empire in Twentieth-Century China: Towards a Framework of Analysis', in Wolfgang J. Mommsen (ed.), *Imperialism and After: Continuities and Discontinuities*. London: Allen & Unwin, 1986, 290–314.

——. *The Transformation of the World. A Global History of the Nineteenth Century*. Princeton & Oxford: Princeton University Press, 2014.

Panessa, Giangiacomo. *Le Comunita Greche a Livorno. Vicende fra integrazione e chiusura nazionale*. Livorno: Books & Company, 1991.

Papadia-Lala, A. O thesmos ton astikon koinotiton ston elliniko choro kata tin period tis venetokratias (13ος–18ος aionas). Mia synthetiki proseggisi. Venice: Elliniko Institouto Vyzantinon kai Metavyzantinon Spoudon, No. 24, 2004.

Papadopoulos, Thomas. *Ioniki Vivliografia. 16ος-19ος aionas*. Vol. B, 1851–1880. Athens, 2000.

Papageorgiou G. 'Dimografika kai Oikonomika Megethi sta Agglokratoumena Eptanisa (1824–1826), me vasi to aporrito arheio tou Vatikanou', *Praktika E' Panioniou Synedriou*. Athens: Etaireia Kefalliniakon Istorikon Erevnon, 1986, 83–94.

Papakonstantinou, Katerina. 'The Port of Messolonghi: Spatial Allocation and Maritime Expansion in the Eighteenth Century', *The Historical Review / La Revue Historique*, Vol. VII (2010): 277–97.

Papanikolas, Georgios Drakatos. 'The Ionian Islands : what they have lost and suffered under the thirty-five years' administration of the Lord High Commissioners sent to govern them : in reply to a pamphlet entitled "The Ionian Islands under British Protection"'. London, 1851.

Papathanasopoulos, Konstantinos. *Elliniki emporiki naftilia*. Athens: MIET, 1983.

———. 'Naftilia, Kratos kai Politiki sto 19o aiona', in V. Kremmydas (ed.), *Eisagogi sti Neoelliniki Oikonomiki Istoria 18os–20os aionas*. Athens: Typothito, 1999.
Paschalidi, M. 'Constructing Ionian Identities: The Ionian Islands in British Official Discourses, 1815–1864'. Doctoral thesis, University College London, 2010.
Patricios, Nicholas N. *Kefallinia and Ithaki: A Historical and Architectural Odyssey*. Danbury, CT: Rutledge Books, 2002.
Patronis, V. 'Stafida kai agrotiki metarrithmisi', in T. Sakellaropoulos (ed.), *Neoelliniki Koinonia. Istorikes kai Kritikes Proseggiseis*. Athens: Kritiki, 1993.
Paximadopoulou-Stavrinou, M. *Oi eksegerseis tis Kefallinias kata ta eti 1848 kai 1849*. Athens: Etaireia Kefalliniakon Istorikon Erevnon, 1980.
———. *Politeiografika Ionion Nison epi Agglikis Kyriarchias 1815–1864. Oi etisies ektheseis tis Armosteias pros to Ypourgeio ton Apoikion*, Vol. I. Athens: Etaireia Kefalliniakon Istorikon Erevnon, 1997.
Peers, Douglas. *Between Mars and Mammon: Colonial Armies and the Garrison State in Early Nineteenth-Century India*. London, 1995.
Pels, Peter. 'The Anthropology of Colonialism: Culture, History, and the Emergence of Western Governmentality', *Annual Review of Anthropology* 26 (1997): 163–83.
Pentogalos, G.H. 'The Medical School of Ionian Academy (1824–1828 and 1844–1865)'. Ph.D. Thesis, University of Thessaloniki, 1980.
———. *Giatroi kai Iatriki Kefalonias sta chronia ton ksenon kyriarchion (1500–1864)*. Thessaloniki: University Studio Press, 2004.
Petrakis, P.E. 'The Borrowing Requirements of the Greek Public Sector, 1844–1869', *Journal of the Hellenic Diaspora* 12 (1985).
Petropoulos, John Anthony. *Politics and Statecraft in the Kingdom of Greece, 1833–1843*. Princeton, NJ: Princeton University Press, 1968.
———. 'Introduction', in N. Diamantouros et al. (eds), *Hellenism and the Greek War of Liberation (1821–1830)*. Thessaloniki: Insitute for Balkan Studies, 1976.
Phylliou, Christine. *Biography of an Empire: Governing Ottomans in an Age of Revolution*. Berkeley and Los Angeles: University of California Press, 2011.
Pierron, Bernard. *Evraioi kai christianoi sti neoteri Ellada: istoria ton diakoinotikon scheseon apo to 1821 os to 1945*. Athens: Polis Editions, 2004.
Pizanias. P. 'Daneistikes sxeseis ke oikonomiki kiriarxia stin Ellada tou 19ou aiona. H idrisi tis Ethnikis Trapezas tis Ellados 1841–1847', *O Politis* 64–65 (1983): 47–58.
Porter, Andrew, 'Introduction', in A. Porter (ed.), *The Oxford History of the British Empire, Vol. 3*. Oxford: Oxford University Press, 1999, 4.
Postnikov, Aleksey V. 'From Charting to Mapping: Russian Military Mapping of Corfu in the Early Nineteenth Century', *Imago Mundi: The International Journal for the History of Cartography* 53(1) (2001): 83–96.
Poulantzas, Nikos. *Keimena. Marxism, Dikaio, Kratos*. Athens: Nisos, 2009.
Pratt, Michael. *Britain's Greek Empire*. London: Rex Collings, 1978.

Pretenteris Typaldos, Iakovos. *Peri tis en Kerkyra choleras kata to 1855*. Corfu: Typografeio tis Kyvernisis, 1856.
Progoulakis, Giorgos. *Anamesa stin timi kai to chrima. I Kerkyra sta chronia tis agglikis kyriarchias 1814–1864*. Athens: Istoriko Archeio-Emporiki Trapeza, 2003.
Prontzas, Evangelos. *Oikonomia kai Geoktisia sti Thessalia (1881–1912)*. Athens: MIET, 1992.
——. 'Oikonomikes epidoseis tou 19ou aiona stin Eptaniso'. Praktika *I enosi tis Eptanisou stin Ellada*, vol. I. Athens: Akadimia Athinon, 2005, 531–44.
Prontzas, E., and D. Anoyatis-Pele. *Kerkyra 1830–1832. Metaksi Feoydarchias kai apoikiokratias*. Thessaloniki: University Studio Press, 2002.
Psara, Ioannou D. 'Peina sta Kythera (1666–1673)', *Praktika E Panioniou Synedriou*, vol. 1, Argostoli: Etaireia Kefalliniakon Istorikon Erevnon, 1986, 139–51.
Raman, Kartik Kalian. 'Utilitarianism and the Criminal Code in Colonial India: A Study of the Practical Limits of Utilitarian Jurisprudence', *Modern Asian Studies* 28(4) (Oct. 1994): 739–40.
Rapp, R. 'The Unmaking of the Mediterranean Trade Hegemony: International Trade Rivalry and the Commercial Revolution', *The Journal of Economic History* 35(3) (1975): 499–525.
Reinhart, Carmen, and Kenneth Rogoff. *This Time Is Different: Eight Centuries of Financial Folly*. Princeton, NJ: Princeton University Press, 2009.
Riall, Lucy. *Under the Volcano: Revolution in a Sicilian Town*. Oxford: Oxford University Press, 2013.
Roldan, Vera Eugenia, and Marcelo Caruso. *Imported Modernity in Post-Colonial State Formation*. Frankfurt: Peter Lang, 2007.
Rontoyannis, Panos G. *I Ekpaidefsi sti Lefkada, 1613–1950*. Athens, 1994.
Rothman, David. The Discovery of the Asylum: *Social Order and Disorder in the New Republic*. Boston and Toronto: Little, Brown and Company, 1971.
Salomon, Marino. *La statistica generale dell' isola di Cefalonia. Una delle sette componenti lo stato politico Jonio sotto la denominazione di Stati Uniti delle Isole Jonie*. Corfu: "Jonia", 1859; Athens, 1996.
Saul, Norman E. *Russian and the Mediterranean 1797–1807*. Chicago: University of Chicago Press, 1970.
Savvidis, G.P., and Niki Kykourgou (eds). *Aristotelis Valaoritis. Vios, Epistoles kai Politika Keimena, v. A*. Athens: Ikaros, 1980.
Schumann, Christoph (ed.). *Liberal Thought in the Eastern Mediterranean: Late 19th Century until the 1960s*. Leiden and Boston: Brill, 2008.
Scott, David. 'Colonial Governmentality', *Social Text* 43 (1995): 191–220.
Sen, S. 'Uncertain Dominance: The Colonial State and its Contradictions (with notes on the history of early British India)', *Nepantla: Views from South* 3(2) (2002): 391–406.
——. 'Liberal Empire and Illiberal Trade: The Political Economy of "Responsible Government" in Early British India', in Kathleen Wilson (ed.), *A New Imperial History. Culture, Identity and Modernity in Britain and the Empire 1660–1840*. Cambridge: Cambridge University Press, 2004, 136–54.

Seymour, A.A.D. 'How to Work the System and Thrive: Ionians and Pseudo-Ionians in the Levant, 1815–1964', in Anthony Hirst and Patrick Sammon (eds), *The Ionian Islands: Aspects of their History and Culture*. Cambridge: Cambridge Scholars Publishing, 2014, 75–105.

Sharma Sanjay. *Famine, Philanthropy and the Colonial State: North India in the Early Nineteenth Century*. New Delhi: Oxford University Press, 2001.

Sideri, Aloe. *Ellines foitites sto Panepistimio tis Pizas (1806–1861)*, Vols. A–B. Athens: IEAN, 1989–94.

Sklavenitis, Triantafyllos E. 'Ioannis N. Stamatelos (1822–1881). O logios kai o daskalos – ta dimosievmata – ta kataloipa – ta cheirografa tis vivliothikis tou', *Praktika IA Symposiou*. Athens: Etaireia Lefkadikon Meleton, 2007, 63–142.

Smith, S.A. *Like Cattle and Horses: Nationalism and Labour in Shangai, 1895–1927*. Durham, NC and London: Duke University Press, 2002.

Smith, William Henry. *The Mediterranean: A Memoir Physical, Historical, and Nautical*. London: John W. Parker & Son, 1854.

Solimano, Stefano. 'I Francesi e le Isole Ionie. Imperialismo Giuridico in difficolta spunti per un approfondimento', in S. Vinciguerrra (ed.), *Codice Penale degli Stati Uniti delle Isole Jonie (1841)*, CEDAM Padova, 2008, XXV–LIV.

Solomos, Marinos-Panagis. Geniki Dimosionomia tis Kefallinias. Etos syntheseos 1859. Athens, 1996.

Sotiropoulos, Michail. 'European Jurisprudence and the Intellectual Origins of the Greek State: The Greek Jurists and Liberal Reforms (ca. 1830–1880)'. Ph.D. thesis, Queen Mary, University of London, 2014.

Stavrinou, Miranta. 'Stoicheia tis dimosias zois sta notia Eptanisa, symfona me anekdoti anaphora tou antistratigou James Campbell (1813)', *Kerkyraika Chronika*, vol. XXVI. Corfu, 1982.

Steinmenz, George. 'The Colonial State as a Social Field: Ethnographic Capital and Native Plocit in the German Overseas Empire before 1914', *American Sociological Review* 73 (2008): 589–612.

Streets-Salter, Heather and Trevor Getz. *Empires and Colonies in the Modern World. A Global Perspective*. New York & Oxford: Oxford University Press, 2016.

Substance of Sir Thomas Maitland's Address to the Legislative Assembly of the Ionian Islands, 4th March 1822. London, 1822.

Sutherland, David. *Managing the British Empire: The Crown Agents, 1833–1914*. Royal Historical Society: Boydell Press, 2004.

`Svoronos, Nikos. *Episkopisi tis Neoellinikis Istorias*. Athens: Themelio, 1985.

Taft Manning, Helen. British Colonial Government after the American Revolution, 1782–1820. New Haven, CT: Yale University Press, 1933.

Tenenti, A. *Piracy and the Decline of Venice 1580–1615*. Berkeley & Los Angeles: University of California Press, 1967.

Theodorou, V. 'Peitharchika systimata kai ergasia sta orfanotrofeia to B miso tou 19ou aiona', *Mnemon* XXI (1999): 55–84.

Theotokis, M. *O Ioannis Kapodistrias en Kefallinia kai e staseis aftis en etesi 1800, 1801, 1802. Istorikai simioseis eksaxthise ek ton eggrafon tou archeiou tis Eptanisou Politeias*. Corfu, 1889.

Theotokis, Sp. 'I Ekpaideusis en Eptaniso (1453–1864)', *Kerkyraika Chronia* 5 (1956).

Theotoky, Em. *Details sur Corfou*. Corfu, 1826.

Thompson, Edward Palmer. 'The Moral Economy of the English Crowd in the 18th Century', *Past & Present* 50 (1971): 76–136.

Todorov, Varban N. *Greek Federalism during the Nineteenth century (Ideas and Projects)*. New York: Columbia University Press, 1995.

Tsiknakis, Kostas G. 'O ellinikos choros sti diarkeia tis Venetokratias', in Chrysa Maltezou (ed.), *Venetokratoumeni Ellada, Proseggizontas tin Istoria tis*. Athens and Venice: Elliniko Institouto Byzantinon kai Metavyzantinon Spoudon, No. 10, 2010, 21–70.

Tsirigotou, Chr. *Statistiki tou en Kerkyra Frenokomeiou tou etous 1877. Ypovlitheisa eis to Ypourgeion Esoterikon*. Athens, 1878.

Tsoukalas, Konstantinos. *Eksartisi kai Anaparagogi: O Kinonikos Rolos ton Ekpedeftikon Mihanismon stin Ellada 1830–1922*. Athens: Themelio, 1977.

———. *Koinoniki Anaptyksi kai Kratos. I Sygkrotisi tou Dimosiou Chorou stin Ellada*, 6th edn. Athens: Themelio, 1999.

Tully, James Dillon. *The History of the Plague, as It Has Lately Appeared in the Islands of Malta, Goza, Corfu, Cephalonia & c. Detailing Important Facts, Illustrative of the Specific Contagion of that Disease, with Particulars of the Means Adopted for Its Eradication*. London, 1821.

Tzavara, Panayoti. *Scholeia kai daskaloi sti venetokratoumeni Kerkyra (16os–18os ai.)*. Athens: Stamouli, 2003.

Varnava, Andrekos. *British Imperialism in Cyprus, 1878–1915: The Inconsequential Possession*. Manchester: Manchester University Press, 2009.

Varvaritis, Dimitrios.'"The Jews have got into trouble again…": Responses to the Publication of "*Cronaca Israelitica*" and the Question of Jewish Emancipation in the Ionian Islands (1861–1863)', in *Quest. Issues in Contemporary Jewish History. Journal of Fondazione CDEC* 7 (July 2014): 30–51. www.quest-cdecjournal.it/focus.php?id=355.

Vaudoncourt, Frédéric Guillaume de. *Memoirs on the Ionian Islands, Considered in a Commercial, Political and Military Point of View*. London, 1816.

Vervitsiotou, Ioannou. *Ekthesis ton gegonoton osa synevisan meta tin parachorisin tis Pargas. Syggrama ekdothen en Parisiois Gallisti kata to 1820 etos nyn the metafrasthen ypo Ioannou Varvitsiotou*. Corfu, 1851.

Vikelas, Demetrius. 'Statistics of the Kingdom of Greece', *Journal of the Statistical Society of London* 31(3) (Sept. 1868): 265–98.

Vinciguerra, Sergio (ed.). *Codice Penale Degli Stati Uniti Delle Isole Jonie*. Padova: CEDAM, 2008.

Vlachos, G. 'Ta prota Ionika Atmoploia', *Kefalliniaka Chronika* 10 (Argostoli 2005): 491–500.

Vlachos-Politis, X. 'To Telos ton Evgenon', *Deltio Anagnostikis Eterias Kerkyras* 24 (2001): 141–86.

Vlami, D. *To fiorini, to sitari kai i odos tou kipou. Ellines emporoi sto Livorno.* Athens: Themelio, 2000.

Vlassi, Despoina E. 'I anamorfosi toy Symvouliou tis Kefalonias apo to Geniko Provlepti tis Thalassas Giovanni Battista Vitturi (1751)', 6th Panionio Synedrio. Thessaloniki: University Studio Press, 2000, 321–35.

Vlassopoulos, Nikos St. *I Naftilia ton Ionion Nison 1700–1864.* Athens: Elliniki Evroekdotiki, 1995.

Vlassopoulos, Stylianos. *Statistikai – Istorikai peri Kerkyras Eidiseis.* Kerkyraika Chronika, Vol. 21, (1822) 1977.

Vrailas-Armenis, Petros. *Scheseis tis viomixanias pros tin ithikin kai noitikin anaptyksin.* Corfu, 1853.

Walker, B.E. *A History of Banking in Canada.* Toronto, 1899.

William, Henry Smith. *The Mediterranean: A Memoir Physical, Historical and Nautical.* London, 1854.

Williams, J.B. *British Commercial Policy and Trade Expansion, 1750–1850.* Oxford: Clarendon Press, 1972.

Wilson, Kathleen. 'Rethinking the Colonial State: Family, Gender, and Governmentality in Eighteenth-Century British Frontiers', *American Historical Review* 116(5) (2011): 1294–1322.

Wood, Alfred. C. *A History of the Levant Company.* London: Routledge, 1965.

Woolf, Stuart. *The Poor in Western Europe in the Eighteenth and Nineteenth Centuries.* London and New York: Methuen, 1986.

Wrigley W.D. *The Diplomatic Significance of Ionian Neutrality, 1821–1831.* London: Peter Lang, 1988.

Yang, A.A. 'Disciplining "Natives": Prison and Prisoners in Early Nineteenth-Century India. South Asia', *Journal of South Asian Studies* 10(2) (1987): 29–45.

——. *Crime and Criminality in British India.* Tucson: University of Arizona Press, 1985.

Yannitsiotis, Yannis. *I Koinoniki Istoria tou Peiraia 1860–1910. I sygkrotisi tis astikis taksis.* Athens: Ekdoseis Nefeli, 2006.

——. 'Social History in Greece: New Perspectives', *East Central Europe* 34–35 (2007–8): 1–2, 101–30.

Yotopoulou-Sisilianou, E. 'I Eptanisiaki paideia sta chronia tis ksenokratias', *Kerkyraika Chronika* XV, 1970, 101–21.

Young, D.M. *The Colonial Office in the Early Nineteenth Century.* London: Longmans, 1961.

Zambeliou, Napoleontos. *Praktika Ioniou Eterias 1860–1, Vol. A*, Ekdothenta ypo, Tamiou kai Iakovou Polyla, Grammateos. Corfu, 1861 (British Library).

Zamit, L. *Oi Maltezoi stin Kerkyra kais ton eyrytero mesogeiako choro. Synthikes pou tous odigisan se metanastefsi.* Corfu: Etaireia Kerkyraikon Spoudon, 1995.

Zanden, Jan Luiten van. 'Colonial State Formation and Patterns of Economic Development in Java', *Economic History of Developing Regions* 25(2) (2010).

Zapanti, Stamatoula. *Kefalonia 1500–1571. I sigkrotisi tis koinonias tou nisiou.* Thessaloniki: University Studio Press, 1999.

Ze'evi, Dror. 'Back to Napoleon? Thoughts on the Beginning of the Modern Era in the Middle East', *Mediterranean Historical Review* 19(1) (2004): 73–94.

Zervos-Iakovatos, E. *I epi tis Agglikis Prostasias Eptanisios Politeia kai ta kommata*. Athens, 1969.
Zivas, Dionisis. *I Architektoniki tis Zakynthou apo ton 16o mechri ton 19o aiona*. Athens, 1970.
Zoes, L. *Ai en Zakyntho Syntechniai*. Zakynthos, 1893.
Zucconi, G. 'Corfu brittanica: Architettura e strategie urbanistiche nella capitale dello Stato Ionio', in A. Nikiforou (ed.), *Corfu: Storia, Vita urbana e Architettura, 14o–19o secc*. Corfu: Archivi di Stato di Corfù, 1994, 95–103.

Index

Adam, Frederick, 7, 46, 53, 63–66, 68, 72, 88, 92, 102, 108, 145, 157, 158, 178, 179, 181, 182, 199, 200, 206, 213, 260, 293, 294, 310,
Ali Pasha, 37, 68, 69, 74, 119, 120, 125
Athens, 12, 35, 158, 159, 161, 166, 168, 195, 205, 222, 278, 279, 280, 300, 303, 309, 312, 330, 333, 334, 335,
Assembly, Ionian, 5, 27, 29, 55, 57, 58, 60, 61, 65, 66, 92, 95, 96, 120, 141, 148, 163, 177, 179, 182, 186–190, 200, 267, 276, 288, 302, 309–321, 328

Black Sea, 24, 109, 110, 112, 133, 145, 149, 150, 152–156, 161, 165, 166
Blue Books, 14, 101, 106, 107, 109, 110, 133, 265, 266, 283, 328
Bourgeoisie, 2, 10, 11, 12, 17, 18, 19, 28, 81, 144, 163, 187, 208, 245, 254, 255, 256, 261, 267, 269, 270, 280, 281, 287, 288, 289, 291, 293, 295, 297, 299, 301, 303, 305, 306, 307, 308, 330, 333, 335
Budget, 15, 39, 58, 66, 174–180, 188, 193, 229, 291, 295, 310, 313
Bureaucracy, 2, 5, 12, 13, 24, 51, 58, 79, 88, 92, 101, 105, 109, 174, 188, 192, 228, 230, 242, 277, 328, 329

Candonis, Antonios, 152, 153, 215, 254, 255
Ceylon, 4, 5, 13, 36, 37, 52, 58, 79, 80, 83, 84, 85, 87, 102, 175, 176, 177, 191
Chamber of Commerce, 163, 164, 220, 243

Civil society, 2, 3, 80, 87, 91, 104, 290, 307, 314, 317, 329
Cholera, 18, 43, 109, 111, 112, 115, 195, 218, 225, 240, 269–276, 278, 280, 283, 285
Civil war, 41, 59, 60, 73, 96
Class, 2, 3, 9–19, 23, 28–31, 34, 35, 53, 59, 60, 63, 74, 80, 89, 93, 96, 118, 126, 133–136, 152, 153, 162, 168, 181, 193, 196, 201–203, 208, 215, 216, 219, 228, 230, 231, 244–247, 251, 253, 259, 261, 262, 265, 266, 270–275, 279, 287–290, 302, 304, 307, 315, 319, 325–333
Codes, 15, 90–94, 102, 183, 266
Colonial Office, 13, 14, 51, 52, 55, 63, 73, 84, 85, 105, 107, 108, 109, 119, 139, 142, 158, 160, 166, 184, 260, 311, 313, 329
Colony, 1, 3, 4, 14, 15, 60, 61, 122, 123, 130, 143, 177, 191, 256, 298, 327, 335, 336
Courts, 40, 57, 64, 79–83, 85, 89, 90–92, 108, 164, 165, 179, 180, 189, 207, 218, 299, 301, 309, 313
Crimean War, 109, 115, 132, 143, 151, 152, 155
Criminal justice, 80–83, 87–90, 92, 95, 188, 266
Currants, 16, 37, 111–115, 125, 133–145, 160, 161, 176, 177, 179, 184, 185, 189, 193, 205, 206, 306
Cyprus, 2, 4, 6, 123, 326, 329, 335

De Bosset, 32, 38, 39, 49, 63, 119, 202, 222
Decolonization, 2, 80, 326, 330

366 • *Index*

Development
  Ionian, 2, 9, 13, 14, 16, 19, 24, 31, 32, 34, 35, 37, 56, 68, 70, 80, 90, 101, 103, 108, 119, 165, 166, 168, 174, 177, 183, 199, 200, 204, 213, 215, 219, 223, 227, 229, 231, 232, 250, 265, 302, 305, 306, 310, 329, 335
Diaspora bourgeoisie, 18
Diaspora Greeks, 25, 155
Dimas, 152, 153, 215, 254, 255, 303, 305
Doctors, 17, 30, 32–35, 41–46, 50, 148, 227, 234, 235, 239, 257, 269–271, 275, 277, 280, 285, 304, 319
Douglas, 36, 120, 143, 147, 179, 182–185, 205, 215, 229, 246, 252, 258–260, 267, 298, 299, 310–313

Egypt, 6, 23, 36, 42, 74, 161, 193, 329, 335
Empire, 4, 7, 79
  Austro-Hungarian, 275
  British, 3, 4, 6, 12–15, 38, 53–56, 64, 67, 69, 71, 76, 80, 81, 83, 101, 106, 118, 119, 130, 136, 145, 174, 175, 216, 219, 265, 278, 326
  Ottoman, 1, 8, 23, 25, 42, 51, 57, 63, 68, 69, 71, 73, 74, 119, 125, 131, 177, 186, 330, 334
Ermoupoli, 165–167, 205, 278, 279, 288
Expenditure, 57, 175–179, 182, 188–192, 213, 240, 261, 318
Exports, 16, 65, 81, 106, 107, 131, 132, 133, 134, 135, 136, 137, 152, 174, 176, 177, 179, 185, 190, 193, 227, 307

Finances, 2, 15, 87, 101, 112, 132, 133, 141, 142, 174, 177–182, 185, 187–193, 196, 200, 202, 205, 239, 290, 299, 310–313, 316, 320, 326
France, 8, 23, 37, 38, 39, 75, 82, 83, 119, 122, 187, 193, 291, 303, 308, 334

Governmentality, 6, 7, 11, 13, 14, 17, 23, 29, 30, 34, 35, 65, 76, 80, 88, 96, 101–105, 107, 201, 212, 267–289, 304, 328, 333
Greek Orthodox, 8, 16, 25, 122, 165, 215, 216, 220, 221, 234, 244, 331

identity,
  Class, 10, 11, 30, 215, 244–246, 254, 287, 288, 333
  National, 6, 16, 297
Imports, 37, 106, 107, 113, 131, 132, 143, 144, 146, 154, 155, 174, 193
India, 4, 5, 7, 12, 15, 36, 37, 55, 64, 79, 80, 88, 91, 94, 102, 108, 179, 180, 199, 250, 273
Ionian Academy, 33, 34, 35, 93, 104, 213, 233, 262, 293, 300, 303, 304,
Ionian Bank, 109, 125, 136, 157, 160, 161, 165, 167, 174, 183, 184, 185, 186, 187, 188, 190, 193, 207, 213, 254, 261, 262, 304
Intellectuals, 3, 12, 18, 30, 32, 35, 73, 104, 163, 186, 201, 214, 303, 304, 327, 330, 334

Jews, 16, 126, 164, 215–220, 256, 274, 301, 331,

Kandonis & Seremetis. *See* Candonis, Antonios
Kapodistrias, 33, 39, 54, 70, 74, 117, 181, 193, 290, 309
Kingdom, Greek, 8, 9, 11, 12, 41, 51, 60, 73, 76, 106, 109–113, 122, 130, 131, 135, 143, 158, 159, 177, 189–194, 199, 205, 217, 222, 250, 273, 278, 289, 301, 306–309, 314, 315, 320, 330–334

Lawyers, 3, 11, 18, 19, 30, 92, 181, 186, 208, 218, 227, 255, 262, 269, 280, 300–303, 319
Liberals, 1, 2, 5, 15, 17, 24, 30, 39, 61, 174, 212, 214, 219, 253, 262, 269, 287, 304, 304, 307–309, 311, 315, 316, 331, 334

Maitland, 13, 29, 37–39, 42, 44–46, 51, 54–72, 75, 79–89, 92, 95, 102, 103, 108, 118, 119, 145, 176–182, 189–191, 194, 200, 202, 212, 232, 310–312, 327
Malta, 4, 5, 37, 42, 43, 45, 46, 51, 53, 54, 56, 58, 66, 79, 80, 83, 84, 85, 86, 87, 89, 107, 108, 118, 123, 125, 157, 158, 175, 191, 192, 207, 213, 228, 237, 245, 294, 299
Maltese, 16, 36, 85, 92, 118, 122, 123, 157, 178, 215, 217
  society, 13, 80, 83
Mandouki, 120, 121, 227, 241, 242, 257, 270, 271, 274–277, 279, 293, 294, 301
Martial law, 13, 57, 64, 67, 71, 76, 89, 94, 335
Mediterranean, 2–4, 6, 8, 9, 13, 19, 23, 36, 37, 40, 42, 53, 54, 56, 58, 79, 80, 91, 102, 103, 105, 107, 112, 117, 118, 121, 123, 125, 134, 155–157, 175, 176, 179, 201, 207, 210, 215, 260, 266, 307, 308, 326, 329, 335
Merchants, 3, 11, 15, 16, 18, 23, 24, 27, 28, 59, 60, 67, 104, 105, 118, 122, 123, 125, 126, 128–133, 135, 137–156, 158–167, 181, 184–187, 194, 200, 206–208, 213–221, 230, 231, 234, 236, 237, 243–246, 254, 255, 262, 263, 269, 271, 273–280, 289, 298, 299, 302–308, 319, 327, 329–332
Militia, 13, 29, 45, 62, 64, 76, 180, 202, 203, 231, 232
Modernity, 2, 3, 7, 11, 12, 16, 36, 67, 73, 80, 81, 102–104, 199, 200, 212, 266, 268, 329–334
Modernization, 15–17, 81, 102, 104, 113, 174, 289, 316
Moncenigo, 28, 31, 33, 39, 117
Mustoxidi, 85, 161, 254, 282, 294, 297, 298, 304–306, 308, 311–313

Napier, Charles James, 52, 53, 58, 89, 102–105, 122, 136, 138–140, 154, 178–182, 193, 199, 200, 203, 204, 206, 213, 214, 252, 253, 266
Newspapers, 3, 19, 35, 36, 163, 278, 287, 303, 311, 313–316, 318, 327
Nugent, 82, 94, 95, 136, 138, 139, 140, 141, 142, 146, 158, 178, 179, 182, 183, 184, 206, 258, 293, 294, 297, 302, 310, 313

Olive oil, 16, 113, 126, 133, 134, 135, 137, 144, 182, 184, 189, 220, 229, 230, 306
Otto, King, 2, 70, 74, 205, 314, 330

Palace of St Michael and St George, 65, 118, 178, 181, 212, 325
Parga, 16, 68, 71, 102, 118–121, 125, 221, 242, 279
Paris, 4, 5, 13, 54, 56, 80, 81, 83, 119, 149, 228, 270, 272, 305, 311, 326, 328
Peasants, 3, 29, 67
Poorhouse, 212, 242, 258–261, 264–266, 278, 279, 280,
Population, Ionian, 13–17, 33–35, 40, 42, 45, 46, 53, 56, 62, 63–68, 71–76, 79, 88, 96, 101–116, 121–124, 130, 135, 144–147, 149, 176, 179, 180, 190, 192, 200–204, 207, 215–221, 245, 250, 254, 269, 274, 276–278, 294, 295, 313, 316, 328
Poverty, 17, 42, 64, 74, 120, 121, 131, 141, 168, 190, 203, 243, 247, 250–252, 256–265, 271, 274, 278, 279, 281, 287
Proprietor, 65, 67, 135, 138, 140, 141, 160, 161, 163, 167, 207, 220, 229–232, 236, 247
Protectorate, 1–6, 9, 13–15, 24, 29, 32, 36, 46, 52–55, 60, 62, 67, 68, 75, 79, 81, 84–86, 89, 102, 105, 107, 108, 111–113, 119, 122, 125, 131, 135, 143, 145, 158, 162, 174, 179, 182, 185, 189, 190, 191, 194, 201, 206, 216, 217, 222, 237, 238, 246, 256, 267, 290, 294, 295, 298–300, 302, 304, 307, 309–311, 313, 314, 316, 318, 321, 326, 327–331, 335

Public works, 2, 3, 14–16, 61, 101, 113, 133, 143, 174, 177, 178, 181, 187–194, 199, 200–202, 205, 207, 222, 227, 232, 250, 327, 329

Radicals, 2, 31, 263, 308, 309, 314–318, 320, 321, 330, 334
Reformists, 19, 263, 288, 314–321, 334
Revenue, 14–16, 28, 52, 64, 66, 81, 101, 109, 112, 133, 134, 135, 137, 138, 140, 143, 144, 148, 158, 162, 174, 176–182, 188–194, 200, 227, 234, 252, 268, 290, 304, 327
Revolutions of 1848, 316
Revolution of 1862, 330
Revolution, French, 7, 55, 225, 333
Revolution, Greek, 1, 6, 8, 9, 13, 41, 57, 62, 64, 65, 67–70, 72–76, 102, 119, 137, 154, 161, 193, 222, 317, 327
Revolution, Haitian, 37
Revolution, industrial, 137, 215
Roman Catholics, 123, 216, 256, 331
Royal Navy, 68, 118
Russia
  Russian, 2, 7, 8, 23, 24, 25, 26, 27, 28, 29, 31, 32, 33, 38, 39, 40, 53, 55, 68, 69, 70, 74, 75, 80, 81, 82, 150, 152, 155, 165, 181, 201, 208, 217, 290, 328, 334

Schools, 14, 38, 102, 135, 175, 178, 195, 212, 213, 222, 277, 290–299, 310, 319
Seaton, John Colbourne, 1, 15, 142, 163, 179, 182, 188, 191, 222, 241, 261, 262, 267, 309, 315–317

Semi-colonial, 1, 3, 8, 10, 11, 15, 20, 112, 143, 174, 328
Septinsular Republic, 7, 8, 11, 24, 27–29, 33, 34, 37, 39, 41, 53–56, 59, 68, 70, 80–82, 84, 88, 89, 91, 117, 210, 232, 275, 290, 302, 308, 326–328, 332
Shipping, 14, 18, 24, 25, 91, 101, 113, 116, 125, 130, 131, 151, 154, 155, 165, 166, 167, 168, 195, 213, 242, 277, 287, 305
Sicily, 4, 37, 53, 56, 118, 122, 192
Statistics, 7, 14, 101, 102, 103, 104, 105, 106, 107, 109, 110, 111, 113, 116, 132, 265, 268
Steamships, 11, 121, 125, 162, 206, 330
Storks, 305, 325

Taxation, 23, 27, 63, 65, 132, 133, 142, 154, 180, 189, 193, 194, 200, 201

Uprisings, 13, 27, 29, 33, 62, 63, 65, 66, 69, 70, 71, 72, 96, 201, 206, 230, 267, 310, 313, 317

Venice, 23, 26, 53, 60, 82, 121, 134, 145, 159, 165, 208, 215, 256

Ward, 52, 67, 121, 188, 230, 267, 276, 279, 313, 317, 318

Xenocracy, 1, 2, 8, 17, 19, 26, 80, 308, 314

Zervos Iakovatos, 288, 309, 316, 317, 319, 320

www.ingramcontent.com/pod-product-compliance
Lightning Source LLC
Chambersburg PA
CBHW071330080526
44587CB00017B/2790